A BULL FOR ALL SEASONS

A BULL FOR ALL SEASONS

Main Street Strategies
for Finding the Money
in Any Market

Dr. Bob Froehlich

New York   Chicago   San Francisco   Lisbon   London
Madrid   Mexico City   Milan   New Delhi
San Juan   Seoul   Singapore   Sydney   Toronto

The **McGraw·Hill** Companies

1 2 3 4 5 6 7 8 9 0   DOC/DOC   0 1 0 9 8

ISBN: 978–0–07–160002–6
MHID: 0–07–160002–7

This publication is designed to provide accurate and authoritative information in regard to the subject matter covered. It is sold with the understanding that the publisher is not engaged in rendering legal, accounting, or other professional service. If legal advice or other expert assistance is required, the services of a competent professional person should be sought.

—From a declaration of principles jointly adopted by a committee of the American Bar Association and a committee of publishers.

McGraw-Hill books are available at special quantity discounts to use as premiums and sales promotions, or for use in corporate training programs. To contact a representative please visit the Contact Us pages at www.mhprofessional.com.

Dedicated to the loving memory of my father,
Robert Joseph Froehlich, Sr. (1920–1991)

Who for 45 years drove a local delivery truck for Gimbels department store in Pittsburgh, all the while showing me by example
what loyalty, passion, and enthusiasm for your job are all about.

CONTENTS

Chapter 4

Investment Strategy   **183**

Chapter 5

Policy and Politics   **253**

Chapter 6

Global Investing 311

ACKNOWLEDGMENTS

Because my book is a culmination of a decade's worth of writings, a great deal of people played a role in its becoming a reality. And while my name appears as the author, this book could never have been written without the assistance of my family, friends, colleagues, coworkers, and clients. Thanks to everyone I have worked with and worked for over the past decade. While you may not recognize it, there is a part of you in this book as well.

I want especially to thank the thousands of financial advisors who I have worked with over the past decade. They gave me the forum to develop, debate, and challenge the world of investing through my market commentaries. Over the years they have provided me with critical analysis, guidance, and insight that was invaluable to me as I wrote these commentaries.

A large debt of gratitude is owed to all the great salespeople I have had the honor to work with. While in our industry we call them "wholesalers," they are salespeople; not just any salespeople, but rather some of the very best in the entire mutual fund industry. I have been through a lot with this sales force over the past decade, including company name changes from "Kemper" to "Zurich Kemper" to "Zurich Scudder Kemper" to "Zurich Scudder" to "Scudder Kemper" to "Scudder" to "DWS Scudder," and now to "DWS." Through all these changes one thing remained constant, and that was our sales force's unwavering encouragement for me to keep writing these commentaries whether I was right or wrong, in good markets and in bad, as it was a great way for them to "add value" by sending my commentaries on to their best clients.

Next I want to thank all my good friends and colleagues in the media at CNBC, FOX, CNN, and Bloomberg. They provided me with the opportunity to bring my market commentaries to life on the air in front of thousands of their viewers at a time. Special thanks goes to Nick Dunn at CNBC, along with on-air personalities Mark Haines, Maria Bartiromo, and Larry Kudlow. At FOX, I especially want to thank Gary Schreier, along with on-air personalities Neil Cavuto, Brenda Buttner, and Liz Claman. These people are not just colleagues, but rather good friends as well.

I also want to thank everyone at McGraw-Hill for their tireless editorial and production efforts in making this book happen; especially Jeanne Glasser, who actually came to me with the idea of writing this book and who was instrumental in developing the concept along the way. Thanks to Pattie Amoroso as well for her hard work during the editing and production process.

Thanks also to my administrative assistant, Michelle Pilota, who has been my assistant for over a decade. She has witnessed the evolution of these commentaries from handwritten notes that I would fax to her to type to now, where I write all my commentaries, with my thumbs, on my BlackBerry while I am traveling. Whether they were written by hand or on the BlackBerry, many of the facts and figures found in these commentaries were researched by Michelle over the years as she has evolved from, not just my administrative assistant, but my research assistant as well.

The biggest thanks of all, however, goes to my family. A book like this is not just the product of one's current research and opinions, but rather a person's views are the product of a lifetime of development. I am so lucky and so blessed in my lifetime to have such a wonderful and loving family, beginning with my sister Mary Ann Mays, who has always been my biggest cheerleader as well as my unofficial public relations agent in my hometown of Pittsburgh. Mary Ann probably single-handedly passed out more copies of my commentaries to anyone and everyone she crossed paths with at work, at church, or even while picking up groceries at Giant Eagle.

Next I want to thank my parents, who both passed away before I wrote my very first market commentary over a decade ago. They provided me with constant encouragement and support while they were alive and they instilled in me a self-belief that I could do anything I set out to do. They are also the only two people who would have handed out more copies of my commentaries than my sister had they been alive. I hope and pray that they can see me now and are as proud of me as I only wish I could tell them that I am of them. I miss them both dearly.

I am also very fortunate to have a wonderfully loving, caring, and supportive father-in-law and mother-in-law in Richard and Marianne Andre. In many ways after the passing away of both my parents, Rich and Marianne became like parents to me. They treat me like the son they never had. They have two daughters and no sons, as did I.

Speaking of daughters, I am so blessed with two of the greatest daughters that a father could ever hope for in Marianne and Stephanie. They are bright, loving, caring, and simply a joy to be around. I can't even count the number of these commentaries that they were subjected to listen to and read while my commentaries were in the development stage. If the commentary didn't pass their review, it never got published. I am also blessed to have a great son-in-law in Chris Neidhart, Marianne's husband. Chris jumped right in and became a part of the family, adding his views, insight, and per-spectives to my commentaries as well. I consider Chris like the son I never had. Together my two daughters and son-in-law have become my sounding board, listening to all my investment ideas and con-cepts all of the time. Their input, answers, suggestions, and some-times "just that look" have helped guide me more than any of you will ever know. I do not have the words to convey my gratitude to them adequately nor to tell them how proud I am of what they are and, what they have become. The three of them, along with my wife and me, have become, and affectionately refer to ourselves as "The Fro Fam Five." We are not just family, but we are all friends as well.

Finally, the love of my life, my wife, Cheryl, is my most valu-able asset. She was subjected to the development of every single one of these commentaries, suggesting that I add this or delete that. She also was the source for so many of the great quotes and one-liners that I used in many of these commentaries (like "The Fro Fam Five" I referenced above, which was actually her idea). Cheryl was always there for me all the time, and I do indeed thank her for her patience, suggestions, and steady guidance. In many respects Cheryl deserves a byline as the coauthor on these commentaries. I am so lucky to have a wife who is so interested in her husband's work and who is so witty as well. Almost all my funny one-liners and stories and quotes and even jokes I stole from Cheryl. Not only is Cheryl an understanding wife and a great and caring mother, but she is my most sensitive and meticulous critic as well. She is both my ghost writer and the love of my life as we have been married now for over three decades. I love and respect you more than words can express, and I am thankful every day that I have you as my wife.

As I close my acknowledgments I want to go back to thanking my parents again, this time specifically my father, to whom this book is dedicated. While I learned many things from my dad, there is one thing he taught me that I will take to the grave with me, and for that I cannot thank him enough, instilling this principle in me: "It's not what you do in life that matters, but rather how you do it." Thanks, dad.

A great Wall Street strategist must have the ability to foretell what is going to happen in the markets tomorrow, next week, next month, and next year, as well as five years from now. But even more important, he or she must also have the ability afterward to explain why it didn't happen.

I consider myself a Wall Street survivor. I have now survived over 30 years of employment in and around the Wall Street community, beginning with my career as a municipal bond issuer in Ohio to my current role as one of the highest-profile strategists on all of Wall Street. Certainly I have had as much television time on CNBC, Fox News, Fox Business News, CNN, and Bloomberg as most other Wall Street strategists combined.

That now makes me the mutual fund industry's most media-genic investment professional. What began from humble television beginnings in December 1995 when I was selected as one of the original regular guest commentators on CNN's new financial news network, CNNfn, has now evolved to my having been a guest on every single CNBC program. In addition, I was one of the very first guests on CNBC's most innovative programming concept, a show called *Worldwide Exchange*. It is the first financial news program ever to be simulcast around the world "live." It is anchored in London and coanchored in New York and Singapore. The only event in broadcast history to be simulcast around the world live prior to *Worldwide Exchange* was the World Cup Soccer matches.

I am the only person ever to have been a CNBC *Squawk Box* guest host in all three *Squawk Box* locations: New York, London, and Singapore. At Fox News, meanwhile, I have also become a regular special guest on their highest-rated weekend show, *Bulls n' Bears*; when Fox News launched its new business network, Fox Business News, I appeared as a guest the day the network was launched. I have been interviewed on some of the industry's most prestigious investment programs, including *Wall Street Week*, with Louis Rukeyser, *Money Line*, with Lou Dobbs, *MacNeil/Lehrer NewsHour*, and *World Business*, with Alexander Haig.

This television exposure and high-profile role have prompted financial advisors and individual investors alike to constantly seek my opinion and analysis of the current investment events driving the global markets.

Even with all this media exposure, though, I still cannot appear as a guest on financial television every day, commenting on every investment-moving event. So, instead, I had to create an outlet to let people know what I was thinking between public television appearances.

Hence, my investment commentaries were born over a decade ago. They have no set schedule. I don't do one every Monday morning to try to predict the investment swings of the market that week. Instead, I do one whenever the mood hits. If there is an investment issue out there that needs to be analyzed, I will analyze it and write an investment commentary about it. If there are no pressing issues, I don't make one up just to write a weekly commentary about it.

I write these commentaries for Main Street, not Wall Street, because I am from Main Street, not Wall Street. I was born and raised on the North Side of Pittsburgh. And even though I was the first person in my family to graduate from college, I have never forgotten my Main Street roots. It's the people on Main Street who need help most when the market is turning upside down. I have never wanted to talk down to people on Main Street, nor did I ever have the desire to "preach" to people about how much I knew about the markets. Instead, all I ever wanted to do was to teach and inform Main Street people about the markets.

As a result of this down-to-earth approach, my investment commentaries, interpreting current events driving the markets, have gained me recognition with the brokerage community on Wall Street as one of the most important investment strategists of our day. Financial advisors on Wall Street , and investors on Main Street the world over now look to me to be in the forefront, explaining with my investment commentaries major investment events and issues around the globe as they happen.

This book looks back at a decade's worth of these investment commentaries. Some things I got dead right, like my view that Y2K would be a nonevent for the markets. Other things I didn't get as right, like missing the outperformance of small-cap stocks. But right or wrong, you always knew exactly where I stood because of these investment commentaries. And right or wrong, you could always learn something from them. That's as true today as the day I wrote them. At the end of each of these commentaries, I include an updated synopsis of what actually occurred. Consider these an after-the-fact report card on my commentaries.

This book's look back over the past decade begins with Chapter 1, which is focused on the economy and ends with Chapter 6, which is focused on global investing. The chapters in between focus on the Federal Reserve Board, the markets, investment strategy, and public policy and politics. Through it all you will see that the issues and opportunities discussed in these commentaries have stood the test of time; their advice is as pertinent today as it was on the day they were published.

During this past decade, while I wrote these commentaries on a variety of subjects, I had no variety in employment. I have held the same job, in the same building in downtown Chicago. In fact, over the past 20-plus years I have changed jobs only once; this loyalty is something I learned from my Dad, to whom the book is dedicated. Here is a man who worked his entire truck-driving career for one company; this kind of loyalty is almost unheard of on Wall Street these days. My father started working full time as a helper on a Gimbels delivery truck when he left high school at age 16 after both his parents passed away. At 17 he was a driver and, other than serving his tour of duty in the army, he spent his entire working life working for only one company, Gimbels.

Likewise, nothing much has changed for me professionally over this past decade, except that I did move from the thirty-second floor to the twenty-eighth floor, then up to the thirty-fourth floor, and now down to the twenty-fourth floor, so I have actually been on four different floors.

The only other thing to change was who my boss was. In the last decade, through a series of mergers and acquisitions and strategic realignments and consultant reorganizations, I have actually reported to 12 different people or, in other words, I have had 12 different bosses. Maybe that tells you all you really need to know about the constant change on Wall Street in the financial services industry.

All 12 of my bosses had one trait in common: they allowed me the editorial investment license to write exactly what I think.

There was never any pressure from them to write a positive commentary about technology or anything else for that matter, nor was there ever any pressure to not write something negative about Korea, or any other topic I was concerned about. I have been very blessed, indeed, to have worked for all 12 of these executives, beginning with Jack Neal, over a decade ago to my current boss, Axel Schwarzer, and my 10 bosses in between: Steve Reynolds, Cornelia Small, Ted Truscott, Mark Casady, Tom Littauer, Lin Coughlin, Dean Barr, Leo Grohowski, Bill Shiebler, and Tom Eggers. I thank each and every one of them, because without their faith and confidence in me and my investment views, there would have been no commentaries, and if there were no commentaries, there would be no book today.

As I bring this introduction to a close, I want to once again focus on my father, who never set foot on Wall Street in his entire life. In his own way, however, he taught me everything I needed to know to be successful there. He taught me that what you end up doing in life is not as important as how you do it. Whatever you do, you need to do it with passion and enthusiasm. And when someone gives you an opportunity, the greatest thing that you can give them in return is your loyalty. That is exactly how he lived every day of his working life; for 45 years, he was one of the most loyal employees Gimbels department store in Pittsburgh ever had. I saw firsthand, as a child, the passion and enthusiasm he took to his job every day. Each and every day of my summer vacation, while I was in grade school, I would spend a half day with him in his truck, delivering packages all over the North Side of Pittsburgh. He was so proud of what he did for a living, and how he did it, that he wanted to share it with me firsthand. Maybe that's the reason, 20 years later, both of my daughters, Marianne and Stephanie, have traveled with me on "Daddy dates" to see firsthand what I do for a living.

Customers even wrote complimentary letters about my father to Gimbels' senior management about the way he delivered packages to their homes. He had an impact on people's lives, and all he did was drive a truck to deliver packages. To him, it was never about what he did, but rather how he did it. If my father could bring passion and enthusiasm to driving a local delivery truck, how could I not be passionate and enthusiastic about the opportunity afforded to me to actually work on Wall Street? I have tried to live up to the high standards he set on Main Street as a truck driver every day I have worked as a strategist all these years on Wall Street. With loyalty, passion, and enthusiasm, you can accomplish anything that you set out to do.

Whether you read my commentaries for the first time or the fifth time, you will quickly realize that I am a man not lacking in opinions, and I love to share them without hesitation. I try to mix my boundless enthusiasm, common-sense approach, and occasional wit with my "contrarian" investment insights. This combination has enabled me to offer enlightened ways to view the world of investing. I do this by trying to fill readers' minds with wonderful personal anecdotes, facts, and stories from my travels around the globe, searching for investment opportunities.

This led my hometown paper, the *Chicago Tribune*, to write this about me a decade ago: "The error-prone strategists and economists make the mistake of believing that the future will unfold just like the past. There are others, however, who have the eyes to see the dust in the distance, ears to hear the hoofbeats of the thundering herd, and noses to *smell the money to be made*. One of those is Dr. Bob."

I hope that you enjoy, once again, reading my commentaries as much as I have enjoyed writing them over the past decade, all the while trying to help you *smell the money to be made!*

A BULL FOR ALL SEASONS

CHAPTER 1

The Economy

The only function of economic forecasting is to make astrology look respectable.

JOHN KENNETH GALBRAITH
Canadian-American economist and author

INTRODUCTION

In its purest sense the economy is merely a system of human activities related to the production, distribution, exchange, and consumption of goods and services of a country. The economy of a country is measured by something we call *gross domestic product*, or GDP. The GDP of a country is defined as the total market value of all final goods and services produced within a given period of time, typically a quarter or a calendar year.

The GDP is also considered the sum or value that is added at every stage of production of all final goods and services produced within a country within that given period of time. From an investment perspective, however, it is much more than that. It's about interest, consumption, inflation, and unemployment, to name a few.

Interest is a fee paid on borrowed capital. By far the most common form in which these assets are lent is money; however, other assets may be lent to the borrower: assets such as shares, major assets such as aircraft, and even entire factories in lease arrangements.

In each case the interest is calculated upon the value of the assets in the same manner as it is upon money. Interest should be looked at as "paying rent on money."

One of the main reasons we borrow is to consume. From an economic perspective, consumption was a concept actually developed by John Maynard Keynes. According to Keynes, consumption actually consisted of two main categories: *induced consumption* and *autonomous consumption*. Induced consumption refers to increases in consumer spending that occur as disposable income rises. In economic theory this increase in consumption as a result of an increase in disposable income is referred to as the "marginal propensity to consume."

Meanwhile, autonomous consumption refers to spending that is done as part of long-term plans for the future, usually driven more by habit or even contractual commitments. Changes in plans or goals, and expectations or habits, are what drive this type of consumption, not changes in income. Put these two types of consumption together and you will realize that consumer spending accounts for over two-thirds of the U.S. economy, which is why it is so important to investors. But consumption is not the only important factor; investors the world over are also worried about inflation.

From a classical economic theory perspective, *inflation* means increasing the money supply, while *deflation* means decreasing it. In layman's terms inflation would be referred to as "expansionary" monetary policy and deflation as "contractionary" monetary policy. But Wall Street is worried about so much more than just inflation (increasing the money supply) and deflation (decreasing the money supply). We're also concerned about *hyperinflation*, which is an out-of-control inflationary spiral. *Stagflation* is a combination of inflation and rising unemployment. And don't forget about *reflation*, which is an attempt to raise prices to counteract deflationary pressures. However, the real reason that investors focus so much time and effort on inflation is because there are actually six separate measures of inflation that we have to worry about.

First we have the *Consumer Price Index* (CPI), which measures the price of a selection of goods purchased by a "typical" consumer. Second, we have the *Producer Price Index* (PPI), which measures the price received by a producer. Keep in mind that PPI differs from CPI in that profits and taxes may cause the amount received by the producer to differ from what the consumer paid. There is also typically a delay between an increase in the PPI and any resulting increase in the CPI. Producer price inflation measures the pressure being put on producers by the costs of their raw materials. This can be "passed on" as consumer inflation, or it can be absorbed by profits, or offset by increasing productivity. Third, we have *wholesale price indices*, which measure the price of a selection of goods at wholesale, prior to retail markups and sales taxes. Wholesale price indices are very similar to the producer price index. Fourth, we have the cost-of-living indices (COLI), which often adjust fixed incomes and contractual incomes based on measures of price changes of goods and services. Fifth, we have the *GDP deflator*, which is a measure of the price of all the goods and services included in the GDP. Sixth, and finally, we have the *commodity price index*, which measures the price of a selection of commodities. Currently, commodity prices are weighted by the relative importance of each commodity. Now it is easy to see why just about every minute of every day someone on Wall Street has something to say about inflation.

As I bring this introduction to the economy to a close, let's focus on unemployment, certainly one of the most important economic components that drives our markets. *Unemployment*, as defined by the International Labor Organization, is the condition of those individuals who are currently not working but are willing and able to work for pay, who are currently available to work, and who have actively searched for work.

In the United States, the Bureau of Labor Statistics measures employment and unemployment using two different labor force surveys. The first is the Current Population Survey (CPS), which is referred to on Wall Street as the "household survey." The CPS conducts a survey based on a sample of 60,000 households. The second is the Current Employment Statistics (CES) survey, which is referred to on Wall Street as the "payroll survey." The payroll survey is based on a sample of 160,000 businesses and government agencies that represent 400,000 individual employers.

Let's think for a minute about just how confusing these numbers can be. The unemployment figures indicate how many are not working for pay, but are seeking employment for pay. These figures are only indirectly connected with the number of people who are actually not working at all or working without pay. Therefore, the actual methods of measuring unemployment may be flawed, especially when you take into account the almost 2 percent of the available working population incarcerated in U.S. prisons; those who have lost their jobs and have become discouraged over time from actively looking for work; those who are self-employed or wish to become self-employed, such as computer consultants, tradespeople, or building contractors; those who have been laid off before the official retirement age but who would still like to work (involuntary early retirees); those on disability pensions, who, while not possessing full health still wish to work in occupations suitable for their medical conditions; and those who work for payment for as little as one hour per week but would like to work full time.

Workers in the latter category are considered "involuntary part-time" workers: for example, those who are underemployed (a computer programmer who is working in a retail store until he can find a permanent job), involuntary stay-at-home mothers who would prefer to work, or graduate students who were unable to find worthwhile jobs after they received their Bachelor's degrees.

But wait, it gets even better. There is another school of thought on Wall Street that claims the estimates of employment and unemployment may be "too high." In some countries the availability of unemployment benefits can inflate statistics because they give people an incentive to register as unemployed. People who do not really seek work may choose to declare themselves unemployed in order to get benefits; people with undeclared paid occupations may try to get unemployment benefits in addition to the money they earn from their work. Conversely, if there is an absence of any tangible benefit for registering as unemployed, people will not bother to register.

On the pages that follow you will get my perspectives and insights about exactly how and why the economy will impact your investments.

The Rules Have Changed

JUNE 1, 1998

In the "old world" of investing, success was determined by one's ability to discover some little-known facts or figures regarding a company, industry, or market influence. Whoever obtained this information first might have a considerable advantage over others in the financial marketplace. But today the technology revolution has leveled the playing field. With the Internet and news providers like CNN and Bloomberg, now essentially everyone has immediate access to the same vast store of information. In the new world order, success is not determined by who secures the information first, but by how the information is analyzed. And to analyze the information accurately today, investors need to toss out a few of the old economic rules.

One former rule of thumb was that our nation's savings rate was an indicator of how much money would eventually flow into the financial markets. Today, that concept is outdated. Our economy has shifted from a manufacturing economy to a service economy. This shift has activated a new flow of money into our markets, particularly in the first quarter of each year. In a manufacturing sector, if an employee works 5 or 10 hours of overtime, the employee's next paycheck will reflect overtime compensation. That additional compensation will probably be spent immediately, because the employee views it as "extra" money. In the service sector, an employee can work 5, 10, or even 25 extra hours, but the employee's paycheck will remain the same. Compensation for extra hard work will usually come in the form of a year-end bonus or commission. Rather than being spent, this lump sum most often finds its way into the market during the first quarter of the year.

Another old economic rule was that holiday retail sales could be used to evaluate how strong gift-buying was and, in turn, how strong our economy would be. But today, many holiday gifts aren't reflected in retail store sales. Counting how many Barbie dolls are sold just doesn't make it anymore. Baby boomers are giving gifts in the form of plane tickets, weekend getaways, gift certificates, luxury cruises, and tickets to sporting events. These gifts aren't reported in the traditional retail sales figures.

Yet another old economic rule was that if unemployment was low, inflation would rise. This was based on the simple fact that if everyone had a job, workers could demand higher wages, thus causing an increase in prices. Today's global economy has made this rule obsolete. Unemployment is the lowest it has been in 25 years, yet we still have low and stable inflation. In a global marketplace, jobs can be easily moved anywhere in the world, keeping inflation in check.

So in the new world order, the rules have changed. Successful investors will be those who can keep pace with the new rules, as they continue to emerge and evolve.

Investment Footnote . . . What actually happened

In the third quarter of 1998 our economy, as measured by GDP, grew at a whopping 4.7 percent. The fourth quarter of 1998 was even better, posting a 6.2 percent growth rate.

Rate Cut Is Second Key to Rebound—What to Look for Next

SEPTEMBER 29, 1998

The Federal Open Markets Committee, referred to in financial circles as the FOMC or the Fed, cut interest rates today by one-fourth of a point (25 basis points) to 5.25 percent. Finally, Federal Reserve Board Chairman Alan Greenspan and the FOMC realized that the inflation bogeyman that they have been looking for under the bed is dead.

For the past two years, Maureen Allyn, our chief economist, has insightfully and correctly been predicting that "the new risks would be deflationary, not inflationary." In my recent book, *The Three Bears*

Are Dead, I concluded that "two powerful factors have combined to kill inflation: the global economy and productivity."

On September 23, Greenspan said, "Deteriorating foreign economies and their spillover to domestic markets have increased the possibility that the slowdown in the growth of the American economy will be more than sufficient to hold inflation in check." Welcome home, Alan!

Don't underestimate the significance of this interest rate cut. It was one of my four keys to the stock market continuing its rebound and the Dow Jones Industrial Average charging forward to 10,000 by the end of the year. Almost one month ago, on August 31, I told you that interest rates will be cut now, at the next meeting of the Fed. I'm changing my forecast of no interest rate movements in 1998 to one, if not two interest rate cuts in 1998. The Fed can no longer afford to sit on the sidelines. I believe rates will be cut 25 to 50 basis points between now and October 1.

LET'S REVIEW MY FOUR KEYS

On August 31, I identified four keys to the turnaround in the U.S. stock market. Let's review the status of those four keys today:

Key: Corporate Stock Buybacks

Status: What does CMNPLBPENEPUBM spell? It spells a parade of companies doing exactly what I said they would—stepping up to the plate and buying back their own stocks in the open market. Oh, and in case you're interested in the details, here is a list of companies that have announced major stock buybacks in September:

C—Continental Airlines

M—Mattel

N—Nations Bank

P—Pfizer

L—Lehman Brothers

B—Bell Atlantic

P—PhyCor

E—Estee Lauder

N—Neiman Marcus

E—Equitable Companies

P—Pier 1 Imports

U—United Airlines

B—Boeing

M—McDonalds

Key: Rescue Package for Russia

Status: No more worry about bombs for food and medicine. A rescue package has not been put together for Russia yet. However, now that we actually have a government in place, since Russian President Boris Yeltsin has named Yevgeny Primakov prime minister, the risks of having no government in place and the potential for trading bombs for food and medicine by angry soldiers have been dramatically, if not completely, reduced.

Simply put, the Russian crisis has dropped in order of global significance compared to other global events that have a higher priority. However, I still feel there will be a new aid package for Russia.

Key: Interest Rate Cut

Status: I told you that a rate cut was in the bank. Greenspan does not like to surprise the financial markets; he's been telling us that he's going to cut interest rates, and today he finally made good on his word.

Key: International Monetary Fund (IMF) Appropriation and Fast-Track Trade Authority

Status: We still need help from Congress . . . write your representatives now! Fast-track trade authority is now officially dead; it failed in the House of Representatives by a 243–180 vote on Friday, September 25. Meanwhile, on the International Monetary Fund appropriation front, we are halfway there. The Senate has approved the Treasury Department's full $17.9 billion request to replenish IMF reserves and double an existing credit line for future financial crises. The House meanwhile rejected an amendment that would have added $14.5 billion to $3.4 billion already pegged for IMF in a foreign aid bill. A House–Senate negotiating session is the next step in determining final IMF funding.

A NEW FOCUS GOING FORWARD

With two of my four keys to the stock market rebound behind us (stock buybacks and interest rate cut), I would like to sharpen my focus on the new keys that will provide the fuel to take our stock market to 10,000 in the fourth quarter.

Key 1: Earnings

Let's not forget that it's earnings that drive our markets; everything else is noise that creates short-term volatility (Monicagate, Russian crisis, Hedge Fund bailout, etc., etc.). I expect earnings to surprise on the high side in the fourth quarter. Now, that doesn't mean that profits and growth haven't deteriorated—they have. However, expectations have fallen through the roof. A short six weeks ago, earnings expectations for profit growth for the fourth quarter were +10 percent; today expectations have fallen to −1 percent. This dramatic reduction of expectations is also one of the reasons that we have had a very small parade of pre-earnings disappointments announcements. Granted, we had our high-profile announcements from Coca-Cola, Procter & Gamble, and Gillette, but the preannouncements have been few and far between. There's a good chance, if the economy doesn't slow too fast, that earnings could surprise on the high side of painfully revised expectations.

Key 2: Global Rate Cuts

Japan has already cut rates and there's no more room to cut—current rates are at one-fourth of 1 percent. The United States has now also cut rates. I expect the talk of a coordinated interest rate cut to emerge again. If you recall a few weeks ago, the German central bank president, Hans Tietmeyer, said "No way" to a German rate cut. That was because of the election. With the German elections behind us, we need a rate cut from Germany and the United Kingdom. I look for both countries to cut rates before year end.

Key 3: International Monetary Fund Appropriation

I will be the first to admit that the IMF has its flaws. However, it's the best thing we have. We must find a way to both fund it and fix it at the same time. I think the volatility in the global capital markets will pressure Congress into fully funding the IMF before the end of the year.

Key 4: Japanese Bank Reform

Japan must adopt a credible plan to reform its banking system. Depending on whose figures you believe, bad loans in Japan range from $600 billion to $1 trillion. At least we can say that they are trying. They first planned to establish a bridge bank to take over weak banks until sources of funding could be found for bad loans. Next there was a plan to nationalize weak banks and then sell off their parts over a fixed period of time. Third came the plan to establish a new ministry/agency equal to others in Japan to take over the weak banks and manage dissolution of them in a way similar to the U.S. savings and loan crisis. It's also important to note that this is not just about Japan; it's about all emerging markets as well. The single most important event to turn around emerging markets and to restore investor confidence is not within any emerging market; it's within Japan—in the name of banking reform. While experts on Wall Street are clearly divided on what will happen next, I belong to the camp that believes Japan will enact some positive banking reform by the end of the year.

A SEPTEMBER TO REMEMBER!

September has certainly been a great month for our stock market. In fact, three of the top five biggest point gains in the history of the Dow Jones Industrial Average occurred in September 1998. On September 8, the market rose 380 points—high enough to rank it as the number 1 gaining day of all time. On September 1, the market rose 288 points, which ranked it as the third highest. And on September 23, the market rose 257 points—a gain that ranked as the fifth all-time high.

As we make our final turn and head into the fourth quarter, keep focused on my four new keys: earnings, global rate cuts, International Monetary Fund funding, and Japan banking reform.

Have you noticed what one of my four keys isn't? It's the Bill Clinton, Ken Starr, Monica Lewinsky saga. While the Clinton scandal will continue to be headline news that can have an influence on the short-term volatility of our markets, it will not influence the ultimate long-term direction of our markets. Rest assured the media hype will eventually pass. When you are living through it, you think that it will never end, but it will. Despite the headlines it will attract, the Clinton saga will not determine where our stock market is headed. The following will determine it.

- Earnings
- Global rate cuts
- International Monetary Fund funding
- Japan banking reform

Have a great day and I'll see ya at 10,000!

PS: In case you haven't noticed, in each of the three weeks since Labor Day, the markets have posted triple-digit positive gains for the week (week of September 7, +155; week of September 14, +100; and last week, the week of September 21, +133).

PPS: Thank you, Mr. Greenspan!

Investment Footnote . . . What actually happened

The Federal Reserve Board did indeed cut interest rates two more times in 1998, once on October 15, 1998, and again on November 17, 1998. And the Dow did reach 10,000; in fact, by the end of 1999 the Dow stood at 11,497.

What's the Significance of 6–15–22–36?

May 1, 1999

No, this is not the latest prefix to the newest low-cost, long-distance carrier. Instead, it may hold the key to one of the reasons why our economy has surprised all of the so-called experts with record growth continuing through the first part of 1999.

The key is taxes—specifically, tax refunds. In order to understand the significance of these tax refunds, let me explain it to you in terms of 6–15–22–36.

6 Represents the 6 percent increase in the number of individuals who received income tax refunds this year. A 6 percent increase means that more than 76 million individuals received an income tax refund check from Uncle Sam.

15 Stands for the 15 percent average increase in the amount of the refund that these 76 million taxpayers received. As a result of this 15 percent increase, the average refund for these 76 million people was $1,531.

22 Represents the total aggregate increase in tax refunds this year: 22 percent. This is the single largest year-over-year increase since the Tax Reform Act of 1986. You see, when 6 percent more people receive refunds and refunds on average increase 15 percent, the impact on the total in tax refunds can be profound. This 22 percent increase means that individual taxpayers received a whopping $116 billion in refund checks.

You need to understand that when they receive that check, they don't invest the money. They spend it. Taxpayers view anything that they get back from the federal government as discretionary income—icing on the cake, if you will. They don't save; they celebrate by spending it.

36 Accounts for the fact that an amazing 36 percent of all refund checks were electronically transferred straight into bank accounts. This allowed the impact to be immediate. Taxpayers didn't have to wait for the check in the mail.

One of the reasons that these large increases in refunds have caught the market off guard is that there were no landmark changes in the tax code, so no one was looking for a dramatic increase in refunds. There were, however, three tax code changes, and it was the combination of these three changes that fueled the explosion in refunds. First, there was a Child Tax Credit, followed by two different education tax credits that fueled the refunds.

When someone comes to you and complains that they just can't figure out how this economy has stayed so strong, simply look them in the eye and say 6–15–22–36.

Investment Footnote . . . What actually happened

In the second quarter of 1999 our economy grew at 3.4 percent, as measured by GDP. Growth in the third quarter was even faster, at 4.8 percent, while the fourth quarter was faster still at 7.3 percent.

The Phantom Menace—Inflation!

JUNE 2, 1999

While summertime moviegoers and Star Wars loyalists are being thrilled by the new George Lucas movie, *The Phantom Menace,* summer investors are being thrilled and chilled by the investment world's phantom menace—this year, inflation.

A little over a year ago the consensus of Wall Street economists was that deflation, not inflation, would finally bring this bull market to an abrupt halt. Well now those same economists have shifted gears 180 degrees and have the entire investment world on the lookout for our new enemy—inflation. In all likelihood, the world's most renowned economist, the chairman of the Federal Reserve Board, Alan Greenspan, is so worried about inflation that he even convinced the Fed to change its policy direction toward a bias to tighten (raise rates) from a neutral policy. While the great inflation debate will last well through the summer, let me share with you why I believe we will not see a rise in inflation.

SLOWER SECOND-HALF U.S. GROWTH

The U.S. economy will slow down on its own in the second half of the year, based on four developments. First, there will be no record tax refunds to fuel the economy in the second half. Second, interest rates are much higher today than they were when the year began. When the year began, interest rates, as measured by the yield on the benchmark 30-year Treasury bond, stood a little above 5 percent. Now, as we enter into the second half of the year, it is a little above 6 percent. This 100-basis-point move will slow consumers' purchases of housing and automobiles in the second half. Third, the first half of the year received a tremendous boost from mortgage refinancing due to falling rates. This has all but dried up. Mortgage refinancing is off a whopping 75 percent. Fourth, and finally, oil prices are up almost 40 percent since we started the year. The rising price of oil has a key psychological impact on consumers because they see it every time they drive into the gas station.

PRODUCTIVITY WILL CONTINUE TO IMPROVE

The technology revolution is far from over. This boom in technology will continue to improve productivity. Improved productivity enables business to keep prices down because they are producing more with the same number of or sometimes fewer employees.

STRONG DOLLAR

Our economy remains one of the strongest economies anywhere in the world. Thus, I don't look for our dollar to weaken anytime soon. Remember, the key to a strong dollar is that it keeps the prices of imports down because they are cheaper when purchased with a strong dollar. Meanwhile, domestic prices have to stay low to compete with these low-priced imports.

COMPETITION IN EUROLAND

The launching of the euro, the common currency for the 11 countries that make up Euroland, is also serving to keep a lid on prices because of the increased competition within Europe. This new Euroland is now the second largest economy in the world at over $6 trillion, trailing only the United States. Meanwhile, there are more people in Euroland than there are in the United States. With everyone in Euroland focused on competition, this also means that they are focusing on keeping prices down, which is good for inflation.

RISING MEDICAL COSTS?

There's a growing consensus that the recent rise in medical costs is proof that inflation is coming back. Well I believe that the recent rise in medical costs will actually be deflationary not inflationary, and here is why. The rise in medical costs is due to dramatic increases in medical technology. Don't forget this medical technology is actually substituting capital for labor. Over time when you substitute capital for labor, costs go down, not up. And even though I'm not an economist, I know that when costs go down, it is not inflationary.

COMMODITY PRICES ARE DOWN

Once you get past the bellwether headline-grabbing price of oil, which is up, you get a much different picture of commodity prices. The price of lead is down. The price of tin is down. The prices of nickel, zinc, and copper all are down. Meanwhile the price of gold is in a freefall downward. Again, it's hard to get inflation with commodity prices falling.

I would strongly suggest that investors join the ranks with moviegoers this summer because if you are looking for the phantom menace—inflation—the only place I see a phantom menace will be at the movie theater. May the force be with you!

Investment Footnote . . . What actually happened ↓

Inflation, as measured by CPI, stood at 1.97 percent in June 1999. One year later it actually soared to 3.73 percent.

A Golden Oldie?

OCTOBER 2, 1999

The recent meteoric rise in the price of gold has given new life to the "old school" economists and strategists who have historically warned us that rising gold prices will always be followed by rising inflation. The old school is wrong. This recent rise in gold prices is not an indicator of future inflation.

Let's take a closer look at some of the recent issues surrounding this meteoric rise in prices.

SUPPLY NOT DEMAND

The recent move in gold was not fueled by some great "demand" for gold over other financial assets such as stocks and bonds. In other words, people aren't dumping their stock and bond portfolios en masse to buy gold. Rather, this is a "supply"-driven rally. There will be less gold on the open market to buy, which always pushes prices higher. This supply-side rally was fueled in late September when the European Central Bank, along with 14 other individual nations who were all part of the International Monetary Fund, decided not to sell or to lease any "additional" gold holdings for the next five years.

VOLATILE SWINGS

The price of gold is a volatile commodity. It tends to overreact on both the high side and the low side. The typical gold investor is very focused on inflationary developments. Thus any inflationary signals are usually interpreted to be much better or much worse than they actually are. In other words, the price of gold tends to overreact to "potential inflationary" signs— even if these signs never live up to their much-hyped inflation potential.

GOLD IS STILL DOWN

Sometimes we get so excited about where the price of an asset has been the past few days or weeks, we tend to lose sight of the bigger picture. In other words, where has it been the past few years? Just as it is important to be a long-term investor looking forward with a longer-term time horizon, it is equally important to use a longer-term time horizon when looking backward to get a truer picture.

I would be the first to admit that from a short-term perspective, gold's meteoric rise from its low of $252 an ounce in August to above $300 an ounce could appear alarming. However, if you simply look back to its peak in January 1996 at $412 an ounce you get a much different picture. Did gold move up from $252 to $300 or down from $412 to $300? It all depends on your frame of reference. Given the choice, I like to believe the glass is half full not half empty.

GOLD TOO NARROW?

Watching any one commodity to determine inflation is a losing proposition. If you want to focus on gold, focus on it in the context of the CRB Commodity Index. After all, this broad-based index includes gold as well as other precious metals, oil and energy, grains, industrials, etc. This broad-based index, even with the recent rise in both gold and oil, continues to show no inflation on the horizon.

Y2K GOLD BUG

One other factor that is playing out in the price of gold is the Y2K bug factor. There is no doubt that some nervous investors want to head into the new millennium with some small piece of their assets in a hard, tangible investment that they can hold in their hands even if the lights go out on December 31, 1999. Don't forget, however, once these investors realize the world didn't end, they will be selling their gold coins en masse.

Help your clients keep the meteoric rise of gold in perspective. I've often wondered why we call it a meteoric rise anyway. After all meteors fall—they don't rise. Maybe gold and meteors do have something in common. They both will continue falling!

Investment Footnote . . . What actually happened ⟷

In October 1999 the CPI stood at 2.56 percent and one year later it had risen to 3.45 percent. Meanwhile, gold stood at $298 an ounce in October 1999 and one year later it did indeed fall all the way to $264 an ounce.

Three Reasons We Have a "New" Economy

MARCH 13, 2000

As we entered the year 2000, our economic expansion officially became our longest running ever. This current expansion, which began in the second quarter of 1991, now eclipses the previous record, which spanned second-quarter 1961 to fourth-quarter 1969.

Everyone seems to agree we're in a "new economy" of some sort. But I'd like to ask, just what the heck is so "new" about this economy, anyway?

To answer that question, I thought it might be interesting to look back at the most recent record economic expansion (1961–1969) and compare it to our current economic expansion to see if we could find out exactly what's new or different.

Actually, there are three key differences that make this current economic expansion new: productivity, unemployment, and the Internet.

PRODUCTIVITY

Technological improvements and cost cutting continue to push productivity growth to new record levels. When our last record economic expansion ended in 1969, productivity was actually decreasing at a 0.3 percent rate. Current productivity growth, on a year-over-year basis, stands at a whopping +3.4 percent. That's quite a stark contrast.

The fact remains that everywhere you look, we are figuring out how to do things better, faster, and cheaper, and that's fueling productivity. The technology revolution is just showing the tip of the iceberg, and we can expect record productivity enhancements to be the order of the day for some time.

If you want some idea of how great this productivity explosion is, consider this: In the most recent government productivity release (fourth quarter, 1999), worker efficiency increased at an astonishing 6 percent annual rate. Even more amazing, manufacturing productivity, which is easier to measure and is much more accurate, increased at an unbelievable 10.9 percent pace. Wow!

UNEMPLOYMENT

In the old economy, low unemployment led to higher wages, which led to inflation, which led to higher interest rates, which stopped the economic expansion. Today we have historically low unemployment but no wage inflation. Why? I can think of three reasons.

First is the explosion of mergers and acquisitions everywhere. Just think of the recent megamerger between Time Warner and America Online. Do you really think anyone at Time Warner or AOL is worried about what his or her salary increase will be next year? Absolutely not. Their concern is whether they will have a job next year.

And what about the two accounting firms that work for Time Warner and AOL? Soon there will only be one accounting firm and one law firm—not two. Do you get the picture?

Second, corporate cost cutting and downsizing are continuing everywhere, even with the bluest of the blue chip companies. Boeing is laying off 7,000; Procter & Gamble, 15,000; Kodak, 20,000. Meanwhile, AT&T is launching a $2 billion cost-cutting program while British Telecom is cutting $1 billion. With all of this cost cutting and downsizing, it's tough to ask for a raise.

Third, the way we compensate employees has changed. Today employees want stock and stock options and stock appreciation rights and stock warrants. As Corporate America has been successful in pushing ownership down to all levels of employees, it has been successful in keeping wage increases relatively small because the real wealth accumulation comes in the form of stock, not wages.

THE INTERNET

Maybe the biggest new thing in this economy is the Internet. The growth in the Internet has been amazing. Just recently, both Ford Motor Co. and Delta Airlines offered home personal computers to workers so they can access the Internet. Meanwhile, President Clinton recently unveiled a $2 billion proposal to get more minorities and lower-income citizens online.

Some people think the Internet can't continue to grow. I think they are dead wrong and here is why. There are currently 100 million homes in the United States—79 million have personal computers, while only 35 million have Internet access. Meanwhile, in the rest of the world there are 1.1 billion homes and both personal computers and Internet usage are in single digits.

Just think how big the Internet has become. It now generates as much revenue as the auto industry. In 1998 (1999 figures are not yet available) more than half the jobs created were Internet-related.

Meanwhile, Toyota recently disclosed that the Internet is its largest source of sales leads, providing more than 1.5 million per month. And finally, consider this: In 1998, the United States Post Office delivered 104 billion pieces of first-class mail. Meanwhile, for every one letter that was sent, more than 30 e-mails were sent. That's right; in 1998 the Internet handled a whopping 3.4 trillion e-mails. In 1969 there were no e-mails, at least not as we know them today.

The next time someone asks you what's so new about this new economy, look him or her in the eye and tell them productivity, unemployment, and the Internet.

Investment Footnote . . . What actually happened ↑

The next quarterly productivity number showed a booming increase from 2.18 percent on March 31, 2000, to 3.84 percent on June 30, 2000. September 30, 2000, wasn't bad either, posting a 2.89 percent gain.

It's the "Old Economy," Stupid!

April 3, 2000

With this being a presidential election year, it's only fitting that we dust off one of the most famous one-liners in presidential politics: "It's the economy, stupid." President Clinton's political advisor James Carville made that catchy one-liner famous. Well, I've updated that famous presidential campaign quote; now it's "It's the old economy, stupid."

Everywhere you turn the debate continues—will it be the new economy companies that continue to drive the market or will it be the old economy companies that regain market leadership? How about both?

It is a mistake to think that our technology revolution is just about new economy companies. The technology revolution is not just about these new dot-com companies that seem to be launched almost daily. It's really about the old economy companies embracing the new economy of technology and the Internet. Once the old economy companies get hooked on the Internet, they will take both the old economy companies and the new economy companies to even higher levels. Some of the old economy companies are getting hooked already.

Maybe the oldest of the old economy industries is the transportation industry. Let me share with you what that old economy industry is doing today. First, the big three automakers created a web-based auto parts supply exchange to transact over $250 billion of auto parts a year. This high-tech solution will save the big three millions of dollars. So who is the beneficiary? Is it the new economy technology industry or the old economy automobile industry, which will reap the millions of dollars of savings? How about both?

In addition, demonstrating that this revolution in transportation isn't restricted to the ground, Southwest Airlines hit a new milestone recently. More than one-quarter of its passenger revenues came from bookings over its Web site. That's an old economy company making money using a new economy tool.

In fact, the best way to look at the lynchpin of the new economy, namely the Internet, is to look at it as a tool. Once we realize that the Internet is only a tool, we will also realize that not every tool or, specifically, not every company that puts a dot-com on its name, will be successful. What all this means is that maybe the real beneficiaries of the Internet and the technology revolution just might be the old economy companies that figure out how to use the new economy tools. Remember, it's all these old economy companies like the big three automakers that are actually giving substance to the potential of the Internet.

With all of the hoopla of the Internet and the new economy, we forget that most Americans still work for "old economy" companies. And it's these old economy companies that are largely driving the technology revolution, which in turn is driving the new economy companies.

This is not just a debate of old versus new. Simply put, you can't have one without the other—the new economy companies will soar only if the old economy companies fuel the technology revolution and take them there.

It might be helpful to think of the old economy companies in this way the next time someone tries to tell you that the old economy is dead. Just remember how you start most of your days. You wake up after sleeping under a blanket made by an old economy company on a mattress made by another old economy company. You then shave with a razor made by an old economy company and brush your teeth with toothpaste made by another old economy company. And finally it's off to work in your car made by still another old economy company.

It's the "old" economy, stupid!

Things Just Don't Measure Up!

JUNE 1, 2000

It seems as though as each week goes by we have another economic release that causes our market either to rally or to crash. While I will be the first to admit that it is important to monitor these releases, it is also important to remember that measuring our economy is not an exact science, and maybe—just maybe—some of these releases aren't telling the whole story. Currently, there are three economic indicators that are causing great concern in our market. The first is gross domestic product (the broadest measure of our economy). The "bears" say it's growing too fast. The second is our nation's savings rate, where the bears again point out that it is way too low. Third, and finally, is our unemployment rate, where the bears are again concerned that it is way too low.

I would like to address these three negative economic indicators and see if they measure up.

GROSS DOMESTIC PRODUCT

To anyone who watches how economists measure things it should be a surprise to no one that the past two economic quarters were some of the strongest back-to-back quarters in decades. The reason isn't just because the economy is strong—it's because we also changed how we measure gross domestic product (GDP), starting in the fourth quarter of 1999.

Starting this past October, economists revised how we measure GDP. If you recall, over the past few years economists have been engaged in a great debate regarding how we measure inflation in the consumer price index. Well, economists finally agreed to change how we measure inflation. We changed how we measure the consumer price index to better capture new pricing issues. These revisions to how we capture inflation in the consumer price index, however, were never reflected in our GDP release—until this past October. Thus, this past October we began revising inflation downward when measuring GDP. And if you revise inflation down, it will, as a result, produce an upward revision to economic growth (as measured by GDP).

Also, this past October for the first time ever, computer software was counted in capital expenditures and government spending, which are part of GDP. It's amazing to think that this booming segment of our economy was never counted before. I don't know about you but I find it extremely difficult to do anything with my computer if I don't have any software. The fact that economists are finally counting the fastest-growing component of our economy and that it is pushing economic growth higher should surprise no one.

SAVINGS RATE

In my opinion, the single greatest reason why we have such a low savings rate is the way in which economists calculate the number. They begin by estimating personal income. Then, actual taxes paid are subtracted from that number. Then, actual consumption expenditures are subtracted from that number, and what is left is what we call our savings rate.

Now think about this for a minute. In the past few years of this unbelievably strong bull market, capital gains (as a result of stock price appreciation) have been rapidly and dramatically rising along with a sharp increase in capital gains taxes. Now get this. While the capital gains taxes are subtracted from current income, the actual capital gains as a result of rising stock values are not counted as income. And to make matters worse, if people spend some of these capital gains, it makes the consumption figure go up, which in turn lowers our savings rate.

Without the tax distortion, I believe our actual savings rate would be twice what it is. While I will be the first to admit that we still have a long way to go, I also strongly believe that it's not nearly as bad as the numbers lead you to believe.

UNEMPLOYMENT RATE

There is a common belief in economic circles that low unemployment will cause higher inflation. This concept is commonly referred to as the Phillips curve of the NAIRU concept. The foundation of the Phillips curve theory is this: low employment causes high inflation. NAIRU, which stands for *nonaccelerating inflation rate of unemployment*, is simply another way of saying exactly the same thing. In other words, these concepts have convinced the market that wage inflation is caused by too many people working!

Economists, however, can't explain how we can have record-low unemployment levels with virtually no inflation. Thus, they are attempting to convince the market that inflation is right around the corner. Well, I for one am not convinced. Most of the problem is rooted in the way economists and the federal government calculate the unemployment rate.

While we currently find ourselves in the midst of the year 2000 census, let me fall back to the last official census we took in 1990 to show you what I mean. In 1990, the census tracked 6.8 million Americans unemployed, while 133.1 million were employed. However, consider this: Another 50 million (actually 49.9 million) healthy, able-to-work adults were omitted from the employment category and the unemployment category. They weren't counted as part of the 133.1 million employed because they didn't have a job. (I can understand that.) However, get this—they weren't counted as unemployed either. The reason is that the Labor Department doesn't count them as unemployed unless they are actually seeking a job. I guess we should consider these people invisible. So the 1990 census should actually read 133.1 million employed, 6.8 million unemployed, and

49.9 million invisible. Give me a break. It's the so-called invisible work force that is helping to keep a lid on wage inflation.

In my way of thinking, you're either employed or unemployed. Maybe the 1990 census should read 133.1 million employed and 56.7 unemployed, some of which are invisible. Thus, maybe our labor markets aren't so tight after all. And maybe—just maybe—our record-low unemployment rate will not cause inflation.

As investors, it's important to remember that sometimes how we measure a number is more important than the number that we are trying to measure. After all, if you look closely, you too will realize that these economic releases that we are so afraid of as investors just don't measure up!

Investment Footnote . . . What actually happened

Our economy, as measured by GDP, did indeed boom in the second quarter of 2000, up 6.4 percent for the quarter and 4.9 percent on a year-over-year basis. And even though employment fell for June 2000, as we had negative job growth of −43,000, it more than rebounded the next month, growing 176,000 new jobs.

What's New about the New Economy?

July 1, 2000

Now that we find ourselves in the midst of the longest-running economic expansion in the history of the United States, we hear a lot of talk about something called the "new economy." Just what about our economy is so new? To answer that question, I compared our current economic expansion to the last record economic expansion, which took place from 1961 and 1969. I found three key differences: productivity, unemployment, and the Internet.

A PRODUCTIVITY EXPLOSION

We're in the midst of a productivity explosion: Fourth-quarter productivity increased an astonishing 6 percent from the previous quarter, and manufacturing productivity, which is much more accurate, increased an unbelievable 10.9 percent. To give you some idea of what that means, when our last record economic expansion ended eight years after it began, productivity was decreasing by 0.3 percent per year. In contrast, we're nine years into our current economic expansion and productivity is increasing at 3.4 percent per year. Behind those numbers is evidence that technological improvements are helping us do things better, faster, and cheaper—and that's fueling productivity.

LOW UNEMPLOYMENT WITHOUT INFLATION

If low unemployment leads to higher wages, which leads to inflation, which leads to higher interest rates, which halts economic expansion—then why do we currently see record low unemployment with no signs of wage inflation? To start, corporate cost-cutting and mergers mean that workers are more worried about keeping their jobs than increasing their salaries. But the way we compensate employees has also changed. Today, it's all about stock: Employees want stock options, stock appreciation rights, and stock warrants. As corporations have pushed ownership down to all levels, they've succeeded in keeping wage increases relatively small—because real wealth accumulation comes not from wages, but from stock.

THE INTERNET

The Internet may be the biggest new thing in this new economy. It didn't exist during the 1961–1969 economic expansion, but in this economic expansion, its growth has been amazing. Some people think that the Internet can't continue to grow, but I think they're dead wrong. There are currently 100 million homes in the United States. Although 79 million have personal computers, only 35 million have Internet access. And think about the rest of the world, in which there are 1.1 billion homes but only a fraction of them have personal computers and use the Internet. If you're looking for proof that the unconnected will soon be online, you don't have to look far. President Clinton recently unveiled a $2 billion proposal to bring the Internet to the underprivileged.

Investment Footnote . . . What actually happened ⟷

For the third quarter of 2000 our economy did not grow; it fell −0.5 percent. However, on a year-over-year basis it was still growing at a whopping 3.5 percent level.

The Real "Survivor"—Our Economy

SEPTEMBER 7, 2000

Recently, viewers all across the United States were glued to their television screens watching CBS's new hit series *Survivor*. One question hung in the air: who would be the lone survivor and million-dollar winner?

Meanwhile, there was another even more interesting survivor story unfolding. And this story line evolved around this question: could any economy around the world survive a major year-end slowdown in economic growth?

While most Wall Street strategists and many Wall Street economists are predicting gloom and doom for our domestic economy for the remainder of the year, I think that our robust economy could be the lone survivor of a global economic slowdown.

RATE HIKES AND ENERGY

The "bears" certainly have rather compelling plot points in their story to explain why our economy will slow down during the remainder of this year. These are rate hikes and energy costs.

The bears' first assertion is that interest-rate hikes both here and abroad will finally cause the world's economies to fall back to earth. Ever since the Federal Open Markets Committee (FOMC) began tightening rates, starting in June 1999, other central banks around the world followed suit. You see, in many respects our FOMC is not just our central bank, it is becoming the central bank of the world. Where it goes other nations soon follow. From June 1999 through this month, most investors are well aware that there have been six separate FOMC rate hikes totaling 1.75 percent (or basis points). What few if any investors realize is the ripple effect that this change in monetary policy has had around the globe. Following the FOMC lead in June 1999 there have been 125 central bank tightenings around the world in the past 14 months. It usually takes around 6 to 9 months for these rate hikes to work their way into economic releases, so we are just now beginning to see their impact.

As their second argument, the bears point to the skyrocketing price of oil and energy. The most important part of this energy cost story is "consumer energy costs," because after all it is the consumer that has become the driver of most economies. Consumer energy costs are up a whopping +18.4 percent this year in the United States. Outside the United States the story is almost as bad. Consumer energy costs are up +17.3 percent in Canada, and in Europe the United Kingdom has witnessed a +16.0 percent increase while France has had to deal with a +13.1 percent increase. Thus when you combine the impact of interest rate hikes with rising energy costs, it's easy to see how most analysts will conclude that our economy must slow down.

I, however, do not believe that our economy will slow down much. The reason is that we have two wild cards in our economy that no one else has: *existing home sales* and *state and local government spending*. You see, while our economy will feel the impact like all the other economies around the globe regarding rate hikes and the rising cost of energy, our wild cards will save the day.

EXISTING HOME SALES

Everyone knows that the housing market is in trouble. The housing market began to slow down when the FOMC began raising interest rates, which caused mortgage rates to rise as well. When mortgage rates rise, building permits drop, new housing starts drop, and new home sales decline; in other words, the housing market is in trouble. What we sometimes overlook, however, is that not the entire housing market is in trouble. If your employer transfers you from Chicago to New York or Los Angeles you are going to buy a house regardless of where mortgage rates are. And guess what? If there is not a good selection of new homes, you find yourself shopping in the existing home market. And this existing home market has been on a tear for the first six months of the year. In fact, existing home sales went up every month for the first six months of this year. Watch what will happen next; existing home sales have a much more dramatic positive impact on our economy than new home sales. You see, when you buy a new home you don't walk into it and say, "Oh my gosh, I hate that wallpaper in the dining room." You can't hate it because you picked it. However, in an existing home the conversation usually goes like this: "I love the house but I hate the carpet" (chalk up new carpet for the whole house). This is followed by "Our furniture doesn't go with this color paint" (chalk up a new paint job). Then comes the "This house has everything we wanted except the custom back deck" (chalk up a deck as well). New home sales are a great leading indicator because they create a ripple effect throughout our economy. Look for a strong ripple in our economy the second half of the year because of a strong existing home sale market in the first half.

STATE AND LOCAL GOVERNMENT SPENDING

State and local government spending is exploding and no one is even noticing. The reason is that state and local budget deficits are actually falling. You see, this defies all fiscal logic: when state and local government spending increases, the budget deficit is supposed to get bigger not smaller. The problem with this outdated logic is our economy. This record long economic expansion has stuffed the coffers of state and local governments. They have more sales taxes coming in than they ever dreamed of, more property tax receipts than they know what to do with. And the same goes for individual and corporate income taxes. With so much money coming in, state and local governments can actually spend more and still allow the budget deficit to go down. State and local government spending is captured on a quarterly basis. The most recent numbers are still from the first quarter of this year where state and local government spending is up a whopping 9.2 percent. That's not a little . . . that's a lot. And more state and local government spending has a greater impact on our economy because it stays right here. Think about it for a minute—regardless of where you are from, state governments all around the United States always ask the question, "Isn't there someone in our state who can do this project?" And every local government dollar that is spent is only spent after someone answers the question, "Isn't there a local business who can do that?"

In other words, an explosion in state and local government spending is not a boom for Europe because money is not making its way across the Atlantic; it's a boom for the good old U.S. of A.

The real survivor story wasn't one to be watched on television this summer when Richard Hatch became the lone survivor on *Survivor*. Rather it was one to be witnessed all across the United States as our economy survives yet another set of gloom-and-doom forecasts from the bears of Wall Street.

Have a great day everyone, keep a positive attitude, and please join me in resolving to remain a long-term investor in a short-term world.

Investment Footnote . . . What actually happened

Our economy as measured by GDP did indeed grow in the fourth quarter of 2000 as it was up 2.1 percent. On a year-over-year basis the economy continued to grow at a 2.2 percent clip.

"They're Outta Here"

September 15, 2000

Traditionally, the investment world has had "three bears" that could spoil everyone's porridge: inflation, interest rates, and government spending. But historic changes have diminished the negative effects these forces have on our markets. True, we can sometimes get so caught up in the economic news of the week that we lose sight of the larger economic picture. But the taming of the "three bears," combined with our strong domestic economy, makes the long-term outlook very bright indeed.

Let's take a closer look at why the three bears—inflation, interest rates, and government spending—are outta here!

INFLATION

Two powerful forces have combined to keep a lid on inflation: the global economy and productivity. Our global economy and global competition really kicked into full force with the end of the Cold War. All markets are becoming more competitive globally as trade barriers continue to fall. The ultimate collapse of the Iron Curtain has created the largest global market in the history of the world. This intense global competition keeps a lid on prices. What the Industrial Revolution did to manufacturing, the "global revolution" will do to inflation. Now the second powerful factor is that productivity improvements driven by technological improvements allow us to do everything faster and with more flexibility than ever before. Think about this: 10 years ago most libraries in the United States still used a manual index card catalogue system. Today almost all are computerized, and many libraries are connected to the Internet, which enables you to look up a book, check it out, and have it mailed to you without ever leaving your living room. I'm not sure where we will be 10 years from now, but I can guarantee that it will make today's high-tech library Internet system seem as much a part of the dark ages as a manual index card system in a library seems today. When you overlay these technology-driven productivity improvements with corporate restructuring, deregulation, and privatization, there is simply no way to have inflation; that bear is outta here.

INTEREST RATES

Interest rates will continue to trend lower because of a combination of two factors: the continual rise in our savings rate, which is largely being driven by an aging population, and a stronger inclination toward private supplemental savings as baby boomers continue to lose confidence in both their public and private retirement plans. This renewed focus on savings is very bullish for interest rates. One of the reasons most investors can't accept that the interest rate bear is outta here is that they first must overcome a problem I call "generational conditioning." You see, investors are still convinced that interest rates will rise, and once again the yield on the benchmark 30-year Treasury bond will be above 10 percent. Some investors are even waiting for the yield to break the 14.8 percent record level it set in 1981. Well, they are going to have a long wait because it is never going to happen. The problem with investors waiting on the sidelines for interest rates to rise and yields to cross 10 percent again is generational conditioning. Here's what I mean: if you look back 200 years from today at the yield on the long Treasury bond and, before that, the highest-grade taxable bonds, and before that the railroad bonds, here is what you would find: the yield on the highest-grade, prime taxable bond over the last 200 years has only been over 6 percent 14 percent of the time. The problem is that all of this 14 percent has occurred since 1968! In essence, our generation has been conditioned to expect interest rates and bond yields that are unreasonable. Interest rates aren't supposed to stay over 6 percent; they are supposed to stay under 6 percent. The interest rate bear is outta here.

GOVERNMENT SPENDING

Neither government spending nor our budget deficit is a problem now that we have adopted our landmark balanced budget agreement. Let me put this in some perspective for you. While keeping track of our deficit, it is important not to look at it in isolation; the deficit should be looked at as a percentage of gross domestic product (GDP). This is the most important way of looking at the deficit because it reflects our economy's ability to absorb the federal deficit. This is one reason why one of the key economic measurements for a country to become eligible for membership in the European Monetary Union is that their deficit as a percentage of GDP must be 3 percent or less. This 3 percent level sets the new threshold by which all government spending and deficits will be judged in the future. In the United States our deficit as a percent of GDP stands at less than one-half of 1 percent. To give you some historical perspective, the highest our deficit ever was as a percentage of GDP was back in 1943 when it was an unbelievable 31.1 percent of GDP. The highest level that our deficit has reached in the last 50 years as a percentage of GDP was in 1983 when it stood at 6.3 percent. The government spending bear is outta here.

Have a great day, keep a positive attitude, and please join me in resolving to remain a long-term investor in a short-term world. After all, the three bears are outta here!

Investment Footnote . . . What actually happened

Inflation as measured by CPI stood at 3.46 percent in September 2000. One year later it stood at 2.59 percent. Interest rates as measured by the yield on the 10-year Treasury stood at 5.73 percent in September 2000, and one year later they dropped all the way down to 4.73 percent. Regarding government spending at the end of 2000, our budget deficit as a percent of GDP stood at 2.4 percent. For each of the next seven years that number dropped.

Don't Give Up on This "Old" Economy Just Yet!

January 11, 2001

The list of economic "bears" keeps growing and growing. You can hardly turn on a business news channel or pick up a newspaper without some investment pundit claiming the United States is in an economic recession or heading into one.

Remember what the definition of a recession is. It's two or more consecutive quarters of zero or negative growth as measured by our gross domestic product. Why are most investors already giving up on the economy for the first quarter and hoping that we can dodge a recession by having some economic growth in the second quarter, following the lead of those doomsayer economists?

As an investment strategist I refuse to give up on the first quarter of our U.S. economy just yet. And don't get me wrong. I would be the first to admit that our economy has dramatically slowed down; however, I do not believe that it will slow all the way down to zero or below in the first quarter.

There are three factors that I believe are going to come together and surprise economists and investors alike by displaying a much stronger than expected first quarter. Two of the three factors are unique to the first quarter; they are employees' bonus pay and tax refunds. The third is not unique to the first quarter; however, it only occurs when the Fed is cutting rates, like it is today. That factor is an explosion in mortgage refinancing. Let me briefly touch on these three factors.

BONUS PAY

Bonus payments and incentives continue to become a much larger component of overall wages and total compensations as companies continue the push to pay for performance. Even though many businesses may not have had as good a year in 2000 as they did in 1999, they are still going to pay bonuses, especially in this record competitive employment market. Oh, and did I mention that the majority of those bonuses are paid in the first quarter of each year?

TAX REFUNDS

We all know that tax day is April 15, the day our tax filings are due. However, that's not tax day for taxpayers getting a refund. When we have to pay Uncle Sam, we wait until the second quarter and on April 15 stand in line at the U.S. Post Office to mail in our check. That's not what people who are getting a tax refund do. Their forms are filled out in January or early February. They want their money now! Combine this with the explosion in online filings and direct deposit of tax refunds and you too will quickly realize why this will drive our economy in the first quarter.

MORTGAGE REFINANCING

Now that the Federal Reserve Board has reversed monetary policy after raising interest rates six separate times for a total of 175 basis points, the floodgates to mortgage refinancing will begin. As interest rates fall as a result of the Fed's rate cut, bankers will follow suit and cut their mortgage rates. As mortgage rates continue to fall, refinancing becomes an option of putting more money in your pocket by lowering your mortgage payment through refinancing.

While the bears will continue to get their gloom-and-doom headlines for now, when the first quarter economic numbers are in sometime in early April, investors will wish that they hadn't given up on our economy just yet!

Have a great day, keep a positive attitude, and I'll see ya at 12,500!

Investment Footnote . . . What actually happened ⟷

First quarter GDP for 2001 came in at −0.5 percent, but on a year-over-year basis it was still a positive 1.9 percent.

Can We Break This Cycle?

April 1, 2001

The current cycle that we are in began with business and consumer spending slowing, which in turn caused the economy to slow, which in turn caused earnings to slow, which in turn caused stock prices to fall.

In the second quarter, this cycle will reverse itself. This cycle reversal will set the stage for the investment foundation for the remainder of the year. In addition, there will be three issues that will weigh heavily on investors' minds in the second quarter: the California utility crisis, cash, and blizzards.

THE CALIFORNIA UTILITY CRISIS

The California electric utility crisis has taken center stage as the event that will finally undo the U.S. economy and our stock market. Sorry to inform all you doomsayers, but this crisis will come and go just like prior events that were supposed to rock our economy.

Investors need to remember that deregulation actually works. The problem is not about deregulation but rather the misguided public policy approach to implement deregulation in California. Three separate components of this deregulation combined to guarantee failure California style.

First, this deregulation experience freed wholesale prices for electricity, while at the same time it put a price freeze on the retail price of electricity that could be charged to the ultimate California utility consumer.

Second, the utilities are forbidden from entering into long-term supply contracts. They have to buy electricity on the skyrocketed stock market while paying the current rate. Third, you won't believe what they did to all the big power-generating plants built before 1996. The state agreed to richly compensate the utilities for what they defined as stranded assets. California valued those assets at a much greater value than their fair market value. California then decided that any new entrant to the California utility market must pick up part of the cost of the stranded assets. Wonder why there's no new competition in California? It's because once these competitors are strapped with these old stranded asset costs, they simply can't compete on a price basis.

Despite what's happening in California, deregulation of electric utilities works. The deregulation problems in California are unique to California; they will not spread to the other states and they certainly will not stop our economy or our markets.

CASH

Most investors feel that the investing world is about to end. After all, the NASDAQ dropped below 2000 for the first time since 1998. And the S&P 500 is officially in bear market territory. Forget about all this gloom and listen to why cash is important.

You've heard the investment term, "money sitting on the sidelines." That's the industry slang for money currently invested in money market mutual funds. Today there is roughly $1.7 trillion in mutual fund money market accounts. And $900 billion in accounts controlled by individual households. In addition to those money market accounts, these same individual households have savings accounts in short-term time deposits of less than one year. With the total equity market fluctuating at about $19 trillion, that means we have the equivalent of more than 20 percent of the entire equity market sitting on the sidelines controlled by individual households waiting to make money.

In addition to individual households, mutual fund money managers are also raising cash. In fact, current cash levels in the entire mutual fund industry stand at a little over 6 percent. That's the highest level since the middle of 1997 when the Asian currency crisis threatened a run on the mutual fund banks and everyone was raising cash.

BLIZZARDS

I'm not talking about the recent weather blizzards but the investment blizzards on Wall Street. We sometimes forget that all investment issues can be classified as either blizzards or icebergs.

Blizzards are the investment issues that can be measured in days or hours or minutes. And when these events occur, we're hit with a blizzard of information.

Short-term investors follow blizzards religiously. They're focused on the crisis of the day and then try to base their investment decisions accordingly. Thus, if you're a short-term investor, these blizzards will keep you on the sidelines or they'll put you there.

Unlike blizzards, icebergs take a much longer time to impact the markets. A long-term investor, like me, follows the icebergs.

There are four investment icebergs that are set to drive our markets to new levels. The first investment iceberg is *budget surpluses*. When governments quit competing with the private sector for capital, more capital flows to business, which is bullish long-term for our market.

The second iceberg is *technology*. This technology revolution is for real; it'll continue to fuel productivity around the globe. Everything we do we are able to do faster, more efficiently, and less expensively. Technology is enabling every business everywhere to do things better.

The third iceberg is *global free trade*, which began with the collapse of the Berlin Wall. All of the markets and the economies of the world are now connected. That means you can sell your products just about anywhere. It also means you can produce your products just about anywhere, as well. Global free trade allows businesses everywhere to produce their products where it makes the most economical sense and then sell them everywhere.

The fourth and final iceberg is *demographics*. The baby boomers will strike again in the United States. Those 76 million people are now entering their 50s, which will be their peak earning years. Also their homes are about paid for and their children have moved out. They will make these their peak savings years as well. Savings and investing are about to explode in the United States.

What you do next is up to you. If you are a short-term investor you will follow the blizzards, stay on the sidelines, and miss this bull market as it runs to the next level. On the other hand, if you are a long-term investor focusing on the investment icebergs, these blizzards don't bother you because you know what is really important: budget surpluses, technology-driven productivity, global free trade, and demographics. And you have seen all of these issues coming for years. Like me, you never left this market, and together we will ride it to new highs.

By the end of the year the blizzard will have passed and our icebergs will be clear to everyone. Perhaps we can wave to them from the top of our icebergs.

Have a great day everyone, keep a positive attitude, and please join me in resolving to remain a long-term investor in a short-term world. I'll see ya at 12,500!

PS: Look out, here comes another blizzard. I see Alan Greenspan opening his mouth. Ah, forget it—he was just yawning.

Investment Footnote . . . What actually happened

Both business spending and consumer spending broke the cycle in May 2001 and surprised everyone to the high side. Business spending was up 1.69 percent after falling −5.76 percent the previous month. Consumer spending was up threefold at 0.73 percent over the previous month's level of 0.26 percent.

The Economy May Not Be as Bad as You Think

JUNE 1, 2001

The debate continues in economic circles: is our economy heading for a hard or soft landing? While our economy is slower today than it was a year ago, I don't think we're in a lot of trouble—and here are what I believe will be the four keys to our continuing economic miracle.

First, consider interest rate cuts. From June 1999 through December 2000, the Federal Reserve Board raised interest rates six

times, a total of 1.75 percent—and central banks around the world
followed suit and raised their rates as well. Now that the Fed has cut
rates by 1.5 percent, you can expect other global central banks to do
so as well. And what if the Fed completely reverses itself and cuts
rates by a total of 1.75 percent, which I believe it will? Look for central banks around the world to aggressively cut interest rates. That's
good news. Falling interest rates are just the medicine that our sick
consumer confidence needs. And remember: consumers account for
two-thirds of our economy, so when they're confident, watch out!

Next, look at tax cuts. There's little doubt that some major tax
reform program will be enacted this year and that program will
most likely be retroactive to January 1, 2001. And the beauty of the
American way is that if it's known that you're getting a tax cut,
some business somewhere will find a way to advance you that
money so you can spend it today. And when people spend money,
our economy responds favorably.

Now, think about the housing market. What's impacted first
when interest rates fall? The housing market, of course. Watch for
mortgage refinancing booms in 2001. If they happen—which I believe
they will—the economy may not be as bad off as most economists
think. And don't forget that a housing uptick is a leading economic
indicator. Once you buy a house, I'm willing to bet you consider buying new furniture and new electronics as well. Nothing has a greater
ripple effect on our economy than a strong housing market.

Finally, remember the job market. Our employment market
has weakened in recent months, but that's nothing to be alarmed
about. After all, it's extremely difficult for the unemployment rate
to stay at record 30-year lows month after month. Try to look past
today's headline-grabbing layoffs—which are payment for yesterday's mistakes—and focus on the future. The future direction of the
job market will be determined by business confidence. If we continue to see global interest rate cuts and an aggressive tax cut
agenda retroactive to January 1 of this year, I believe that business
confidence will respond favorably. A confident business environment creates a positive employment market, and when people have
jobs, they spend money. And, as I mentioned above, when people
spend money, our economy responds favorably.

Investment Footnote . . . What actually happened ↑

Business confidence, as measured by the NFIB Small
Business Conference Index, did improve in both July and
August above its June level of 97.2. In September and
October it slipped back below that level again until it
rebounded above it for the next 15 consecutive months.

Glory Days!

SEPTEMBER 2, 2003

Probably no song captures the mood of our markets better than
Bruce Springsteen's "Glory Days." Think about it for a minute. What
more could you ask for as we begin this week after the long Labor
Day weekend? The Standard & Poor's 500 Index is up 14.6 percent
year-to-date; NASDAQ is up 35.6 percent year-to-date; and the Dow
Jones Industrial Average is up 12.9 percent year-to-date. In addition,
the NASDAQ at 1810, the Russell 2000 at 497, Value Line at 1345, and
the Wilshire 5000 at 9770 are all at new 12-month highs. These truly
are glory days. What more could we possibly need as we start the
final stretch of the year following Labor Day? Then it hit me—the
significance of Labor Day, our labor market, and, most important,
jobs. That is the one missing link for our markets. I can tell you firsthand from my travels all across the United States, employment and
unemployment are the issues that top most investors' worry lists.
The media has been debating this so long they have actually given it
a slogan. They are calling it the "jobless recovery."

Let me attempt to put the employment market in some perspective for you so we can get on to celebrating our "glory days."

Y2K STRIKES AGAIN

Let's start with understanding the basis for this "jobless recovery"
so far. It's Y2K. While I spoke long, loud, and often that Y2K would
not cause a market collapse or a global economic meltdown, I must

admit I didn't see it impacting the labor market the way it has. Here is what I mean. Our economy has been growing for nine consecutive quarters, but it hasn't had to add jobs to keep up with that growth. The reason is the unprecedented business capital spending leading up to the year 2000, most of which was driven by Y2K fears. This record buildup is the underlying reason why productivity has soared and why employment has not rebounded as quickly. That's right; you can blame it on Y2K.

NOT JUST MANUFACTURING

One other perspective regarding employment is to look past just manufacturing employment. This is easier said than done, however, because the media constantly brings our attention to all of the manufacturing jobs we lost to Mexico as a result of the North American Free Trade Agreement and all of the manufacturing jobs we are losing to China because of granting them most-favored-nation trading status. While I would be the first to agree that we have lost manufacturing jobs, I also think it is important to keep this in some perspective. Manufacturing employment certainly has collapsed over the past few years to the point that manufacturing employment has now fallen to where it was in 1958. And while that certainly sounds alarming, let me remind you of something. Using 1958 as a base year, industrial production is up over 300 percent. In other words, productivity has skyrocketed and we can now do much more in manufacturing with fewer employees. And again, if you take a broader perspective beyond just manufacturing, here is what has happened since 1958. Total employment is actually up 152 percent since that time. We aren't losing jobs, we are creating them.

EMPLOYMENT REBOUND IS COMING

Looking forward, I firmly believe an employment rebound is taking hold. Employment always follows a logical investment cycle. It has four parts: the economy, profits, business spending, then employment. Briefly, before employment can pick up, first the economy has to improve. And it has now, for nine consecutive quarters. Then profits have to improve, and they have—the Standard & Poor's 500 Index has now posted positive profits on a year-over-year basis for five consecutive quarters. Then business spending must improve, and we're finally seeing signs of life in that area. Only after these three legs of the cycle are complete, does the employment market finally pick up. And that is exactly where we are today. There is some anecdotal evidence. Microsoft is adding 5,000 jobs worldwide and is increasing its research and development spending by 8 percent.

IT'S ALL ABOUT CONFIDENCE

In closing, the employment market is all about business confidence. No business is going to hire new employees if it is not confident about the future. Well, guess what? Everywhere you look, business confidence is improving. First, the latest reading of the Pricewaterhouse Coopers Management barometer (which measures the sentiments of top executives at U.S. multinational companies) shows that 63 percent of those executives are now optimistic about the U.S. economy over the next 12 months. That's up from 34 percent last quarter. Second, Goldman Sachs surveyed their top 100 global clients and found that confidence has risen strongly with expectations for big spending increases on the horizon. Third, the Business Roundtable, a quarterly economic survey of America's top executives, showed more CEOs expecting sales and employment to increase. Fourth, U.S. business confidence, as measured by the Conference Board, has dramatically rebounded this year. Fifth, and finally, the newest kid on the block measuring business confidence is "economy.com." They have only been measuring business confidence since January of this year so there is not much historical reference; however, their most recent survey hit an all-time record high.

I hope that everyone had a wonderful Labor Day weekend. Don't worry about our labor markets, they are just fine. The cycle after all is now working in our favor. These truly are "Glory Days"—crank it up, Bruce!

Investment Footnote . . . What actually happened

Employment growth, as measured by nonfarm payrolls, did indeed rebound in September 2003 and posted positive monthly gains for the next consecutive 52 months all the way through December 2007.

You Can't Always Get What You Want
SEPTEMBER 22, 2003

It's pretty easy to figure out what investors want today. They want employment to improve. It has become the single most important issue facing our markets, especially now that the consensus on Wall Street has finally joined me in concluding that both the third and fourth quarters of this year will reflect extremely strong economic growth (i.e., there is nothing to worry about). So the new worry is how to sustain this growth. In other words, even if the third and fourth quarters post strong growth due to the front-end-loaded nature of the economic stimulus package, it can't be sustained if the employment market doesn't pick back up. Remember, we have lost 3.3 million jobs since the peak of our market in early 2000. And, while I empathize with everyone who has been laid off and is still looking for a job, the fact of the matter is if you look at the employment cycle, we are right where we are supposed to be.

The employment cycle has four growth stages: economic growth, profit growth, business spending growth and, finally, employment growth. Let's briefly look at all four, beginning with economic growth.

ECONOMIC GROWTH

Our economy, as measured by gross domestic product (GDP), has clearly turned the corner. The third quarter GDP number will be released in the next few weeks. Through the second quarter of this year, we have had nine consecutive quarters of *positive* year-over-year economic growth in our economy. The great hype and concerns of a prolonged recession or even a depression are now clearly in the rearview mirror. From an economic perspective I think it's safe to say that it's clear sailing ahead. Let's move on to stage two, profit growth.

PROFIT GROWTH

While we anxiously await the third quarter earnings season to begin, here is where we currently stand. Through the second quarter, earnings as measured by the S&P 500 have posted five consecutive quarters of year-over-year profit growth. So the worst of the profit collapse is clearly behind us as well. Remember a while back when everyone was screaming, "Why aren't businesses spending any money? If it weren't for the consumer, our economy would be in a complete collapse." Well, here is why. I don't care how many consecutive quarters of economic growth we have, if business profits don't grow, businesses will not spend. And that is exactly what happened. As the economy was growing for nine consecutive quarters, profits have been growing for only five. So even though the economy was strong, business spending was weak. Let's move to the third stage, business spending growth.

BUSINESS SPENDING GROWTH

Everywhere you look business spending is now also growing. In fact capital spending for equipment increased at an annual rate of 8.2 percent in the second quarter of this year. And capital spending on facilities and plants paints an even more compelling picture. Capital expenditures for facilities and plants have reached all-time highs in both educational buildings and hospitals, and mining and exploration have posted tremendous gains all year as well. Josh Feinman, the chief economist of Deutsche Asset Management, Americas, astutely points out: "The recent evidence on investments is encouraging and we expect it to continue as firms respond to the declining relative price of capital goods to rebuild the capital stock and reap gains in efficiency."

One way to substantiate business confidence and spending is to look at the increased spending in advertising. The media sector tends to be the focus in the back end of an economic recovery as businesses finally increase their advertising budgets. A recent survey conducted by International Strategy & Investment in New York showed U.S. ad spending jumped 6.8 percent in the first half of this year following a three-year drought. In addition, Joann Barry, global sector team leader of Deutsche Asset Management, insightfully points out that in addition to ad spending rebounding off its lows, next year the pace should continue as ad spending reaps the one-two benefit of the Olympics and a presidential election year. I think that Joann is absolutely right about the potential impact of these two news sources for 2004. Let's now move on to the fourth and final stage, employment growth.

EMPLOYMENT GROWTH

We are sitting at the doorstep of the next stage, employment growth. We are not in trouble. Quite to the contrary, we are right where we are supposed to be. First we needed economic growth, which we have. Then we needed profit growth, which we also have. Then we needed business spending growth, which we also have. It is only after we have those three stages that employment growth can kick in, which it is about to do. I will caution you, however, to be patient because of where we are in the calendar year. Most companies in the S&P 500 have a fiscal year that is the same as the calendar year, ending December 31. Thus, even though the cycle calls for employment growth, I now suspect it will be postponed to help profits in the short run. In other words, most companies will be interviewing, recruiting, and even making offers for employment; however, the start date will not be until next year because companies will put off adding the expense of new hires and health benefits and instead let that cost savings fall right to the bottom line fueling profit growth instead. If you can step back from all the noise, you will see that we are exactly where we should be in employment.

One final note: Steven Bell, Deutsche Asset Management global chief economist in London, reminds us, "After a series of strong and stronger-than-expected U.S. data, only the labor market shows weakness. But this is a lagging indicator and should improve soon."

Remember, you can't always get what you want, but from an employment perspective, I know that we are about to get "just what we need!"

Investment Footnote . . . What actually happened ↑

Unemployment stood at 6.1 percent in September 2003. One year later, in September 2004, it had fallen all the way down to 5.4 percent.

How Do You Spell Relief? J – O – B – S

APRIL 22, 2004

There may not be a more important issue for our markets, our economy, or our presidential election than jobs. There was a sigh of relief from all fronts when the most recent payroll employment number expanded by over 300,000 in the most recent employment release. With this issue on everyone's mind, I thought I would give you a few perspectives on jobs.

THREE IS BETTER THAN ONE

While everyone knows that I am extremely bullish on the employment turnaround in the United States, I am not going to gloat or even focus on that blockbuster, headline-breaking number. This is because any one month can overstate or understate the employment numbers. Thus, I think the best barometer when looking at payroll employment numbers is not monthly numbers but rather payroll numbers over the past three months. By looking at three months, there is enough time to iron out distractions. While I am still celebrating the one-month 300,000 number, the even more important number is 171,000. You see, over the past three months payroll employment has averaged 171,000 new jobs per month. That is the strongest three-month period in almost four years. There is absolutely no doubt in my mind that the labor markets have clearly turned the corner.

IT'S THE DATA, STUPID

The second point regarding jobs is that even when we count them we tend to underestimate what is actually happening. In other words, I believe the revised data will show us that this wasn't a jobless recovery after all. The differences between first-reported payroll employment numbers and the final, final revisions are huge. Many times these numbers actually understate employment by 100,000!

In fact, this error in data collection can even have a major influence on who ends up in the White House. Remember back in 1992, Bill Clinton ran his presidential campaign on the theme, "It's the Economy, Stupid," focusing on the so-called jobless recovery in 1992. Well, guess what: the so-called jobless recovery of 1992 was a statistical illusion. As first reported, payroll employment rose only 423,000 during all of 1992. That meant we only averaged 35,250 jobs a month. Subsequent revisions raised the 1992 numbers up from 423,000 all the way to 1,157,000. That means we were actually adding almost 100,000 new jobs per month versus the 35,250 first reported.

I firmly believe that once again our economy is actually creating more jobs than those captured by the initial Labor Department numbers.

OUTSOURCING CAN CREATE U.S. JOBS

No commentary on jobs would ever be complete without at least making some comment about outsourcing all of American jobs to India and China. I want to relay a fact to you that was first reported in the *Wall Street Journal* on March 16, 2004. It was a real-life example of how outsourcing actually ended up creating more jobs in the United States.

A medical billing service in New Jersey called Claimpower Inc. wanted to expand so they decided to outsource jobs to India. Claimpower Inc., by the way, had only five employees at the time. So in 2001, Claimpower hired four locals in Bombay, India, to help file insurance claims on behalf of New Jersey doctors. Today, they employ 35 people in India. They are paid the equivalent of $133 to $663 a month, which is good pay by Indian standards. As a result, Claimpower can charge their doctors less while giving even more specialized service. The end result is that the business is booming, and Claimpower is looking to add a dozen new jobs in the United States as it expands nationally. These new jobs, by the way, are higher paying jobs than the four that were outsourced. Do the math. We outsource four jobs and create 12—by my count we are up eight. I'll take that trade any day of the week. This proves that outsourcing is not a one-way street. Outsourcing is clearly a new means to lowering costs and actually creating jobs.

TAKE A LONG-TERM VIEW

In closing, one of the best perspectives that you can take on anything is to take a long-term view. I am talking really long—not 5 or 10 years, but rather 50. I know that a lot of bears are still complaining about how weak our employment market is. Well, the unemployment rate is currently 5.7 percent. Taking a longer-term view, the 50-year average of the unemployment rate in the United States is—you guessed it, 5.7 percent. Can things be really all that bad if the worst thing about employment is that our current unemployment number is sitting right on its 50-year average?

How do you spell relief? I spell it J – O – B – S.

Oh, I almost forgot one more long-term trend. The Conference Board's business confidence survey for the first quarter of this year indicated that 50 percent of CEOs expect employment in their industry to rise. That's the highest survey number ever in the entire history of The Conference Board, which, by the way, began these surveys in 1976. That makes it the best sign in only 28 years for job growth.

Like I said before, how do you spell relief? I spell it J – O – B – S!

> ### Investment Footnote . . . What actually happened ↑
>
> Unemployment did indeed take a dramatic drop. One year later, in April 2005, the unemployment rate fell from 5.7 percent to 5.1 percent. A year after that, in April 2006, it continued to fall to 4.7 percent. Finally, a year after that, in April 2007, it was still falling . . . all the way to 4.5 percent.

Debunking the Most Popular Economic Myths: Why the Market Will Rally into 2006

OCTOBER 1, 2005

Everywhere I turn, I keep hearing that the U.S. economy is going to falter, taking the markets with it. And I just don't get it, because the problems many economists see, I don't. So I set about identifying the areas in which economists and I just don't see eye to eye. And I came up with four myths. Now I'm going to debunk them.

MYTH 1: CHINA MUST SLOW DOWN AND TAKE THE COMMODITIES MARKET WITH IT

Most economists are convinced that China's economic growth must slow, taking the commodities bull market with it. And I just don't understand that.

China's economy, as measured by gross domestic product (GDP), grew at an annual pace of 9.5 percent for 2004 and the first six months of 2005. Just how fast is that? Well, if the U.S. economy were to hit annual GDP growth of 4 percent, economists would be opening the champagne.

Commodities are also performing well. Chinese industrial production is up almost 17 percent on a year-over-year basis, with steel production up an astounding 33 percent.

At the same time the Chinese economy is growing at this stellar pace, its inflation, as measured by the Consumer Price Index (CPI), remains under 2 percent. That's really low, folks.

I haven't seen any reason to think that will change. In fact, I only see good things for China. Beijing is gearing up to host the Olympics in 2008. Two years after that, Shanghai will host the World's Fair. That creates jobs. When people have jobs, they buy things. When people buy things, manufacturing prospers.

The way I see it, it's only going to get better for China, folks.

MYTH 2: HIGHER LABOR COSTS MUST EAT INTO CORPORATE PROFITS

Many economists are worried about higher labor costs. As the theory goes, they could eat into corporate profits, and that could cause a market downturn. And again, I don't get it.

It seems as if a day doesn't go by that more layoffs are in the news. Reuters is cutting 500 jobs. Sun Microsystems is slashing 1,000.

In that environment, a lot of workers are taking pay cuts. United Airlines got its union to agree to major labor concessions (but went into bankruptcy anyway). Northwest Airlines is headed in the same direction. The National Hockey League Players Association Union has agreed to a 24 percent salary cut.

But the real icing on the cake may be that the French government is actually considering a law that would make it easier to fire employees. The French, fire employees? I never thought I'd see that day.

So you see, workers aren't in a position to demand higher wages that will eat into corporate profits. And that's because the labor landscape has changed completely. The confluence of competition, technology, and globalization has tipped the scales against them.

MYTH 3: EARNINGS GROWTH MUST SLOW

Many economists are convinced that earnings growth must slow, and that this will lead to a market downturn. But why?

Since the market hit its low in 2001, earnings of companies in the Standard & Poor's 500 (S&P 500) Stock Index have increased by more than 80 percent. In fact, corporate earnings are growing at about 11 percent on a year-over-year basis—more than economists had predicted.

Moreover, earnings *lead* the market. Since the market hit its low in 2001, during the time that earnings grew by 80 percent, the S&P 500 stock market itself only grew by 40 percent. Where do you think earnings will lead the S&P 500 next?

MYTH 4: COMPANIES MUST STOP PAYING HIGH DIVIDENDS

Dividends have been big news since the Jobs and Growth Tax Relief Reconciliation Act of 2003 cut the federal tax rate on stock dividends from a maximum of 38.6 percent to 15 percent. But many economists think that's almost over. I just don't see why.

Currently, somewhere around 400 of the 500 companies in the S&P 500 pay a dividend. That's an improvement over 2002, when 351 companies paid a dividend. But we still have a long way to go before we get back to the 1980s when 469 companies in the S&P 500 paid a dividend.

So you see, it's getting better, not worse. And until I see a fall in the number of companies paying dividends, I'm going to think the dividend story is just beginning.

THE REALITY: PREPARE FOR A MARKET UPTURN

If those are the myths, what's the reality? When I look at the facts, I see no reason to expect the worst. I see continued growth in China, which could create demand throughout the world. I see continued labor concessions. I see solid corporate earnings. And I think companies are going to keep paying dividends. And that's all good. In fact, it's so good, I think the markets are going to rally—and keep rallying well into 2006.

HURRICANE HAVOC AND OIL OBSESSION

A lot of people ask me how Hurricane Katrina and Hurricane Rita affect my economic and market outlook. And I tell them, they don't.

Before I explain that, I want to say this: One of the great things about my job is that I get to formulate an investment strategy in response to every world event. The only thing I hate about my job is that I get to formulate an investment strategy in response to every world event. And I don't *want* to formulate an investment strategy in response to disasters such as hurricanes. But it's my job, so here it is.

There's no doubt that the hurricanes will negatively impact the economy of the Gulf states. Cities were evacuated. Ports were closed. Tourism stopped. The regional economy will certainly take a hit in the short term. But watch what will happen in the fourth quarter of 2005 or early 2006. Yes, we can expect an economic boom. The affected cities will rebuild. Rebuilding will involve major demolition, reconstruction, construction, and engineering projects. And the economic boom should more than offset the loss of business caused by the hurricanes. So in economic terms, at least, we come out even, or a little better off.

As for how the loss of oil capacity will affect the rest of the country . . . yes, the Gulf of Mexico produces more than 10 percent of all the oil and natural gas that is consumed in the United States. And more important, it accounts for more than 15 percent of gasoline refinery capacity. But those refineries were up and running fairly quickly after the hurricane. The biggest problem I see, then, isn't too little oil, but too much panic. If consumers start lining up at the gas station because they think there won't be enough gasoline, consumer confidence and spending could take a big hit. But this hasn't happened yet, and I have faith in the American consumer. So I'm not worried yet.

Investment Footnote . . . What actually happened

The stock market really did rally all the way through 2006. The S&P 500 was up 13.6 percent, the DJIA was up 16.3 percent, and the NASDAQ was up 9.5 percent for 2006.

The $684,000 Question

OCTOBER 17, 2005

Even though we are more than halfway through the month of October, it seems we're still being bombarded with what the market did or did not do through the first nine months of the year.

NINE-MONTH MARKET RECAP

Let me jump on that bandwagon as well before I get to the $684,000 question. From an overall market perspective, the first nine months pretty much appeared to be a nonevent as measured by the leading market indices. The S&P 500 was slightly up by 1.4 percent. The Dow Jones Industrial Average was down by 2 percent, while NASDAQ was down 1.1 percent. Maybe the real story of the first nine months is not told by these overall market indices. In my opinion, there were actually four dramatic developments through the first nine months.

The first development was that the value style of investing clearly outperformed the growth style. As of September 30, the BARRA Growth Index was up 0.9 percent year-to-date, while the BARRA Value Index more than doubled that gain, rising 1.9 percent for the nine-month period.

I think the second important development was that the real story on the equity markets actually occurred outside the United States. While our market was basically flat through the first nine months of the year, the United Kingdom's FTSE 100 Stock Market was up 14.3 percent; Japan's Nikkei Stock Market was up 18.2 percent; Germany's DAX Stock Market was up 19.1 percent; and France's CAC 40 Stock Market was up 21.0 percent.

Now, let's go back to the United States for the third development, which was narrow market leadership. Of the 10 sectors that comprise the S&P 500, only four had positive returns through the first nine months. Two of them barely did that with health care up only 3.8 percent and consumer staples just barely positive at

1.5 percent. It was the remaining two sectors that provided all the leadership to our markets. The utility sector was up 20 percent and energy was up 40 percent; keep in mind this was occurring when the overall market was up a mere 1.4 percent.

Fourth, and finally, was the continued commodity boom, especially in oil and natural gas. Through the first nine months of this year, oil was up 52.7 percent while natural gas was up a whopping 128.5 percent. Even with all of these underlying major developments, the one development that is clearly the most dramatic and most important to me and to our markets is one I call the $684,000 question.

684,000 MISSING!

Let me explain what I mean. But first let me set the framework for just how important I believe this issue is to our market. I have always believed that the single most important economic indicator is the employment report. That's because I think employment does the best job of telling you where the overall economy is headed. Figuring out where the economy is headed sets the foundation for figuring what direction our markets will be moving. Remember it all starts with employment. Employment drives our economy and our economy drives our markets.

Now back to my $684,000 question. Believe it or not, there are actually two different major economic releases that attempt to capture the employment picture. The first and most popular is the nonfarm payroll employment report. The second is the household employment survey. The more widely followed nonfarm payroll employment report tells us that through the first nine months of 2005, we have created 1,592,000 jobs. That's not bad when you consider the backdrop of rising interest rates and rising energy prices.

At the same time, the Household Employment Survey says we have created 2,276,000 jobs through the first nine months. That's a difference of—you guessed it, 684,000 jobs. Where are all those missing jobs, anyway?

WHAT'S THE DIFFERENCE WITH THESE EMPLOYMENT REPORTS?

Here is the basic difference between these two employment reports. The nonfarm payroll employment report surveys actual payroll data from 400,000 companies, while the Household Employment Survey report surveys 60,000 individual households regarding employment. The reason more people focus on the nonfarm payroll employment report is twofold. First, most people think that more has got to be better (except my wife, Cheryl, who taught me that less is more). So a survey of 400,000 has got to be better than a survey of 60,000. To even think that a survey of 60,000 cannot reflect what is going on in our population is silly, from my perspective. Need I remind you that most election polls survey a mere 1,500 people to reflect how 180 million people will vote? If we can project elections with a 1,500-person survey I am sure we can also project employment with a survey that is 40 times larger. We don't need a survey of 400,000 to tell us what is going on in employment. Remember, less is more.

Now the second reason why everyone focuses on the nonfarm payroll employment report is that Alan Greenspan likes it better. I quote Alan Greenspan on this matter: "I wish I could say the household survey were the more accurate. Everything we've looked at suggests that the data on the so-called payrolls survey is surely the more accurate of the two." I beg to disagree. I think that the nonfarm payroll employment report only captures the "old" economy jobs while the household employment survey captures the "new" economy jobs as well.

MISSING JOBS

I think I can tell you exactly where those missing jobs are. They may be in the office or cubical right next to you at work. You see, the nonfarm payroll employment report *does not* count independent contractors who work in a company side by side with full-time employees. They have the exact same boss, are working on the exact same project, doing the exact same job, attending the exact same company picnic and holiday parties, and many are even in the exact same employee stock option plan. The *only* difference is that "payroll" doesn't pay them. Instead, they invoice the company and are typically paid from a vendor account. The nonfarm payroll employment report considers these people "not working"!

I suspect that whatever numbers of the 684,000 not in the independent contractor group are probably working for small startup businesses that were not surveyed in the 400,000 non-farm payroll employment survey. Or maybe they are self-employed. That's a whole other group that is missed by the non-farm payroll report.

Let me make one final point about why I do not like the non-farm payroll report. In boom times, it actually double counts jobs. Here is exactly what I mean. If, for example, I were working for Microsoft and quit my job on October 17 and went to work at Cisco on October 18 (which happens all the time when the job market is hot), I would be counted as working for *both* Microsoft and Cisco that week. I call that *irrational job exuberance*, Mr. Greenspan!

FOLLOW THE JOBS

In closing, I believe this $684,000 question is the biggest issue our markets are facing, bigger in my opinion than interest rates or the price of oil. If there are 684,000 more jobs than Wall Street thinks, then the economy will be stronger than Wall Street thinks. And if the economy is stronger than Wall Street thinks, we have a foundation for the market to move higher.

From my perspective, a fourth quarter stock market rally is not out of the question. In fact, I can give you 684,000 reasons why!

Investment Footnote . . . What actually happened ↑

The stock market did indeed rally in the fourth quarter of 2005 and posted a +3.0 percent gain for the entire year for the S&P 500 Index.

CHAPTER 2

The Federal Reserve Board

The Fed's job is to take away the punchbowl before the party gets really going.

WILLIAM MCCHESNEY MARTIN
Federal Reserve Board Chairman (1951–1970)

INTRODUCTION

The Federal Reserve Board, the Federal Reserve System, or simply, as we call it on Wall Street, "the Fed," is the Central Bank of the United States. It was created in 1913 by the adoption of the Federal Reserve Act. In its role as the Central Bank of the United States, the Fed serves as a banker's bank, and as the government's bank. As a banker's bank, it helps assure the safety and efficiency of the payment system. As the government's bank, or fiscal agent, the Fed processes a variety of financial transactions involving trillions of dollars. The U.S. Treasury keeps a checking account with the Federal Reserve through which incoming federal tax deposits and outgoing government payments are handled. As part of this unique relationship, the Fed sells and redeems U.S. government securities such as savings bonds and Treasury bills, notes, and bonds. It also issues the nation's coin and paper currency. The U.S. Treasury, through its Bureau of the Mint and Bureau of Engraving and Printing, actually produces the nation's cash supply; the Fed's banks then distribute it to financial institutions.

The Fed is actually considered an independent agency within government. It was set up that way so that special interests in Congress or the presidency would not abuse the power to create money or abuse the government regulations with regard to banks. In order to accomplish this, the Federal Reserve System was organized to be separate from the three branches of the federal government. This structure was set up to make it impartial to special interests so that it could make policies that are good for all of the people and all of the businesses in the United States.

The members of its Board of Governors are appointed for long, staggered terms, limiting the influence of day-to-day political considerations. The Fed's unique structure also provides internal checks and balances, ensuring that its decisions and operations are not dominated by any one part of the system.

The system is organized much like private corporations so it can generate revenue independently without the need for Congress. Since it was designed to be independent while also remaining within the government of the United States, it is therefore positioned as "independent within the government."

Think about it like this. The Federal Reserve System or the Fed is not "owned" by anyone and is not a private, profit-making institution. Instead, it is an independent entity within the government, having both public purposes and private purposes. As the nation's central bank, the Federal Reserve derives its authority from the U.S. Congress. It is considered an independent central bank because its decisions do not have to be ratified by the president or anyone else in the executive or legislative branch of government. It does not receive funding appropriated by Congress, and the terms of the members of the Board of Governors span multiple presidential and congressional terms.

However, the Federal Reserve is subject to oversight by Congress, which periodically reviews its activities and can alter its responsibilities by statute. Also, the Fed must work within the framework of the overall objectives of economic and financial policy established by the government.

The seven-member Board of Governors is the main governing body of the Federal Reserve System. It is charged with overseeing the 12 district reserve banks and with helping implement national monetary policy. Governors are appointed by the president of the United States and confirmed by the Senate for a 14-year term. Once a member of the Board of Governors is appointed by the president, he or she functions mostly independently. The Board is required to make an annual report of operations to the Speaker of the U.S. House of Representatives. The Federal Board of Governors also supervises and regulates the operations of the Federal Reserve Banks and the U.S. banking system in general.

Membership on the Board is generally limited to one term. However, if someone is appointed to serve the remainder of another member's uncompleted term, he or she may be reappointed to serve an additional 14-year term.

Of special interest to everyone on Wall Street is the Federal Open Markets Committee or FOMC. The FOMC is comprised of the seven members of the Board of Governors and five representatives selected from the regional Federal Reserve Banks. The representative from New York, which is actually referred to as the Second District, is a permanent member, while the rest of the banks rotate at two- and three-year intervals.

These 12 regional Federal Reserve Banks have a board of directors whose members work closely with their Reserve Bank president to provide economic information and input on management and monetary policy decisions. These boards are drawn from the general public and the banking community and oversee the activities of the organization. They also appoint the presidents of the Reserve Banks, subject to approval of the Board of Governors.

The 12 actual regional districts and regional Federal Reserve Banks are as follows: First District: Boston, Second District: New York, Third District: Philadelphia, Fourth District: Cleveland, Fifth District: Richmond, Sixth District: Atlanta, Seventh District: Chicago, Eighth District: St. Louis, Ninth District: Minneapolis, Tenth District: Kansas City, Eleventh District: Dallas, and the Twelfth District: San Francisco.

At the end of the day, the reason why Wall Street is so focused on the Fed is because the Fed is the key to monetary policy. You see, monetary policy refers to the actions undertaken by a central bank to influence the availability and cost of money and credit to help promote national economic goals. What happens to money and credit affects interest rates and the performance of the U.S. economy as well as the performance of stock markets around the world.

The Fed implements monetary policy largely by targeting the federal funds rate. This is the rate that banks charge each other for overnight loans of federal funds, which are the reserves held by banks at the Fed. This rate is actually determined by the market and is not explicitly mandated by the Fed. The Fed therefore tries to align the effective federal funds rate with the targeted rate by adding or subtracting from the money supply through open market operations.

The Federal Reserve System also directly sets the "discount rate," which is the interest rate that banks pay the Fed to borrow directly from it. This rate is generally set at a rate close to 100 points above the target federal funds rate. The idea is to encourage banks to seek alternative funding before using the "discount rate" option.

Both of these rates influence the prime rate, which is usually about 3 percentage points higher than the federal funds rate.

Lower interest rates stimulate economic activity by lowering the cost of borrowing, making it easier for consumers and businesses to buy and build; however, this is at the cost of promoting the expansion of the money supply and thus, greater inflation. Higher interest rates slow the economy by increasing the cost of borrowing. The Federal Reserve System usually adjusts the federal funds rate by 0.25 percent or 0.50 percent at a time.

The Fed might also attempt to use open market operations to change long-term interest rates, but its "buying power" on the market is significantly smaller than that of private institutions. The Fed can also attempt to "jawbone" the markets into moving toward the Fed's desired rates, but this is not always effective.

On the pages that follow you will get my "jawboning" and perspectives and insights on exactly how and why the Fed has such a great impact on your investments.

"Irrational Trepidation": Exuberance Has Become Uncertainty in the Wake of World Leaders' Economic and Military Chaos

AUGUST 31, 1998

August 31 marked the second largest single point decline in the history of the Dow Jones Industrial Average. Its 512-point decline was second only to last October's 554-point drop. Before I explain what I believe to be the forces behind this market-driven correction—and what I expect to happen to reverse it—it's important to keep the relative importance of this most recent decline in perspective. While the 512-point loss ranks in the top 10 market declines on a percentage basis, it's nowhere near the second largest drop on a percentage basis.

As investors and financial advisors struggle to look for the reason behind this volatile one-day move, my suggestion is to quit looking. There is no single event that caused this sell-off—it was the result of market uncertainty.

Investors lost confidence—at least for one day—in our market. This lack of confidence isn't just about our market; it also has something to do with a fear that the world is collapsing. Such a shakeup in confidence is being driven by the fact that no matter how you measure global might—whether it's in terms of financial or military power—there is a major question of leadership, which will always equate with uncertainty.

First, let's focus on the measure of financial might. We measure financial power by the size of a country's economy. The two largest economies in the world today are the United States, which is number one, and Japan, which is number two. Both of these economic powerhouses have major political uncertainties hanging over them. Japan had the resignation of the prime minister and continued uncertainty over what public policies will be put forward by the new administration to turn the country's problems around. Meanwhile, in the United States, the largest economy in the world, we have continuing questions surrounding President Bill Clinton and the Monica Lewinsky scandal, and Vice President Al Gore and the fund-raising scandal. International investors are still struggling to find the real meaning of the movie *Wag the Dog*.

When you have a tremendous amount of uncertainty at the highest political level for the two largest economies in the world, it creates uncertainty for investors.

Shift gears for a minute to look at another way to analyze nations. If we don't focus on economic might, we focus on military power. Here again, we find political leadership chaos among the two largest military powers in the world. The second largest military power as measured by nuclear capability is Russia. The future of Boris Yeltsin remains a very serious question, and whether any fundamental changes can be made between his administration and parliament remains to be seen. Of course, then you have the number one nuclear power of the world, the United States, being questioned about using military force for the political advantage of an embattled president. Never before in the history of the stock market has there been such uncertainty among both economic leaders of the globe and the major political and military leaders of the globe. In my opinion, investors finally had enough and decided to go to cash.

For this market to turn around it will take a combination of events, all of which I firmly believe will still happen between now and the end of the year. There will be four keys to the turnaround in the U.S. stock market:

- I firmly believe that stock buybacks will take off. Corporations will support their own stock prices as individuals in those corporations will also support their stock prices. In aggregate, I expect it to be one of the largest corporate stock buybacks ever. After all, it's in the best interest of everyone who has an option to support the price of that option.

- President Clinton will unveil a major rescue package for Russia. Make no mistake about this. President Clinton is probably the smoothest presidential politician we have ever seen—there is no way in the world he would ever travel halfway around the globe with nothing dramatic to tell. He needs a strong and positive public relations event and this may be just what he's looking for. Also, ask yourself this: Where has Bob Rubin been the last two weeks? In the midst of the greatest financial meltdown in the Clinton administration, the secretary of the Treasury has disappeared. I contend he's in the backroom putting together a bigger bailout package than he and President Clinton authored for Mexico.

- Interest rates will be cut now, at the next meeting of the Federal Reserve Board. I'm changing my forecast of no interest rate movements in 1998 to one, if not two, interest rates cuts in 1998. The Fed can no longer afford to sit on the sidelines. I believe rates will be cut 25 to 50 basis points between now and October 1. The Fed has no choice but to unleash the only economy around the globe that's hitting on all cylinders.

- International Monetary Fund funding and fast track trade legislation get approved. Congress has remained helpless during this financial market meltdown. They need something to show their voters that they not only are sympathetic to what's going on but that they, too, are going to help solve this global crisis. The only tools at the disposal of Congress to help address this issue are funding for the IMF and anything that will improve global trade, namely fast-track trade legislation.

My year-end market forecast remains at 10,000. I want everyone to remember that when the market was screaming through 9300 back in mid-July I didn't jump in and change my forecast upward. Likewise, I haven't jumped in to pare back my forecast of 10,000 by the end of this year.

However, the events this week will really set the foundation for the rest of the year. If we have a negative week in the market, the market will be under pressure it may not be able to overcome in time to achieve 10,000 by December. We need a positive week before Labor Day. The week after Labor Day begins the start of a new season—a pre-earnings disappointments season, which always is bad news for the market.

This week will be the most important week in the entire year for the market. I will revise my forecast after Labor Day based on the events of this week, which I feel will determine the ultimate direction and strength of our market.

For investors around the globe who have been waiting for the last year and a half to see what phrase Fed Chairman Alan Greenspan would use to replace his now famous speech of "irrational exuberance," I have a suggestion. I'll call it "irrational trepidation."

This recent decline in the market has absolutely, positively nothing to do with market fundamentals. I've said it once and I will say it again. This market is driven by low interest rates, which are now even lower; inflation, which is now invisible, is driven by strong consumers who—regardless where the stock market is—still have jobs and still get paid every day of the week.

Just as irrational exuberance became a distant memory, so will irrational trepidation. Oh, and here's one final thought. Since July 17, when the market closed at 9337, it has lost 1,798 points and currently stands at 7,539. If the market would have gained 1,798 points instead, the market would have closed today at 11,135. Just as 11,135 is irrational exuberance, 7,539 is irrational trepidation. See you at 10,000!

Investment Footnote . . . What actually happened   ←→

While the Dow didn't close above 10,000 at the end of the year, it did rebound to 9,181, which was a whopping 16.1 percent gain for the year.

Alan Greenspan Uttered the Magic Words: "Irrational Trepidation"

SEPTEMBER 9, 1998

As the entire world anxiously waited to hear what Alan Greenspan would say regarding the financial markets during his speech at the University of California at Berkeley last Friday, he uttered the two words that I needed him to say: "irrational trepidation" (even if he didn't say it exactly like that).

Here is exactly what Alan Greenspan said: "Just as a bull stock market feels unending and secure as an economy and stock market move forward [*irrational exuberance*], so it can feel when markets contract that recovery is inconceivable [*irrational trepidation*]. Both, of course, are wrong."

Right on, Alan!

Remember, for this market to right itself, we need support from four fronts and guess what? We're getting it.

First we need corporate stock buybacks to increase to support falling stock prices and the declining stock market. Last week one of the bluest of the "blue chips," Boeing, announced such a plan . . . let the games begin!

Second, the United States must brokerage a financial support plan for Russia to assure that their nuclear weapons aren't traded for food and medical supplies. And while no rescue plan has been announced yet, President Clinton's comments while he was in Russia made it very clear where he is heading. "If the reform process can be completed, then I for one would be strongly supportive of greater assistance to Russia from the United States and other big economic powers." It won't be long until we show them the money.

Third, U.S. interest rates need to be cut. Even Alan Greenspan now admits that a rate cut is more likely now than it was at the beginning of the summer and that an outbreak of inflation is no longer the near-term worry. No kidding—welcome down from the ivory tower, Alan & Company. A rate cut is as good as in the bank.

Fourth, Congress must approve the International Monetary Fund appropriation. Well, guess what? Late last week the Senate approved the Treasury Department's full $17.9 billion request to replenish IMF reserves and double an existing credit line for future financial crises. Now it's on to the House of Representatives—one down and one to go.

I promised after Labor Day that I would revise (revisit) my forecast for the stock market for the remainder of the year. Well, the summer and Labor Day are now over; however, before I give you my market forecast I want to remind you that investment strategists such as me should never be allowed to change their yearly stock market forecast. I for one have been appalled at all of these so-called experts who have been flip-flopping their market forecasts over the past few weeks. My forecast for the Dow when we started the year was 10,000. Before I should be able to change that forecast, I first should have to admit to you that . . . I was wrong. Then and only then should I be given the opportunity to change my thinking. After all, if we expect President Clinton to publicly apologize, we should at least expect investment strategists to say they were wrong before they change their forecast.

Everything came into perspective for me while I was watching our community's annual Labor Day parade with my family. After the high school bands and Governor Jim Edgar and others (there are too many politicians in parades), came a group with a sign that said "481 days until the next millennium."

After I got home that sign got me thinking. How many days until the end of the year? There are 116. Then I thought, how many more days will the stock market be open—81 days. Then I wondered how much the stock market would need to gain each of those 81 days to get to 10,000 by the end of the year. The answer is 29 points. If you think about it, at 29 points a day, 10,000 is still doable.

This is not about market fundamentals. Low interest rates, no inflation, and a strong consumer virtually assure us of strong market fundamentals during the remainder of the year. This is about investor confidence.

For our stock market to be standing at 7,640 on Labor Day is "irrational trepidation" (even Alan Greenspan thinks so). Inch by inch anything is a cinch. With the market standing at 7,640 and 81 trading days left for our stock market in the year, even if the market only moves an average 29 points a day, the Dow Jones Industrial Average will actually close at 9,989!

With low interest rates, no inflation, and a strong consumer providing the foundation (and then we add in corporate stock buy-backs, a bailout plan for Russia, an interest rate cut from the Fed, and congressional funding for the IMF) 29 points a day is doable.

It is important to keep things in their proper perspective—many things that appear insurmountable really are not. For you baseball fans consider this: Before the season began, if someone would have told you that Mark McGwire would hit 61 home runs and tie the all-time baseball home-run record *by Labor Day*, you would have said impossible, that record is surely insurmountable, especially by Labor Day. Yet yesterday, what six months ago appeared impossible happened when Mark McGwire hit his sixty-first home run on Labor Day.

For many investors, a Dow 10,000 by the end of the year seems equally insurmountable. However, at 29 points a day, anything is possible.

Maybe this is the year that seemingly insurmountable records were made to be broken. Remember anything is possible. If Mark McGwire can hit 61 home runs by Labor Day and Alan Greenspan can imply the stock market is being driven by *irrational trepidation*, then surely the Dow can be at 10,000 by the end of the year.

In case you haven't figured it out, I still believe in my original forecast of the Dow at 10,000 by the year-end.

Have a great day and I'll see ya at 10,000!

Investment Footnote . . . What actually happened ←→

The Dow rebounded to 9,181, and thus fell short of 10,000. But at 9,181, that was a 16.1 percent gain.

Who in the World Is Humphrey-Hawkins Anyway?

FEBRUARY 25, 1999

For the past two days all the financial markets around the world held their collective breath as Alan Greenspan delivered his Humphrey-Hawkins testimony to Congress. From Wall Street to Main Street to Tokyo to Brazil everyone was focusing on "Humphrey-Hawkins." While everyone knows who Alan Greenspan is, I thought it might be useful to revisit just who this Humphrey-Hawkins character is and why is it so important.

In 1913 Congress passed the Federal Reserve Act, which created the Federal Reserve Banking system and the Federal Reserve Board. Throughout history numerous other laws were passed to clarify and refocus the original 1913 law. None of these additional laws was as significant as the Full Employment and Balanced Growth Act of 1978. This act redefined the primary goal of national economic policy to include four objectives:

1. Economic growth in line with the economy's potential to expand
2. High level of employment
3. Stable prices
4. Moderate long-term interest rates

The original sponsors of the Full Employment and Balanced Growth Act of 1978 were Senator Hubert *Humphrey* and Representative Augustus *Hawkins*. Thus this landmark piece of legislation is fondly referred to as "Humphrey-Hawkins" after its original sponsors. Under the Humphrey-Hawkins Act, the Chairman of the Federal Reserve Board must deliver a report to Congress twice a year—once in February and once in July—addressing the objectives of the Humphrey-Hawkins Act.

A quick review of these objectives will show you why this testimony keeps the global markets on edge.

1. *Economic growth.* Nothing really to discuss here as the U.S. economy continues to hit on all cylinders.

2. *Employment.* With our unemployment rate hovering at the lowest level in 30 years, there is certainly nothing to discuss here.

3. *Stable prices.* Stable prices really meant stability in the purchasing power of the dollar, and with prices actually falling (deflation not inflation), there is nothing to discuss here either.

4. *Moderate long-term interest rates.* Even with the recent uptick in interest rates, they remain at record low levels; nothing to discuss here either.

All right now, if you don't focus on growth or employment or prices or interest rates, the only thing left to focus on is, you guessed it—"the stock market." That is the reason why Humphrey-Hawkins is so important. When the most influential financial figure in the world (Alan Greenspan) talks about the most influential financial market in the world (our stock market), everyone hangs on every word. What will he say about valuations, or the wealth effect, or the Internet investing craze? The best thing about the Humphrey-Hawkins testimony is that it's over; there were no bombshells dropped (even though he did again warn that stocks might be overvalued).

Now that we are done with this brief history lesson it's time to focus on two other historic events that will combine to move our markets forward.

Don't forget that when the year began, the markets were faced with three unprecedented historic events that no investor has ever experienced in his or her lifetime. The three historic events were the creation of the European Monetary Union (EMU), President Clinton's impeachment trial, and the one-year countdown to Y2K.

Well, guess what? Two of these three events are now history, and together they will serve as a springboard to move our markets higher.

EMU. There was tremendous concern that the EMU would never happen—not just for political reasons, but because the technology glitches of creating a common currency were to be a preview of what will happen with Y2K. Well, the EMU is here and, from a technology standpoint, it went off without a hitch. Take that, you Y2K doomsayers! I've said it once and I'll say it again: this event will go down in history as the greatest economic miracle in the past 50 years. And remember, a strong Europe means a stronger United States.

Impeachment. I only have two words to say about this—"it's over!" The significance is that now that this historic event is behind us, I look for the foreign flow of capital to return to our equity markets. Foreign investors stayed on the sidelines while they attempted to figure out what all this impeachment debate meant. When this foreign flow of money returns, look out.

With Humphrey-Hawkins now history (at least until July) and two of the monumental historic events, EMU and impeachment, behind us, all that is left is Y2K. I'll be back another time to address Y2K in greater detail; however, before I do I want you worriers who think the world is going to end on January 1, 2000, because of Y2K to remember that we were all supposed to be dead by the year 2000 anyway. That's right, remember that killer bees were supposed to come up from Brazil and Mexico and kill us all by Y2K.

Have a great day, keep a positive attitude, and please join me in resolving to remain a long-term investor in a short-term world.

Investment Footnote . . . What actually happened

Y2K went down in history as the most hyped disaster that never occurred . . . just as I predicted.

The "Fat Lady" Just Sang . . . It's Over!

JUNE 30, 1999

One of the most famous lines in the Monday night football broadcast booth over the years was "It's not over 'til the fat lady sings." This comment was in reference to the opera, where traditionally the "fat lady" would sing the last song and that was your sign that the opera was about to end.

Well, when the Fed raised rates today and changed their bias to neutral in opera terms, it was the same as the "fat lady singing." In other words, it's over not, just for today but for the rest of the year as well. Four factors will combine to keep the Federal Reserve Board in a holding pattern the remainder of the year.

NO INFLATION

In the simplest of terms, the Federal Reserve Board's job is to fight inflation and quite simply there is no inflation to fight. The technology revolution, which has been turbocharged by the rapid expansion and acceptance of the Internet, is providing a one-two punch to inflation. Whether we are at home or at work, everything we want to do can now be done faster, better and, more important, cheaper because of technology. It doesn't matter if you are talking about buying a book or an airline ticket or even a house; the Internet is serving as an efficient engine to keep a lid on prices.

Also, don't forget about the impact of Euroland. The launching of the European Monetary and Economic Union (EMU) created the second largest economy in the world, trailing only the United States. The EMU has increased competition—and increased competition lowers prices.

MIXED GLOBAL GROWTH

While there is no doubt that the global economic distress that engulfed our markets last year has subsided, the turnaround in the global landscape is still at a very early and very fragile stage. There is still tremendous downside global economic risk and, as a result, the United States cannot afford to slow down the only economy that is hitting on all cylinders. Here are some of the global stress points that the Fed must consider.

- *Japan.* Industrial production plunged to its lowest level in five years.

- *France.* Imports continue to fall at a record pace.
- *Argentina.* The economy remains on the brink of a recession with no end in sight.
- *Germany.* Unemployment remains at double-digit levels.

With so much global uncertainty, the Federal Reserve must look beyond just domestic issues and assume the role of the world's central bank.

CUTTING THE TREND

It is extremely important to remember that when the Fed cut rates three times last fall it wasn't because our domestic economy needed a boost; it was in recognition that global economic growth was a problem. In other words, central banks can no longer operate in a vacuum. What they do or do not do will have a major influence on other central banks around the world. Since January 1, there have been 91 central bank interest rate cuts. Count 'em. I said 91.

There Have Been 91 Interest Rate Cuts So Far This Year			
U.K.	Colombia	Belgium	Brazil
Denmark	Philippines	Austria	Philippines
Hungary	South Africa	Portugal	Brazil
Greece	Chile	Luxembourg	Brazil
Philippines	Colombia	Switzerland	Philippines
Brazil	Sweden	Denmark	New Zealand
Chile	Brazil	Hong Kong	Colombia
Norway	Israel	Hungary	Chile
Czech Republic	Canada	South Africa	Philippines
Thailand	Pakistan	Philippines	South Africa
Philippines	Brazil	Brazil	Brazil
Taiwan	Pakistan	China	China

U.K.	South Africa	India	U.K.
Denmark	Sweden	Norway	Philippines
Columbia	Chile	Philippines	South Africa
Japan	U.K.	Ukraine	Denmark
Sweden	Germany	Hungary	Norway
South Africa	France	Brazil	South Africa
Philippines	Italy	Hong Kong	Philippines
South Africa	Spain	Malaysia	Hungary
Denmark	Ireland	Czech Republic	Chile
India	Finland	Canada	Thailand
Norway	Netherlands	Chile	

The Fed simply cannot risk undoing those 91 rate cuts that are serving as the foundation to global economic recovery.

WHAT ABOUT BILL?

Earlier this week, President Bill Clinton joyfully reported that we have created a $1 trillion surplus, a budget windfall if you will. The "we" he was talking about was not Democrats and Republicans—it was you and me. That's right, you and me and all the other consumers in the United States who account for more than two-thirds of our economy. And our budget surplus is being created by strong economic growth. President Bill Clinton made numerous references to the benefits of low interest rates. Low rates encouraged capital spending by corporations. Low rates encouraged home consumption. Low rates enabled more students to be educated by providing lower interest student loans. In other words, all of the budget celebration in Washington is really about low rates. It's one thing for the Fed to take the punch bowl away from our party. It's another if they try to take the punch bowl away from a Washington party.

FIFTY-FIVE AND COUNTING

In closing, just imagine now that this much-hyped Fed meeting is over—we have to wait only 55 more days until the next one on August 24, 1999. In the meantime, look for our markets to continue to post strong gains as earnings will surprise on the high side when they are released for the second quarter of 1999. And investors will continue to pour money into the market as consumer and investor confidence remains at record highs. Don't worry about the next Fed meeting; if you listen closely, you can still hear the "fat lady" singing.

Have a great day, keep a positive attitude, and please join me in resolving to remain a long-term investor in a short-term world.

Investment Footnote . . . What actually happened

Dead wrong on this one, as the Fed cut rates two more times in 1999: once by 25 basis points on August 24, 1999, and again by 25 basis points on November 16, 1999.

Stocks, Bonds, and Dictionaries

OCTOBER 6, 1999

As investors attempt to figure out where their investments are heading the remainder of the year, the biggest clue may not be found in the stock market or bond market, but rather in the dictionary.

You see, yesterday the Federal Reserve Board left interest rates unchanged (which is good for investments); however, they surprised the market by changing their bias from "neutral" to "tighten" (which is a negative for investments because it increases uncertainty).

Starting this year, after each Federal Reserve Board meeting the Fed issues a public statement so the markets get a better understanding of what the Fed is thinking. Along with that statement, the Fed announces its bias. Now perhaps the most important issue facing investors for the remainder of the year is exactly what is the definition of *tighten*?

Well, on page 924 of my Webster's dictionary, one of the definitions of *tight* is "fixed very firmly in place." And that is exactly where interest rates are going to be for the reminder of the year: "fixed" very firmly in place exactly where they are today.

Here are five compelling reasons why the Fed will not move rates the rest of the year.

CONSUMER PRICES SHOW NO INFLATION

Consumer prices, as measured by the Consumer Price Index, are up less than 2 percent from a year-over-year basis. Consumer prices that rise less than 3 percent are considered excellent; less than 2 percent is the most perfect environment you could ask for. There will always be the headline-grabbing commodity of the day that will give the appearance of inflation, whether it's oil or gold or whatever; however, the fact of the matter remains that we are in a service-driven economy and the spike up of any one or several commodity prices will have little if any negative impact on inflation. Also, don't forget the impact of technology on productivity. Everything we do today is better, faster, and cheaper than five years ago. Our technology revolution is also keeping a lid on inflation.

Y2K AND COUNTING

With less than 100 days until we enter the new millennium, the only thing we know for sure is that no one, not even Alan Greenspan, knows anything for sure. Y2K is creating one of the greatest uncertainties our market has ever seen. Economists' forecasts range from Y2K causing a global economic meltdown to it being the most hyped disaster that never happened (I'm in this camp). I do not believe that the Fed would risk changing monetary policy in the face of such major uncertainty.

WHAT WAGE INCREASE?

While the Fed remains concerned about our extremely tight labor market and the fact that the record low unemployment rates will lead to higher wages, I feel that the Fed may be focusing on the wrong thing. Mergers and acquisitions are having a greater impact on wages than low unemployment. In fact the single largest constraint on keeping wages intact is the record number of mergers and acquisitions. Looking for a reason? I'll give you 140,000 of them. When MCI WorldCom merges with Sprint Corp., their new company, WorldCom, will have 140,000 employees. And guess what? Not one of those employees is worried about what their wage increase will be next year. However, all 140,000 are worried if they will have a job next year. It's mergers and acquisitions, not the unemployment rate, that is the driving influence on wages.

REMEMBER FLOYD?

Hurricane Floyd has virtually rendered our economic releases for the next two to three months useless. The employment picture will be tainted first by the evacuation and work stoppage. Then these releases will be infected by the startup. Building activity and permits will be useless to look at for a clue regarding how the economy is doing because of the repair and renovation explosion. Regardless of what any economic release shows, you can make a case, because of Floyd, that the release is not presenting a clear picture. I don't think the Fed will change monetary policy with tainted economic data.

NOW WE CAN GO TO NEUTRAL

Possibly the real reason the Fed moved to a tightening bias was so that they would have some policy flexibility at the next FOMC meeting on November 16, 1999. If liquidity is drying up because of fears of Y2K, the Fed will now have the flexibility of calming the market without lowering interest rates. All they have to do is change their bias from tighten to neutral—which is exactly what I think they are planning to do on November 16, 1999.

In closing, 1999 will go down in history as the year that you truly needed a dictionary to figure out what's going on in Washington, D.C. It is only fitting for a year that began with the most powerful person in Washington, D.C., President Clinton, saying, "Well, that all depends on what your definition of 'is' is." If the most powerful person in Washington can change the definition of *is*, I'm guessing the second most powerful, Alan Greenspan (sorry, Mr. Gore), can change the definition of *tighten*.

Remember when the Fed had a neutral bias, they actually tightened rates twice; now that they have tightening bias, they will be neutral on rates. Would somebody pass me that dictionary again?

Have a great day, keep a positive attitude, and please join me in resolving to remain a long-term investor in a short-term world.

Investment Footnote . . . What actually happened

Wrong again, as the Fed moved rates one last time in 1999. On November 26 they raised rates 25 basis points.

Back to the Future!

NOVEMBER 17, 1999

With the Federal Reserve Board's Federal Open Market Committee (FOMC) decision to raise interest rates another 25 basis points, investors can finally stop worrying if and when the FOMC is going to "take back" its three 1998 rate cuts. The November 16 hike of 25 basis points is the third this year, which puts us right back where we started before the FOMC's cuts. Now it's time to stop looking backward and start thinking about where rates could be going next. It's time to get "back to the future."

I think there are three areas to look at when trying to determine where rates are heading: labor, Y2K, and elections.

WHAT TIGHT LABOR MARKETS?

If you analyze the statement issued by the Fed on November 16, it's clear that the organization's greatest inflation concern is labor markets—and with the Fed worried about wage inflation, you shouldn't have to worry about a rate hike. That's because there are three powerful forces that keep wage inflation in check that the Fed can't capture in its models:

MERGERS AND ACQUISITIONS

Every day, some company is merging with some other company. Just look at the past two weeks in the pharmaceutical industry. American Home Products and Warner Lambert announced their plans to merge. Then Pfizer entered into the negotiations. A few days later Monsanto announced its desire to be acquired. Now I'm not sure who will finally acquire whom, but I am sure of one thing—the 54,000 employees at American Home Products aren't trying to figure out what their wage increase will be next year. The same goes for the 43,000 employees at Warner Lambert, 46,000 employees at Pfizer, and 30,000 employees at Monsanto. Those 173,000 employees are more worried about whether they'll have a job than what their wage increases will be next year.

DOWNSIZING

Companies around the world are getting leaner and meaner. Boeing and British Telecom both have $1 billion cost-cutting programs. AT&T is trying to cut $2 billion in costs. General Electric and Johnson & Johnson are cutting jobs. And if you think companies can't succeed with such drastic cuts, think again: Renault Motor Company in France produced 220,000 more vehicles with 20,000 fewer employees. Do you really think employees at Renault have any leverage to ask for a pay raise?

CAPITAL GAINS

At some point the Fed will realize that workers focus on "capital gains," not on wage gains. Think about it for a minute. Employees have profit-sharing plans, company stock, ESOP plans, warrants, options, shadow stock, or "rights." Wealth isn't accumulated by wage gains anymore; it's accumulating by capital gains. Employers can keep a lid on wage gains by compensating employees with potential "capital gains."

Y2K: IT ISN'T OVER 'TIL IT'S OVER

The millennium bug is about to take center stage with the FOMC. The FOMC won't raise rates at its next meeting, which takes place on December 21, because changing monetary policy in the face of Y2K-related hype and investor uncertainty could disrupt the markets. I also doubt that the FOMC will raise rates at its next two meetings, on February 1 and 2 and March 21. While no one knows for sure what will happen with Y2K, there seems to be a consensus that first-quarter economic data will be distorted as both individuals and businesses prepare and respond to Y2K. In the short run, then, I think we can expect the FOMC to keep interest rates where they are.

IT'S ELECTION TIME!

When the Y2K influence stops somewhere around March 21, the election influence will begin. The next FOMC meeting after March 21 isn't until May 16, when we'll be in the heat of the presidential and congressional election cycles. And in a presidential election year, the FOMC tends to be more reactionary than preemptive. It is much more difficult for the FOMC to say it's raising rates because it sees something no one else sees, so it will have to offer concrete proof of inflation before raising rates in March—and I don't think they'll be able to offer that proof.

BACK TO THE FUTURE

We had three rate cuts in 1998 and three rate increases in 1999, so we haven't really gained or lost anything. And with the influence of Y2K, the labor markets, and the election year, we probably won't gain or lose anything anytime soon. So sit back, relax, and join me in resolving to remain a long-term investor in a short-term world!

Investment Footnote . . . What actually happened

I was wrong, since the Fed didn't stop until it raised rates three more times in 2000 by 25 basis points on each occasion. First, on February 2, 2000, next on March 21, 2000, and finally on May 16, 2000.

Hackers and Yackers

FEBRUARY 11, 2000

As if nervous investors didn't have enough to worry about this week, we've come up with two new threats to end our bull market: *yackers* (Treasury Undersecretary Gary Gensler and Treasury Secretary Lawrence Summers yacking mixed messages about what the Treasury Department plans to do about paying down debt) and *hackers* (the computer hackers who are launching a cyberattack that shut down some of the highest profile Web sites on the Internet).

FIRST, THE YACKERS

Let's start with the yackers. With interest rates rising around the globe, fueled by central bank rate hikes in the United States, Canada, England, Euroland, South Korea, and so on, equity investors are paying very close attention to where bond yields (interest rates) are heading. Thus, with equity investors nervously watching the bond market, the Treasury Department made its first policy misstep under Secretary Summers, which whipsawed the bond market and turned the stock market on its ear as well. You see, First Treasury Undersecretary Gensler publicly stated that the Treasury Department will be deemphasizing the use of the benchmark 30-year Treasury bond and focusing on the 10-year note instead. The markets reacted with a strong bond market rally in the 30-year Treasury bond. (Because, after all, if the Treasury Department would be using our new government surplus to buy up 30-year Treasury bonds, that means that there would be less supply and the ones left would have greater value.)

That all came to a sudden halt a few days later when Treasury Secretary Summers said that the Treasury Department planned to continue to use all aspects of the yield curve including the 30-year Treasury bond. The bond market immediately collapsed and turned the equity market upside down once again.

Does the left hand of the Treasury have any idea what the right hand is doing? To make matters even worse, in his most recent Senate Committee testimony, Mr. Summers chose to exit through the back door to avoid talking to reporters.

The bottom line is that the bond market doesn't like surprises. When Mr. Rubin was secretary of the Treasury, he always kept the markets well informed and always knew just what to say. Mr. Summers' missteps will take months to recover from as the markets don't give back credibility too quickly. Although this policy misstep doesn't really change anything, it will increase the volatility in an already volatile bond market—which will certainly spill over into volatility in the stock market as well.

NOW THE HACKERS

A few misguided computer hackers have attacked some of the highest-flying Web sites; suddenly we are supposed to think that the Internet is going to collapse, which would crush our economy, which in turn would cause our markets to crash. Adding fuel to this high-profile fire alarm is President Clinton's decision to hold an Internet security summit. (It never ceases to amaze me how many excuses politicians can find to hold a news conference in an election year.) We don't need the federal government to stop the few misguided computer hackers. The technology industry will stop them on their own.

Keep in mind the Internet is an evolving industry that has experienced explosive growth. Sometimes that growth can get in front of the infrastructure, which creates a window of opportunity for the "criminal element" that surfs the Web. Don't worry, though,

the industry will try to quickly catch up and contain these few misguided hackers. What nervous investors need to remember is that
with every technology advancement, pranks will occur as the
industry evolves.

When the telephone was first gaining popularity in the United
States, the popular prank was to get 20 people to make a call to the
switchboard operator at a certain time. The goal was to overload
the system and the poor switchboard operator at the same time. The
industry responded by hiring more switchboard operators, which
in the early 1900s was one of the hottest jobs around. In fact, in 1908
a Bell Company engineer forecast that by 1930 every female in the
United States age 17 to 30 would have to be a telephone switchboard operator based on explosive growth projections for the Bell
Company's telephone. Ever wonder what happened to those great
jobs? Well, two years later, in 1910, automatic switches were
invented. And the prank of overloading the switchboard operator
was dead.

Now, I'm not sure who will invent the modern day "automatic
switches" to stop these computer hackers, but I am confident someone will. These computer hackers will not stop the Internet; they
will not stop our economy.

While hackers and yackers can add to its volatility, the overall
direction of our market will continue to be fueled by an economy
that is now in the largest economic expansion in our country's history and profits that continue to surprise on the high side, fueled by
the most productive companies anywhere in the world.

Have a great day, keep a positive attitude, and please join me
in resolving to remain a long-term investor in a short-term world!

Investment Footnote . . . What actually happened

They didn't stop our economy, since GDP grew at 1.0 percent
for the first quarter of 2000 and at a whopping 6.4 percent for
the second quarter.

Goodnight, Mr. Greenspan!

JUNE 28, 2000

Finally, the Federal Reserve Board has decided to take a rest from raising interest rates in the year 2000. In each of the prior three meetings this year, the Federal Reserve Board has raised interest rates. Now they are finally resting, not just this month, but, I believe, for the remainder of the year.

Let's look at why they stopped raising interest rates. I believe that there were two overriding issues: time and gasoline.

TIME IS ON OUR SIDE

First, it takes time for a rise in interest rates to work its way through the economy before it has any impact. In this short-term world that we live in, investors expect that if the Federal Reserve Board raises rates on Monday, by Wednesday the economic releases will reflect a slowdown. The Federal Reserve Board knows better. They realize that it takes approximately nine months before a rate hike will work its way into the economy. This weakness we are seeing in some economic releases is the cumulative result of what the Fed has done over the past year, not the past week.

Remember, it was June 30, 1999, when the Fed started their first of six interest rate hikes. On June 30, 1999, they moved the Fed fund rate from 4.75 to 5 percent. Then, on August 24, they moved rates again to 5.25 percent, followed by another rate hike on November 16 to 5.5 percent. This year they had been relentless, hiking rates at every single meeting. On February 2, 2000, they went to 5.75 percent,, followed by a March 21 move to 6 percent, and then the May 16 granddaddy move of them all, a whopping one-half percent move to 6.5 percent. Thus, in the last year the Fed has raised rates six separate times—a total of 1.75 percent from a Fed fund rate of 4.75 percent to its current level of 6.5 percent.

All of these prior rate hikes are now just beginning to start to have an impact on our economy. Thus, the Fed can afford to sit on the sidelines and monitor the impact of the past year's work.

In addition, don't forget that our Fed has become the de facto central bank of the world. What we do, everyone else seems to follow. From June 30 of last year, when the Fed raised rates for the first time, there have been 102 central bank rate hikes. The Fed realized that they risk slowing down the global economy if they continue to move rates higher.

LIFE IS NOT A GAS

Second, the skyrocketing price of gasoline also served as a key reason to keep the Fed on hold. Now I know that this runs against all economic logic, because conventional wisdom says that rising gas prices prove inflation is a problem so you raise rates. Right? Wrong. This gasoline price spike is very unconventional. The Fed knows it is not a sign of inflation because, other than oil, commodity inflation is tame. Rather it's a sign that OPEC again has figured out how to hold us hostage by limiting supply and watching the price go to the moon.

Getting back to why this influenced the Fed . . . it's all about confidence. The price of gas is on everyone's mind. We usually get reminded of it at least twice a week when we drive up to the pump. The price of gasoline has a great impact on consumer confidence, both positive and negative. And the Fed was worried that if the high price of gas erodes consumer confidence and the consumer slows down too much, this, combined with the impact of their six previous rate hikes, could slow things down way too fast too soon. After all, remember that the consumer accounts for two-thirds of our economy, and if the consumer isn't confident, the economy slows.

EARNINGS, NOT INTEREST

Going forward, there are only two more meetings between now and the presidential election: August 22 and October 3. Unless we have an outrageous outbreak of inflation, which I firmly believe we will not, the Fed will continue to stay on hold. And after the election, the impact of prior rate hikes will take hold, giving the Fed a rest for the remainder of the year.

These are great times for our markets. Finally, for the first time this year, we can move investors' focus away from interest rates and on to earnings. With our focus on earnings, I believe that the overall market fundamentals will improve. Earnings for the remainder of the year will stay exceedingly strong across most industries. Better-than-expected earnings, combined with the Fed taking a rest, should mean a better-than-expected market the second half of the year.

I have been waiting for the Fed to take a rest all year and now I finally get to say it: "Good night, Mr. Greenspan."

Have a great day, keep a positive attitude, and please join me in resolving to remain a long-term investor in a short-term world.

Investment Footnote . . . What actually happened

I was dead right, since the Fed didn't move rates again in 2000.

We've Only Just Begun (to Cut)

JANUARY 4, 2001

On the surface, yesterday's Federal Reserve Board's 50-basis-point rate cut appeared to some market participants to be bold and dramatic. After all, it didn't come as part of a regularly scheduled meeting and it wasn't the typical Greenspan gradualist approach of 25 basis points. It was a whopping 50 basis points. However, there was nothing bold or dramatic about it if you look back over the past two years.

In 1999, in the last six months of the year, the Fed raised rates three separate times, at 25 basis points each. In 2000 they raised rates three more times: 25 basis points twice and 50 basis points once. Thus, over the past two years, we have endured six separate

rate hikes, raising rates 175 basis points. Thus, from that perspective, one rate cut at 50 basis points isn't all that bold after all. From my perspective, it's one rate cut down and five more to go, or 50 basis points down and 125 more to go. However you look at it, the important thing to remember is that the trend has turned. Just as the Fed raised rates for almost a two-year period, I look for them to continue lowering rates, especially over the next 12 months.

And don't forget, when the Fed moves monetary policy by cutting rates, the rest of the central banks around the world usually soon follow. One sure way to offset any global slowdown is to have central banks around the globe embarking on a series of interest rate cuts.

When rates fall, businesses tend to invest more in their businesses, which in turn keeps the productivity story alive. And when rates fall, we will have another refinancing of mortgage boom, which will fuel consumption and our economy. And finally, nothing brings the confidence back to equity investors faster than falling interest rates.

While you are celebrating all of this good news, don't forget that we haven't even begun to talk about tax cuts yet.

Have a great day, keep a positive attitude, and I'll see ya at 12,500!

Investment Footnote . . . What actually happened ↑

I was correct, because the Fed did indeed continue to cut rates; in fact, the Fed cut rates 11 more times and didn't stop cutting rates until June 25, 2003.

Give Me a Price Break!

FEBRUARY 16, 2001

As our markets continue to struggle to find a direction in which to go, it's always useful to remember how we got here in the first place so that we can figure out where we are heading.

The underperforming equity markets over the past year or so were the result of two independent factors that combined to hit business and consumers around the globe. These caused economies to slow down, which, in turn, caused markets to slow down. The two negative forces were rising interest rates and rising energy rates. If you think about it, we are already addressing half of these negative market forces.

Remember, if you will, how this rising interest rate force began. Back in June 1999, the Fed began a cycle of rising interest rates that encompassed six separate rate hikes, totaling 175 basis points, from June 1999 through the end of last year. During that same time period, there were 200 other central bank interest rate hikes from around the globe. Remember, the Fed is very respected and very influential, and the rest of the world tends to follow where they go with their policy directives.

Let's fast-forward to today. So far this year, the Fed has reversed policy and has cut interest rates twice in a rather dramatic fashion, totaling 100 basis points already. And just like last time, the rest of the world is following the lead of our Fed. There have already been 25 central bank rate cuts from around the globe in the first two months of this year.

We're halfway home; the interest rate scare is now behind us. And, in fact, interest rate cuts will help move both the economy and the markets forward. And that brings us right back to energy.

The price of oil jumped from a little over $10 a barrel to a little over $35 a barrel in an 18-month period. Add on top of that the record cold winter all across the United States and natural gas, heating oil, and, most important, heating bills shot up as well. Nothing hurts consumer confidence like high heating or cooling bills. Oh, and in case you need some proof of how rising prices can affect the economy, consider this: The consumption of gasoline rose every single year for 10 years straight—a whole decade of gasoline consumption rising. Last year in the United States, for the first time in a decade, gasoline consumption actually fell by 1 percent.

I believe that the worst is behind us on oil, which means that the worst is behind us on energy costs as well. And here is why: first of all the OPEC (Organization of Petroleum Exporting Countries) cartel doesn't want prices to stay too high because higher prices stimulate new exploration activity and more competition weakens OPEC's control of the oil market.

Second, I firmly believe that my good friend, technology, will finally break up the OPEC cartel. You see, technology is creating new approaches to improve the success rate of exploration activity, which leads to new reserves. Also, technology is dramatically reducing the cost of producing oil, making production at high-cost locations more feasible than ever. And, in the long run, technology will ultimately lead to the development of alternative fuels, which will lower the demand for oil, which in turn will lower the cost.

Don't forget, we're already halfway through February, spring is right around the corner, and the memory of those sky-high winter heating bills is about to be a thing of the past as well.

Finally, we are about to get a much-deserved price break on oil. Oh, and did I mention there already is a great price break on stocks and bonds? Think about it: stocks . . . bonds . . . gasoline. I think that we just found the missing fuel to drive our markets higher.

Let me close with this one thought for you to keep in mind when "gloom and doom," also known as rising interest rates and rising energy prices, are the story of the day: I want you to remember just how vibrant our global economy is.

Even in the face of record-high energy prices and rising interest rates, watch how the economies around the world performed. There are 190 countries around the globe. And, of those 190 countries, how many do you think experienced a decline in their economy in 2000 as a result of Drs. Doom and Gloom? You better sit down for this: four. That's right, despite all the problems, 186 countries experienced economic growth while only four experienced a decline in 2000.

Have a great day everyone. The price is about to be right, and I'll see ya at 12,500!

PS: For anyone who's interested, the four countries were the Congo, Ivory Coast, Zimbabwe, and Moldova.

Investment Footnote . . . What actually happened

I was wrong, because our economy did not grow in the first quarter of 2001; it contracted −0.5 percent even though it continued to post positive growth on a year-over-year basis at 1.9 percent.

What's 175 Got to Do with It? Plenty!

APRIL 9, 2002

The 175 I'm talking about is 175 basis points—investment jargon for 1.75 percent. And you probably know that refers to interest rates. I'm amazed that I'm talking about interest rates, with so many things to worry about: the war on terrorism and our military action in Afghanistan, the conflict in the Middle East and the Enron and Arthur Andersen debacles. But investors across the United States have chosen to focus on interest rates, so I will as well. Investors are concerned that interest rates will rise, and that's where my 175 comes into play. But let me show you why rising interest rates will not derail our stock market.

WHERE THEY'VE COME FROM

First of all, you should never look at interest rates in isolation. It's just as important to focus on where they've come from as it is to focus on where they are today. So let's remember that we started the year 2001 with the Federal Reserve Board's federal funds rate at 6.50 percent.

Interest rates began to rise when the Fed began an aggressive easing in an attempt to stimulate our sagging economy. It cut rates seven separate times during the first eight months of the year. The first five interest rate cuts were 50 basis points each, and the next two were 25 basis points.

That was the Fed's way of signaling to the market that they were just about done. You see, first they cut 50 basis points, then they cut 25 basis points, then they did nothing. And with the federal funds rate standing at 3.50 percent as we entered September of last year, the Fed was preparing to continue to do absolutely nothing.

Then, unexpectedly, along came the horrific events of September 11. Suddenly the Fed felt the need to jump in and help. When our stock market reopened after closing due to September 11, the Fed cut rates four more times. The first three cuts were 50 basis points, and the fourth one was 25 basis points. Those four interest rate cuts—which wouldn't have happened without the horrific events of September 11—trimmed rates another 175 basis points.

Do you see where I'm going with this? When the year ended, interest rates were cut 11 times for a total of 475 basis points. This caused the federal funds rate, which began the year at 6.50 percent, to end the year at—do you sense a theme?—1.75 percent. That, by the way, is the lowest federal funds rate we've seen in 40 years.

OBVIOUSLY, THE NEXT MOVE IS UP

With the federal funds rate at 1.75 percent, the next move is obviously up—especially when Fed Chairman Alan Greenspan describes the federal funds rate as "very low."

When the Fed starts to increase rates (and notice that I said "when," not "if"), don't think of it as a means of slowing our economy or our markets. Instead, think of it as a removal of the "emergency insurance rate cuts" made in response to the September 11 terrorist attacks. You remember the ones I'm talking about: those four cuts that totaled 175 basis points. The most I could see the Fed moving rates over the next two years is—you guessed it—175 basis points.

There's some recent history to give us a clue as to how the Fed might respond. Recall, if you will, 1998. The crisis that was supposed to hit our economy and markets at that time was long-term capital management's collapse. Within three months after the collapse, the Fed cut interest rates three separate times for a total of

75 basis points. Once the predicted disaster did not come to pass, the Fed took back all three of those emergency insurance rate cuts.

WE'RE STILL LOW

Even if the Fed takes back all 175 basis points of its emergency insurance rate cuts, the federal funds rate will still be extremely low at 3.50 percent. In fact, there has only been one other period in the past decade (1990 through today) during which the federal funds rate was lower than 3.50 percent. That was a brief 20-month period between July 1992 and March 1994 when we were in our last recession. So I fail to see what everyone is so worried about.

One fact is perfectly clear though: in the past 40 years, we haven't started raising rates from such a low level. Thus, I think the impact will be different from any other interest rate increase in the past 40 years. I don't think a couple of hikes will stop our market.

NOT SO FAST!

Let me close by reminding you that the focus on interest rate hikes is "when," not "if." While many so-called Fed watchers are calling for the Fed to raise rates at its next meeting on May 7, and the consensus of economic forecasters calls for numerous interest rate hikes to begin this fall, I disagree. The reason is because of—you guessed it—175. But this is a totally different 175 basis points that I'm talking about. Let me explain.

In my opinion, Greenspan may very well go down in history as the greatest Fed chairman ever. History will also point out that the greatest policy mistake he made in his illustrious career is when he inadvertently caused our latest recession by raising interest rates at the same time the prices of oil and energy were surging. It was June of 1999 when the Fed began to raise rates six separate times for a total of—you guessed it—175 basis points. That deadly one-two punch of higher interest rates and rising energy costs is what brought our record economic expansion to a close.

Greenspan is a student of history. He recalls that the only blemish to his wonderful career is when he began raising rates at the same time the price of oil began creeping upward. Today, once again, the price of oil is creeping upward and the current unstable nature of the Middle East could deliver an oil price shock at any time. As a result, I believe that Greenspan and company will remain on the sidelines until our economy and markets are on firm footing—all year, I'm guessing.

Greenspan knows what 175 has got to do with it. Now so do you!

Investment Footnote . . . What actually happened   ←→

Almost right, since the Fed couldn't quite stay on the sidelines all year. . . . But instead of raising rates, they actually lowered rates 50 basis points on November 6, 2002.

J.O.B.S.

NOVEMBER 14, 2003

There is no more important issue today than jobs. Investors are focusing on it, businesses are focusing on it, and so are politicians at both the state and federal level. Why? The single biggest story to come out of the last Federal Reserve Board meeting was that the Fed replaced three simple words with four new ones in its directive. The Fed removed the words "has been weakening" and replaced them with "appears to be stabilizing." This was important because the Fed was talking about—you guessed it—the labor market.

The reason that jobs are so important is that they are the vital link to sustaining our economic recovery. Higher personal income and dividend and long-term capital gains tax cuts were great. So was the mortgage refinancing explosion fueled by record low mortgage rates and zero-percent financing to buy cars. However, these things are simply tools to jump-start the economy. To keep it going after jump-starting it, you need jobs. In addition to the economy, the job market is a key driver in where the stock market is headed and has great influence in determining the direction of the dollar. And if that isn't important enough, jobs will probably also play a significant role in deciding the 2004 presidential election. With all of the focus and importance being placed on jobs, I want to spell out what I see happening in the job market.

"J" IS FOR JOB LOSS

"J" is for job loss. There appears to be a newfound fear that every service job is now suddenly moving overseas. Let me make two important points here. First, weakness in the service sector is due to the sudden loss of all the Internet startup and Internet spinoff companies that suddenly disappeared. When they did, so did a lot of the service-related jobs that supported them. This service sector job collapse had nothing to do with foreign competition or the overseas outsourcing of service jobs. It had to do with the Internet bubble bursting.

Second, I will admit that there is a trend developing in which U.S. service workers are being replaced with less expensive foreign service workers in far-off places like India, especially in call centers and telemarketing. There is another side to this trend that is also going on, especially as it relates to call centers in India. Wages for call center service workers have risen 20 percent in the past year and turnover is above 30 percent. Despite a perception among investors that India has an unlimited labor force that speaks fluent English and can replace the entire U.S. service sector, I think these numbers are actually pointing to a different trend. A 20 percent increase in wages to get employees to stay on the job and a 30 percent turnover rate tells me that many college-educated workers in India may not be satisfied with a career answering customer service calls and pretending they are in Iowa. As technology recovers, so will our service sector jobs.

"O" IS FOR OUTPUT

Well, we spelled out "J," so now let's move on to "O," which stands for output. You cannot simply look at jobs in isolation. You have to look at them in terms of output as well. While everyone is complaining about all the automotive industry jobs we have lost, let me put something in perspective. Currently, total employment in the U.S. auto industry has fallen to the same level it was in 1950, well off the go-go years of the 1960s and the 1970s. On the surface, in isolation, having employment at the same level as 1950 may seem like a bad thing—until you consider output. Industrial production is up an astonishing 550 percent since 1950. That's the result of productivity growing at approximately 5 percent a year. Is it really such a bad thing when each employee is 550 percent more productive than his or her 1950 counterparts? The loss of manufacturing jobs in the automotive industry does not signal a problem with American manufacturing, but rather faster growth in manufacturing productivity than in the economy as a whole.

"B" IS FOR BUSINESS CONFIDENCE

Now let's move on to "B," which stands for business confidence. Everywhere you look there are signs that business confidence is improving. Capital expenditures have already turned around and are now poised to increase at a 10 percent quarterly clip. Temporary employment, which historically leads to an uptick in permanent employment, has been trending higher for months. And finally, advertising spending is up 6 percent on a year-over-year basis and is up 14 percent from its post- 9/11 recession low. When businesses begin spending on advertising again, along with temporary employment and major capital outlays, you have a good sign of increased business confidence. And that is a key link to the turnaround in jobs. In addition, business confidence can be a key driver in the consumer goods sector. Earlier this year when I met with Sangita Uberol, Deutsche Asset Management, global sector team leader for consumer goods, retail, and leisure in our London office, she astutely pointed out that "business pessimism fuels negative consumer sentiment." That is exactly where we were earlier in the year. However, the current upturn in business confidence, if it is followed by an uptick in employment, bodes extremely well for consumer confidence. And that should mean good things for the consumer goods sector going forward.

"S" IS FOR SARBANES-OXLEY

Finally, let's move on to "S," which stands for Sarbanes-Oxley. You remember Sarbanes-Oxley, don't you? That was the landmark corporate regulation that was put in place in the aftermath of the Enron, WorldCom, Arthur Andersen, et al., scandals. While this law was not intended to do anything about jobs, it actually has. The regulatory climate has caused companies to retain more accountants in order to stay in compliance with Sarbanes-Oxley. Companies are hiring more legal staff as well. And they are increasing both public relations and investor relations staff to deal with this sensitive issue. I haven't even begun to touch upon the increase in compliance personnel and internal auditors. In addition, with all this new disclosure, and footnotes that now read like a short story, printing companies are staffing up to meet this newfound printing demand. Who knows? Maybe Sarbanes-Oxley will go down in history as the "full employment act."

In closing, here is some important anecdotal evidence. United Airlines is rehiring 300 flight attendants. IBS has announced plans to add 10,000 employees. Who knows? Maybe there is more to jobs than simply J-O-B-S.

Investment Footnote . . . What actually happened

I was dead right, as the November 2003 employment numbers released in December 2003 showed that the unemployment rate had dropped from 6.0 percent to 5.8 percent and 55,000 jobs were created. That trend continued the next month as well, when were the unemployment rate dropped again to 5.7 percent and a whopping 168,000 new jobs were created.

Hurricane Alan

OCTOBER 3, 2005

As we head into the fourth quarter we are still on hurricane watch as the season is not over. From an investment watch I have good news and bad news as we enter the fourth quarter. The good news is that the most recent U.S. manufacturing activity economic releases confirm what I have been saying all along on www.scudder.com regarding the impact of Hurricanes Katrina and Rita: "The economic impact will be regional, not national."

The bad news is that these extremely strong economic releases appear to have the market convinced that the Federal Reserve Board, under the direction of Alan Greenspan, will continue its current approach and move interest rates higher. Alan Greenspan has already raised interest rates 11 times by moving the Fed Funds Rate (the interest rate that banks charge other banks to borrow money overnight) from 1 percent to its current level of 3.75 percent. Wall Street seems to be much more worried about Hurricane Alan than it was about Hurricanes Katrina or Rita. Let's explore what all this may mean for our stock market in the fourth quarter.

EARNINGS MATTER

Sometimes we forget that the ultimate driver of our equity markets is earnings. And I believe that third quarter earnings (the report will be released in the fourth quarter) will be staggering! I forecast the operating earnings of the Standard & Poor's 500 to increase a whopping 20 percent on a year-over-year basis.

I think we spend way too much time worrying about the weather and budget deficits and the price of oil. Never forget that it is earnings that ultimately matter, because earnings ultimately drive our market. The only reason to even look at these other things is to see if they will have any impact on earnings, either positively or negatively. From my perspective, the earnings picture has never looked better in this new century and I think this will eventually be reflected in stock prices.

IN NEED OF A CATALYST—OIL

I think what we need in the fourth quarter is a catalyst for investors to refocus on earnings. One possible catalyst would be a correction in the price of oil, heading closer to $50 a barrel rather than $100 a barrel. I believe that is exactly what we are going to see in the fourth quarter.

Supply/demand fundamentals set the foundation for a weakening of oil prices. From a supply standpoint, more than one million barrels of oil a day are being added to new capacity in 2006. Nigeria is increasing production by 390,000 barrels; Libya, 225,000 barrels; Algeria, 50,000 barrels; Saudi Arabia, 300,000 barrels; UAE, 100,000 barrels; Iran, 105,000 barrels, and, finally, Venezuela will add 70,000 barrels a day. All told we will have more than 1,240,000 barrels of new oil every day next year.

Now, from a demand perspective, keep an eye on what China is doing. China's National Development Reform Commission is developing projects to reduce China's consumption of energy. This is going to be achieved by implementing a series of energy-saving practices that will ultimately change energy consumption. And, by the way, this has never been done in China before. Never. With more supply and lower demand, which way do you think oil prices are headed?

CATALYST—INTEREST RATES

Well, if the price of oil falling doesn't provide our markets with a catalyst, perhaps Hurricane Alan and the Fed stopping their interest rate hikes would. And even though virtually everyone on Wall Street is convinced Hurricane Alan is not slowing down anytime soon—especially with these most recent bullish manufacturing economic releases—I disagree. Let me give you two reasons why I believe Hurricane Alan needs to stop raising interest rates.

First, consider this tremendous manufacturing number that caught all of Wall Street off guard. I believe this figure was impacted positively by Katrina and Rita. You see, I feel this big uptick in manufacturing was a panic reaction to place orders and secure goods that were feared to be in short supply post-Katrina and -Rita.

In other words manufacturing may be strong but not that strong. So, in my opinion, we really don't need to slow it down by raising interest rates again.

Second, let me remind you that the consumer is more important to our economy than manufacturing. After all, the consumer accounts for two-thirds of our economy. And just last week consumer confidence (as measured by the University of Michigan's Consumer Sentiment Survey) showed the largest single drop in the past 25 years! When two-thirds of your economy has just experienced the largest drop in confidence in 25 years, what in the world is Hurricane Alan trying to slow down? If I am correct and Hurricane Alan turns into a tropical storm, it would become the best catalyst the market could have hoped for in the fourth quarter.

FOLLOW THE MONEY

Regardless of which catalyst gets us looking at earnings again, I want to remind you of just how much cash is sitting on the sidelines waiting to drive our markets higher in the fourth quarter. Ten years ago individual cash savings stood at $2.5 trillion. (By the way, individual cash savings are comprised of money market accounts, certificates of deposits that mature in one year or less, and savings accounts.) Today, one decade later, individual cash savings stand at over $5 trillion! Individual cash savings have more than doubled in 10 years. The actual amount is $5,132,900,000. That's a lot of cash to fuel our markets higher once we get our catalyst.

FOURTH QUARTER HISTORY LESSON

Let me close with one more historical perspective for you regarding our markets in the fourth quarter. In each of the past four years our market, as measured by the S&P 500, rose each and every year by at least 8 percent. I firmly believe that 2005 will make it five in a row.

Here is a little more history for you. Back in 1981 the Pittsburgh Steelers, winners of four Super Bowls, adopted the slogan "One for the Thumb." Actually, it was their Hall of Fame defensive lineman "Mean" Joe Greene who said he had four Super Bowl rings for all of his fingers; all he needed was "one for the thumb." What a great slogan. I am sorry to say that my beloved Steelers are still searching for that "one for the thumb."

In the meantime, I will borrow Mean Joe Green's slogan and say that earnings will be our "one for the thumb." I expect that once again we will see at least an 8 percent rise in our market for the fifth year in a row during the fourth quarter. And that will be one for each finger plus one for our thumb. And I'll go as far as saying that in the first quarter of 2006, the Pittsburgh Steelers will finally get their "one for the thumb" as well!!

PS: In case you were wondering, I believe Hurricane Alan is a Category "1" storm, which doesn't matter nearly as much as earnings, which are a Category "5."

Investment Footnote . . . What actually happened

Third-quarter earnings for the S&P 500 didn't quite make it to the 20 percent level as I forecasted. They came in at 18.84 percent. But in the fourth quarter of 2005 they did indeed come in above 20 percent at 20.19 percent. (There is such a fine line in this business between being wrong and being early.)

The Newest "Big Ben"
OCTOBER 27, 2005

Now we have yet another Big Ben to worry about. The original "Big Ben" is the clock tower at Parliament in London. Next came Big Ben Roethlisberger, the young star quarterback of my beloved Pittsburgh

Steelers. And now along comes the newest Big Ben—as in Ben Bernanke, who was nominated by President Bush to be the next Chairman of the Federal Reserve Board.

NO SURPRISE

Certainly the choice of Ben Bernanke was not a surprise. He emerged as the leading candidate in a small group rumored to be under consideration by President Bush. After nominating two Supreme Court Justices from somewhat out in left field, the president was determined not to make this appointment appear to be a big surprise as well.

And it certainly was no surprise to our loyal Scudder.com readers because you already knew this was probably going to happen four days before the president made his announcement. You'll recall that I told you in my latest commentary posted on scudder.com " . . . Alan Greenspan is retiring and the next Federal Reserve Board Chairman, in my humble opinion, will be Ben Bernanke . . . "

Not only is his appointment not a surprise, but I think he should easily gain Senate confirmation. In addition to his current experience in the White House as Chairman of the President's Council of Economic Advisors, he also served as a Governor on the Federal Reserve Board. Before he began his political career he was a top academic economist at Princeton after having been educated at Harvard and the Massachusetts Institute of Technology.

WHERE'S BOB?

Despite all of his experience and training I suspect there will be great concern that no one will ever be able to replace Mr. Greenspan. Those of us who have been in this business for over 20 years will recall that's exactly what was being said in 1987 when the great concern was that no one would ever be able to replace Mr. Volker (the then retiring Chairman of the Federal Reserve

Board). Well, things seemed to have worked out just fine back then, and I am sure they will today as well.

But I want to give you a more recent reminder of how things work out. Prior to Alan Greenspan's departure, the great concern on Wall Street was that no one would be able to replace Bob Rubin, the Secretary of the Treasury in the Clinton Administration who saved the world from financial disaster when he solved the Mexican peso crisis. And because he came to Washington, D.C., from Wall Street, he was very well respected on Wall Street.

You may recall several years ago when suddenly, out of left field, Bob Rubin resigned. What in the world would happen to us now? I remember that day like it was yesterday because I was actually traveling in Boston and my cell phone and voice messages would not stop with clients calling me wanting to know what this would mean for our markets.

It was my lucky day because one of my meetings was with my friend and investment guru Peter Lynch of Fidelity Investments. I couldn't wait to meet with him to ask for myself what this means for the markets. When I got together with Peter later that afternoon, that was my first question and I will never forget his answer. He said to me, "I have no idea; let me check." He then spun his computer screen around so I could see what he was doing as he took his finger and pointed to each stock on the screen one at a time. When he finished he looked at me and said, "I am going to be OK. I just checked and I didn't make a single one of my investment choices because Bob Rubin was Secretary of the Treasury."

I am willing to bet the same is true today regarding Alan Greenspan. I can't imagine anyone making their investment decisions based on the fact that Alan Greenspan is the Federal Reserve Board Chairman.

BACK TO BEN

Now let's get back to the newest Big Ben. I firmly believe that there will be some changes under Ben Bernanke's leadership. For one, I expect he will set a target for inflation. This is something that Alan

Greenspan was opposed to doing, while Ben Bernanke argued that it would improve the transparency of the Federal Reserve Board if all investors knew what the inflation target was. Inflation targets are nothing new for central banks to be public about. In fact the Bank of England has used an inflation target since 1992. So while it would be new to the United States, it is not a new tool to central bankers.

RISING ABOVE IT ALL

In closing, I can tell you from firsthand experience what a great Federal Reserve Board Chairman Ben Bernanke will be. You see, Ben Bernanke joined me seven months ago as one of the keynote speakers on the campus of the University of Dayton for the Redefining Investment Strategy Education (RISE) student forum, which is the largest student investment forum in the world. Ben gave the luncheon address, which I moderated. Two things struck me in the time I got to spend with Ben Bernanke in person. First, he is a conceptual thinker. That is, he links concepts that on the surface appear unrelated and connects the dots for you. Second, he is still a teacher committed to education. This was again proven by the fact that he took time out of his hectic schedule as a Federal Reserve Board Governor to come to the University of Dayton's RISE Forum. You could see the spark in his eye when students from around the world began asking him questions as he knew each answer would be a teaching experience.

I think all investors are about to learn some great lessons from the newest Big Ben.

Investment Footnote . . . What actually happened

I was right. Ben Bernanke is nothing like Alan Greenspan.

Hurricane Ben

June 21, 2006

As we survive the first tropical storm of the season, "Alberto," I am afraid that the current storm, "Hurricane Ben," could wreak havoc across the United States and possibly even around the world as well. Hurricane Ben is not a storm off the Gulf Coast; it's the nickname I have given to new Federal Reserve Board Chairman, Ben Bernanke, who is destroying more value than 100 tropical storms combined with his ill-advised and misguided interest rate tightening policy. The policy is ill-advised for two reasons, in my opinion. Let me explore both of them now, beginning with rental inflation, which I refer to as the puppy dog chasing its tail.

RENTAL INFLATION—THE PUPPY DOG CHASING ITS TAIL

If the Federal Reserve Board is raising interest rates to protect us from inflation, I demand to know exactly what inflation they are protecting us from. Here are the simple facts: Owners' equivalent rent (OER) and apartment rents together account for almost 40 percent of the core Consumer Price Index (CPI) that we are so worried about. The reason why these two areas of the inflation picture are dramatically picking up steam is due to the lagged effect of raising interest rates (from a 1.00 Fed Funds rate to a 5.00 Fed Funds rate), which in turn depresses homeownership and lifts apartment demand, which in turn pulls apartment vacancy rates down and rental rates up. In other words, this is a case where the Fed's rate hikes are actually contributing to the higher inflation rate instead of protecting us from it. It is the classic case of the puppy dog chasing its tail and never knowing when to stop. Let me help. Hurricane Ben, it is time to stop.

GLOBAL RATE AND LIQUIDITY SQUEEZE

The second issue is the synchronized global rate hike strategy, which in turn causes a liquidity squeeze. This so-called liquidity squeeze is in response to the fact that we now have two-thirds of the world's central banks raising interest rates in the past year, and the list is growing. Just this month alone we have seen the European Central Bank, Thailand, Turkey, India, Korea, Denmark, South Africa, Sweden, and Switzerland join the fray by raising interest rates. And last Friday, China lifted the reserve requirement ratio for its banks to 8 percent from 7.5 percent to help cool the credit-induced investment boom in China. It is interesting to note that this is in addition to the 27-basis-point tightening in lending rates that was initiated by China at the end of April. The global landscape has already completely changed. We are now in the middle of a synchronized global tightening cycle that can only stop when the Fed does so. So just do it. Hurricane Ben, it is time to stop.

TWO KEYS

From my perspective, there will be two key reflection points that will determine if we can survive the impact of Hurricane Ben. The first reflection point will be the June 29 FOMC statement issued after the meeting. In many respects the guidance this statement provides will be more important than the meeting itself.

The second is Ben Bernanke's mid-July Humphrey-Hawkins testimony on the semiannual monetary policy report. This testimony could set the tone for what the Fed will or will not do at its upcoming August FOMC meeting.

In closing, the sooner we can get the Fed to stop chasing the inflation bogeyman that isn't there, the sooner the markets can focus on what really matters—namely, earnings. And I believe when they do that, this market is poised to move higher and faster than any hurricane could ever take it—even Hurricane Ben.

> **Investment Footnote . . . What actually happened** ↑
>
> I was dead right again, as the Consumer Price Index dropped from its June 2006 level of 4.33 percent to 4.15 percent in July and continued to drop for the next 18 consecutive months.

The Fed's "Job" Is Over!

AUGUST 7, 2006

After 17 consecutive interest rate hikes, the Federal Reserve Board, in my opinion, is finally done raising interest rates. They will not move rates higher at tomorrow's Federal Open Market Committee (FOMC) meeting because Friday's jobs report proved the Fed's job is done.

THE JULY JOBS REPORT

No matter what aspect of Friday's jobs report you want to look at, all signs give the Fed reason to stop raising interest rates. First, payroll employment rose only 113,000, well below Wall Street's consensus of how many new jobs would be created. Second, the unemployment rate rose to 4.8 percent. While 4.8 percent is a good long-term trend rate, in the short run, it is the highest unemployment rate that we have experienced in this country since last February—over a year and a half ago. And finally, the Household Employment number, which many Wall Street pros (including me) think does a better job measuring the employment market, was even worse. FYI, while Payroll Employment surveys companies and asks how many new people they hired, the Household Survey goes to households and asks who is working, capturing all of the small business jobs that many people may work on out of their homes. Last month's Household Employment Report showed a gain of 387,000 jobs, while Friday's Household Survey showed a loss of 34,000 jobs. Like I said, the jobs report made it as clear as can be that the Fed's job of raising rates is clearly over.

EARNING NOT OVER

While the Fed's job of raising rates may be over, the second quarter earnings' story has a little way to go yet and, in my opinion, earnings are, in a word, "spectacular." According to Thompson's First Call, here is where we stand with 389 of the 500 companies of the S&P 500 (77.8 percent) reporting. More than 70 percent have beaten earnings expectations, while 18.5 percent of the companies have had negative earnings' surprises, and 10 percent reported earnings right in line with expectations. However, these numbers don't tell the whole story. Of the 70 percent of companies that have beaten earnings expectations, the companies beat earnings expectations by the robust margin of +5 percent. In other words, they didn't exceed earnings by a little margin, they crushed earnings. Before the second quarter earnings season started, the consensus on Wall Street was for earnings to grow 12.2 percent in the second quarter on a year-over-year basis. Wall Street always wants earnings to grow double digits, at least 10 percent, so the forecast of 12.2 percent was actually a bullish forecast. I predicted that second quarter earnings would grow 15 percent! And I said if I am wrong, it will be because I am too *low*, not too *high*. Well, with 389 of 500 of the S&P 500 companies reporting, earnings have grown at a 14.8 percent pace: my 15 percent forecast is a lock.

RATES MATTER MORE THAN EARNINGS

It is interesting to note that, in the short run, on a quarter-by-quarter basis, interest rates are actually more important to moving the markets higher than earnings. International Strategy & Investment Group conducted a study on quarterly stock market performance looking only at interest rates and earnings. If earnings are going down and interest rates are going up, that creates the worst market backdrop, followed by, as the second worst backdrop, when both rates and earnings were going up. Clearly, the market hates rising rates. The single best environment was when rates were going down and earnings were going up—clearly this is the Promised Land. The second best was when rates were going down and earnings were going down as well. In other words, on a quarterly basis, rates matter more than earnings. So here are the final standings.

1. Rates DOWN, earnings UP
2. Rates DOWN, earnings DOWN
3. Rates UP, earnings UP
4. Rates UP, earnings DOWN

READ HIS LIPS

This really means that it is very, very important that I get this interest rate call correct. As a little more proof, all we really have to do is read Ben Bernanke's lips. He gave us a great clue when he testified before Congress on July 19. He said that the Fed must be aware of the full influence of its policy actions, since these actions are felt only after a considerable period of time. He talked a lot about the "lagged" effect of policy changes. In other words, many of these prior 17 rate hikes haven't even made their way into the economy yet to slow it down. He knows that, and I know he is done. Also, he is a pretty smart guy. Anyone who can score a perfect 1600 on his college SAT. exam like Bernanke did is surely smart enough to figure out when enough is enough.

NOT THE END OF THE WORLD

In closing, with all this focus on rising interest rates—17 rate hikes from a 1 percent Fed Funds rate to the current level of 5.25 percent—there has been much talk about how this will be the end of the world for the poor consumer. The reason is quite simple, with interest rates going higher now, all of these consumers with adjustable rate mortgages are going to have to spend more on their mortgage payments, bringing an end to our economy. Great story, too bad it's not true. Here are the facts at the end of the first quarter according to the Federal Reserve Board's "Flow of Funds" report. During the first quarter, consumers had to spend $589 billion on mortgage payments due to higher rates, but that's only half the story. Personal interest income rose to $1.039 billion due to the same higher interest rates. That's over a trillion dollars in personal interest income, which is a record. So let me get this straight; higher interest rates cause us to spend $589 billion on mortgage payments, while we collected almost twice that amount, $1.039 billion or over $1 trillion, in personal interest income. I just don't see how this is the beginning of the end. Oh, and by the way, did I mention that the $589 billion in mortgage interest payments is tax *deductible* as well?

Let me end where I began. The Fed's job is done and your job, as an investor, is just beginning. I personally believe that the biggest risk now is being out of the market and missing this rally. Have a great day, keep a positive attitude, and I'll see ya at 12,500! With Ben as my copilot, we are halfway there!

Investment Footnote . . . What actually happened
I was correct, as the Fed did indeed stop after 17 rate hikes.

Not "If," but "When"

FEBRUARY 22, 2007

I had the pleasure last year of spending several weeks on the road traveling all throughout the United States on our "Global Road Show" with Oliver Kratz, who, in my opinion, is one of the best and brightest investment professionals in the business today. One of the many fascinating things about Oliver is his uncanny ability to uncover investable themes that he classifies as "not if, but when." In other words, these themes are so dramatic and sweeping they are going to happen and the only unanswered investment question is "when." Oliver's tag line of "not if, but when" can actually be applied to explain a lot of investment issues we are facing today.

NOT IF, BUT WHEN—INTEREST RATE CUTS

The first "not if, but when" focuses on interest rate cuts. Last evening, I was on CNBC's Kudlow & Company show and all the rage was the big scare about the Consumer Price Index (CPI), which had just skyrocketed and whether that meant the Federal Reserve Board would now raise interest rates. In a word, *"No."* Here is why. First of all, the consensus of Wall Street economists was for the CPI to come in at 0.2 percent, and it came in at 0.3 percent. In other words, what's the big deal? Also, this is a snapshot in time. It's one number for one month, which really never tells much anyway unless you take the time to look beyond the headline number of 0.3 percent. I did, and here's what I found. Because January has the unusual characteristic of being the first month of the calendar year, it is renowned for being a month when excise tax hikes (on things like tobacco, which happened with this latest CPI number) kick in, and it's the month when Medicare prices get reset. So why was everyone so surprised that we saw a big uptick in tobacco and medical inflation? It happens virtually every year.

Like I said before the year began, it's not a matter of "if," but "when" the Federal Reserve Board will cut interest rates. Even with yesterday's so-called dramatic CPI number, I am sticking with my original forecast of two interest rate cuts to happen sometime in the second half of the year.

NOT IF BUT WHEN—BUDGET DEFICIT FALLS AS TAX RECEIPTS RISE

My second "not if, but when" focuses on the falling budget deficit as tax receipts rise. While any discussion of the budget deficit tends to become highly charged politically, I am going to remove politics from it and show you why the deficit is going down based simply on the facts and not on opinions or forecasts.

Over the past 12 months, our budget deficit (as reported by the Federal Reserve Board) has shrunk $162 billion. In 2004 we had a record budget deficit of $411 billion, which shrunk to $319 billion in 2005 and ended 2006 at only $249 billion. How in the world could this possibly happen? It's simple. It's all about tax receipts. For the federal government, record corporate profits are the driver for generating tax revenues. It's pretty simple to figure out: the more money companies make, the more they have to pay in taxes. But that's only the beginning if it.

Also, when companies make money, they tend to share the wealth with their employees by paying bigger bonuses and increasing salaries and wages. In addition, profitable companies also spend some of their profits by expanding their workforce by hiring more employees. The net result is that individual personal income rises, which again means more tax revenues for the federal government. This time it is from individuals, not corporations.

Want some proof? Over the past 12 months through January of this year (according to the Congressional Budget Office), total tax revenues are up 11.5 percent. Individual taxes were up 13.2 percent, while corporate taxes were up 25.6 percent over that same time frame. Like I said, it's not a matter of "if," but "when" the budget deficit falls as tax receipts rise. How about all year long since we could end this fiscal year with a budget deficit below $200 billion?

NOT IF, BUT WHEN—GLOBAL EXPORT BOOM

The third and final "not if, but when" focuses on the global export boom. While politicians in Washington, D.C., only focus on our terrible trade deficit as a way to bash cheap Chinese imports that are fueling this trade deficit, I would like to take a broader view beyond China. Take a look around the world, outside the United States, and see what countries are experiencing an export boom. In my opinion, the single best indicator of global economic growth is global exports. Here are the facts, according to the World Bank. While everyone blames China for being the biggest exporter, China actually trailed Germany in export growth in 2006. Both China and Germany were part of a five-country ring that watched exports explode above 20 percent last year. Germany exports were up 28.2 percent. China exports were up 24.8 percent. Russia was up 22 percent, while South Korea was up 21.1 percent and Italy was up 20.7 percent. And it doesn't stop there as virtually everywhere you looked last year you found double-digit export growth. South of our border, both Brazil and Argentina witnessed exports boom 17 percent. Back across the "pond" both France and Turkey witnessed double-digit export growth with France weighing in at 14.6 percent and Turkey an amazing 15.3 percent. And back to Asia again, Japan's exports grew 12.2 percent, while Indonesian exports boomed over 16 percent. How do you spell a synchronized global boom? I know how I spell it—E-X-P-O-R-T-S.

One more point before I leave this global export boom. While everyone in Washington always focuses on "the glass half empty," complaining about our terrible trade deficit, no one ever looks below the trade deficit number to see if any industries actually have a trade surplus in the United States. Well, I did, and I think the findings will astound you. According to the Commerce Department, several industries in the United States are not just running a trade surplus, they are running a "record" trade surplus as their exports are booming. The industries are aircraft and parts, jet engines, drilling and oil field machinery, semiconductors, excavating machinery, generators, and agricultural machinery. Who knows? Maybe things aren't so bad after all.

In closing, the single biggest "not if, but when" for individual investors is investing globally. It is not a matter of "if" you should invest more globally, but only a matter of "when" you will do it, in my opinion. How about today?

Go Global, Go Global, and Go even More Global!

Investment Footnote . . . What actually happened

Wow, was I correct! The Fed did exactly what I said: cutting rates two more times in 2007, once on October 30, 2007, and again on December 11, 2007. I was also dead right about the budget deficit as it continued to drop in 2007, as well, from −1.9 percent of the gross domestic product, or GDP, to −1.2 percent in 2007. Last but not least I was right about the economy as well, as first-quarter GDP grew at +0.6 percent, just as I had forecasted. Somehow I should get three stars for this commentary.

CHAPTER 3

The Markets

Markets can remain irrational longer than you can remain solvent.

JOHN MAYNARD KEYNES
British economist and founder of Keynesian economics

INTRODUCTION

When investors hear the word *market* they immediately think *stock market*. The stock market refers to the market that enables the trading of company stocks, other securities, and derivatives. Bonds are still traditionally traded in an informal, over-the-counter market known as the *bond market*. Commodities are traded in commodities markets, and derivatives are traded in a variety of markets but, like bonds, mostly over-the-counter.

To give you some perspective, the actual size of the worldwide bond market is estimated at $45 trillion. The size of the stock market is estimated to be about $51 trillion. The world derivatives market has been estimated at about $480 trillion. Would you like a little perspective on just how big $480 trillion is? Well, compared to the entire U.S. economy, it is 30 times larger. And from a global perspective, the $480 trillion derivatives market is 12 times the size of the entire world economy.

Even though it may not be the biggest, it's the stock market that gathers all of our attention and focus. Let me put this market into some perspective for you. Stocks are listed and traded on stock exchanges that are actual entities, either a corporation or a mutual organization. These exchanges specialize in the business of bringing buyers and sellers of stocks and securities together. Stock exchanges also provide facilities for the issue and redemption of securities as well as other financial instruments and capital events including the payment of income and dividends.

The securities traded on a stock exchange include shares issued by companies, unit trusts, and other pooled investment products and bonds. To be able to trade a security on a certain stock exchange it has to be "listed" there. Usually there is a central location, at least for recordkeeping, but trade is less and less linked to such physical places. Modern markets are electronic networks, which gives them advantages of speed and cost of transactions. Trade on an exchange is by members only. The initial offering of stocks and bonds to investors is, by definition, done in the primary market; subsequent trading is done in the secondary market. A stock exchange is often the most important component of a stock market. Supply and demand in the stock market is driven by various factors, which, as in all free markets, affect the price of stocks.

There is usually no compulsion to issue stock via the stock exchange itself, nor must stock be subsequently traded on the exchange. Such trading is said to be "off exchange" or "over-the-counter." Remember, this is the usual way that bonds are traded. Increasingly, stock exchanges are part of a global market for securities.

Participants in the stock market range from small individual investors to very large pension fund managers. But no matter who you are, your order ends up with a professional at a stock exchange who executes your order.

Some exchanges are physical locations where transactions are carried out on a trading floor by a method known as open outcry. This type of auction is used in stock exchanges and commodity exchanges where the traders may enter "verbal" bids and offers simultaneously. The other type of exchange is a virtual kind, composed of a network of computers where trades are made electronically via traders.

Actual trades are based on an auction market paradigm where a potential buyer bids a specific price for a stock and a potential seller asks a specific price for the stock. When the bid and ask prices match, a sale takes place on a first come, first served basis if there are multiple bidders or askers at a given price.

So, if you think about it, the purpose of a stock exchange is to facilitate the exchanges of securities between buyers and sellers, thus providing a marketplace, either virtual or real. The exchanges provide real-time information on the listed securities, facilitating price discovery.

Let's think about how these virtual or real exchanges work and differ. The New York Stock Exchange is a physical exchange. On Wall Street we call it a "listed" exchange, meaning only stocks listed with the exchange may be traded. Orders enter by way of exchange members and flow down to a specialist who goes to the floor trading post to trade stock. The specialist's job is to match buy and sell orders using open outcry. If a spread exists between bid and ask, no trade immediately takes place. This is where the specialist uses his or her own resources, either cash or stock, to close the difference between the bid and ask price. Once an actual trade has been made, the details are reported on the "tap" and sent back to the brokerage firm, which then notifies the investors who placed the order. Although there is a significant amount of human contact in this process, computers play an important role, especially for program trading.

Meanwhile, Nasdaq is a virtual listed exchange where all the trading is done over a computer network. The process is similar to the New York Stock Exchange; however, buyers and sellers are electronically matched. One or more Nasdaq market makers will always provide a bid and ask price at which they will always purchase or sell these stocks.

Whether virtual or real, the stock market is one of the most important sources for companies to raise money. It allows businesses to go public or raise additional capital for expansion. The liquidity that an exchange provides affords investors the ability to quickly and easily sell securities. This is an attractive feature of investing in stocks compared to other less liquid investments, such as real estate.

History has shown that the price of shares and other assets is an important part of the dynamics of economic activity, and can influence, or be an indicator in, public mood. Rising share prices, for instance, tend to be associated with increased business investment and vice versa. Share prices also affect the wealth of households and their consumption. Therefore, central banks tend to keep an eye on the control and behavior of the stock market and, in general, on the smooth operation of financial system functions.

History has also shown us that individual investors can temporarily pull financial prices away from their long-term trend level. Overreactions may occur so that excessive optimism or euphoria may drive prices unduly high or excessive pessimism may drive prices unduly low. Theoretical and empirical arguments have been put forward against the notion that stock markets are efficient.

According to the *efficient market hypothesis*, only changes in fundamental factors, such as profits or dividends, ought to affect share prices. Then along came Black Monday. On October 19, 1987, the Dow Jones Industrial Average fell by 22.6 percent in one day, after completing a five-year rise in stock prices. This event not only shook the United States but quickly spread across the world. By the end of October 1987, stock exchanges in Australia lost over 40 percent, Canada lost almost 25 percent, Hong Kong lost almost 50 percent, and Great Britain approached 30 percent.

The visible reasons for the Black Monday stock market collapse were never identified. This event did put many important assumptions on the defensive, namely the theory of rational conduct of human beings and the hypothesis of market efficiency.

In conclusion, sometimes the market tends to react irrationally to economic news, even if that news has no real effect on the technical value of the securities itself. Therefore, the stock market can be swayed tremendously in either direction by press releases, rumor, euphoria, and mass panic. Over the short term, stocks and other securities can be battered or buoyed by any number of fast market-changing events, making the stock market difficult to predict.

On the pages that follow, I will give you my predictions on where the market is going and how and why it will impact your investments.

Market Drop? Relax—It's the "B Team" Overreacting

AUGUST 27, 1998

Thursday, August 27, marked the third largest point drop in the history of the Dow Jones Industrial Average, trailing only the largest market decline in October 1987 and the second largest decline in October 1997. This drop was fueled by the ongoing currency and economic crisis in Russia.

As unsettling as it may have been today, it's important for investors to understand how the market really dodged a bullet— the fundamentals were in place for this market to experience the single largest drop in the history of the stock market. But, because the Securities and Exchange Commission changed its circuit breaker rules from triggering in response to an absolute point drop in favor of a system that would trigger the circuit breakers in response to a percentage point decline, the market never closed today, panic selling never set in, and the market actually rallied back from its low before it settled in at 357 points down.

It's important to keep a perspective on the events in Russia that are fueling this market decline. Russia will have very little, if any, impact on our economy and overall stock market. Fundamentally, Russia is not important to our economy or stock market. In 1997, U.S. exports to Russia (the former U.S.S.R.) accounted for seven-tenths of 1 percent of all U.S. exports. That's no more than a rounding error, irrelevant to our economy.

It will have impact, selectively, on those financial institutions that have loaned money to Russia and hedge funds that have money in Russia. But the Russian bear will not be the overall issue that turns the U.S. stock market into a bear market.

Why did the market overreact today? It's the end of August and the B team is running the show. The A team is on vacation, celebrating all the money that was made this year. We tend to have larger market gyrations at this time of year, when the B team is left behind to mind the trading floors.

My message to investors is "relax." There are two fundamental issues that I think will combine to provide this market support. I look for major corporations across the United States to step up their plans for stock buybacks. The fact of the matter is that we've all become greedy. Corporate America is compensated in stock options. I look for companies across all industries to spring to the defense of the stock market, in support of their shares—and more important the price of their stock options—by buying the discounted stock back. What executive wouldn't buy his or her stock at a 20 percent discount? It's a no-brainer.

Second, I firmly believe that Treasury Secretary Bob Rubin will embark on an ambitious plan to support Russia. President Clinton is already scheduled to visit Russia, and I think that we're going to see the Clinton administration pull out all the stops to come up with some combination of International Monetary Fund or additional G–7 assistance. I'm convinced that the potential single greatest loser from the events in Russia would not be individual investors—it would be Bill Clinton. It's a lot easier to be a popular president when the Dow is at 9,300 than when the market has fallen to 8,100. This administration will do everything it can to rally around Russia and provide a level of support.

The money that has left the U.S. stock market has created a tremendous rally in the bond market, but I see that as a short-term effect. I doubt that investors will be satisfied with the 5 percent return they can get from bonds. As these events pass, I look for money to flow back to the stock market in even greater waves than when the money went out. In fact, as things settle down and it becomes obvious that other markets have more direct exposure to Russia, the U.S. market will be the market of choice. The fundamentals that are driving our market keep getting better instead of worse: low interest rates, which are now even lower; low inflation, which is now no inflation; and the strong consumer, who I think is going to continue to get stronger even with this market pullback.

The single most important message that investors have to remember is that it is never wise to disrupt your long-term portfolio strategy in response to short-term market fluctuations.

The markets will undoubtedly remain volatile over the next two weeks, but when we're sitting at 10,000 and looking backward, we'll see this drop, we'll circle it, and remember it as "the Russian buying opportunity." Those who weren't invested or didn't remain invested may have wished they had. I still say, "Low interest rates, low inflation, and the strong consumer will drive our market to 10,000 by the end of this year."

Investment Footnote . . . What actually happened

The Dow didn't quite make it to 10,000, and it closed the year at 9,181, a 16.1 percent gain for the year.

It's Weight Watcher Time!

DECEMBER 4, 1998

Before we even had time to celebrate the fact that our stock market had completed its unbelievable and dramatic rebound and had actually recouped all of its losses from our brief bear market this past summer, volatility has quickly returned and the market is having trouble convincing itself to stay above 9,000.

This latest mini "bear" market scare appears to have been driven by three independent issues.

- Boeing announces production cutbacks and layoffs because of the crisis in Southeast Asia.
- Sears announces pre-earnings disappointments.
- Brazil's parliament fails to pass the necessary tax increases promised to the International Monetary Fund.

Let me give you my quick perspective on these three events:

- *Boeing announces cutbacks.* It's never good news for the market when such a bellwether stock as Boeing has problems; however, don't underestimate how quickly oil can turn around the entire aerospace industry. You see, even though there are production concerns now because of the global slowdown in Southeast Asia, the falling price of oil may be more than an offset. Think of it this way: There are two major operating cost components for the airline industry—labor cost and energy cost. With energy cost (oil) falling to record low levels, what happens if the airline industry starts posting huge profits? One major possibility is that they will start buying planes again. Stay tuned—this is far from over.

- *Sears announces pre-earnings disappointments.* The news, remember, is always bad. After all, you don't have to prepare the market for good news. I would ask you to think about this for the upcoming earnings season (fourth quarter): Our economy grew an unbelievable 3.9 percent in the third quarter as measured by gross domestic product. It exceeded even the rosiest economists' forecasts. So we have an economy growing at 4 percent and, on the next to the last day of the third quarter (September 29), the Fed cut rates to spur the economy. Then they cut rates in October. Then they cut rates in November. Talk about momentum. You see, with an economy growing at 4 percent, followed by 3 rate cuts, there just might be more momentum to our economy than people realize. A stronger economy could mean stronger profits . . . stay tuned.

- *Brazil's parliament fails to pass necessary tax increases.* Don't overreact; this should not surprise anyone. After all, Brazil is working with what I call a dead duck parliament. First, remember that tax increases are not popular in Brazil, so we knew this would be a difficult vote. It became an impossible vote with their dead duck parliament. In our recent congressional election, we returned 99 percent of incumbents to office; however, we still call this a lame duck Congress as we await the new one to take over. Well, in Brazil's recent election they returned less than 50 percent of their incumbents back to parliament. Well, if 99 percent is a lame duck, less than 50 percent has got to be a "dead duck." Once the new parliament is sworn in, I am convinced Brazil will continue to do the right things. Stay tuned— this is far from over.

In closing, don't forget the positive impact that global rate cuts will have on our market. Remember, on November 6, I told you, "We look for the United States to cut rates once and possibly twice this year" (which they did on November 17), and "Germany and France will finally follow with a rate cut before the end of the year" (well, they finally did on December 3).

Since the United States started this global rate cut explosion back on September 29, there have been 61 separate interest rate cuts by 33 different countries.

- One country, Sweden, has cut rates *four* times.
- Nine countries have cut rates *three* times:
  United States
  Canada
  Spain
  Ireland
  Portugal
  Denmark
  Singapore
  Malaysia
  Chile

- Seven countries have cut rates *twice*:
  England
  Thailand
  Indonesia
  Italy
  Taiwan
  Hungary
  Brazil

- Sixteen countries have cut rates *once*:
South Korea
Greece
Czech Republic
China
Poland
Russia
Japan
New Zealand
Philippines
Australia
Germany
France
Finland
Netherlands
Belgium
Austria

The most important thing to remember is that *none* of these 61 rate cuts by 33 different countries has had any impact yet. The impact of a rate cut usually takes about six months. It's like Weight Watchers. The fact that you joined Weight Watchers today didn't change anything today. The impact will happen six months from now. That's exactly the same with rate cuts; the real impact of this explosion in rates is yet to come.

As always, have a great day, keep a positive attitude, and I'll see ya at 10,000!

PS: Don't eat too much during the holidays!

Investment Footnote . . . What actually happened

Wow, was I correct on this one. Twelve months later, the Dow closed the year at 11,497, a 25.2 percent gain.

I Was Wrong!

January 4, 1999

The Dow Jones Industrial Average closed the year on December 31, 1998, at 9,181. My yearlong, unwavering investment forecast called for a Dow 10,000 by December 31, 1998; facts do not lie . . . I was wrong.

While I may have been wrong regarding the year-end value of the Dow, I was right on several issues that fueled the Dow to rebound from its low on August 31 of 7,539 (which was down 19.2 percent from the July high), to an all-time high of 9,374 on November 23, to finally giving back some of those gains to close the year at 9,181.

- Remember, I said, "Congress will fully fund the International Monetary Fund (IMF) before the end of the year." Well, by the end of October, Congress fully funded the IMF with $17.9 billion . . . I was right!
- Remember, I said that with the German elections behind us, we need a rate cut from Germany and the United Kingdom, and I look for both countries to cut rates before year-end. Well, England cut rates twice, and Germany cut rates once . . . I was right!
- Remember, I said, "I expect earnings to surprise on the high side for the third quarter." Well, third quarter earnings season is over, and in the S&P 500, 28.2 percent of the companies had negative surprises while 48.9 percent had positive earnings surprises . . . I was right!
- Remember, I said that the United States would cut rates once and possibly twice. Well, the United States cut rates three times . . . I was right!
- Remember, I said, "Corporate stock buybacks would explode in September, October, and November." Well, in September, October, and November 1998 there were 1,732 corporate stock buybacks announced. That compares to only 329 for the same time period in 1997. That's a whopping 525 percent increase . . . I was right!

- Remember, I said, "Japanese bank reform will be implemented." Well, both Long Term Credit Bank of Japan and Nippon Credit Bank are being nationalized. While banking reform still has a long way to go, it is being implemented . . . I was right!
- Remember, I said, "The IMF would approve a bailout package for Brazil in excess of $25 billion." Well, the IMF put together a bailout package for Brazil in excess of $40 billion . . . I was right!
- Remember, I said, "There would be major increases in mergers and acquisitions." Well, just look at these megamergers: AOL–Netscape, Deutsche Bank–Bankers Trust, Exxon–Mobil. For the entire year, mergers and acquisitions were up an astonishing 78 percent . . . I was right!

In closing, all of these "rights" do not change the one simple fact that I was "wrong" with my Dow 10,000 market call. To put this in some perspective for you, the Dow began 1998 at 7,908; thus, a Dow 10,000 forecast meant the stock market would have to climb 26.5 percent. And while this forecast may have appeared outlandish to some investors, the stock market as measured by the S&P 500 actually gained 26.6 percent, and the stock market as measured by Nasdaq actually gained 39.6 percent. You see, even though the Dow did not hit 10,000, it was still a very good year.

In the investment forecasting business, there is a very fine line between being "wrong" and simply being "early." Was the Dow 10,000 forecast by December 31, 1998, really wrong, or was it simply a few weeks early?

Have a great day, keep a positive attitude, and please join me in resolving to remain a long-term investor in a short-term world.

Investment Footnote . . . What actually happened

The Dow didn't quite make it to 10,000 in 1998, falling short at 9,181.

10K Is Not a Race!

MARCH 16, 1999

Well, we finally did it. The Dow Jones Industrial Average crossed 10,000 today. While the meteoric rise of our stock market has caught many investment gurus and investors by surprise, some of us did see it coming. In fact, some of us were even early. Many of you will recall my January 4, 1999, market commentary titled, "I Was Wrong!" in which I pointed out, "In the investment forecasting business there is a very fine line between being 'wrong' and simply being 'early.' Was the Dow 10,000 forecast by December 31, 1998, wrong or was it simply a few weeks early?"

I guess we now know it wasn't wrong, it was simply a few weeks early—10 weeks to be exact.

IT'S NOT OVER

While it is fun to celebrate market milestones, we must remember that just because the Dow crossed 10,000 doesn't all of a sudden mean the end of something. This move to 10,000 wasn't a race; investing is a journey and this is simply one stop along the way to your ultimate investment goals.

Don't get so caught up in the celebration that when the market goes back below 10,000 you consider panic selling. After all, the market will close below 10,000 numerous times this year. With each of the two most recent 1,000-point milestones, the market had trouble staying above that new milestone. On July 16, 1997, the Dow closed above 8,000 for the first time. Then, on 105 separate occasions, it closed below that milestone 8,000 level. Then, on April 16, 1998, the Dow closed above 9,000 for the first time. On 93 separate occasions after that it closed below the milestone 9,000 level.

At 8,000 we fell below 105 times and at 9,000 we fell below 93 times. Don't be fooled into thinking that just because we crossed 10,000 once doesn't mean we won't cross it numerous more times in the weeks ahead.

Instead of thinking about 10,000 as only the end of something, think of it as the beginning of something as well. The lyrics of the hit song "Closing Time," by Semisonic, may give you the best perspective of all: "Every new beginning comes from some other beginning's end." Today we officially begin our journey to the next 10,000 points. I can't wait!

MORE THAN JUST A NUMBER

The significance of the Dow breaking 10,000 is not just that we crossed another 1,000-point threshold; it is significant because the market came back from what some market and economic forecasters were claiming was the beginning of a *bear market*. Don't forget, on Labor Day, around six months ago, the Dow was hovering a little over 7,500 at 7,640. These so-called bear watchers were telling us that the next stop would be 5,000! The real excitement about 10,000 is not simply because we crossed another 1,000-point level; it's because in six short months the Dow came back from the brink of disaster at 7,640 to break through 10,000. Wow!

CLINTON RELIEF RALLY?

When we started the year at 9,181, many investors felt it was within the realm of possibility for the Dow to cross 10,000 sometime this year, but certainly not as early as March. If you are looking for a reason this happened so soon, look no further than the White House.

In my market commentary on January 20, 1999, titled "This Is (Un) Real," I wrote: "Expect a Clinton Relief Rally. When this sad chapter in American history finally closes, you may wish you were fully invested so you could have participated in the Clinton Relief Rally."

You see, the market hates uncertainty and once President Clinton was acquitted and the impeachment saga was over, a major uncertainty was removed from the marketplace.

Want proof? From January 1, 1999, until February 12, 1999, the day President Clinton was acquitted, the market rose 93.46 points over 29 trading days. Since the president's acquittal, the market has been open only 21 days, and in those 21 days it has surged 655 points. That's over a 600 percent increase in one quarter. How do you spell relief?

SWEET "16"

Here's something to ponder. The first day of trading in the stock market after the Clinton impeachment saga ended was February 16. A month later, on March 16, the Dow breaks 10,000. The Dow broke 9,000 on April 16, 1998. The Dow broke 8,000 on July 16, 1997. The NCAA Men's Basketball Tournament, CBS coverage of which Kemper Funds is a proud sponsor, is now down to the Sweet "16." Last, but not least, my youngest daughter, Stephanie, just celebrated her *sixteenth* birthday last month. Come to think of it, the Dow was up *16* percent last year. There may be an investment theme somewhere in here; I just haven't found it yet. Remember, 10K is not a race, even though we got here faster than most investors ever dreamed possible.

Have a great day, keep a positive attitude, and please join me in resolving to remain a long-term investor in a short-term world!

PS: *It's great to finally see ya at 10,000!*

Investment Footnote . . . What actually happened

Just as I predicted, the Dow breaks through the 10,000 level.

Should Russell 2000 Be Called the Animal Farm Index?

August 1, 1999

In this index-crazy investment world that we live in, there are three indices that dominate the focus and attention of investors and the media: the Dow Jones Industrial Average (representing the "bluest" of the blue chip stocks), the Standard & Poor's 500 (representing the overall stock market), and the Russell 2000 (representing the small capitalization market).

Investors make the mistake of comparing these indices to one another to determine where to invest. That is the worst mistake an investor can make. You cannot compare these indices to try to determine where to invest because they are not all created equal. It would be like comparing the performance of a gas-efficient economy car to a formula one race car and saying, "They are both cars. I can't understand why the formula one race car goes faster all the time!"

WHAT'S IN AN INDEX?

While many talk fluently about the three major indices that drive our market, I am not convinced that they know the actual definition of those indices. Thus, I thought it would be useful to begin there:

- *Dow Jones Industrial Average (DJIA).* The DJIA is an index used to measure the performance of the U.S. stock market by analyzing the stock of a select group of the largest and most profitable companies in our market. This index, which started out in 1896, is a price-weighted index. In other words, the stocks that comprise the Dow are given their relative importance and impact on the index based on their price. The 30 stocks that comprise the Dow are continually updated to keep the index in touch with our changing corporate and economic landscapes.

- *Standard & Poor's 500 (S&P 500).* The S&P 500 was established in 1922 as a broader market index than the DJIA. The S&P 500 index covers about 70 percent of the value of the overall U.S. stock market. Individual companies are added or subtracted from the S&P 500 throughout the year based on market value,

capitalization, trading, and a number of other
subjective criteria.

- *Russell 2000*. In 1984, the Frank Russell Company created
  the Russell 2000 to provide a measurement tool for one
  aspect of the overall market. Unlike the Dow and the S&P
  500, which use secretive committees to determine whether
  a stock is in or out of the index, the Russell 2000 is very
  objective. First, the Russell 3000 is constructed from the
  3,000 largest companies headquartered in the United
  States. Of those, the top 1,000 companies become the
  Russell 1000. The 2,000 companies that remain become the
  Russell 2000. Each of the stocks in the Russell indices is
  capitalization-weighted, which reflects the market value of
  each share of stock. Thus, as stock prices change, stocks
  will be moved into and out of the Russell 1000 and Russell
  2000. However, unlike the Dow and the S&P 500, where
  changes can occur at any point in time, the Russell indices
  are reconstituted once every year on June 30.

CHANGES MATTER!

Changes that are made to an index can have a major impact on the
performance of that index. Let's take a look at one of the four
changes that was made to the Dow in 1997. From March 17, 1997,
until December 31, 1998, the price of Hewlett-Packard moved to
$68.312 from $55.625, a 22.81 percent increase. Meanwhile, the company it replaced, Bethlehem Steel, moved to $8.375 on December 31,
1998, from $8.500 on March 17, 1997, a –1.47 percent decrease.

RUSSELL 2000's HANDICAP

Given what we have already discussed, think for a minute why
the Russell 2000 Small-Cap Index always seems to be lagging the
other two benchmarks. First, the Dow and the S&P 500 will change
at any point in time to reflect the proper mix of companies that will
serve as a benchmark for our markets and our economy. In other

words, they are cherry picking. As long as you stay a top performer, you are in the index. Once you become laggardly, a secret committee subjectively kicks you out.

This is not so with the poor Russell 2000. Changes are made only once a year. The companies that have been the most successful and have grown their market capitalization will be moved out of the Russell 2000 to the Russell 1000. Meanwhile, the laggards or "fallen angels" of the Russell 1000 fall back to the Russell 2000. Can you imagine the performance of the S&P 500 or the Dow if they were constrained by the same objective criteria for moving companies in and out of the index?

If you are waiting for a sign from the Russell 2000 about when to invest in small caps, it's never coming. I would suggest you focus on three much more important indicators for the small-cap market.

1. *Economic strength.* Our economy is still strong.
2. *High consumer confidence.* High confidence means investors will broaden out to small caps.
3. *Strong global liquidity.* The more money there is, the more demand for small caps. All three of these signs are flashing a *go* signal to invest in small-cap stocks.

In closing, I propose we change the name of the Russell 2000 Small-Cap Index to the Animal Farm Index. Just think back to that moment in George Orwell's classic *Animal Farm* when the animals peer into the window and see the pigs playing poker in plush settings with the farmers. It was the pigs who had, just days before, left only a single commandment on the wall: "All animals are equal, but some animals are more equal than others."

Ironically, the Russell 2000 was launched in the same year as the title of Orwell's other classic, *1984.*

Investment Footnote . . . What actually happened

I was right about small-cap outperformance in 1999 as the Russell 2000 Small-Cap Index posted a 19.6 percent return.

Market Worries

July 2, 2000

As we approach the third quarter of 2000, I think there will be five dominant investment issues that may cause some concern in our market: our savings rate, the weak U.S. dollar, China and the World Trade Organization, stock dividends, and the Internet in Europe.

OUR SAVINGS RATE

In my opinion, the single greatest reason we have such a low savings rate is the way in which economists calculate this number. They begin by estimating personal income. Then, actual taxes paid are subtracted from that number. Then, actual consumption expenditures are subtracted from that number, and what is left is what we call our savings rate.

In the past few years, capital gains have been rising dramatically, along with a sharp increase in capital gains taxes. While the capital gains taxes are subtracted from current income, the actual capital gains as a result of rising stock values are not even counted as income. And to make matters worse, if people spend some of their capital gains, it makes the consumption figure go up, which in turn lowers our savings rate.

Without this tax distortion, I believe our actual savings rate would be twice what has been reported.

THE WEAK U.S. DOLLAR

A temporary decline in our dollar's value certainly has positive investment ramifications that ripple across the globe.

First, a weaker dollar strengthens the yen, which in turn limits the risk of another round of the Asian currency meltdown. Second, a weaker dollar is good for Latin America and Brazil, who are leading trading partners south of the border. Third, a weaker dollar benefits global consumers who will be able to buy more American products. And finally, a weaker dollar eases the debt burden of countries trying to finance their dollar-denominated debt.

CHINA AND THE WORLD TRADE ORGANIZATION

Who's the big winner—the United States or China? The answer is actually both. The United States will be the real winner first. However, the long-term impact will rest on China's shoulders. The reason that the United States will win initially is that it will be much easier for U.S. companies to actually make a profit in China. First of all, they'll pay lower tariffs on all the parts that they import from the United States. Second, they are no longer obligated to purchase all their parts from local Chinese suppliers.

However, long term the real winner is China. U.S. companies doing business in China can now import better products than the ones currently being produced by Chinese enterprises. Eventually, workers at these enterprises will be redeployed to more productive firms that would continue to lower inflation and raise the standard of living.

STOCK DIVIDENDS

I think that there are very logical reasons why stock dividends have declined and will continue to do so. The first is taxes. Stock dividends are a form of income. Income in our country is taxed at a top rate of 40 percent. However, if the profits stay in a firm, investors can defer this tax. Or, if they need the cash, they can lock in a capital gain that is taxed at only half the amount. The second reason is the explosion in stock buybacks. Companies are very focused on the value of their stocks. And instead of using idle cash to pay dividends, it is being used to support the value of the stock price.

THE INTERNET IN EUROPE

Now that the dot-com bubble has burst here, everyone is searching for the next Internet run-up. And the consensus is that it will be in Europe.

However, in order to reach 75 percent of the population in Europe, your Internet site would need to be translated into five different languages. Second, to purchase an item on the Internet, you need a credit card. In Germany, less than 15 percent of the entire population has one credit card. While I continue to believe that Europe is a great investment, I'm not so sure that business-to-consumer Web sites will be the next great investment craze.

Let's quickly recap my five investment themes for the third quarter. Our savings rate looks bad because of the way it is calculated. It is not as bad as it appears. Second, we explored some positive ramifications of a weaker dollar. Third, we examined China and concluded that China being part of the World Trade Organization is good for the United States and China. Fourth, we concluded that even though stock dividends are down, U.S. companies are choosing not to pay dividends for tax and stock buyback reasons. And finally, we looked at the Internet in Europe and concluded that there are several obstacles that will keep this segment under pressure for years to come.

Investment Footnote . . . What actually happened ↑

I was correct about the third quarter of 2000. Earnings for the S&P 500 grew at a respectable 14.17 percent.

Something Old, Something New, Something Borrowed, Something Blue

OCTOBER 12, 2000

Let me begin by saying that neither of my grownup daughters is getting married anytime soon. While I've been struggling to explain just what the heck is going on with our markets, however, this wedding jingle popped into my head—and suddenly I got it! Let's look at the jingle and try to make some sense of the recent market sell-off, starting with "something old."

SOMETHING OLD

Even though it's old news, the Federal Reserve Board's interest rate hikes over the past 16 months are taking some of the steam out of our markets. Remember, we've had six separate interest rate hikes totaling 1.75 percent. That's enough to take some wind out of any economy's sail, regardless of how strong it is! Plus, this old news is even more important when we realize that all of the other central banks around the world have followed suit and raised their rates as well. All told, there have been 130 interest rate hikes since June 1999. Maybe the market is finally realizing that all of these rate hikes will actually slow global growth a little.

SOMETHING NEW

Let's keep on singing our jingle and move on to "something new." Violence in the Middle East has suddenly unglued our markets. Fifteen days of violence have resulted in more than 100 deaths, including the deaths of four U.S. sailors who perished on their Navy destroyer in a suspected terrorist bomb attack. This latest round of violence has sent the price of oil through the roof. It's currently higher than $36 a barrel, and the possibility of supply shortages is greater today than anytime in the past decade. This new political uncertainty is causing investors to take their money off the table.

SOMETHING BORROWED

Well, we did "something old" and "something new," so now it's time to look at "something borrowed." What did we borrow? Technology demand. You see, the great technology boom, both in demand and the markets, was fueled by the Y2K scare. Because of the Y2K scare, much of the technology spending that would have happened this year happened in the fourth quarter of last year. We borrowed that spending from this year, so to speak. As a result, at the end of last year, technology spending was off the charts, and that fueled an unbelievable run-up in the Nasdaq. I, for one, have absolutely no sympathy for Nasdaq technology investors who are screaming that the Nasdaq is down 30 percent. So what? It was up

86 percent in 1999—so by my math, it's still up 56 percent over the past two years. I don't want to hear any complaints from someone who has averaged 23 percent gains over the past two years.

SOMETHING BLUE

Finally, let's move on to "something blue." Make no mistake about it. Blue chip companies have certainly been crying the earnings blues. Intel, Lucent, Home Depot—the bluest of the blue are continuing to issue earnings warnings. And even though things seem really blue now, I want you to remember that it's pre-earnings season, and in pre-earnings season, we always get the negative surprises, not the positive ones. Remember, the market doesn't need to be prepared for good news.

A GIFT FOR YOU

No one would go to a wedding without a present, so let me close my wedding theme with a present for you. Open it up and you'll find that none of the issues we discussed change the long-term positive fundamentals of our markets. Inflation is still falling, even with the recent spike in oil prices. Interest rates are still low. (Remember, the long bond is well under 6 percent.) The productivity boom continues, as month after month this amazing story keeps getting better. And, we're no longer debating budget deficits; we're debating what to do with budget surpluses. If you want to figure out the direction of our markets in the long run, forget the song, and focus on the present.

Have a great day, keep a positive attitude, and please join me in resolving to remain a long-term investor in a short-term world.

Investment Footnote . . . What actually happened

I was correct about the long-term positive trends in our markets. Three years later, in 2003, the Dow gained 25.3 percent as all the positive forces that I discussed came into play.

A New Dawn for Graduates and Markets
JUNE 20, 2001

The month of June not only signifies the official start of summer, it also marks the beginning of a new stage in many young people's lives as they now find themselves new graduates from high school or from college. The Froehlich household, like many other households all across the United States, is entering into a new dawn, if you will. Stephanie, our youngest of two daughters, just graduated from Neuqua Valley High School in a Chicago, Illinois, suburb. Stephanie and the other high school and college graduates all across the United States are about to enter into a new dawn unlike anything we have ever witnessed or experienced before.

Just in case you are one of those cynics who doesn't believe in this new dawn stuff, let me remind you of this startling fact—by the end of 2002, the number of U.S. households that receive Internet service will exceed the number of households that receive a daily newspaper! This is truly a new dawn. Also, when you tell these new graduates "You've got mail," they don't run to the mailbox outside; they run to their computer to check their e-mail.

Our graduates are not the only ones embarking on an exciting new dawn journey. The markets are also about to enter a new dawn that is every bit as exciting and could be just as rewarding as the new dawn journey of the graduates.

The fundamental reason that our markets are about to enter into a new dawn is that the key issues that had a strong negative influence on the overall markets are now behind us. There was not just one, but six, negative influences keeping our markets from entering into a new dawn.

First was the presidential election uncertainty and bitter political partisanship battles in the Florida courtrooms that mesmerized the entire world. This influence is no longer a drag as George Bush has comfortably settled into the White House.

Second was the unpredictable and severe weather across much of the United States this winter. This unusual weather pattern made economic releases more misleading than they already are as the weather played havoc on both shoppers and businesses as well. I am happy to report that this influence is also gone.

Third was the skyrocketing oil and energy prices shock. And even though energy prices are still somewhat higher than they were two years ago, the "shock" effect is now behind us as businesses and consumers are no longer as worried about this issue.

Fourth was rising interest rates. As we entered the year 2001, the Fed had embarked on a series of six interest rate hikes, and over 200 other central banks around the globe followed suit. Now the Fed is cutting rates and over 75 other central banks have joined them so far this year.

Fifth was tax shock. Many investors, especially mutual fund investors, found themselves hit with a capital gains tax due to the rise in stock prices. However, when it came time to pay it, all the price rise had disappeared; yet they still had to pay the tax bill. Many investors were forced to sell stocks and mutual funds simply to pay taxes on gains that were no longer there. Thank goodness tax day only comes once a year, and it's over.

Sixth, and finally, was the U.S.–Chinese spy-plane controversy. There are a few words that our stock market doesn't like: one is "bear" and the other is "hostages." This spy-plane gridlock created a new uncertainty, the impact of which was difficult to analyze. Thank goodness all of our crew is back, safe and sound.

With these six influences now clearly behind us, I look for our markets to join our new graduates by embarking on a new dawn journey filled with many happy returns.

To all of the graduates across the United States, especially my daughter Stephanie, I wish you luck and happiness on your new dawn journey. And remember, you don't have to be a new graduate to experience this new dawn journey. Our markets are about to take investors on a new dawn journey as well; the only requirement is you have to be invested in the market. Happy trails, everyone. I'll see ya at 12,500!

Investment Footnote . . . What actually happened ↓

Wrong, the Dow didn't recover in 2001, losing −7.1 percent
to close at 10,021.

Happy Birthday!
JULY 2, 2001

The first week in July marks a major birthday celebration in this
country—the birth of this great land of ours, which this year is 226
years old. In the Froehlich household, the first week in July marks
two major birthday celebrations: one is for our country and the
other is for our eldest daughter, Marianne, who turns 21 this year!

There are a lot of important milestone birthdays as we grow
up. For me, age 10 was especially important—I just couldn't wait to
be in double digits. My two daughters' "sweet 16" birthdays were
extra special, giving them the opportunity to get behind the wheel.
And don't forget that eighteenth birthday: you finally are old
enough to vote and offset your parents' political influence. None of
these birthdays, however, is as instrumental as the twenty-first one.

You see, your twenty-first birthday is your official pass into
adulthood. As I think about my daughter Marianne and what the
future holds for her, as well as all the other young adults in this
country, this is truly a remarkable time.

Our economy is stronger and more diversified today than at
anytime in the past 50 years. Inflation is falling, not rising. This
great country has moved from budget deficits to budget surpluses,
as we have become the envy of the world on government downsizing and spending. The technology revolution, which is still in its
infancy, has pushed productivity to all-time highs. The globalization of economies and markets allows us to work, play, shop, and
travel virtually anywhere in the world today. What a great time to
be a 21-year-old in this country. And think about this—what a great
time to be an investor in this country.

The future simply couldn't be brighter for a 21-year-old investor in this country. Quite frankly, the future looks bright for all investors in this country, regardless of age. Happy birthday, America, and happy birthday, Marianne. I'll see ya both at 12,500!

Investment Footnote . . . What actually happened

Wrong, as the Dow continued to struggle, barely closing above 10,000 at 10,021, a −7.1 percent loss.

Forget January . . . It's December That Really Matters!

FEBRUARY 3, 2003

Well, now that the month of January is behind us, all the "bears" on Wall Street are pointing to the "January effect" as proof we are heading for a fourth straight down year in our stock market.

AS JANUARY GOES, SO GOES THE YEAR

This particular January effect is based on the principle that as January goes, so goes the year. And because the Standard & Poor's 500 was down—2.7 percent for January—the bears are latching on to this January effect. I will have to admit that, historically, it's been a pretty good market indicator, correctly predicting the direction of the market 78 percent of the time. However, it is also important to remember that this January may be unlike any other January the markets have ever seen because of the focus on the potential war with Iraq. And while our markets have prepared for wars before, those preparations have usually been similar; whether it was the Korean War, World War I or World War II, Vietnam, etc., we prepared to send our troops to battle "over there," September 11 changed all that. When we send our troops "over there" now, there is concern, fear, and anxiety that the battlefield may also be "over here," with terrorist acts breaking out in major metropolitan areas. It's one thing for the market to prepare for a war "over there"; it is a completely new experience preparing for the possibility of a war "over here" as well. I would not read too much into this January effect, because we have never seen a January like this before . . . even if the indicator is 78 percent accurate.

85 PERCENT IS BETTER THAN 78 PERCENT

If you do need to focus on indicators like the January effect, why not focus on something that has been more accurate, such as, let's say, the "Super Bowl effect." The Super Bowl is played every year when teams from the National Football Conference play teams from the American Football Conference. When the NFC team wins the Super Bowl, the market has been up 17 of 20 times. That's an accuracy rate of 85 percent. This year's Super Bowl winner was Tampa Bay. And for any of you diehard investors who are not football fans, Tampa Bay is in the NFC. Last time I checked, 85 percent was better than 78 percent.

I'LL TAKE 100 PERCENT

Finally, if you still need to focus on an indicator like the January effect, why not focus on the one that has been accurate 100 percent of the time, not just 78 or 85 percent. This particular indicator doesn't have a name so I am taking the liberty of naming it . . . I call it the "Rule of 3" and it is 100 percent accurate. Here is how the Rule of 3 works. Over the past 60 years, the third year of a presidential term has never, ever, ever had a down market. The average stock market return was 22 percent. Now, for any of you who didn't do so well in government class in high school, I bring up this Rule of 3 because this year is the third year of a presidential term.

INDICATOR OVERLOAD

For as long as I can remember, investors have longed for an indicator to accurately predict the market. Whether it was the "hemline" indicator, which was supposed to give us the direction of the market based on whether skirt hemlines moved higher or lower that fashion year, or our January effect, Super Bowl effect, or my Rule of 3, all of these indicators have one thing in common: they take our focus away from what is really important in determining the ultimate direction of the markets.

KEY MARKET DRIVERS

While you will continue to get bombarded about the January effect, I want you to remember that January is not going to determine how the market ends up in December. The direction of our markets will be influenced by productivity, which continues to come in at record levels. It will be influenced by cost-cutting. Don't forget that company after company and industry after industry have spent the last two years cutting costs, which will improve their profit picture when the economy turns. Add to all of that the supportive monetary policy of the Federal Reserve Board to support our stock market. I could not agree with Josh Feinman, chief economist at Deutsche Asset Management, any more than when he points out, "The Federal Reserve likely sees the very accommodative monetary policy they have put in place as sufficient to ensure a gradually strengthening economy by 2003, led by an improvement in business investment." That's the type of thing that tends to happen in up markets, not down markets. So if you are looking for indicators, look at productivity, cost-cutting, and monetary policy. I could go on and on; you know I haven't even touched upon the president's landmark economic and savings stimulus package and its positive impact on the market.

I am going to close this commentary where I began, by telling you that it's December that's important, not January. It's not how we start the year, but rather how we finish it that really matters. Now I can't stop all the "bears" from drowning you in information about the January effect, but I would ask you to remember this as they try to convince you of how accurate this indicator is: There was a time in this world when all of the smartest and brightest influential minds looked at all of the accurate indicators and thought the world was flat. History proved them all wrong. In my opinion, history will also prove this year's January effect wrong as our markets post double-digit gains when we close the year in December.

PS: For any of you indicator junkies out there, here's one last one for you: it's the "terrible towel" indicator. Every year that the terrible towel-waving Pittsburgh Steelers won the Super Bowl (four and counting), the market had an up year. The average return was 22 percent. From my perspective, that's the only thing that could have made this a better year.

PPS: As a Pittsburgh native, yes, I am still crying in my terrible towel!

Investment Footnote . . . What actually happened

I was dead right on this one. January really didn't matter as the Dow soared the remainder of 2003, posting a 25.3 percent gain to close at 10,453.

The Triple Crown of Investing

May 21, 2003

Now that Funny Cide has won the first two legs of horse racing's Triple Crown—the Kentucky Derby and the Preakness—all eyes are now focused on the third and final leg—the Belmont Stakes—to see if Funny Cide can be a Triple Crown winner. I have to admit that, growing up in Pittsburgh, I never was much of a horse racing fan. I was a baseball fan. I spent my time at old Forbes Field watching the likes of Roberto Clemente. Come to think of it, there is a triple crown in baseball as well. You have to lead the league in three categories to win baseball's triple crown: home runs, runs batted in, and batting average. Well, if there is a triple crown in horse racing and baseball, why not investing? The three reasons why the markets will continue to move higher make up my triple crown of investing.

QUALITY OF EARNINGS

The first leg in the triple crown of investing is *quality of earnings*. One of the great debates on Wall Street, in light of Arthur Andersen's collapse and the lack of confidence in financial reporting, is that investors are constantly receiving mixed signals regarding what a company actually earns. That's because companies would give two earnings-per-share numbers—operating earnings per share and reported earnings per share. And the differences were huge. Last quarter (fourth quarter of 2002), the difference between reported earnings per share and operating earnings per share for the Standard & Poor's 500 Index was $9. That number got way out of line because of the monumental disparity in AOL operating earnings per share and reported earnings per share. Simply subtracting the AOL disaster, the difference would drop from $9 to $3. I think the $3 frame of reference is a more accurate perception of what is actually going on. First quarter earnings for the first quarter of 2003 are almost complete. Let me give you a reference to the first quarters of 2001 and 2002. In the first quarter of 2001, the difference between operating earnings per share and reported earnings per share for the S&P 500 was over $3. In the first quarter of 2002, the difference between operating earnings per share and reported earnings per share for the S&P 500 was over $2. Now, for the good news—remember that I said the quality of earnings was a reason the market would move higher—well, in the first quarter of 2003, the difference between operating earnings per share and reported earnings per share has almost vanished. While all the final numbers are not in yet, the difference is expected to be about 25 cents. So last quarter the difference was either $9 or $3. A year ago it was over $2, and in the first quarter two years ago, it was over $3; now it has collapsed to 25 cents. The reason is quite simple: Regulation G. You see, Regulation G forces companies to explain any differences between operating earnings per share and reported earnings per share. It's simply amazing that when you force companies to explain how this game is played, they quit playing. Regardless of the motivation, there is no better sign regarding the improvement in the quality of earnings than the narrowing of the gap between operating earnings per share and reported earnings per share.

MERGERS AND ACQUISITIONS

The second leg in the triple crown of investing is *mergers and acquisitions*. Two elements are coming together to fuel mergers and acquisitions. First, with the collapse of corporate bond yields, it makes for a compelling vehicle for corporations to buy other companies. The explosion of stock prices in the 1990s meant that companies used those increased stock prices as a form of currency to buy other companies. Now, the currency has changed: instead of using equity, they will use debt, especially now that rates are so low. Second, because of the improved cash position and credit quality of corporate America's balance sheets, banks are now much more willing to expand their commercial loan portfolios. These two sources of currency are the missing links to fueling a rebound in merger and acquisition activity.

CHINA

The final leg in the triple crown of investing is China. I know that there has been great concern regarding China in light of the severe acute respiratory syndrome (SARS) epidemic. Let me help you put something in perspective: Chinese consumers buy more cell phones than consumers anywhere else in the world today. Chinese consumers buy more film than the Japanese consumers, who have long been synonymous with the camera and film industry. The Chinese consumers now buy more vehicles than the Germans, who have long been synonymous with the automotive industry. In fact, if the Chinese had the same auto ownership rates as Americans, the number of cars in the world would double. Now here's where things get interesting . . . while all the bears on Wall Street have focused on SARS and China and all of the negative implications, let me remind you of one simple fact: all industries are not treated equally. Yes, SARS has hurt retail and entertainment, but look at what it is doing to the automotive industry. Beijing, China, is the most SARS-infected city in the world. Automobile sales have more than doubled to 900 per day in Beijing. The reason is that people are avoiding trains and buses to avoid catching the disease and instead are buying cars. In the marketplace, when one door is closed, another is usually opened.

WHICH ONE ARE YOU?

In closing, let me remind you of a popular scene in most movies during the Cold War: a close-up of someone's finger about to push the red button. Back then, that dreaded red button signified the launch of nuclear weapons that could lead to a global meltdown. Now that the Cold War is over, the meltdown most people are concerned about is a stock market meltdown. Well, as an investor, you have one of two choices: you are either the finger or the red button. If you can't figure out which one you are or which one you want to be, call your financial advisors. They can help. They also know that the most important triple crown is not in racing or in baseball, but rather in investing.

PS: Stay away from the red button!

Investment Footnote . . . What actually happened ↑

I was right, as the Dow climbed 25.3 percent to close at 10,453.

And Now . . . the Rest of the Story
MARCH 9, 2004

In this fast-paced world that we live in today, most investors have little time to catch more than the headlines of what is moving the markets. There is little, if any, time to reflect on these issues, and certainly precious little time to dig a little deeper into the issues.

Thus, I thought I would stop the clock for you and give you the rest of the story on the two issues that dominated our market as the first week of March came to a close: the weak employment report and Martha Stewart's conviction.

JUST THE FACTS

Let's start looking at weak employment by only looking at the facts:

1. The unemployment rate remained at 5.6 percent. It was not too many years ago that I recall Alan Greenspan testifying to Congress that he felt a 6 percent unemployment rate would put this country at "full employment." Remember, things can't be all that bad if your national unemployment rate is 5.6 percent.
2. Nonfarm payrolls rose 21,000. That means we only created 21,000 new payroll jobs; the consensus of the best and brightest economists on Wall Street was predicting 130,000 new jobs.

Wall Street economists continue to embarrass themselves over this employment issue. Remember, in December of last year, only 1,000 payroll jobs were created and the consensus of economists was calling for 150,000 new jobs. What is going on here?

THE REST OF THE JOBS STORY

Now that we all have the facts, let me give you the rest of the story as it relates to the employment markets. The rest of the story is all about unemployment claims, benefits, and cash. I want to touch briefly upon all three, beginning with unemployment claims.

Initial weekly unemployment claims have been trending lower, which is a very important leading indicator for the overall employment market. However, what is even more important is the reason why initial unemployment claims are falling—namely, profits. You see, this is not rocket science here, but rather a basic premise that initial unemployment claims and profits have an inverse correlation. Think about it. When profits are going down, businesses do not hire and, therefore, initial unemployment claims go up. Thus, I believe that, currently, the reason initial unemployment claims are down is because profits are up, which creates a strong foundation for the future of our employment markets.

Next, let's look at benefits. I believe that this just might hold the key to why our economy's payroll employment numbers and household employment numbers are so different. (Remember, if you will, that the household employment number better captures small businesses and self-employed contractors.) Over the past six to nine months, the household employment number has been much stronger than the payroll employment number that the market focuses so closely on—and maybe, just maybe, it can all be explained away through benefits. Currently, benefit growth is outpacing wage growth by more than a two-to-one margin.

Think about what this means. These increasing benefit costs are now taking up a bigger and bigger piece of the total compensation picture. This trend in benefits is actually encouraging companies to substitute nonpayroll workers (whom they do not have to pay benefits) for payroll workers (whom companies must compensate for those higher benefit costs). Oh, and in case you haven't connected the dots, nonpayroll workers are all captured in the household employment numbers.

Third, and finally, let's look at cash. Corporate America is currently generating more than twice the cash as is normal for where we are in the economic recovery. This is because these companies are still paying the price for all of the excesses associated with the dot-com boom, and our renewed focus on corporate governance has pushed company after company to raise large amounts of cash to shore up their balance sheets. But now what? They are now sitting on a ton of cash. I believe businesses will do three things with all this cash: First, there will be a surge in business capital spending, which we are already starting to see. Second, they will return some of that cash to their shareholders in the form of larger dividends. Remember, this quality dividend trade I have been talking about is for real. Third, and finally, they will hire more employees. Think about what is happening here. Companies are increasing their capacity, and when you increase your capacity, you ultimately must increase employment to keep it going. Now you have the rest of the story regarding jobs.

JUST THE FACTS, AGAIN

Let's bring the commentary to a close by looking at just the facts of the Martha Stewart trial. There is only one fact that matters—she was found guilty on all four charges that were brought against her.

THE REST OF THE MARTHA STEWART STORY

Now that we have all the facts, let me give you the rest of the story and put this issue in some perspective for you. This is not just about Martha Stewart. This is about changing corporate America and, more important, holding corporate America accountable. I believe that it's time we send the white collar criminals to jail. It is the only way we will influence the future business leaders of this great country of ours. If you do the crime, you do the time.

It shouldn't stop there. It's not just about what's right or wrong; it's also about perception. If it looks like it could be wrong, then it is. No more hiding behind corporate attorneys to argue all of these gray areas of the law. I believe our market will be a much better place when we finally see the people sitting on the very top of their organizations held accountable: Bernie Ebbers of WorldCom, Ken Lay of Enron, Martha Stewart, et al.

Who knows, if we really get serious about holding corporate America responsible, CNBC's *Squawk Box* may have a new road trip to take. Instead of going to Boca Raton, Florida, or Greenbrier, West Virginia, to follow the business roundtable of corporate CEOs, they can instead follow them to prison and do a show behind bars interviewing only former CEOs who are "doing time for doing the crime."

Now you know the rest of the story!

Here Come the Whales!

May 19, 2004

It's over! I believe the major downturn in our equity market is about to turn around because I can now see the whales. Here is what I mean. When there is an explosion underwater, the small fish are killed first and they come to the surface almost immediately. The big fish can withstand the blast much longer, and it sometimes takes days for them to finally show up on the surface. For the whales, however, it can take weeks after the explosion before they finally come to the surface.

It's the same with our stock market. The explosion in our stock market was the one-two punch of the Federal Reserve changing its interest rate language from "considerable period" to "patient" and the market's immediate overreaction to the concern of rising interest rates. Then the news and pictures of the Iraqi prison scandal hit the market. This one-two punch, in essence, created an explosion of bad news for our markets.

In keeping with my underwater analogy, here is what happened in our market. The small fish got killed first. Our market's small fish are the companies with weak balance sheets and questionable earnings. Next, the explosion killed the big fish. The market's big fish are companies that are profitable and experiencing both top-line revenue growth and bottom-line profitability growth. Now, we are killing the whales as well. The whales in our market are the large-cap multinational companies with strong balance sheets, diversified revenue streams, global brands, strategic direction, and (most important) *big dividends*!

Let's reflect for a moment on what has been going on in our markets. If there is a bad economic release or earnings report, the market goes down that day. If there is no news from an economic or earnings perspective, the market goes down that day as well. When there is good news from an economic or earning perspective, the market still goes down. Bad news the market goes down; no news the market goes down; good news the market goes down. That is irrational.

It is somewhat fitting that I am calling this market "irrational" the day after President Bush renominates Alan Greenspan for another term as Chairman of the Federal Reserve Board. After all, it was Greenspan who made "irrational" a household word and a Wall Street focus in the go-go late 1990s when he said our markets were experiencing "irrational exuberance." Come on, Alan, don't fail me now. If the late 1990s saw irrational exuberance, the markets today are demonstrating irrational fear. How can we be afraid of bad news, no news, and good news all at the same time? There is no doubt in my mind that the market is turning because of both short- and long-term indicators.

SHORT-TERM DRIVERS

In the short run, I see two critical issues that I believe will move our markets forward. First is the job market. Keep in mind that our economy and our markets to date have been doing everything without the help of the labor market. Now that the job market is growing, our economy should have new strength in the second half of 2004 and throughout 2005. That means the economy can still grow, which is bullish for our markets as well as for profits. That, by the way, is my second short-term critical issue: profits. At the end of the day, profits always determine the long-term direction of our markets. First quarter profits were up 27 percent on a year-over-year basis. Profit growth for all of 2004 is now forecasted to be an eye-popping +18 percent on a year-over-year basis. (I personally think it will be +20 percent.) There is no way the market can continue to sell off in the long run with profits this strong.

LONG-TERM DRIVERS

Speaking of the long run, in addition to the short-term drivers of employment and profits, don't lose sight of some key long-term issues that continue to paint a bullish case for our equity market.

Focus on these two important long-term trends: money and brands. First, from a money perspective, if you follow the money, you end up in the United States. Never forget that U.S. consumers spend $7 trillion annually. That is more than three times more than the second largest economy, Japan. Only in the United States can a product be launched into a 290-million consumer pool that will spend $7 trillion.

Second, look at where all the strong global brands are today. They are in the United States. According to data compiled by Interbrand, which annually ranks the top 25 global brands, an astonishing 17 of the top 25 global brands are U.S. companies. These strong global brands attract global capital because these brand leaders are industry and market leaders as well. By the way, the top five global brands are a U.S. sweep: (1) Coca-Cola, (2) Microsoft, (3) IBM, (4) GE, and (5) Intel. In the long run, when you have both the money and the brands that attract the money, your market is bound to benefit.

In closing, I expect that it is going to be a long hot summer for investors. Take my advice: turn off the TV (except when I am on CNBC), buy some dividend-paying stocks, and go outside, sit under a tree, and read *Moby Dick*. You will be both a better person and a better investor!

Investment Footnote . . . What actually happened

I was right. The Dow stayed positive for the year, posting a 3.1 percent gain to close at 10,783.

D-Day for the Markets . . . June 30

June 23, 2004

It's only fitting that right on the heels of the 60-year anniversary of D-Day, which immortalized forever the storming of the beaches of Normandy, the markets have created their own sort of D-Day. The market's D-Day is June 30, when four events weighing on the overall market will be decided. Those four events are the Federal Reserve Board meeting, the turning over of power to the Iraqi government, the annual reconstitution of the Russell equity indices, and mid-year portfolio rebalancing. Let's briefly look at all four of these market D-Day events starting with the Federal Reserve Board meeting.

FEDERAL RESERVE BOARD MEETING

I don't believe it matters whether the Fed raises rates or not at the June 2004 meeting. I don't expect it to play out like 1994, which was another Fed rate hike period that was the beginning of a bear market for stocks and bonds. And the simple reason is *transparency*. Back in 1994 the Fed shocked the markets by raising rates. Today, the market is already doing the job for the Fed. Remember, the yield on the benchmark 10-year Treasury bond has already backed up 100 basis points, so there will be no surprises about whether the Fed moves 25 basis points, 50 basis points, or doesn't move at all. Also, it is important to keep in perspective that even if the Fed raises rates, they are raising them from 46-year lows. Thus, from a historic context, even after a series of Fed rate hikes, interest rates will still be at historically low levels.

NEW IRAQI GOVERNMENT

The second issue that gets closure on June 30 is that the United States will officially turn over all power and control to the new Iraqi government. This is truly a landmark event that culminates the overthrow of Saddam Hussein's terrorist-ridden empire. As long as the United States remained in control of Iraq, investors could never get beyond those headlines. Now, at least from an investment perspective, once the transition of power is complete, Iraq will simply become another spot in the world that has problems. These problems, however, will no longer consume U.S. investors.

RUSSELL EQUITY INDICES

The third issue is which stock is going where in which Russell Equity Index. You see, once a year the Russell Equity Indices are reconstructed based on a company's new market capitalization. Some companies will no longer find themselves in the small-cap index, for instance. Their market caps may have shrunk so much that they will be dropped off the index completely. And this means that anyone trying to shadow this index will no longer need to buy that stock. Alternatively, a stock could be moved to another Russell index if its market capitalization level has grown so much that it is no longer a small-cap stock. Anyway, all the guessing and forecasting of who goes where ends on June 30 when the indices are officially reconstructed.

WINDOW DRESSING TIME

Fourth, and finally, it's window dressing time for all portfolios, both retail and institutional. This happens at the end of every quarter as retail portfolio managers clean up their portfolios preparing for the quarterly report to shareholders. Even though we do this four times a year, the mid-year window dressing, if you will, tends to drive the most action because everyone wants to know exactly what is going on at the halfway point. In addition to the retail investors, most institutional portfolios are also cleaned up for mid-year reviews by institutional clients.

UP NEXT . . . SECOND QUARTER EARNINGS

As D-Day comes and goes, our markets will no longer be focused upon the Fed's June 30 meetings, the transition of power in Iraq, the new Russell indices, or all the portfolio window dressing. All that will be left to focus on is earnings. When that happens, get ready for a red-hot summer where I believe the U.S. equity markets will begin a second-half push to double-digit equity returns by the end of the year.

Think about this for a minute. The overall market and earnings have been disconnected due to these D-Day events. How else can you explain earnings up 28 percent on a year-over-year basis in the first quarter while the market is essentially flat? Second quarter earnings could also approach 20 percent. Keep in mind that, from a historical perspective, the annual earnings growth for the S&P 500 over the past 20 years is only 8.3 percent.

D-Day can't come soon enough. Once these events pass and investors once again begin to focus on earnings, these outstanding earnings fundamentals should finally be reflected in the overall markets' performance.

From a market perspective, D-Day was a long time coming!

Investment Footnote . . . What actually happened

I was right. Second-quarter earnings were strong and did approach 20 percent as they came in at 16.98 percent growth on a year-over-year basis.

Why Am I So Bullish?

July 23, 2004

As I travel across the country—and even around the world—investors everywhere ask me why I'm so bullish on the U.S. equity market. What do I see that no one else sees? I tell those investors that I see what everyone else sees; the difference is that I also try to think what no one else has thought. For example, here are my thoughts about four trends that I believe will set the foundation for a bullish U.S. equity market.

1. INTEREST RATES

While there is great concern among investors about the now rising interest rate cycle, we must keep everything in perspective. My perspective became much clearer last week when I had the opportunity to travel with Tom Sassi, lead portfolio manager of Scudder Large Cap Value Fund. When asked about interest rates, Tom astutely asked advisors to keep things in proper perspective. Here is what he meant. Four years ago, interest rates, as measured by the yield on the 10-year Treasury, were at 6.5 percent, and, if you measured them by the Fed funds rate, they stood at 5 percent. Back then, the price/earnings ratio for the S&P 500 stood at 32x, and you could not find one news article alarming investors about high interest rates with the 10-year Treasury at 6.5 percent and Fed funds at 5 percent. Maybe Alan Greenspan was correct when he called that period "irrational exuberance."

Fast forward, if you will, to today. The 10-year Treasury is trading at about 4.5 percent versus 6.5 percent four years ago. Meanwhile, the Fed funds rate is at 1.25 percent versus 5 percent four years ago. And, everywhere you look, the media are talking about how these high interest rates will destroy equity returns. If we had irrational exuberance four years ago, what do we have today? And here is one more thought for your frame of reference. Today the S&P 500 P/E ratio stands at 17x, compared to 32x four years ago. And, for some reason, investors are still on the sidelines. This is one of the primary reasons that I remain so bullish. Thank you, Tom, for that great perspective!

2. PERFECT STORM

My second thought is that when we find ourselves in the perfect storm, we never recognize it until it's too late. Well, it's not too late to recognize the perfect storm that is driving our equity markets. It is a confluence of three things—a strong and robust economy, record productivity gains, and a relatively weak labor market. If you gave any strategist on Wall Street a blank piece of paper and asked him or her what is necessary to have our equity markets outperform, most would reply (as I would),"a robust economy, strong productivity, and a weak labor market." And that is exactly where we are today. It simply is not reflected in the price of the equity markets.

3. DEMOGRAPHICS AND DIVIDENDS

My third thought is demographics and dividends. While I have been a very outspoken advocate for dividend-paying stocks, I never connected this short-term strategy to the long-term demographic trends. So I will do it now. As baby boomers get older, they will become more conservative with their investments. However, at the same time, they are demanding higher yield and income to support their active lifestyles. The answer is dividend-paying stocks; it is the only investment vehicle that gives baby boomers that much-needed income plus the possibility of capital appreciation. I firmly believe that the portfolios of baby boomers will be increasingly loaded with dividend-paying stocks in the future.

4. NOT JUST A JOB

Fourth, and finally, I firmly believe that the main reason our employment market took so long to recover—and, consequently, why we were beaten to death with all the talk of a "jobless recovery"—is because people were just not looking for a new job. Think about it; in a true global economy, which we are in, a person who is laid off may need to find a new career, not just a new job. This has happened before. If you were a candlestick maker and were laid off after the invention of Thomas Edison's light bulb, first, you looked for a job in the candle-making industry, and then you looked in an associated industry. When you realized none were hiring, you also realized that you had to not only change jobs but change careers as well. It takes a lot more time to change careers than it does to simply change jobs. That is why employment actually looked weaker than it was. In our global economy, people were not simply changing jobs, they were changing careers.

In closing, I am an investment optimist. I will always see the glass half full as opposed to half empty—especially when I have interest rates, a perfect storm, dividends, and employment on my side.

> **Investment Footnote . . . What actually happened** ↑
>
> I was right, as the Dow posted positive returns for the year, closing at 10,783, a 3.1 percent gain.

See Ya at 10,000—Again!

SEPTEMBER 28, 2004

The Dow Jones Industrial Average has once again dropped below the historic 10,000-point level. At first blush, our equity markets at below 10,000 may be viewed as a negative development by most retail investors. But, after the initial shock, I suggest that you focus on two things: First, keep this number in perspective. Second, what lessons, if any, can we learn from the U.S. equity markets' never-ending battle with the Dow 10,000 level?

5½-YEAR PERSPECTIVE

Let's begin by putting things in proper perspective. While in many respects it seems like just yesterday, it was actually five and a half years ago—almost to the day—when the Dow first crossed the 10,000 level on March 29, 1999. Since that historic day we have crossed, recrossed, and uncrossed that level too many times to count. An important perspective to remember is that things are actually much better *today* in our stock market than they were five and a half years ago when we were gleefully celebrating Dow 10,000.

Consider these four aspects that are much better today than they were back then. First, even with three interest rate hikes this year, interest rates are still much lower today than they were when the Dow crossed 10,000 on March 29, 1999. Back then, the benchmark 10-year Treasury bond was trading above 5.25 percent, while today it's at 4 percent. Second, dividends were not important to most companies, or even to most investors, back then. But today, dividends are front and center on most investors' minds and a priority for most companies. We're seeing company after company raising its dividend or establishing a dividend if it does not have one. Sometimes as you live through history you do not realize the significance of an event. However, consider this: Five and a half years ago, if I had told you that one of the highest-flying growth companies of all time—Microsoft—would be paying a dividend today, you would have called me crazy! Who's crazy now? Third, the tax situation is better. While things weren't bad five and a half years ago—if you were in the top tax bracket back then, you were paying 39.6 percent in taxes on dividends—today it's only 15 percent. And back then you were paying a 20 percent long-term capital gains tax, while today it's only 15 percent. The tax landscape is much better today than it was five and a half years ago. Fourth, and finally, is the quality of earnings. While this point is impossible to quantify, it is nonetheless very important. Think about five and a half years ago: that was before Enron, WorldCom, Arthur Andersen, et al., and most important, it was before Sarbanes-Oxley corporate reform legislation. While it was painful to live through those scandals, today we find ourselves with better corporate accountability than ever before, which in turn means the quality of the earnings is much better today than five and a half years ago. Keeping things in proper perspective, we are much better off today in our stock market than we were five and a half years ago.

LESSONS LEARNED

Let me move on to my second point. What can we learn from the U.S. equity market's seemingly never-ending battle with the Dow 10,000 level? The answer is the most basic of all investing principles: asset allocation. The constant battle in the U.S. equity market is a reminder to never, ever, ever, put all of your eggs into one basket—even if the U.S. stock market is the largest and best market in the world. Savvy investors with proper asset allocation stay exposed to fixed income and, to them, Dow 10,000 doesn't matter. In addition to U.S. stocks and bonds, remember to consider rounding out your portfolio with some exposure to real estate and commodities as well.

And finally, with oil above $50 a barrel, don't forget to look at our emerging markets. The economics of many emerging markets, such as Mexico and Venezuela, are driven solely by oil. And, at $50 a barrel, these emerging markets may also deserve consideration for a place in your asset allocation strategy.

In closing, if you keep Dow 10,000 in perspective, things aren't all that bad. And more important, let it remind you that asset allocation is the second most important decision you will ever make as an investor. The most important decision is being smart enough to realize you need a financial advisor to help you design an asset allocation strategy that works for you.

PS: I'll see ya at 10,000!

Investment Footnote . . . What actually happened

I was right, as the Dow closed above 10,000 at 10,783 at the end of 2004.

The Stock Market Is Not One-Dimensional!
FEBRUARY 25, 2005

The price of oil is above $50 a barrel; most investors are overreacting, and are convinced the market must go down. Boy, do I wish it were that easy. My job would be so simple if the stock market were that one-dimensional. Think about it for a minute. Oil goes up, the market must go down. Oil goes down, the market must go up. That is exactly the way it would work if the market were one-dimensional, but it's not! It's not that easy to look at just one thing to forecast the market, whether it is oil or interest rates or whatever. The market is multidimensional. Yes, oil above $50 a barrel is not good for our overall market; however, there are four other issues that

I believe are much more important in the long run to the overall direction of our stock market. And I believe these four issues will more than offset the one-dimensional impact of the high price of oil.

CORPORATE DEFAULTS

The first of these four issues is *corporate defaults*. The reason no one is talking about corporate defaults anymore is because it is good news, not bad. Let me put this important issue in perspective for you and show you just how far we have come in a very short time. Just two short years ago, in 2002, 5 percent of the U.S. corporate sector had defaulted on its debt. That 5 percent peak matched the default peak of our savings and loan crisis in the late 1980s and was the highwater mark for corporate defaults over the past 35 years. In addition, since the start of the new millennium, the U.S. corporate sector had just experienced 10 out of 20 of the largest bankruptcies in the nation's history. Where are we now? Corporate defaults have dropped 90 percent and currently stand at less than one-half of one percent. This amazing turnaround has been fueled by strong corporate profits and record-high cash levels on corporate balance sheets. It would be front-page news if corporate defaults climbed 90 percent.

EMPLOYMENT

The second of the market's four multidimensional issues is employment. In many respects, employment just might be the single most important economic indicator we have. Once employment kicks in, it creates a ripple effect throughout the economy. Did you know that our employment is currently at an all-time high? You probably didn't realize it because it is good news and no one focuses on the good stuff. Let me give you just the facts. In January 1997 there were 121,000,000 people employed in the United States. As the "bull market" began to take off, fueled by the dot-com craze, employment soared over the next three years to 132,500,000. Then the dot-com bubble burst, the market collapsed, and so did employment, as a result of downsizing, cost-cutting, and outsourcing. Now, let me give you the rest of the story. Five short years later employment is back to its all-time high once again. As of January 2005, there are 132,500,000 Americans who have a job!

CONSUMER DELINQUENCY RATE

The third of four multidimensional issues is the consumer delinquency rate. Remember, the consumer still accounts for two-thirds of our economy, so we always must keep at least one eye on the consumer. I believe that one of the best indicators to take the financial pulse of the consumer is the delinquency rate on loans. It is a great leading indicator of things to come. First, a consumer is delinquent in making a payment on a loan and, before we know it, being delinquent moves to being in default.

Let me give you some perspective on this largely ignored indicator. Over the past 20 years, the highest point that the consumer delinquency rate ever reached was 4.2 percent. That was in 1991. When the dot-com bubble burst and the market collapsed, the delinquency rate stood at 3.4 percent. It dramatically shot up to 3.7 percent, which, to this day, remains the highwater mark for the new millennium. Today, the consumer delinquency rate is below 3 percent. And, you guessed it, that's the lowest rate of the new millennium and one of the lowest rates in the past 20 years. While many market bears continue to predict that the U.S. consumer is on the brink of collapse, the consumer delinquency rate tells us a completely different story!

WALL STREET RECOMMENDATIONS

The fourth, and final, multidimensional issue hinges on Wall Street recommendations. At the turn of the millennium and the peak of the bull market, virtually everything on Wall Street was a "buy." Looking back, one has to wonder why we didn't question these Wall Street analysts more back then. Here are the numbers. From January 2000, 75.7 percent of all recommendations were "buy," 22.6 percent were "hold," and a mere 1.7 percent were "sell." No wonder "irrational exuberance" was the term of the day. In five short years, and with a little prodding from the SEC and Elliott Spitzer, Wall Street has changed its tune completely. In January 2005, only 46.2 percent of all recommendations were "buy"; 43.4 percent were "hold," and a record 10.4 percent were "sell."

Do not underestimate the landmark importance of keeping investors' expectations in line with reality. Think about it. Five short years ago, three-fourths of all recommendations were a "buy." Today, fewer than one-half are a "buy." And five years ago, only a little over 1 percent were a "sell." Today over 10 percent are a "sell." Not only do I believe that we have more realistic recommendations from Wall Street, I also believe we have better research than ever before, based upon the improved corporate accounting we have today. It's a pretty simple concept: if you give Wall Street better information (as we do today), it only stands to reason that in return you will get better research.

In closing, I will remind you that we always attempt to make the market appear one-dimensional so we can better understand it. But, in reality, it is multidimensional. Yes, oil above $50 is a negative for our markets. However, collapsing corporate default rates, record employment, falling consumer delinquency rates, and more realistic Wall Street recommendations are all positives. And the last time I checked, four positives still beat one negative!

PS: Even though I am still in Asia, I am not going to forget about our market in the good old U.S. of A.!

Investment Footnote . . . What actually happened

I was correct, getting two out of three markets right for 2005. While the Dow was down −0.6 percent for the year, both of our broader markets, the S&P 500, which gained 3.0 percent, and the Nasdaq, which gained 1.4 percent, posted positive returns, just as I predicted.

Convergence!

June 28, 2005

The issues facing our market used to be so clearly defined. The "wall of worry" was limited to three issues: oil, interest rates, and the falling dollar. While in many ways these are still the primary issues investors worry about, they can no longer be looked at in isolation. These issues are becoming increasingly connected to one another and feeding off each other. To get an idea where the market may be going, you now have to look at these issues together, and as they converge with other issues.

OIL

Let's begin with oil. The new issue is no longer just price, although that is still a concern. Now, merger mania has taken center stage in this industry as well. A rival bid by China National Offshore Oil Corporation (CNOOC) over Chevron's planned acquisition of Unocal Corporation is the new story of the day. And let me point out that this story is bigger than the entire energy sector. It is one more example of the merger and acquisition boom that we are experiencing. These deals are changing entire industries. Think, Procter & Gamble acquiring Gillette. Think, SBC acquiring AT&T (which led to Verizon acquiring MCI). Or think, Time Warner acquiring Comcast, or MetLife acquiring Travelers, or Federated Department Stores acquiring May Department Stores to combine Macy's, Bloomingdales, Lord & Taylor, and Marshall Field under one roof. The significance of these landmark deals is that they so dramatically change the competitive landscape that other M&A deals will soon follow.

Maybe the single best example of how the more things change the more they remain the same would be to think about the telecommunications industry. Remember, it was 1984 when the Department of Justice split the Bell System up into local and long distance. Now, after a boom of mergers, we are almost right back where we started, with only the names having changed. Verizon's acquisition of MCI was the final dramatic change to this landscape. The games began in February 2004 when Cingular Wireless acquired AT&T Wireless. Later that year, Sprint Corp. acquired Nextel Communications. That led to the SBC/AT&T blockbuster deal, which brings us back to the Verizon/MCI deal. And, in the end, the financial services industry through its investment banking operations may be the biggest winner. That's why, in my mind, the real issue in the energy sector right now is merger and acquisitions rather than price.

INTEREST RATES

Let's move on to investor worry number two: interest rates. There is great speculation in the markets this week regarding what the Federal Reserve Board will do regarding rates. They have already raised rates eight consecutive times, at 25 basis points each time, moving the federal funds rate (the rate at which banks can borrow money overnight) from 1 percent to the current level of 3 percent. Will this week make it nine in a row? I don't think so. In my opinion, rates are now more about oil. And this goes back to my convergence theme. Here's what I mean. When the Federal Reserve Board began raising interest rates a year ago, the Fed funds rate was at 1 percent. But even more important, oil was under $40 a barrel (actually trading at $38). Now the Federal Reserve Board has raised interest rates from 1 to 3 percent. But I think the real story is that oil has risen from $38 a barrel, when the Federal Reserve Board began raising rates, to $60 today. Looked at another way, the high price of oil is already doing the Fed's job for it by slowing the economy. That's why I think that if you want to understand rates, you have to look at oil. And if I am correct and the Fed stops raising rates—or even if I am wrong and they raise them one more time and then quit at 3.25 percent—it's time to look at which industries do best six months after the Fed stops raising rates. Historically, two industries have posted almost 30 percent gains six months after the Fed stopped raising short-term interest rates. One is the investment banking and brokerage industry and the other is wireless communications. Again, the convergence continues.

DOLLAR

Third, and finally, the dollar has a new concern. It is no longer falling; in fact, it is actually gaining strength. When the dollar strengthens, it makes sense to look at sectors that derive the smallest amount of their sales outside the United States. This is so because, with a stronger dollar, everything sold outside the United States will be worth much less when it is converted to dollars. Of the 10 sectors that comprise the Standard & Poor's 500 Index, the one that has the least amount of foreign sales is telecommunications, at 4.8 percent. For a frame of reference, the entire S&P 500 derives about 33 percent of its sales outside the United States. In addition to telecommunications, one other sector stands to be a big winner because it only derives 13.3 percent of sales outside the United States; that sector is financial services. Telecommunications and financials are both big players in the merger and acquisition boom. And this convergence continues. Could it be that the dollar is now more about merger and acquisition than anything else?

In closing, let me tell you what I think this convergence means. Oil will begin to trend down, rates are not going to continue rising, the merger and acquisition boom will continue, the financial services sector may provide the biggest upside surprise, and the overall stock market will be up by double digits (10 to 12 percent) by year end. Now that's what I call convergence.

And one final thing: Let me remind you what my role is as a high-profile Wall Street strategist. I have to have the ability to foretell what is going to happen in the market tomorrow, next week, next month, next year, and five years from now. And more important, I must have the ability afterward to explain why it didn't happen.

Investment Footnote . . . What actually happened

I was right, as financials led the stock market rally; however, they were not as strong as I thought, gaining 3.7 percent, not 10 to 12 percent.

Big, Better, Best

March 24, 2006

It is amazing how things that we learn in childhood stay with us the rest of our lives. I know that all of you baby boomers out there are already humming, "Good, better, best, never let it rest until your good is better and your better's best."

As you can see, I have taken some liberty with that childhood jingle and replaced "good" with "big." And for the purposes of this commentary, those words are one and the same—big is good and good is big, especially in terms of the U.S. stock market.

BIG IS BETTER

I believe that *large-cap stocks* will finally outperform small-cap stocks in 2006. The confluence of three issues makes the case for large-cap stocks. First, large-cap stocks have higher dividend yields. During every single day that goes by, the baby boomer generation that was humming my jingle at the start of this commentary is marching closer toward retirement. The closer these 76 million baby boomers get to retirement, the more important retirement income becomes to them. I believe the best source of income available in the investment world today is dividend-paying stocks. As baby boom investors search for dividend-paying stocks, they will quickly realize that most dividend-paying stocks are also large-cap stocks. This unprecedented baby boom demographic shift is about to dramatically tilt the investment landscape in favor of large-cap stocks for a long, long time.

The second issue is that we are finally seeing a rebound in the *initial public offering*, or IPO market. IPOs are typically smaller companies that decide to go public for the first time, giving individual investors a chance to invest in them for the first time. These new IPO companies tend to be small-cap companies. Rather than support the remaining universe of small-cap stocks, any money looking to invest in small cap will more than likely invest in these brand-new IPOs, which tend to come to the market for the first time with a great deal of hype and excitement.

The third issue is *greater foreign exposure*. Large-cap multinational stocks tend to derive a greater amount of their revenue from outside the United States than small-cap stocks. That becomes extremely important because we are embarking on a synchronized global recovery in the United States, Asia, and now, Europe. There are more people outside the United States than inside. There are also more commodities and more capital flowing outside the United States than within it. This, in turn, means that greater investment opportunities exist outside the United States as well. Large-cap stocks are much better positioned than small-cap stocks to benefit from this boom happening outside the United States.

IT'S A SMALL WORLD

It's not enough to simply understand the issues that will make large-cap stocks outperform. We also need to understand why small-cap stocks outperformed for six straight years. I believe it was a combination of two things, both of which are going away. The first reason was interest rates at 40-year lows. When you have a federal funds rate (the rate banks charge other banks to borrow money overnight) at 1 percent, that low rate can help bail out even the most speculative companies (usually small cap) because their cost of getting capital is so low. Now the federal funds rate stands at 4.5 percent and at that level it no longer will be bailing out the risky and speculative companies.

The second issue was that large-cap companies were content to grow very slowly and simply build up cash as they were trying to figure out exactly what life after Sarbanes-Oxley would be like. After building up cash for the last five years, large-cap stocks are on a buying and spending spree, buying other companies (merger and acquisition boom) in order to buy growth, and spending on capital equipment to help them become more productive and grow faster. When the two issues that lead to small-cap outperformance are reversing themselves, it is good news for large-cap stocks.

FOLLOW THE MONEY

Finally, don't forget to follow the money. There is one final issue that makes an extremely compelling case for large-cap stocks to outperform small-cap stocks this year. It is the amount of retail money that is still on the sidelines. According to the Federal Reserve Board, as of December 31, 2005, retail investors were sitting on $4.7 trillion in cash. Cash, by the way, is defined as a savings account, checking account, money market account, or any time deposit that matures in one year or less.

Let me explain why this $4.7 trillion is so important to large-cap stocks. When this money finally comes off the sidelines out of cash and into our equity market, I believe I have a pretty good idea where it is *not* going. There is simply no way cash from a money market account will be put into some small-cap biotech company whose company name can't even be pronounced and for which you have no idea how it even makes money. Instead, I believe that money will go from cash to large-cap stocks—the bluest of the blue chip companies and the companies with which baby boomers grew up. It will go to the companies that people clearly understand: what they do and how they make money. As this money begins to rotate off the sidelines out of cash into the stock market, I believe that rotation will be the critical catalyst that will allow large-cap stocks to finally outperform small-cap stocks.

Like I said, "Big, better, best, never stay at rest; as long as your big is large cap, you will be happier than the rest!"

Investment Footnote . . . What actually happened

I was wrong, as small cap clearly outperformed large cap in 2006. Large cap, as measured by the S&P 500 Index, was up 13.6 percent. Meanwhile, small cap, as measured by the S&P 600 (small-cap index) was up 14.1 percent and small cap, as measured by the Russell 2000, was up 17 percent.

Forget the Indicators—Let's Get Back to the Basics

MARCH 31, 2006

I'm the first to admit that I contribute to the indicator frenzy that is often rampant among financial advisors and their clients. And it's not just economic indicators I'm talking about. Earlier this year, for example, I discussed a market indicator popularly known as the Super Bowl effect—the notion that the winner of the Super Bowl will tell us where the stock market, as measured by the Standard & Poor's 500 Index (S&P 500),* will be at the end of the year. But it goes further than that. Women's hemlines! The Daytona 500! All these things can allegedly predict the future of the U.S. economy and market. And as much fun as that is, it's sometimes important to remind people of what really matters: consumer spending, business spending, and earnings.

CONSUMER SPENDING

One of the most important traditional economic indicators is consumer spending. When consumers spend money, companies make money and the economy prospers. And consumer spending is strong right now.

On March 1, the Commerce Department reported that the warmest January in more than a century had lured consumers out to the stores. Personal spending shot up by 0.9 percent, the strongest gain in six months.

Now that wasn't surprising, given that personal incomes rose by a solid 0.7 percent in January, the best showing since September. Gains were attributed to a variety of factors, including cost-of-living adjustments for Social Security benefits and the new prescription drug benefit for Medicare recipients.

---

* The S&P 500 is an unmanaged index, widely regarded as representative of the equity market in general. Index returns assume reinvestment of dividends and capital gains and, unlike fund returns, do not reflect fees or expenses. You cannot invest directly in the index.

And I think it's going to continue. Energy prices have retreated, interest rates remain at historical lows, and housing prices are strong. All three of these things make consumers feel like they have more money to spend.

BUSINESS SPENDING

Business spending is also key to any economic expansion. After years of cost-cutting, downsizing, and outsourcing, companies are now in a position to start spending again. I think we're going to see business spend money in a number of ways.

First, I expect to see a big uptick in capital spending, concentrated in two areas. Companies need to replace the technology they put in place in 1998 and 1999 to save us from the Y2K bug. (It's hard to believe, but that equipment is now seven or eight years old!) They also need to add capacity to address the supply-demand imbalance we have in the commodities market. Both of these projects are major long-term capital improvements that will cost millions of dollars and take years to build.

Second, I think companies are going to spend money buying other companies. We saw a merger and acquisition boom in 2005, and it shows no signs of ending anytime soon.

Third, I think companies are going to spend money on employees. The labor market continues to strengthen, with strong job growth persisting in January.

Finally, I think companies will continue to return capital to their shareholders in the form of dividends (regardless of what the dividend tax rate is)! Both individual and institutional investors are demanding higher dividends, and corporate America is responding.

EARNING

At the end of the day, it's always about earnings. Fourth quarter earnings for the S&P 500 posted the fifteenth consecutive quarter of double-digit, year-over-year gains. That has never happened in the modern era of our markets (in other words, after World War II). The previous record of 13 consecutive quarters ended in December 1995.

Why is no one talking about this? Can you even imagine the headlines if it were 15 consecutive quarters of double-digit losses?

But what's really exciting to me about earnings is not where they've been, but where they're going. The S&P 500's historical average earnings growth is a little over 8 percent and I think it's going to get even better. When you combine strong consumer spending with strong business spending, you get an economy that could grow at 5 percent, and that could drive earnings to grow at 15 percent—or almost double the historical average.

THE FUN STUFF

I have watched all 40 Super Bowls and I occasionally watch the Daytona 500. And I'm not immune to women's hemlines, but they can't tell the whole story. History shows us that consumer spending, business spending, and earnings can tell you more than all the hemlines and Daytona 500 winners combined. So don't forget about them—and don't let your clients forget about them.

A GLOBAL INDICATOR

Another indicator I'd like to talk about isn't one you've likely read about, but it's important nonetheless: what's going on in the world. You see, the U.S. economy is increasingly connected to the world economy. And one of the most dramatic investment forces in 2005 was the world economy. Its strength led international stock markets to rise dramatically: France's CAC 40 was up 23.4 percent (even while rioters were "burning" Paris!). Germany's DAX was up 27.1 percent (even in the face of election uncertainties!). And Japan's NIKKEI was up a whopping 40.2 percent. And this shows no sign of letting up in 2006. That doesn't mean the U.S. markets will do the same—but the positive momentum could affect them positively. It's just something you may want to keep an eye on.

Investment Footnote . . . What actually happened ↑

I was right, as the Dow posted double-digit gains of
16.3 percent, closing at 12,463 at year-end.

God Bless America—and Goldilocks, Too

MAY 1, 2006

I have recently returned from almost three weeks of international
travel that took me from the Middle East to Africa and then to
Europe. I can sum up all my travels with three simple words: "God
Bless America."

To understand just how great our country is, one simply has to
spend some time in other parts of the world. Not that our country
doesn't have its share of problems; of course it does. But despite all
of our problems we remain, in many respects, the greatest country
on the face of the earth. We have the most diversified economy, a
resilient stock market, and the strongest consumer base anywhere
in the world. And, let me remind you that we are doing pretty well
from an investment perspective as well.

In fact, from my perspective, we again find ourselves with a
Goldilocks economy—not too hot and not too cold. You see, you
don't want inflation to be too hot, but at the same time you don't
want the economy to be too cold. Currently, we seem to have the
best of both worlds. The economy is hot but not too hot, and inflation is cold but not too cold.

EMPLOYMENT COST INDEX

Let me point to two recent quarterly economic reports to prove my
point: the employment cost index and the gross domestic product
(GDP). Let's begin with the employment cost index.

This is one of my most favorite employment reports because it is the only one that measures both wages and benefits. The employment cost index rose only 0.6 percent in the first quarter of 2006. This translates into a year-over-year gain of only 2.8 percent. Just last June, those annual gains were 3.2 percent. The wages and salaries component climbed 0.7 percent, putting the year-over-year increase at 2.7 percent. The benefits component was the big surprise. It grew at just 0.5 percent, substantially less than expected.

This means that both components—benefits and wages—slowed, the former more so than the latter. However, the fear was that the wage component was going to accelerate, confirming the recent steady increase in the weekly average hourly earnings reports. This very bullish employment cost index report, from an inflation standpoint, is very positive for corporate earnings and profits. At this time there are simply no evident wage and benefit pressures anywhere.

GROSS DOMESTIC PRODUCT

Let's now move on to gross domestic product, the broadest measure of our economy. Our economy, as measured by gross domestic product, advanced 4.8 percent in the first quarter of 2006. Consumer spending, corporate capital spending, and government spending all posted good gains. It simply doesn't get any better than this.

DON'T FORGET FINANCIALS

What does all of this mean for the U.S. stock market? Look no further than the largest sector and the basic bellwether for the overall markets: the financial sector. Last week the financial sector reached a new 12-month high. Why? It rallied on the back of Fed Chairman Bernanke's suggestion that Fed tightening was coming to an end. The basic bet is that the margin squeeze on spread lending is coming to an end, which is good news for both the financial services sector as well as the overall market. Remember, as soon as the Fed stops raising rates, financials and the market are likely to do better.

BEST OF BOTH WORLDS

Even with all of the great things going on in the United States, I still believe that the most compelling investment opportunities are currently outside our borders. As a U.S. investor you get to enjoy the best of both worlds. You get to live in the greatest country in the world, and invest in international markets to capture the opportunity they present. It simply doesn't get any better than this. Let me end where I began: God bless America! Oh, and I almost forgot— God bless Goldilocks, too!

Investment Footnote . . . What actually happened

I was right. While the Dow gained 16.3 percent for the year, international markets boomed almost twice as much at 29.2 percent as measured by MSCI–EAFE (Morgan Stanley Capital International–Europe, Australia, and the Far East).

When the Dust Settles

AUGUST 14, 2006

As the second quarter earnings season draws to a close, I am not sure what more investors could have hoped for, other than the U.S. market reflecting the strong earnings.

CRAZY MARKETS

I don't know that I would go so far as to say our markets are crazy, but I would say that last week was one of the craziest weeks that I can remember. First the Federal Reserve Board paused its interest rate tightening cycle after 17 consecutive rate hikes. When the Fed stops raising interest rates, it is bullish for the market. So how did the market respond to this great news? Like I said, things are crazy; it actually went down. Second, a major terrorist plot was uncovered in the United Kingdom aimed at flights heading into the United States. The terror alert level was raised. There was chaos at most U.S. airports, as I witnessed firsthand at the two busiest airports in the United States: Atlanta and Chicago. So with this new terror and uncertainty (which always spook the markets), how did the market react? It was crazy again. It actually went up. Third, and finally, when the week ended, the single biggest economic surprise of the week was the robust retail sales numbers. This was so important because the consumer accounts for two-thirds of our economy. With the high price of gasoline, many economists were predicting that the consumer is essentially dead. This number proved that the U.S. consumer is alive and well, and shopping. And that's great news for our market. So how did our market respond? I am sure you guessed it by now; it went down.

BACK TO EARNINGS

Let's get back to earnings for a minute, because it's earnings that will drive our markets. As second quarter earnings season draws to a close, it is now official; we will have double-digit earnings growth for the seventeenth consecutive quarter.

Double-digit, year-over-year earnings growth is what the market hopes for every quarter. Now remember, as we began the earnings season the consensus on Wall Street was calling for 12.2 percent year-over-year earnings growth, which was a bullish forecast. My forecast, on the other hand, called for a 15 percent year-over-year-earnings growth. And when I made that forecast, I said that if I am wrong, I will be wrong because I am too low, not too high. Well, I was wrong. Earnings did not grow at 15 percent; they are now projected to grow at 16.4 percent according to Thompson's First Call, which, quite frankly, is exceptional from an earnings perspective.

Across the board, sector by sector, there was strong earnings growth. From an individual sector perspective, three sectors had the largest percentage of companies beating earnings expectations: telecom, health care, and materials. With materials being one of the three, I guess that means the commodity boom is not dead—just as I have been telling you.

MARKET REBOUND—AXIS OF EVIL

If earnings are so good, why is the market not responding and moving stocks higher? I believe that our stock market has been slow to reward companies for strong earnings due to increased risk premiums associated with what I consider the new axis of evil—the end of the Federal Reserve Board's interest rate hike cycle, geopolitical risks, and high oil prices. Once we begin to see a pull-back in one or more of these three issues, I think the stock market will finally reward U.S. companies for their strong earnings over the past 17 consecutive quarters. In the meantime, if you are tired of waiting on the U.S. markets to respond, why not simply follow theme number 1 of my top 10 investment themes this year: "Go global, global, and even more global"?

GO GLOBAL

Year-to-date, the U.S. market, as measured by the Dow Jones Industrial Average, is up +3.46 percent. Meanwhile, look what is going on outside the United States. China's market, as measured by the CBN China 600, is up +25.4 percent year-to-date; Hong Kong, as measured by the Hang Seng, is up +16.0 percent; Spain, as measured by the IBEX 35, is up +9.7 percent; Brazil, as measured by the Sao Paulo Bovespa, is up +10.4 percent; Mexico is up +13.9 percent as measured by IPC All-Share; Venezuela is up +72.1 percent as measured by the Caracas General Index; and, finally, Chile, as measured by the Santiago IPSA Index, is up +9.0 percent. So remember, as you are waiting for the dust to settle in the United States, you can always go global, go global, and go even more global. And speaking about going global, I am about to embark on an eight-country trip to Europe that includes Sweden, Germany, Denmark, Norway, Scotland, the Netherlands, Belgium, and England.

Investment Footnote . . . What actually happened

I was right, as the Dow gained 16.3 percent. But I was soundly beaten by the international markets as MSCI–EAFE (Morgan Stanley Capital International–Europe, Australia, and the Far East) was up 29.3 percent and MSCI–EM (Morgan Stanley Capital International–Emerging Markets) was up 23.5 percent.

12K Is a Big Deal

OCTOBER 25, 2006

Last week the Dow Jones Industrial Average (Dow) broke a milestone, closing above the coveted 12,000 level for the first time ever. It was pretty much a nonevent with the media and with the markets. The reason is that with each 1,000 point gain on the Dow, the next one becomes easier to achieve as a percent of the overall market. In other words, to move from 1,000 to 2,000 the Dow had to increase by 100 percent, while to move from 11,000 to 12,000 was only a 9 percent move.

I don't care. A thousand points is a thousand points. That is why I simply could not believe it when I went to the end of my driveway on Saturday morning to get my copy of *Barron's*, expecting the cover to be a celebration of Dow 12,000 with a big strong bull on the cover. To my shock and dismay, it wasn't mentioned on the cover at all. While no one else thinks that Dow 12,000 is a big deal, I do. In fact, I think it is a very big deal and let me tell you why.

DOW MILESTONES

First, a little history lesson is in store. The Dow Jones Industrial Average was created on May 26, 1896. It didn't reach 1,000 until November 14, 1972, which was 27,930 days after it was first created.

It reached 2,000 on January 8, 1987, which means it took 5,168 days to double from 1,000 to 2,000. On April 17, 1991—some 1,560 days later—we hit 3,000 and some 1,480 days after that, on February 23, 1995, the Dow hit 4,000. The Dow milestones just kept coming all within a year's time.

It only took 271 days to move to 5,000 on November 21, 1995, and 328 days after that, on October 14, 1996, we topped 6,000. On February 13, 1997—only 122 days later—we crossed 7,000. In the same year, 1997, we crossed 8,000 in 153 days on July 16 and hit 9,000 on April 6, 1998, or 264 days after breaking 8,000. The seemingly insurmountable Dow 10,000 happened a little less than a year later (357 days to be exact, when we crossed Dow 10,000 on March 29, 1999. In the blink of an eye, we were at 11,000, taking 35 days to reach that milestone on May 3, 1999, the quickest 1,000 or more points in history. This brings us back to Dow 12,000. It took us 2,726 days to move this last 1,000 points from 11,000 to 12,000. It was the longest timeframe to reach the 1,000 point milestone since we went from 1,000 to 2,000. So you see, it is a really big deal. In my opinion, this was the single toughest 1,000 point milestone ever for the Dow.

THE DOW AXIS OF EVIL

The reason these 1,000 points were so difficult to achieve was that the Dow was hit with what I am calling the "Dow Axis of Evil." The first axis of evil was the Internet bubble. While I was one of the few Wall Street strategists who did not jump on the Internet stock bandwagon, I also was one of the many who underestimated what would happen when this house of cards folded. I thought it would create a collapse of these high-flying Internet stocks only. Instead, it triggered a complete and total meltdown of our entire stock market, beginning with Internet stocks, followed by all technology stocks and then by the overall stock market. There was nowhere to hide. Even the old economy, blue chip industrial stocks, got crushed as investors ran for the door.

The second axis of evil was the most horrific event I have ever witnessed in my entire life—the merciless terrorist attacks of 9/11. This single event, in one fell swoop, caused the greatest level of uncertainty our markets have ever faced. No one had any idea or any experience as to how our markets would respond after the world's largest economy and world's largest market was attacked on its own soil. The resulting major market sell-off was all about fear and uncertainty.

While this event has been engraved in everyone's mind, in my mind, it had a double engraving. That is because I was actually in the air when 9/11 was unfolding, on one of the last flights to take off from Chicago that day after the first tower had been hit. The consensus was that it was an accident. When the second tower was hit, I was actually in the air—and we knew it was no longer an accident. Exactly one week earlier, I was in that same World Trade Center for a gala book signing of my then new book, *Where the Money Is*, at Borders bookstore. It is times like this when we realize just how fragile life really is.

The third and final axis of evil is a combination of the worst examples of corporate fraud, corporate greed, malfeasance, and totally unethical behavior that has ever occurred in the entire history of Wall Street. Three names together remain engrained in our memories as a constant reminder of the lowest level of corporate governance maybe in the history of our country—Enron, WorldCom, and Arthur Andersen. Combined, these three companies created a complete and total collapse of what little investor confidence remained after the Internet bubble burst and the terrorists attacked on 9/11. Some people questioned if anyone would ever buy a stock again.

On the surface, almost seven-and-a-half years may seem like a lifetime to move from 11,000 to 12,000. However, when you consider the Dow Axis of Evil, I do not believe that there is another market anywhere in the world that could withstand the blows our market did and still continue to move higher, even if it was at a much slower pace. In my opinion, this move from 11,000 to 12,000 is the single most impressive 1,000 point move in the entire history of our stock market.

DOW 13,000

With 12,000 behind us, all eyes are now on the next level—and how long until Dow 13,000. In my opinion, it will happen by early next spring and certainly well less than a year after we crossed 12,000. The fuel for this next 1,000 point move? The price of fuel.

The price of oil has fallen dramatically from almost $80 a barrel a few months ago to below $60 a barrel today. I believe this will go down as the greatest tax cut in the Bush presidency. This collapse in oil prices equates to a $100 billion de facto energy tax cut. This tax cut has consumer and investor confidence soaring. And remember, the U.S. consumer accounts for two-thirds of our economy. Watch for a blowout holiday sales season, which means a stronger economy and in turn stronger profits. Consumers will not just be buying socks for the holidays; they will also be buying stocks.

Have a great day, keep a positive attitude, and I'll see ya at 13,000, I believe sometime before Memorial Day next year, if not sooner!

PS: Happy shopping for stocks and socks.

Investment Footnote . . . What actually happened

I was right, as the Dow hit 13,000 in 2006 and it actually closed the year at 13,264.

CHAPTER 4

Investment Strategy

Strategy is about changing unfavorable circumstances into a favorable situation.

NADER SABRY
Egyptian soccer star

INTRODUCTION

In its purest sense, an investment strategy is a set of rules, behaviors, or procedures designed to guide an investor's selection of an investment portfolio. Usually, an investment strategy will be designed around the investor's risk-return tradeoff. Some individual investors will prefer to maximize expected returns by investing in risky assets, others will prefer to minimize risk, but most will select a strategy somewhere in between. Passive strategies are often used to minimize transaction costs, and active strategies, such as market timing, are an attempt to maximize returns.

One of the better known investment strategies and one of my favorites is *buy and hold*. Buy and hold is a long-term investment strategy, based on the concept that, in the long run, equity markets give a good rate of return despite periods of volatility or decline.

A purely passive approach to this strategy is *indexing*, where an investor buys a small proportion of all the shares in a market index, such as the S&P 500, or, more likely, in a mutual fund called an *index fund*.

This viewpoint also holds that *market timing*, where the investor enters the market on the lows and sells on the highs, does not work, nor does it work for small retail investors; thus, it is better to simply buy and hold. The retail investor more typically uses the buy-and-hold investment strategy in real estate investment where the holding period is typically the lifespan of the mortgage.

Remember, buy and hold is a long-term investment strategy based on the concept that, in the long run, financial markets give a good rate of return despite periods of volatility or decline. This viewpoint also holds that market timing, the concept that one can enter the market on the lows and sell on the highs, does not work, nor does it work for small retail investors, so it is better simply to buy and hold.

On the opposite end of the spectrum of buy and hold is the concept of *day trading*, in which money can be made in the short term if an individual tries to short on the peaks and buy on the lows, with greater money coming during periods of greater volatility. Clearly, one of the strongest arguments for the buy-and-hold strategy is the *efficient market hypothesis*, which states that if every security is fairly valued at all times, there is really no point to trade. Some take the buy-and-hold strategy to an extreme, advocating that you should never sell a security unless you need the money. I am one of those advocates.

Others have advocated buy and hold on purely cost-based grounds, paying no attention to the efficient market hypothesis. In this strategy, costs, such as brokerage and bid/ask spread, are incurred on all transactions, and buy and hold involves the fewest transactions for a given amount invested in the market, all other things being equal.

Investment strategy also must deal with how you construct your investment portfolio. From an investment strategy perspective, a portfolio is an appropriate mix or allocation of investments held by an individual investor or even a major institution, for that matter. In developing an investment portfolio, a major institution will conduct its own investment analysis; meanwhile an individual retail investor should always use the services of a financial advisor. Even if a financial institution offers portfolio management services, you still need a financial advisor. Developing and holding a portfolio is part of an investment and risk-limiting strategy called *diversification*. By owning several assets, certain types of risk, especially specific event risk, can be greatly reduced. The assets in the portfolio might include stocks, bonds, options, warrants, gold, real estate, commodities, futures contracts, or just about any item that is expected to grow in value.

No introduction on investment strategy would be complete without at least briefly touching upon behavioral psychology. Behavioral psychology approaches to stock market trading are being viewed as a classic alternative to efficient market hypothesis. In fact, there are specific investment strategies that seek to exploit exactly such inefficiencies. A growing field of research called *behavioral finance* studies how cognitive or emotional biases, which are individual or collective, create anomalies in market prices and returns that may be inexplicable using efficient market hypothesis alone. However, if and how individual biases manifest inefficiencies in marketwide prices are still open questions. Ironically, the behavioral finance program also can be used tangentially to support efficient market hypothesis, or it can actually explain the skepticism drawn by efficient market hypothesis, in that it helps to explain the human tendency to find and exploit patterns in data even where none exist. Ever look up into the clouds and convince yourself those clouds look like a dog or a bull?

Well, it's time to get your head out of the clouds. On the pages that follow, you will get my perspectives and insights on exactly how and what investment strategies to use in order to best position your investments.

What in the World Went Wrong?

OCTOBER 1, 1998

Only two days ago, everything appeared to be on track as the Federal Open Markets Committee (FOMC) cut interest rates. Lower interest rates not only serve as a stimulus to our economy (which is good for stocks) but also serve as a form of price support when these lower interest rates are placed in financial models that try to determine if stocks are fairly valued (which is also good for stocks). Thus, with this positive event as a backdrop, the market crashes over 448 points during the next two days and is actually 8 points lower than it was on Labor Day, when it stood at 7,640. In two volatile trading days, we have witnessed all the gains from September completely wiped out. What in the world went wrong? Actually, it was the confluence of three unrelated events that put undue pressure on our markets. Two of them are minor in nature and one major. Let me begin with the two minor ones.

SHOW ME THE MONEY

Even though the FOMC cut rates by one-fourth of 1 percent, the global markets were very disappointed that the rate cut was not deeper (one-half of 1 percent). There was also great concern because there was no clear signal from the FOMC about whether this was the first or last rate cut. The FOMC was lagging the markets, not leading the markets. In times of crisis, we need the FOMC to lead, not lag, the markets.

AT LEAST IT WILL LOOK GOOD

The last day of every quarter can be a difficult time for the stock market. You see, it is the last day for money managers to make any final changes to their portfolios before the quarter ends. (September 30 was the last of the third quarter.) When the quarter has not been positive to begin with (just like this quarter, which was the worst quarter in eight years), it becomes difficult to find buyers. Portfolios are both dumping losers that they don't want to be associated with and moving to cash, so they appear more conservative. In financial circles, we call this "window dressing."

CAN YOU IMPEACH A NOBEL LAUREATE?

The failure of Long-Term Capital Management (or, as I like to refer to it, long-term capital mismanagement) continues to send shock waves around the financial world. It adds another level of uncertainty to already uncertain markets. Not only was this hedge fund supposed to be too big to fail (leveraged up to more than $90 billion), it was also supposed to be *too* smart to fail. After all, it combined the best and the brightest from business, government, and academia. From the business world came John Meriwether, legendary Wall Street wizard from Salomon Brothers. From the government sector came David Mullins, former assistant treasurer and vice chairman of the Federal Reserve Board. And from academe came two Nobel award–winning economists, Merton Miller and Myron Scholes (whose award was for their landmark modern options trading theory).

Here are a couple of key points to remember:

- Long-Term Capital Management's hedge *did not* go bankrupt and it *did not* collapse; it was bailed out—the key here being they did not have to unwind their investments immediately in an extremely volatile market, which, due to the sheer size, could have triggered a global meltdown.

- It was a private bailout. Fed officials encouraged the private sector, banks, and broker dealers to come up with private money. No government funds were used. The government *did not* bail out Long-Term Capital Management.

- This isn't a complicated issue. Long-Term Capital Management *did not* make good investment decisions. It made some very bad, very leveraged, and very risky investment decisions that lost billions. Then, 15 of the world's top financial companies provided a $3.5 billion bailout. This will give the fund about six months to unwind some of its poor investment decisions.

This saga is far from over. When a fund this big, managed by bright people, fails, you can see why the markets were worried that other hedge funds could follow. By the way, now that their trading strategy backfired and almost caused a global meltdown, I wonder what the provisions are for impeachment of a Nobel Laureate in Economics?

DON'T FORGET MY NEW KEYS

Even though it's only been two days since my last market update, I want to remind you not to lose sight of the four keys to our stock market in the fourth quarter:

- *Earnings*. There have been no new major pre-earnings disappointment announcements. From my perspective, no news is good news.
- *Global rate cuts*. The Bank of Canada cut interest rates one-fourth of 1 percent. The Bundesbank (Germany) left rates unchanged. Germany will come around. One out of two is not bad.
- *International Monetary Fund approval*. Bob Rubin is now taking this issue on as his personal cause. He figured out a way to bail out Mexico in 1994; I know he can structure a deal to get Congress to fully fund the IMF.
- *Japanese banking reform*. Both the ruling and opposition parties have agreed to transfer significant power from the Finance Ministry to a newly created independent ministry. This had to happen before any bank reform legislation had a prayer. It's not much, but it's better than nothing.

Remember, in every dark cloud there is a silver lining. Sometimes it's easy to lose sight of the fact that interest rates are low and going lower, inflation has disappeared, and the U.S. consumer remains strong. I'm not giving up. What you can lose in two days, you can gain in two days.

What in the world went wrong? Two words come to mind—*irrational trepidation*! I've said it before and so has Alan Greenspan (even if not in exactly the same terms); our stock market at 7,632 is irrational trepidation. It's not been a great day, but I'll still see ya at 10,000!

Investment Footnote . . . What actually happened

Never quite made it to 10,000, but we did cross 9,000, closing at 9,181 at year-end.

EMU, Y2K . . . DJIA!

June 1, 1999

Over the past year, investors have been inundated with information and analysis about the two most recognizable acronyms in the investment world today—EMU (European Economic and Monetary Union) and Y2K (the Year 2000 problem). While most of the focus on these two events has been on their immediate or short-term impact, I would like to suggest that we add another acronym, DJIA (Dow Jones Industrial Average) and another focus (long-term instead of short-term). While there can be no denying that EMU and Y2K have been the dominant short-term focuses of our markets, I would like to take a longer-term perspective and take a peek at what both the EMU and Y2K just might mean for my favorite acronym, DJIA!

EMU

On January 1, 1999, the European Economic and Monetary Union (EMU) was launched. Eleven countries are in the initial group that comprises the EMU: Austria, Belgium, Finland, France, Germany, Ireland, Italy, Luxembourg, the Netherlands, Portugal, and Spain. These countries have given up the authority to set monetary policy to a new European central bank. A new currency called the *euro* will also be launched. While most investors are excited about the prospects of the EMU for European stocks, don't forget what it means to my favorite acronym, DJIA.

Major multinational companies in the United States, with major facilities and operations in Europe, will be big winners as well. This is because the creation of the EMU and its new currency, the euro, will cause European currencies to stabilize and strengthen against the U.S. dollar. What this means is that instead of a strong dollar eating into the profits of our U.S. multinational companies because of currency exchange rate transactions, a weaker dollar can actually help create profits due to the positive currency exchange rate. Think about it this way: If the dollar were 5 to 15 percent higher than the French franc, a U.S. multinational company's profits would decrease 5 to 15 percent, given the exchange rate to dollars. If, however, the dollar were 5 to 15 percent lower than the French franc, a U.S. multinational company's profits would actually increase 5 to 15 percent. Wow, EMU is good for DJIA, as well.

Y2K

I don't deny for a minute that Y2K will be a headache. I also don't deny that it will cost significant money. In addition to being a headache and costing significant money, Y2K will actually turn out to be a net positive for DJIA, and here is why.

Companies around the world are using the Y2K challenge as an opportunity not just to upgrade systems, but to replace entire computer systems. These new systems, by the way, are deploying the latest and greatest technology.

One of the reasons companies are making these changes is because of accounting rules. You see, if you spend money to fix your current system, all of that cost must be expensed in the current period. In other words, it's a direct hit to the bottom line against profits. If, however, you put in a brand new system, you can actually capitalize that cost over several years, reducing the negative impact on profits. Remember, when companies put a new computer system in place, it starts a chain reaction. First efficiency improves. After efficiency improves, productivity increases. Once efficiency improves and productivity increases, profits go up. Efficiency plus productivity equals profits. Y2K is also good for DJIA.

In the short run, much attention will continue to be paid to EMU and Y2K. In the long run, however, it's the DJIA!

Investment Footnote . . . What actually happened

I was dead right on this one, as the Dow gained 25.2 percent for the year, closing at 11,497.

"The Woodshop Syndrome"

OCTOBER 1, 1999

Investors have caught the "woodshop syndrome." It begins by going into your woodshop to build a chair. But after you get into your woodshop, you realize that some of your tools need sharpening. So after you sharpen your tools, you decide to keep a log of when you sharpened them. Finally, you develop a simple instrument to assess the sharpness of your tools without running your fingers over them. But by the time you have all your materials ready, you forgot why you originally went into the woodshop.

Investors have caught the woodshop syndrome and, instead of being distracted by tools, investors are getting distracted by interest rates. Will the Fed move rates up? Will it keep them the same? Did you hear what Greenspan said in his speech yesterday? And so on and so on. Investors are so fixated on interest rates that they've forgotten why they're investors. You save and invest to improve your quality of life, and that means a lot of different things to a lot of different people. It may mean sending your child to the college of his or her choice, or retiring at age 60, or buying your dream home. Interest rates have no effect on why you save. Whether rates go up or go down, you still should be saving, so please—don't get caught up in the woodshop syndrome. Now, on to my fourth-quarter investment outlook.

I believe the economy will grow at above-trend growth in the fourth quarter. The GDP should rise more than 3 percent for the fourth quarter thanks to five factors: a reduced trade deficit record, credit card debt paydowns, inventory buildup due to Y2K, personal bankruptcy dramatically falling, and economic measurement changes that virtually guarantee that our economy will be healthy.

Next, I think our equity market will remain strong, and I'll focus on five issues:

1. *Indexes.* Don't get caught up in comparing them with each other, and consider putting some money in small caps.

2. *Technology.* Technology will continue to drive overall markets higher.

3. *Productivity.* U.S. worker productivity can get better, which in turn will move markets higher.

4. *Valuation.* The Fed's focus on valuation will increase volatility.

5. *Global market capitalization.* Global market capitalization is very important, so focus on the six biggest markets.

And I've got five keys to the fourth-quarter bond market:

1. *Labor market.* Even though it's tight, there's no wage inflation thanks to mergers and acquisitions.

2. *The dollar.* The dollar's weakness can actually help.

3. *Gridlock.* In D.C., gridlock could spell market volatility.

4. *Inflation.* Inflation is only caused by too much money chasing too few goods.

5. *Foreign Treasury owners.* Treasury owners outside the United States should spark a bond market rally.

Finally, I'd like to get back to my main "woodshop syndrome" theory by covering two different approaches to accumulate $1 billion: you can either work to accumulate your $1 billion or you can save and invest.

If you decide to work for your $1 billion and not save and invest, here's what you can look forward to. Let's assume you're lucky enough to land a job that pays you a whopping $100 an hour, you don't pay any taxes, and you work 12 hours a day, 365 days a year. Do you have any idea how long you'll have to work to accumulate $1 billion? You'd better sit down for this answer: you'll have to work 2,283 years.

I'm not sure I like this option, so let's try accumulating $1 billion by saving and investing. If you begin with one lonely dollar bill and are somehow able to save and invest so your money compounds and doubles in value each day, how long will it take to accumulate $1 billion? Well, you really should sit down for this one.

If you're able to double your money every day, after starting with $1, you'll accumulate $1,073,741,824 after only 31 days.

Now I know it's unrealistic to think anyone could work 12 hours every day for 2,283 years. And it's equally impossible to find an investment that would double your money daily. What I've just shown you, however, is a great illustration of the power of compounding. When your money can compound, time is really on your side, because you constantly generate new interest on both your original principal and the added interest. So even though I'm not sure any of us will ever get to be worth $1 billion, we can get a whole lot closer to our financial objectives by making sure we save and invest every day.

Have a great day, keep a positive attitude, and please join me in resolving to remain a long-term investor in a short-term world.

Investment Footnote . . . What actually happened

Boy, did the equity markets remain strong as the Dow posted a 25.2 percent gain for the year.

Heads I Win, Tails You Lose!

MARCH 1, 2000

With the recent volatility in our markets, all of a sudden everyone is talking about "heads" and "tails." Not the old favorite coin-flipping game—heads, I win, tails, you lose. But rather, I'm speaking in terms of headwinds (which slow the market) and tailwinds (which speed the market up).

One way to get some clue as to the overall strength or weakness in our markets is to analyze these headwinds and tailwinds to see which are more likely to influence the overall direction of our markets.

HEADWINDS

There are three headwinds attempting to slow our markets—rising interest rates, surging oil prices, and the Dow Jones Industrial Average sell-off.

1. *Rising interest rates.* These tend to have a chilling effect on economic growth. This effect can either be a slowdown in the housing market, a downtick in auto sales (due to the higher cost of auto loans), or an upward ratcheting in adjustable-rate mortgages that takes a bite out of people's disposable income.

2. *Surging oil prices.* These can not only slow the economy but they also have a tremendous impact on investor confidence as well. There is no commodity price that hits home more often than the price of oil. After all, we are reminded every single time we pull up to the gasoline pump. In addition, rising oil prices will push inflation higher, which also serves as a detriment to our stock market.

3. *Dow Jones Industrial Average (DJIA) correction.* Pundits continue to debate the official yardstick for a correction. Is it a 10 percent decline or a 20 percent decline? Regardless, there can be no mistaking that the DJIA was down more than 15 percent from its high this year. The selloff in the DJIA has tremendous psychological impact on investor confidence. It is the most widely watched market indicator around the world. When it's down, so is investor confidence. When investors aren't confident, they don't invest.

TAILWINDS

There are five key tailwinds that are providing the force to push our markets forward—technology revolution, global acceleration, strong economy, strong corporate profits, and fiscal stimulus.

1. *Technology revolution.* Technology will continue to drive our markets. Every single day another product or another strategic alliance is developed that makes someone do

something better, faster, and, more important, cheaper. We can worry about inflation all we want but the fact of the matter is that the most important inflation fighter is not Alan Greenspan, it's technology—and we have not even seen the tip of the iceberg.

2. *Global acceleration.* This will provide a great foundation to our markets. Almost everywhere you look, economies around the world are better off today than they were a year ago. Mexico received a credit rating upgrade from the Wall Street rating agencies. A positive aspect of the rising price of oil is that it enables those oil-dependent economies like Venezuela and Russia to turn things around. And finally, even the European unemployment rate is dramatically falling.

3. *Strong economy.* A strong economy is occurring as a result of a confluence of three factors. First, bonus pay usually hits in the first half of the year. Second, tax refunds are trending higher (given that refunds are viewed as discretionary, taxpayers immediately spend the money). Finally, warm weather across the United States has caused a construction boom and promoted early spring and summer shopping at the mall.

4. *Strong corporate profits.* Strong corporate profits will continue to move the markets higher. That doesn't mean we won't have our high-profile profit disappointments. However, for the first half of the year, more companies will surprise analysts with earnings that are higher, not lower. These earnings are being driven by the strong economies both here and abroad as well as the productivity boom that is making everyone more profitable.

5. *Fiscal stimulus.* Fiscal stimulus always occurs in presidential election years as politicians rush to spend money to convince voters that they are doing something. In this election cycle, fiscal spending is also happening at the state level as well. And don't forget, 800,000 new census takers are being hired. I'm willing to bet that after they get paid, they will spend their money.

Sometimes trying to figure out where the market is heading is almost a coin toss . . . too close to call.

So you toss the coin, and I'll call it in the air—"heads," the market's going up, "tails," the market's going down. If I win, so do you if you stay in the market.

Investment Footnote . . . What actually happened ↓

The tailwinds didn't help as the Dow stayed negative for the year, falling −6.2 percent.

The Latest Back-to-School Sale
AUGUST 17, 2000

Over the years, I have unwillingly become one of the nation's back-to-school sale experts. Observing my two daughters over the years developed my expertise. Marianne, who is beginning her sophomore year in college, and Stephanie, who is beginning her senior year in high school, have taught me valuable lessons about back-to-school shopping. First, no matter how many clothes you have in your closet or how many gadgets and notebooks you have, you still shop the annual back-to-school sale. You may wonder why. The straightforward answer is because things are on sale. In fact, under the guidance of my lovely wife, Cheryl, my daughters have almost convinced me that they are not spending money; they are actually saving me money by shopping the back-to-school sales. Their shopping-the-back-to-school-sale philosophy got me thinking about the latest back-to-school sale; this sale, however, is actually being conducted by the stock market.

Just think for a moment about the unbelievable opportunity investors have today. Our stock market, as measured by the Dow Jones Industrial Average, is actually lower today than when we started the year (in other words, it's on sale!).

But it's not just the fact that it's on sale that's important. Remember, investors had some pretty strong objections to investing back in January. At the top of the list of reasons to stay on the sidelines back then were inflation, interest rate hikes, and the likelihood of political chaos in Mexico because of the election. Well, let's take a quick look to see if those objections still hold any water today.

INFLATION

The most recent inflation release for consumer price edged up just 0.2 percent for July. Meanwhile, on a year-over-year basis, inflation has actually dropped from 3.7 to 3.6 percent. Inflation under 4 percent will not hinder our economy in the long run. It simply looks high when we compare it to our record low inflation levels of the past few years. Even though inflation is higher than last year, the trend is now down and on a historical basis; inflation is still low.

INTEREST RATE HIKES

When we began the year, the Federal Reserve Board had already increased interest rates three times in 1999, and the consensus was that these rate hikes by the Fed would continue all throughout the year 2000. Well, the consensus was half right. It continued through the first half of the year as the Fed increased rates three more times in 2000 (February, March, and May). The new consensus, with which I strongly concur, is that the Fed is done raising interest rates for the remainder of the year. Even more important, the rules of the game have changed. When we began the year, we needed softer economic numbers to prevent a Fed tightening. Now we need stronger economic numbers to produce a tightening; the burden of proof, if you will, has now shifted.

MEXICAN ELECTION

When the year began, most investors were convinced that the upcoming election in Mexico would result in political, social, and, more important, investment chaos in Mexico, rippling all throughout emerging markets. Well, the election occurred without one single hitch. Vincent Fox's stunning upset ends 71 years of the Institutional Revolutionary Party's control of Mexico. This transfer of political power is occurring flawlessly. In addition, Mr. Fox wants to deregulate both the electricity and energy industries as well as continue the deregulation in telecommunications. He will also be aggressive with his tax reform proposals by broadening the tax base (so it becomes less dependent on oil) without increasing taxes. This potential negative event in Mexico has actually turned into a positive investment event.

Two other things have changed dramatically since the beginning of the year: one is Alan Greenspan and the other is Germany.

ALAN GREENSPAN SEES THE LIGHT ON PRODUCTIVITY

When the year began, Alan Greenspan was cautiously advising the market that this productivity boom, fueled by the technology revolution, cannot continue forever. Now Alan Greenspan has reversed himself and feels that this technology revolution can go on for quite some time. Welcome aboard the information superhighway, Mr. Greenspan. Technology is not going away; it is becoming more and more a part of our daily lives, and the more it becomes part of our lives, the more it becomes part of our economy and, in turn, our markets.

When the year began, investors were concerned that the technology sector accounted for 30 percent of our market's total capitalization. I don't understand why that concerns anyone. During the past five years, the tech sector accounted for 26 percent of gross domestic product growth. Shouldn't something that is responsible for so much of the economic growth be rewarded with a higher market capitalization? Think about it. Five years ago tech accounted for only 15 percent of U.S. markets' capitalization. Oh, and by the way, during the five-year period prior to that, technology accounted for 15 percent of gross domestic product growth. Before you know it, CNBC's "Squawk Box" may have to change their "Alan Greenspan briefcase indicator" to the "laptop indicator."

GERMAN TAX REFORM

When the year began, no one thought that Germany would ever be able to pass comprehensive tax reform. Well, guess what? They did, and it will have ripple effects not just all across Europe, but around the globe as well.

Germany cut the highest personal income tax rate from 51 to 42 percent and cut the lowest rate from 23 to 15 percent. It slashed corporate taxes on certain earnings from 40 to 25 percent and on distributed earnings from 40 to 30 percent. In addition, it has eliminated the 50 percent capital gains tax on corporations that own stock in other German corporations. Not only will these changes cause an economic boom, they will fuel a merger boom as well.

All the reasons that investors had for sitting on the sidelines back in January have disappeared. In addition, conditions are actually better now from the investment perspective (thanks to Germany and Alan Greenspan's change of heart on technology) than they were when the year began. And more important, from the Dow Jones Industrial Average perspective, things are still on sale.

Have a great day everyone, keep a positive attitude, and please join me in resolving to remain a long-term investor in a short-term world.

PS: Remember, the blue light special is not just for Kmart; right now it's for our stock market as well.

Investment Footnote . . . What actually happened

The sale just got better, as the Dow fell even more in 2000, another −6.2 percent.

Wall Street's "Axis of Evil"

July 16, 2002

When the history books tell the story of his presidency, possibly the one-liner most people will remember George W. Bush for is his "axis of evil" comment. The president uttered those now famous words on January 29, 2002, during his State of the Union address. The axis of evil that President Bush was referring to was Iraq, Iran, and North Korea.

When the history books tell the story of our stock market this year, they will highlight the stock market's new axis of evil: accounting issues, corporate governance, and dollar weakness. You see, from the U.S. stock market's perspective, the axis of evil didn't even exist until this year. Think about it for a minute.

ACCOUNTING ISSUES

Up until this year, investors around the globe looked up to the United States as the benchmark to strive to copy with regard to accounting and financial engineering. Then along came Enron, followed by Tyco, followed by WorldCom, with too many others in between. And overnight we went from having the world's best accounting industry to the world's worst.

CORPORATE GOVERNANCE

Again, corporations and investors around the globe looked up to corporate America as the model to copy regarding corporate governance. Focused board of directors' committees such as audit and compensation provided assurance that things would never get out of hand. Once again, this time regarding corporate governance, we went from "first" to "worst."

THE DOLLAR

Finally, the dollar—which for the past three years U.S. investors as well as foreign investors thought could only go up—is now, after a period of overvaluation, finally coming back to reality This minor correction could not be coming at a worse point in time for our markets.

As little as a year ago, even the biggest bears on Wall Street were not able to identify this axis of evil that has brought our stock market to its knees.

Are we at the bottom? I don't know. I do know, however, that our stock market always errs at the extremes. The Nasdaq at 5,048 in March 2002 was indeed one extreme. Today, I feel our markets are close to the other extreme. After all, it's not fundamentals that are driving our markets lower anymore, it's fear. Fear of the axis of evil. And this fear is all emotional.

At some point in the not-too-distant future, fundamentals will matter again. I can't wait because I've got a six-pack of issues for investors to focus upon.

1. *Monetary policy.* The drastic sell-off in equities has kept the Federal Reserve Board on the sidelines much longer than the economic consensus regarding rate hikes. The longer they are on the sidelines, the stronger our economy gets, and the better it is for stocks.

2. *Economic growth.* The U.S. economy has bounced back from its short-lived recession more quickly than anyone would have imagined. Add to that the fact that the global economy today is stronger than at anytime in the past three years. This, too, paints a bullish backdrop for stocks.

3. *Valuations.* If you liked stocks anytime in the past three years, how could you not like them today? . . . Many are on sale for half off. They are the same great companies but at half the price—yet no one is interested.

4. *Inflation.* There is no inflation anywhere. Case closed. This, too, is bullish for stocks.

5. *Profit margins.* Profit margins are on the rebound. Both Josh Feinman, Deutsche Asset Management's chief economist, and I continue to believe that a powerful rebound in corporate profits is under way. Josh has insightfully pointed out, and I agree, "Labor markets have eased up and productivity has remained very strong, causing unit labor

costs to come sharply off the boil, alleviating the main source of the margin squeeze of the past few years."

6. *Don't forget demographics.* Demographics haven't changed and they are still in our favor. There are 76 million baby boomers who have to save and invest for their retirement. With money market returns at near zero, our stock market will again become the asset class of choice.

The market will get over its emotional shock from Wall Street's axis of evil. And when it does, your biggest risk is not being in the market.

Investment Footnote . . . What actually happened

The axis of evil won in 2002 as the market collapsed −16.8 percent and the Dow fell all the way down to 8,341.

Looking for Some Real Guidance? . . . Hit the Mute Button

JANUARY 23, 2003

As we find ourselves right in the middle of earnings season (fourth quarter earnings for 2002), investors have to be wondering what is going on. So far 64 percent of the companies posted positive surprises and only 12 percent posted negative surprises. Company after company and industry after industry are posting better-than-expected earnings. In fact, December earnings revisions are significantly better than the average December revisions over the past five years. So if we are having such a good earnings season, why is the market selling off? The reason is that with each positive earnings report, there appears to almost always be "guidance" from the company expressing caution for future earnings.

Earnings are good, guidance is poor, so everyone focuses on the guidance. I believe investors are making a big mistake. You have to look beyond that guidance and see what is motivating it. When you do, I believe you will find two factors.

WAR WITH IRAQ

The first is the uncertainty regarding the war with Iraq. This is the biggest wild card of all. Forget deflation or inflation or even interest rates, for that matter. The war with Iraq transcends everything else. It is the greatest unknown in the marketplace. You could do everything right with running your company, and a war with Iraq could make everything look bad. Facing such unbelievable uncertainty, why would you provide positive guidance? The market gives you no chance to make excuses. If you give positive guidance regarding your company's earnings and it doesn't come to pass, you don't get to make excuses even if they are good ones, such as . . . "We were on target to meet or exceed all of our forecasts until war broke out." To the market, that is like saying, "The dog ate my homework." Even if it is true, it doesn't matter. In many ways, we ought to be questioning the few companies giving positive guidance instead of the majority of companies signaling caution.

NO ROOM FOR ERROR

The second reason for this guidance is that the market is priced for perfection. There is no room for even the smallest margin of error. Miss your company's earnings by one penny and you could find your stock down 20 percent, losing hundreds of millions of dollars in hours. Is it really worth the risk? I don't think so. In the go-go days of the late nineties, everyone was hyping their stock. Today, I think that we have a new world order in investing . . . it is called "under-promise and over-deliver." Savvy investors will now have to realize that they may need to begin discounting all of the doom and gloom that they are hearing from corporate America.

A BIG MAC AND A COKE!

One final note that may be the most positive trend I have seen in the markets for 20 years is something that Coke and McDonald's now have in common. Neither company will provide forecasts for quarterly or annual earnings. Coke was first and now McDonald's new chairman and CEO, Jim Cantalupo, joined the club. McDonald's will gauge its success based on operations and sales, not on this ill-conceived "beat the street" mentality. Deutsche Asset Management's CEO of asset management, Tom Hughes, actually pointed out to me months ago, when we were discussing the problems in corporate America, that the one common thread he saw between the Enrons and WorldComs of the world was their desire to hit the quarterly earnings number at any cost. And, sad to say, that cost ended up being bankruptcy, loss of lifelong retirement savings, and jail time.

Maybe at long last we have turned the corner. I will call it the "Hughes factor" (after Deutsche Asset Management's chairman, Tom Hughes). The more companies that begin focusing on the long-term prospects, the better off we will all be. In the interim, the next time you are listening to guidance on CNBC, simply hit the mute button . . . you will be a better investor for it. Unless, of course, I'm on CNBC; in that case, mute the next guy.

Investment Footnote . . . What actually happened

I was right, as the Dow climbed 25.3 percent in 2003.

The Good, the Bad, and the Ugly

FEBRUARY 10, 2003

This weekend, when my wife and I were channel surfing, one of the movies that flashed by was Sergio Leone's classic, *The Good, the Bad, and the Ugly,* starring Clint Eastwood. In that brief moment,

I thought to myself, now there's a title that accurately reflects our stock market today . . . the Good . . . the Bad . . . and the Ugly. Even though I don't have my cowboy hat on, let me take a shot at putting this market in perspective for you, starting with the ugly.

THE UGLY: GEOPOLITICAL UNCERTAINTY AND THE RISING PRICE OF OIL

Clearly there are two ugly pressures currently weighing on our markets. The first is the geopolitical uncertainty regarding war with Iraq. This continues to play out like a soap opera with Germany and France on one side . . . Russia's Putin trying to decide which side to be on . . . and, through it all, everyone is really focused on Arms Inspector Hans Blix and what he thinks. Add to the mix the potential threat of terrorist acts at home, and you can see why this is truly ugly for our markets to deal with. The second ugly thing is the skyrocketing price of oil. The price of oil has jumped for two reasons: the first is the above-mentioned geopolitical uncertainty in Iraq, and the second is the oil shortage caused by Venezuela's general strike. With oil at $35 a barrel, don't underestimate how ugly a drag this is on our economy. Oil prices have almost doubled in the past year from $18 per barrel to $35 a barrel. A quick rule of thumb based on historical oil usage theorizes that for every $1 rise in the price of oil, the cost of U.S. energy for businesses and consumers increases by $7 billion. Thus, the recent $17 spike is costing us a whopping $119 billion.

THE BAD: CORPORATE GOVERNANCE AND PENSION EXPENSES

Let's move away from the ugly and look at what bad things are weighing on our markets, namely, corporate governance and pension expenses. Let's start with corporate governance. The memories are still too fresh in investors' minds to forget about Enron and WorldCom and Arthur Andersen. We are making tremendous progress in clearing up our corporate governance mess, especially fueled by changes to accounting oversight and the fact that financial statements now have to be certified under oath. Also, don't forget the parade of companies that began with Coca-Cola Company, which refuses to give earnings guidance and is forcing investors to focus on the long run. The problem, however, is that we need more time. The only thing that will heal this deep wound that hit investors in the pocketbook is time.

The second bad pressure weighing on our market is *increased pension expenses*. You don't have to be an analyst to figure this one out. After three straight down years in our stock market, many pension plans are now underfunded due to the negative stock market returns. As if things aren't bad enough, now businesses have to come up with money to resolve their pension-funding shortfalls, as well.

THE GOOD: POLICY AND PROFITS

I am glad we are done with the bad and the ugly—let's get on to what's good about our markets. There are two things; the first is *policy*. Both monetary policy and fiscal policy could not be more conducive to equity markets. Monetary policy has reduced interest rates so that money is virtually free—witness the ongoing explosion of mortgage refinancing. And fiscal policy has as its cornerstone proposals to encourage people to save and invest—from the elimination of double taxation of dividends, to the establishment of lifetime savings accounts.

The second thing that is good is *profits*. Fourth quarter profits are running 16 percent ahead of fourth quarter profits from a year ago. Remember, first profits, then capital spending, then employment—it all starts with profits.

THE SHOOT-OUT

Let's close this commentary with a good old-fashioned, Clint Eastwood-style shoot-out between the good, the bad, and the ugly to see who is left standing.

Let's end where we began, with the ugly pressures on our market. Remember that these geopolitical uncertainties will be resolved and will become a distant memory. And when they are, the second ugly pressure on our markets, the rising price of oil, will quickly fall and serve as one more tax cut for consumers. All right, I shot down the uglies—bring on the bad. Corporate governance has already turned the corner—companies are more focused on shareholder values today than ever before. I believe the greed, deception, and "hit the numbers at all costs" mentality are a thing of the past, as well. Regarding the other bad pressure, rising pension costs: as our market turns, which it will, the market will help to quickly close that pension liability gap. All right, I shot down those bad pressures as well. Understand that the good things in our market are not just going to suddenly go away. Good monetary and fiscal policy lay a groundwork for years to come in our markets. And profits have turned and will continue to improve, fueled by productivity gains and cost-cutting.

While the bad and ugly pressures may seem like a pretty dominant force, when the dust settles, it's the good that will be left standing. Monetary and fiscal policy, as well as profits, just can't be beaten, no matter how fast a draw you have.

Say, can someone pass me a cowboy hat?

Investment Footnote . . . What actually happened

I was right. The Dow rebounded to 10,453, a 25.3 percent gain. ↑

I'm Still Shopping . . . How about You?
FEBRUARY 18, 2003

For the past three years, all the bears on Wall Street have been predicting that the consumer has finally run out of steam. In fact, the bears have been saying that for at least the past 10 years; it's just that in the past three years they have been screaming it!

The reason they have been screaming it over the past three years is that they think the bear market means that consumer debt is rising and the stock market crash has taken a big bite out of consumers' net worth, as well. The reason consumers are so important is that they account for two-thirds of our economy; so it's pretty clear: as the consumer goes, so goes our economy, and as our economy goes, so goes our market. While this topic has been hotly debated in recent years, I'm about to end the debate. Consumer debt is not rising and the market correction has not taken a big bite out of consumers' net worth.

As proof, I call my star witness, none other than the Federal Reserve Board. The Federal Reserve Board just released its "2001 Survey of Consumer Finances." This survey is conducted every three years based on over 4,000 individual interviews. What's especially interesting in the 2001 survey is that all 4,449 households were interviewed between May and December 2001, right at the heart of the technology bubble burst, market crash, and economic recession.

Here are the results. These aren't guesses, forecasts, or assumptions; they are simply the facts.

NET WORTH

The survey says "median" household net worth in the 1998 survey, which was the last year the survey was taken, was $78,000. In the 2001 survey that was just released, it increased to $86,100. That's not worse off, that's better. Back in 1998, the "mean" household net worth was $307,400. In the new survey, it's $395,500. Again, that's not less net worth, that's more!

TOO MUCH DEBT

Let's move on to this so-called debt burden . . . the survey really buries this myth. First, in 1998, debt as a percentage of total assets stood at 14.3 percent. In 2001, that number dropped to 12.1 percent. This means the consumer is actually better off. Next, how about the ratios of debt payments to family income? In 1998 it stood at 14.4 percent.

In the current survey it dropped to 12.5 percent, which again means the consumer is better off. Finally, how about this one to quiet those bears? In 1998, 8.1 percent of families surveyed had debt payments past due 60 days or more. In the 2001 survey that number dropped down to 7.0 percent, which, one more time, means the consumer is actually better off, not worse off.

While this debate obviously will continue, may I suggest you quit listening to the bears and, if you want, you can quit listening to the bulls, as well. However, when the Federal Reserve Board speaks, especially with their Survey of Consumer Finances, everybody better listen!

DAYTONA 500 MARKET INDICATOR

In closing, I have one additional indicator I want to bring to your attention and that is the "Daytona 500 indicator." My good friend and colleague (and boss), Leo Grohowski, who is the chief investment officer for Deutsche Asset Management in the Americas, brought this one to my attention. You may recall in my February 3, 2003, market commentary I talked about the "January effect," the "Super Bowl effect," and the "Rule of 3" (i.e., third year of a presidential term). Now, thanks to Leo, we have the Daytona 500 indicator. Here's how it works. The Dow Jones Industrial Average (DJIA) returns were analyzed between 1959 and 2002, based upon what make of car won the Daytona 500. For example, the average return for the DJIA when a Dodge won the Daytona 500 was −17 percent, and, for example, the average return for the DJIA when a Pontiac won the Daytona 500 was +6.3 percent. There are only two makes of cars that can boost positive double-digit returns for the DJIA when they win the Daytona 500: Chevrolet and Buick. The reason I reference the importance of double-digit returns is that in my January 2, 2003, market commentary, I forecasted double-digit returns for the DJIA.

Well, the Daytona 500 was run this past Sunday, February 16, 2003, and the winner was Michael Waltrip. More important, from my perspective, guess what make of car he drove? You guessed it . . . a Chevrolet. Average return for the DJIA when a Chevrolet wins the Daytona 500 is +13.3 percent. Last time I checked, that was double digits!

Ladies and Gentlemen, start your investment engines.

Investment Footnote . . . What actually happened

The Dow did indeed post double-digit returns in 2003, gaining 25.3 percent.

It's Time to Double Up!

May 15, 2003

I never was very good at blackjack, so I am not sure if you are actually supposed to double up or double down when you know that you have just been dealt a winning hand. I do know something about recognizing winning hands in the markets, however, and we are clearly experiencing a double up.

STOCKS AND BONDS TOGETHER

A landmark change has occurred that is extremely positive for all investors. Stocks and bonds are rallying together. It just doesn't get any better than that. Bond yields have actually declined as the stock markets went up in price. With bond yields falling, that means bond prices are rising at the same time as stock prices climb higher. What had been happening prior to this landmark change is that each and every time stocks would rally, bond yields would rise, meaning bond prices fell. These rising bond yields increased the likelihood that any recovery would be quickly put on hold by these higher bond yields. It also tends to be a signal that the Federal Reserve Board may soon raise interest rates as well.

But now we have stocks and bonds going up together. Stocks and bonds can rally together only when the market has been dealt a hand that shows economic growth is not going to cause inflation to rise; thus, the Federal Reserve Board will not be raising rates anytime soon. In fact, the next move will most likely be down, not up. This is exactly the hand the market was hoping for . . . both stocks and bonds going up together.

How did we get dealt such a great hand? The market drew five cards:

1. MONETARY POLICY

The first card is monetary policy. Not only are interest rates at record lows here in the United States, central bank rates all around the world are either at or near record low levels as well. And the rate cuts are not stopping anytime soon. Based on the negative gross domestic product number released by Germany today, the German economy has had back-to-back quarters of negative growth. In economic circles that is what we call a recession. Remember, Germany is the largest economy in the European Monetary Union, so I look for the European Central Bank to cut rates soon.

2. FISCAL POLICY

The second card is fiscal policy. Even if absolutely nothing happens in Washington regarding the president's tax cut plan, we still have a $1.1 trillion tax cut coming. Keep in mind, the president's current plan is talking billions . . . I am talking trillions. Investors forget that the 2001 tax cuts were phased in over 11 years. We still have a whopping $1.1 trillion in tax cuts coming our way. Add to that the current tax cut proposal, which ranges from another $200 to $600 billion. If we simply split the difference and agree on $400 billion and add that to the $1.1 trillion already coming, that means we have a $1.5 trillion tax cut to support our markets.

3. MORTGAGE RATES

The third card is mortgage rates. The benchmark 30-year fixed mortgage rates have dropped to another all-time record low level. The collapse of mortgage rates to an even lower level means that two things will happen: first, new mortgage applications will continue to flood the market, and second, we will witness another round of mortgage refinancing.

4. OIL PRICES

The fourth card is oil prices. Oil prices have fallen almost 33 percent from their prewar peak. This is better than any tax cut Washington could give us. Think about it . . . no one needs to vote for it and consumers don't have to wait to file any tax forms; you simply drive up to the gas pump and get your tax cut immediately.

5. THE DOLLAR

The fifth and final card is the falling dollar. The decline in the value of the U.S. dollar means that all of our products are now cheaper around the world. On a trade-weighted basis, our dollar is down almost 15 percent. A 10 percent decline in the value of the dollar on a trade-weighted basis is the same as a 1 percent interest rate cut form the Federal Reserve Board.

In closing, I might not be any good at blackjack, but I love the hand the stock and bond markets have just been dealt. Monetary policy, fiscal policy, mortgage rates, oil prices, and the dollar—what a great time to double up.

Investment Footnote . . . What actually happened

I was so right, as the Dow continued to soar in 2003, gaining 25.3 percent.

Leadership Matters!

JUNE 12, 2003

In all walks of life, in all aspects of life, leadership matters. That is true for investing as well. There is currently a new wave of leadership coming from three different fronts to provide support for our stock market.

PUBLIC POLICY LEADERSHIP

Everywhere you look in Washington, D.C., we have renewed public policy leadership to support our markets—from the Federal Reserve Board, to the U.S. Treasury Department, and to the White House and Congress. Think about it for a minute. Over the past year and a half the Federal Reserve Board's leadership has embarked on one of the most aggressive interest rate–cutting cycles in its history.

Furthermore, the Fed is signaling to the markets that it is not done yet. I think that we could easily see another 75- to 100-basis-point cut by the end of this calendar year. From the U.S. Treasury Department leadership we have support for a weaker dollar. The weaker U.S. dollar puts extra political pressure on foreign governments to cut their interest rates in order to support their export business, which is hurt by our weak dollar. (Witness the European Central Bank's cut last week.) The more rate cuts that occur around the globe, the stronger the global economy and the stronger our market—the largest market in the global economy. Finally, from the White House and Congress we have the recent Tax Relief Act, which supports all aspects of our markets. For the value investor, dividend taxes were slashed from 38.6 to 15 percent. Value investors typically invest in companies that pay a dividend. Now those dividends will be more attractive because of the lower 15 percent tax rate. For the growth investor, long-term capital gains taxes were cut from 20 to 15 percent. Growth investors typically invest in companies that return a capital gain. Those capital gains are now worth more because they are now taxed at only 15 percent as opposed to the

214 A Bull for All Seasons

previous 20 percent. Thus, everywhere you look in Washington, D.C., there is public policy leadership to support our market.

CORPORATE LEADERSHIP

The second area of leadership is corporate leadership. Don't listen to what corporate executives say; watch what they do—especially regarding their own company stock, which they will always know more about than any of us ever will. As a general rule of thumb, corporate executive "insiders" typically sell at twice their rate of buying. Anything below that ratio is considered bullish. Much of the selling is for diversification and tax reasons. Anyway, in 2001 and 2002, corporate insiders sold four times more of their company stock than they bought. This is certainly a bearish sign, especially when you consider that in 1999 and 2000 they were actually net buyers. In other words, they bought more than they sold. What is this insider selling by corporate leadership telling us? It has dropped below twice the rate of buying, which is extremely bullish. The leadership in corporate America is trying to tell us that they like what they see, especially with regard to the prospects for their own companies.

STOCK MARKET SECTOR LEADERSHIP

The third and final area is stock market sector leadership. The top 25 companies of the Standard & Poor's 500 index comprise almost one-half of the market value of that index. Thus, it is important to see what sectors are represented in those top 25 companies. Said another way, where is the sector leadership coming from? At the peak of our market in March of 2000, two-thirds of the top 25 companies in the S&P 500 were from only two sectors—information technology and telecommunications. Remember, there are 10 different sectors that comprise the S&P 500. Only two of those sectors comprised two-thirds of the top 25 companies, which, in turn, comprised half of the market value. How did we not see this narrow sector leadership as a problem? Today that leadership is extremely diversified. Of the top 25 companies, two-thirds are now covered by four sectors with almost equal influence: health care, information technology, consumer discretionary, and consumer staples. What do you think is better stock market leadership, two sectors or four sectors? The leadership in our market today is much more diversified, and that can be extremely positive both on the upside and the downside.

In closing, everywhere we look, leadership is rising to support our stock market—from public policy leadership to corporate leadership to stock market sector leadership. And remember, as Rev. Theodore M. Hesburgh, C.S.C., president emeritus of the University of Notre Dame, once said: "The very essence of leadership is that you have to have vision." All of this leadership is giving me a vision. I'll see ya at 10,000!

Investment Footnote . . . What actually happened

I was right, as the Dow broke 10,000 in 2003, closing the year at 10,453.

The Next "Big" Thing!
OCTOBER 8, 2003

Technology analysts coined the phrase "the next big thing" as their rallying cry while they frantically searched for the next "big" theme after wireless communication and the Internet. The debate still rages on, regarding what will be the next big thing for the technology sector. I know what the next big thing will be for our overall market—and it is BIG! That's the answer: *big*, as in big companies, as in large capitalized stocks. I believe large-cap stocks will begin to outperform the overall market because of five unrelated factors: a weaker dollar, cheaper funding, leverage distribution, new money flows, and higher dividend yields.

WEAKER DOLLAR

First, a weaker U.S. dollar, which we are currently experiencing, actually helps large-cap stocks. The reason is that many large-cap companies are also multinational corporations. These multinational, large-cap stocks have significant foreign exposure. When the dollar weakens, that foreign exposure is worth more, as foreign sales and profits are translated against a weaker U.S. dollar. Thus, profits can rise even with no pickup in revenues or productivity simply because of the positive currency transaction.

CHEAPER FUNDING

The second factor is that these companies have access to cheaper funding sources. This is one of the places where the "scale" of a large-cap company comes into play. When you are borrowing hundreds of millions of dollars as opposed to a few million, you obtain a cheaper rate from the banks. (Banks always want to take care of their biggest and best customers, which are large corporations.) Another reason large-cap companies have access to cheaper funding is that they have large and diversified balance sheets with lots and lots of assets—the same assets that are important when viewed as possible collateral for any funding.

LEVERAGE DISTRIBUTION

The third factor is that these large-cap companies can leverage distribution. This is another example of how "scale" plays into favor for large-cap stocks. Because of their sheer size and importance in any wholesale or retail distribution channel that they are in, they can constantly go back to their various vendors and continue to "squeeze" costs—and, in turn, more savings—out of their distribution channels. Large companies can do this because they are such an important client. Because of their scale, vendors tend to give them anything they want and make up for it in their dealings with other companies. In distribution, size really does matter.

NEW MONEY FLOWS

The fourth factor is all the money still sitting on the sidelines because investors are afraid to get back into the market. There are trillions of dollars today in money market accounts actually earning "real" negative returns—"real" meaning after you subtract taxes and inflation from your less than one-half percent yield. Anyway, as this money looks for a new home in the equity market, I believe it will find it in the large-cap arena. Remember, these are the bluest of the "blue chip" companies, names that investors on the sidelines have grown up with and have known their entire investing lives. These large-cap stocks are also the most liquid, as they are actively traded daily around the world. When nervous investors get back into stocks, they will be looking at the most liquid securities, and names that they recognize. In other words, they will rotate out of negative "real" returns on money markets and into large-cap stocks.

HIGHER DIVIDEND YIELDS

Fifth, and finally, large-cap stocks offer higher dividend yields. This stands to reason because these companies are more established and have long track records to follow, both financially and with regard to their dividend history. Investors will finally catch on that maybe the "biggest" thing that has happened in Washington, D.C., in the past 50 years was the dramatic slashing of dividend taxes from 38.6 to 15 percent. It's not often that we cut taxes by over 60 percent! That is really BIG. And as investors finally understand this dramatic shift, they will be looking for the highest dividend-paying stocks. And we know where they will find them: in large-cap stocks.

The next "BIG" thing is here—overweight large-cap stocks now!

Investment Footnote . . . What actually happened

I really missed this one, as the big story was all about small caps. While the S&P 500 returned 26.4 percent, the S&P 600 (Small-Cap Index) posted a 37.5 percent return and the Russell 2000 Small-Cap Index surged 45.4 percent. Maybe it is a "small" world after all.

The New "Piece" Dividend

OCTOBER 20, 2003

As I am driving by the White House, the Capitol, and various other monuments here in Washington, D.C., my mind wanders to the "peace" dividend. The peace dividend, spelled P-E-A-C-E, was a term coined in Washington political circles after World War II to describe the money that did not have to be spent on war. The logic went like this: if there was peace then we didn't need to replenish bombs or missiles and so this unspent money, this so-called peace dividend, could be spent elsewhere on education, social, or business initiatives.

Well, as I travel around the Washington, D.C., area, I can tell you that no one is talking about a peace dividend while our country continues to develop an exit strategy from the war with Iraq. Any strategy will likely involve even more money, not less. There will probably be no peace dividend.

THE NEW PEACE DIVIDEND

Then it suddenly hit me. There is a new peace dividend—spelled P-I-E-C-E—as in get a piece of earnings with a dividend. And it happened right here in Washington, D.C., with the Jobs and Growth Tax Relief Reconciliation Act, which drastically lowered the taxation of corporate dividends on individuals from 38.6 to 15 percent. That is a 62 percent tax break. Here is what President George W. Bush had to say about it: "The reduced tax rate on dividends will encourage more companies to pay dividends."

IT STARTS WITH EARNINGS

With all of this new excitement about dividends, we cannot forget to focus on earnings. You see, dividends are paid out of earnings. You can't simply buy a stock for the dividend. You better make sure that the company has enough earnings to cover its projected dividend. Thus, from an investment strategy standpoint, if you are interested in dividends you better be interested in earnings first. So, what are earnings currently telling us? Two things: First, earnings estimates are typically revised downward during pre-announcement earnings season. Companies then beat these reduced expectations. But in the third quarter, earnings expectations never declined. In fact, they actually went up a little. Second, company after company is beating those higher earnings expectations. As the week begins, companies meeting or beating expectations, as opposed to failing to meet expectations, are currently running seven to one. That is outstanding. Think about it. For every company that disappoints, we have seven that do not! This suggests that earnings will be even stronger than the current Wall Street consensus, which is 17 percent. That means there is a whole lot of cash to either establish dividends or increase existing dividends.

WATCH THE S&P 500 PAYOUT RATIO

Probably the single best way to monitor where this dividend shift is going is to focus on the Standard & Poor's 500 dividend payout ratio. The S&P 500 dividend payout ratio is measured as dividends per share divided by earnings per share. The dividend payout ratio currently stands at only 31 percent. The historic average since the end of World War II, when the original peace dividend was coined, has been 51 percent. In the early 1960s, this ratio peaked above 70 percent. With the peak since World War II above 70 percent and the average at 51 percent, the fact that we are currently sitting at only 31 percent suggests that companies have plenty of room to either boost or establish dividends.

FOLLOW THE LEADER

In closing, don't forget to follow the leader. Earnings always lead dividends. Thus, this great acceleration in earnings in the third quarter means that dividends should continue to accelerate as well. Speaking of leaders, as I am now squarely in front of the White House, I want to close with a quote from our leader, President George W. Bush: "It's hard to pay dividends unless you've actually got cash flow. The days when people could say invest with me because the sky's the limit will be changed by dividend policy."

Make sure you get a piece of earnings with this new PIECE dividend program. And, as our thoughts and prayers continue to be with our troops, hopefully we can develop a lasting road to peace there as well. When we do, let's spend that entire PEACE dividend on tax cuts and take the dividend tax rate down from 15 to 0 percent. Then you will wish you had a PIECE of the PEACE dividend.

God Bless America!

Investment Footnote . . . What actually happened ↑

I was dead right on this call since value, as measured by S&P 500/CitiGroup Value Index, gained 29 percent while growth, as measured by the S&P 500 Growth Index, only gained 23.9 percent. Value wins.

Indicator Overload

FEBRUARY 6, 2004

Have you ever noticed how investors search tirelessly for that one "magic" indicator that can predict where the equity market is heading in any given year? At the beginning of each year the two most popular indicators are the "January effect" and the "Super Bowl effect." Let's see if either one of those popular indicators give us a reliable clue to where our equity market is headed this year.

JANUARY EFFECT

Let's begin with the January effect. The January effect is based on the principle that as January goes, so goes the rest of the year. While there are numerous ways to slice, dice, and present the January effect, the one that I like the best is the simplest: if January is positive, the year will be positive; if January is negative, the year will be negative. Using that simple approach, the January effect has correctly predicted the direction of the market, as measured by the S&P 500 Index, 78 percent of the time over the past 50 years—39 of 50. Well, the S&P 500 Index ended January up +1.73 percent. So, if historically there is a 78 percent likelihood that the market will close the year positive as well, the January effect may be good news for the equity markets this year.

SUPER BOWL EFFECT

Now, let's move on and see what kind of indicator we get from the Super Bowl. The Super Bowl effect suggests that, depending on whether the National Football Conference (NFC) or the American Football Conference (AFC) wins, you will have a pretty good insight into where the equity markets will end up. In fact, for the first 37 Super Bowls (this year's Super Bowl was number 38), the American Football Conference team has won the Super Bowl 16 times. And of those 16 years, the equity markets ended the year with a positive return only 56 percent of the time (9 of 16). Meanwhile, the National Football Conference champion has won the Super Bowl 21 years, and 90 percent of the time (19 of 21) the year ended positive for the equity market. Thus, from an investor's perspective, if you believe in the Super Bowl effect, you want an NFC team to win the Super Bowl. And this year they almost did—until a last-second field goal made the New England Patriots the 2004 Super Bowl Champions. Sorry to say, New England is from the American Football Conference. Thus, the so-called Super Bowl effect tells us that there is only a 56 percent chance that the equity markets will end the year with a positive return. So this year, the Super Bowl effect is certainly a negative indicator for our markets. Let's see: that's one negative indicator and one positive indicator for our markets, so we can't stop now.

SANTA CLAUS EFFECT

What does the Santa Claus effect show us? The Santa Claus effect goes like this: For any December when the S&P 500 is up 3 percent or more (meaning Santa Claus was good to investors), the first six months of the following year begin with a bang. Well, this past December the S&P 500 gained more than 3 percent. That has only happened 16 times in the entire history of the S&P 500, and when it did, 87 percent of the time the first six months of the following year started strong with an average double-digit gain of 11.4 percent. If you believe in the Santa Claus effect, it is telling you that there is an 87 percent likelihood that the S&P 500 will be up 11.4 percent by midyear. That is certainly a positive indicator for our market. So let's see now: that's two positive indicators and one negative. But I am not stopping now. I'm on a roll. Don't forget my Election effect.

ELECTION EFFECT

The Election effect goes like this: During the past 60 years there have been nine occasions when in the fourth year of a presidential term an incumbent ran for reelection. Each and every time a whopping 100 percent of the total return for the S&P 500 Index was positive. The average total return was 16.25 percent. Don't forget: 2004 is the fourth year of a presidential term with incumbent George W. Bush running for reelection. If you believe (like I do) in the Election effect, this is certainly a positive.

I could go on and on and on. But instead, I am going to share with you my secret indicator, which I believe has the greatest correlation to predict the direction of our markets. Are you ready? Here it is:

I   is for Interest rates at 40 year lows.

N is for No inflation concerns.

D is for Dividend tax cuts.

I   is for Improving, as in improving job market (we've had positive growth for five consecutive months).

C is for Capital gains tax cuts.

A is for Aggressive cost-cutting by corporate America to improve the bottom line.

T is for Top-line revenue growth.

O is for the Orderly decline of the dollar, which is helping fuel large-cap multinational companies.

R is for Record productivity that continues at a torrid pace.

Put them all together and they spell INDICATOR. And to me they spell another strong and positive year for our equity markets.

Investment Footnote . . . What actually happened

I was right. The Dow gained 3.1 percent for the year.

Show Me the Money

JUNE 16, 2004

Maybe one of the most remembered one-liners from modern movies is from *Jerry McGuire*, when Cuba Gooding, Jr., utters that now famous line to Tom Cruise —"Show me the money." Well, in my recent travels across the United States, I have had advisors and clients utter that same line to me, but with a twist: "Show me the money in financials." The reason for this twist is that when the year began, one of my Top Ten Investment Themes was the financial services sector. Many clients and advisors are now concerned that with the expected rise in interest rates by the Federal Reserve Board, I may be changing my mind about financials. I was bullish on financials when the year began, and I am actually even more bullish today. I would encourage you to focus on the following three issues—interest rates, earnings, and wealth—to get a better perspective on why I still believe the financial services sector is positioned to outperform the overall market for 2004. Before I briefly explore these three issues, I want to give you a benchmark of where we are currently.

SECTOR BENCHMARK

Through the first five months of this year, of the 10 sectors that comprise the S&P 500, seven sectors actually posted positive returns through the end of May. And guess what? The financial services sector was one of the seven that posted positive returns. Looking a little closer at the real benchmark, the S&P 500 was up 0.8 percent through the first five months of the year. Only four of the ten sectors that comprise the S&P 500 beat that benchmark. And I'll bet you've guessed by now that the financial services sector was one of the four sectors that outperformed the overall market, even though it was by a very narrow margin. It's important to realize that things are not as bad as they may seem in the financial services sector. Enough about looking backward. Let's look forward and focus on the three issues that I believe paint a bullish picture for the financial services sector.

INTEREST RATES

Let's start with interest rates, where the market consensus is that as soon as they move higher, financial services stocks will move lower. Boy, it would be nice if things were that simple, but they are not. Here are the plain facts. On two occasions in the past two decades (once in 1983 and once in 1994), 12 months following an initial Federal Reserve Board tightening, the financial services sector was down by nearly double digits: −9.5 percent and −9.8 percent. Before you jump to any conclusions, let me give you the rest of the story. You see, there were two other occasions, also in the past two decades, when the Federal Reserve Board began raising interest rates—once in 1988 and again in 1999. On both of those occasions, 12 months following the initial Federal Reserve Board rate hike, the financial services sector was actually up a whopping double digit 16.3 percent! In other words, recent history shows us that just because rates are going up doesn't mean financial services stocks are going down.

EARNINGS

Next, let's look at earnings, because, as I have said many times before, at the end of the day it all comes down to one thing: earnings. According to First Call, the 2004 consensus earnings estimate for the financial services sector when the year began on January 1,

2004, was 10.7 percent. Today, the First Call 2004 consensus earnings estimate for the financial services sector is 15.9 percent. That's a 5.2 percent positive swing in consensus earnings. In other words, the financial services sector is trying to "show you the money."

WEALTH EFFECT

Let's move on to the third and final issue, the Wealth effect. Financial services companies tend to do well when their clients are wealthy. In other words, wealthy clients have more opportunities to save and invest. While there is a great misconception in the media about the U.S. investor being in too much debt, I just give you the facts and let them speak for themselves. In the recently published (first quarter, 2004) Federal Reserve Board's "Flow of Funds" report, which, by the way, is the official scorekeeper of household net worth, it was reported that household net worth is now at the highest level ever! That's right. Not only has household net worth completely recovered from the stock market crash of 2000–2002, but it has blown right by that record to set a new all-time high.

Let me give you a closer peek behind these numbers, along with some historical perspective. Net worth is a pretty simple concept. All you do is subtract your liabilities from your assets and what is left is your net worth, or, in the case of the flow of funds report, a nation's net worth.

In the first quarter of 1995, household net worth stood at $25.4 trillion. Back then, assets were $30.1 trillion minus liabilities of $4.8 trillion, getting to the bottom line household net worth of $25.4 trillion. Fast forward to the first quarter of 2004 and household net worth currently stands at $45.2 trillion. That's a $20 trillion increase in less than 10 years. Currently households have $55 trillion in assets, minus $9.8 trillion in liabilities, which again gets us to the bottom line $45.2 trillion net worth number. In case you need more proof why this is bullish for financial services, all you have to do is peek at where the $55 trillion of assets are. Stocks and bonds account for $29.3 trillion, real estate accounts for $20.1 trillion, and cash then remains at $5.5 trillion. As that money is put in motion, the financial services sector stands to be one of the clear winners.

Let's end where we began. If you want someone to show you the money, you need look no further than the financial services sector.

> **Investment Footnote . . . What actually happened** ↑
>
> Financials didn't let me down, posting a 3.7 percent gain for the year.

Cash Is King—Again

July 19, 2004

If I had but one investment principle to live by, that principle would be "cash is king." All else being equal, always go where the cash is. Would you really expect anything different from someone who wrote a book entitled *Where the Money I$*?

Through all the negative news and headlines regarding the high price of oil, rising interest rates, terrorism, and ongoing concerns about Iraq (not to mention the uncertainty of the upcoming presidential election), something amazing is happening. There is cash everywhere you look—from consumers to governments to corporations. Let's briefly look at all three, starting with consumers.

CONSUMER CASH

While I touched on this in a prior commentary, it is so important that I think we need to look at it again. Currently, consumers hold $5.6 trillion in cash. Their balance sheets simply could not be stronger. At the end of the first quarter of this year, consumer net worth stood at $45.2 trillion. Consumers currently have $55 trillion in assets minus $9.8 trillion in liabilities, which bring us to the $45.2 trillion net worth figure. But I think the real story here is where that $55 trillion of assets is.

Stocks and bonds account for $29.3 trillion, $20.1 trillion is in real estate, and the remaining $5.6 trillion is in cash. I think we can make the case for adding the stocks and bonds number of $29.3 trillion (since it can quickly be turned to cash with as little as a phone call) to the actual cash number of $5.6 trillion. This shows us that the consumer actually controls almost $35 trillion in cash. As a frame of reference, that figure is three times larger than our entire U.S. economy. It's also three times larger than the entire U.S. stock market. The next time you hear someone talk about how "bad off" the poor consumer is, simply remember the $35 trillion in cash consumers control. All of a sudden they don't look so bad.

GOVERNMENT CASH

Two years ago, in June 2002, combined state and local operating budgets were running an almost $50 billion deficit. Today, they are posting a $36 trillion surplus. This is the most dramatic swing from deficit to surplus in the past 50 years. It works every time. A strong economy always will improve government cash flow at both the federal level and the state and local levels as we stuff the government coffers with tax receipts.

CORPORATE CASH

Having touched upon consumer cash and government cash, let's move on to the third and most important focus—corporate cash.

I measure corporate cash by something that is called the *business funding gap*. The business funding gap is the difference between corporate cash flow and capital spending. This business fund gap has seen the most dramatic change in the past 100 years, moving from a massive deficit to a surplus. And this dramatic improvement means corporations are flush with cash.

In March 2000, when our markets peaked, the business funding gap was in a deficit of $334.6 billion. Today it is in surplus of $62.8 billion. However, the story doesn't stop there. There are only five uses for all of that cash, and all five are extremely bullish for our markets. First, corporations can use the cash to increase capital spending, which would be bullish for our stock market. Second, they can use the cash to buy back shares of their stock, which would also be bullish for the stock market. Third, they can use the cash to pay down debt, which would be bullish for the stock market, as well. Fourth, they can use the cash to make acquisitions, which would fuel the merger and acquisition boom, which would also be bullish for the stock market. Fifth, and finally, they could do what I would do, which is to boost dividend payouts. This would be extremely bullish for our market.

When there are five uses for corporate cash and all five are bullish, things cannot be as bad as they are being painted in the financial media.

In closing, from an investment perspective *cash* has always been *king*. Now, everywhere you look, from consumer to government to corporations, cash is going up. I am a firm believer that our markets will soon follow. After all, cash is king!

Investment Footnote . . . What actually happened

I was right. Cash drove our markets higher, gaining 3.1 percent in 2004.

Follow the Money!

April 26, 2005

One of the great lessons that I have learned in almost 30 years on Wall Street is to always follow the money. In this current state of market uncertainty, let me remind you that things become much less uncertain when you simply follow the money. I want to help you follow the money by looking at profits, the consumer, and dividend-paying stocks.

PROFITS

Let's start with profits. We currently find ourselves in the midst of first quarter earnings season. When the earnings season began, analysts expected earnings to grow in the first quarter at 8.6 percent, according to Thompson First Call. Now, less than a week or so into earnings season, expectations have been quickly revised upward to 12.1 percent. When first quarter earnings season ends, I believe earnings growth could exceed 15 percent, which would be almost double the 8.6 percent amount the so-called best and brightest on Wall Street were calling for as first quarter earnings season began.

The numbers are quite staggering so far, with 66 percent of the S&P 500 reporting earnings that "beat" expectations, 17 percent "meeting" expectations, and only 17 percent "missing" or falling short. I call that an 83 percent success rate of corporate earnings.

I believe that one of the real surprises of this earnings season has been this profit margin growth. It is a very simple concept to understand. Companies are showing top-line revenue growth, along with continued productivity, while experiencing little if any wage pressure. One has to look no further than last week's University of Michigan Consumer Sentiment Survey for proof. According to that survey, 46 percent of households are looking for inflation to outpace their wage growth this year. That is the highest level recorded since 1990. This lack of wage pressure on companies falls right to the bottom line, and I believe that is the real reason we are having such a strong earnings season. And it is not simply the earnings, but rather the quality of the earnings as well. After the adoption of Sarbanes-Oxley, the transparency of financial reporting has greatly improved. Now that CEOs are personally responsible, both civically and criminally, the quality of financial reports and footnotes and the clarity of information are better today than at any time in my 30 years of experience. If you follow the money to earnings, you will find a very strong earnings season.

THE CONSUMER

Now, let's follow the money to the consumer. I believe that most economists and strategists are making the wrong bet by saying this lack of wage growth means the consumer is about to slow down, especially when you combine it with the price of oil, which is back up into the mid $50 range. Keep in mind these are the same Wall Street strategists and economists who have been calling for the collapse of the U.S. consumer every year for the past decade. They were wrong before and I believe they are wrong now; here is why.

I am the first to admit that the lack of wage growth and the high price of oil are a drag on the consumer. But those are only two of the six elements that drive the consumer and consumption. The other four are all positive. First, is interest rates, which remain at historic lows and are a great influence on consumption. Second, are stock prices, which have recovered from the bear market that marked the beginning of this millennium. The third element is home prices. Don't forget that more people own homes than own stocks. The increased value of homes has been one of the reasons the consumer stays confident.

Fourth, finally, and most important, is employment. There is nothing more important than employment for the consumer. Let me again remind you what happened last week. The U.S. Labor Department reported that initial jobless claims (the number of U.S. workers filing first-time applications for unemployment benefits) fell to 330,000. To get a better look, you should focus on the four-week average that smoothes out weekly fluctuations. The four-week average stands at 338,000. The rule of thumb for Wall Street economists is that any number below 350,000 indicates job creation. Last time I checked, 338,000 is below 350,000, which means we are still creating jobs. And this means that if you follow the money to the consumer, you too will see that they are doing just fine.

DIVIDEND STOCKS

Third, and finally, let's follow the money to dividend-paying stocks. Companies are flush with cash and one of the uses of that cash is to pay a dividend. When a company has enough cash to pay you a dividend, it typically means that company is in pretty good financial shape; otherwise, it certainly would not be paying you a cash dividend. One of my four major investment themes this year is to invest in the "quality trade" by focusing on dividend-paying companies. That quality trade has certainly worked out great. Over the past 12 months through the first quarter of this year, the average return of a dividend-paying stock in the S&P 500 was 16.5 percent, while a non-dividend-paying stock averaged a return of 3.1 percent.

Now let me get back to my "follow the money" rule to help explain this great outperformance of dividend-paying stocks.

After the Jobs and Growth Tax Relief Reconciliation Act of 2003 lowered the dividend tax rate to 15 percent, mutual fund companies responded with an explosion of closed-end dividend funds. In fact, there were 12 of them launched in late 2003 and early 2004, which raised over $8.3 billion in assets. As you know, one of the great things about closed-end funds is that money never leaves; it never goes away. That is $8.3 billion of dividend stock demand that will always be with us—one of the miracles of closed-end funds. And did I mention that these funds can only buy dividend-paying stocks? If you follow the money, you too will see that the "quality trade dividend-paying stock" story has a long way to go.

In closing, I want to share one final thought about following the money. Taxes on dividends and capital gains are at the lowest level since 1941! It's great when we don't follow the money to Uncle Sam!

Investment Footnote . . . What actually happened ↑

I was correct. Value, as measured by the S&P 500/CitiGroup Value Index, returned 3.5 percent, while growth, as measured by the S&P 500/CitiGroup Growth Index, only returned 2.5 percent.

The Four Ts of Investing during Turkey to Tax Time

OCTOBER 21, 2005

My good friend and colleague, Mark Peterson, head of product development here at Deutsche Asset Management, has provided me with research revealing some compelling stock market performances based on six-month blocks of time. However, these are not the traditional Wall Street six-month blocks of January to June and July to December, to which we have all become accustomed. Instead, the first block of time is November 1 to April 30. Because November is the month of Thanksgiving when we get together for our traditional turkey feast and April is the month in which our dreaded federal income taxes are due, we simply call this period "Turkey (November) to Tax (April) Time." The second block of time, then, is the remaining six months from May 1 to October 31. I'm not giving this period of time a name because I don't want you to focus on that time period. Instead, I want you to focus on the Turkey to Tax Time of November 1 to April 30.

TURKEY TO TAX

If you go back to 1950 and look at the historical returns of the S&P 500 between those two time periods, the results are simply staggering. Since 1950, the average return of the S&P 500 during the six-month Turkey to Tax time frame has been 9 percent. Meanwhile, the average return of the S&P 500 during the remaining six-month period of May 1 to October 31 was only 2.71 percent. Understand the magnitude of what this means: over the past 55 years, 75 percent of the return in the S&P 500 occurred during Turkey to Tax Time.

But wait; I think the story gets even more compelling. There have only been two blocks of time where the Turkey to Tax Time strategy underperformed the historic average of a 9 percent cumulative return for three consecutive years. The first was the period 1980, 1981, and 1982 when the Turkey to Tax Time returns were only 7.30, 6.68, and −1.71 percent, respectively.

It happened again in 1992, 1993, and 1994 when the Turkey to Tax Time returns were 7.31, 6.60, and −2.32 percent, respectively. These two periods were the longest consecutive periods where the Turkey to Tax Time strategy underperformed the historical cumulative average of 9 percent. Keep in mind they were the longest. Currently, for the past six consecutive years, the Turkey to Tax Time strategy has underperformed the historical cumulative average of 9 percent. This had never happened in the previous 55 years. Talk about a trend that is overdue to be broken. I believe this Turkey to Tax Time strategy is about to burst out. And I think it is creating one of the great entry points for investors to get off the sidelines and get into our equity markets prior to the beginning of Turkey to Tax Time. In my perspective, this opportunity creates a renewed sense of urgency to get into the U.S. stock market right now, before this Turkey to Tax Time strategy begins to play out.

UNLUCKY 7

Why do I say this six-year streak of Turkey to Tax Time underperformance has to end? Couldn't it go on to a seventh consecutive year of underperformance? It could. But I don't believe it will, and here is why. I will give you not one or two but rather 10 reasons why I'm convinced this Turkey to Tax Time strategy will exceed the historical cumulative average return of 9 percent.

1. The price of oil is coming down. I think the next stop is $50 a barrel, and that might be the best tax cut we can hope for in 2006.

2. I think interest rates are going to stop going up during Turkey to Tax Time. Why? Because Alan Greenspan is retiring and the next Federal Reserve Board Chairman (Ben Bernanke, in my humble opinion) will not need to continue to raise interest rates to fight inflation that isn't there.

3. Corporate profits are up. Third-quarter profits may be up by as much as 20 percent on a year-over-year basis, and, I believe, all throughout Turkey to Tax Time, profits will be in the double digits.

4. Productivity is up. I believe that productivity will continue to surprise on the high side, growing at over 4 percent a year.
5. I expect the dollar will strengthen. A country's currency is ultimately a reflection of the underlying economy. Our economy is strong, and thus our currency will be strong as well.
6. Our trade deficit should improve. With the price of oil going lower and the dollar going higher, the trade deficit can only get better.
7. The budget deficit ought to improve as well. As corporate profits continue to soar, corporate tax receipts should rise as well, growing faster than government spending. And that should improve our budget deficit.
8. Employment is robust. If you look at the nonfarm payroll employment, we have already added 1.5 million new jobs year-to-date. If you look at the Household Survey Employment report, we have added 2.2 million jobs. No matter how you look at it, employment is robust.
9. Corporate balance sheets remain flush with cash that can be used to hire employees, increase dividends, or fuel a merger and acquisition boom.
10. The so-called housing bubble didn't burst; it simply fizzled. A slight slowdown in home price appreciation is actually a good thing. This may bring more investors to the stock market as they realize that housing doesn't just go up. When you put these 10 issues together, we may even have the single best Turkey to Tax Time ever.

THE FIFTH T—TWELVE (AS IN 12,000)

Let me end my commentary regarding the four Ts of investing by adding a fifth "T." The fifth "T" stands for twelve, as in 12,000. Yes, I am talking about the Dow Jones Industrial Average hitting an all-time high and breaking through 12,000 points. When I said this might be one of the greatest equity entry points ever, I wasn't kidding. By the time Turkey to Tax Time is over, I think the Dow may well be above 12,000.

Turkey, then Taxes, then 12,000, oh my. Turkey, then Taxes, then 12,000, *oh my!* If this sounds a little like *The Wizard of Oz*, that's because it is. Remember, the television networks always show *The Wizard of Oz* around . . . you guessed it, Turkey Time.

When you see *The Wizard of Oz* this year I want you to remember that it's Turkey, then Taxes, then 12,000, Oh my!

Investment Footnote . . . What actually happened

I was correct, as the Dow crossed 12,000, ending 2006 at 12,463.

Follow the Money Again!

DECEMBER 15, 2005

One of the reasons that I think that 2006 is already shaping up to be a great year for global investors is what I see happening right now in the United States. This is important to global investors because the United States remains both the largest stock market and largest economy in the world. Thus, I believe global investors should always keep one eye on the United States.

What I see happening in the United States is that individuals and corporations are flush with cash. As I've said, the U.S. stock market is the largest stock market in the entire world. Because of that, it is always extremely important to follow how much money or cash that stock market is actually sitting on. Second, the U.S. economy is the largest economy in the entire world. And over two-thirds of that economy is driven by the consumer. Because of that, it is always important to follow how much money or cash individuals are sitting on as well. Let's take a closer look as we follow the money and look at both corporate balance sheets and individuals' balance sheets.

CORPORATE CASH

The 500 individual companies that comprise the Standard & Poor's 500 Index are currently sitting on $2.3 trillion of cash (at the end of the third quarter of 2005). That is the highest cash level in the past 30 years. Many stock market bears will want to quickly point out that the reason that number is so high is because financial services companies now comprise almost one quarter of the Standard & Poor's 500 Index and those financial services companies need a lot of cash to run their businesses. While I do not agree with that argument, here is what I am going to do to show you another perspective of how much cash corporations are sitting on.

At the end of the third quarter, if you were to exclude financial services companies, corporations were still sitting on almost $800 billion in cash. Oh, and by the way, that also is the highest cash level in the past 30 years.

In my opinion, the important thing, however, is to watch what is about to happen next. Over the past 30 years the cash/asset ratio (which is Wall Street jargon for the percentage of all of the assets a corporation holds in cash) for the S&P 500 *excluding* financial services companies has averaged 6 percent. Right now it stands at over a whopping 9 percent! If you believe, as I do, that history is a great teacher and that trends will eventually revert back to their longer-term averages, then corporations will most likely be looking to do something in 2006 with that extra 3 percent of cash they are currently sitting on.

Corporations can put their cash to use in one of two ways. And, from my perspective, both paint a bullish foundation for the U.S. market, which in turn can help global markets. One way corporations can spend that money is to "return it to shareholders." You can return money to shareholders either through dividends or through stock buybacks, both of which are bullish for the market.

The second way corporations can spend that money is to "reinvest for their future." Corporations can reinvest for their future in three different ways and all are bullish for the market. One way to reinvest for the future is to hire more employees, which helps the economy and helps the market. Second, they could spend the money on major capital equipment, which would make them more productive, which would again help the economy, and, in turn, help the market. Third, and finally, they can reinvest for their future by making an acquisition of another company. Upticks in mergers and acquisitions are bullish for our stock market as well.

I am not sure that you could ask for anything more as a global investor. U.S. corporations have more cash today than at any time in the past 30 years. And whether they choose to return some of that cash to shareholders or reinvest it for their future growth, either of these uses is bullish for the markets.

INDIVIDUALS' CASH

Let's now move on to individuals' cash where, believe it or not, the story actually gets better. You better sit down while you read this part because you are never going to believe it.

Individuals are currently (*again*, as of the end of the third quarter) sitting on $4.7 *trillion*(!) of *cash*. By the way, I define *cash* as money sitting in checking accounts, money market accounts, and time and savings deposits that mature in one year or less. While all of the "bears" in the media will continue to harp on the so-called negative savings rate of U.S. individuals, I, on the other hand, do not care. I simply follow the money and the money shows me that American consumers are sitting on $4.7 trillion. And that, by the way, is larger than most countries' entire economies! And this $4.7 trillion in cash is only part of the story of individuals' balance sheets.

Individuals' net worth (assets minus liabilities) is at the highest level ever in all of recorded time at $51.1 trillion. And maybe even more remarkable (with all of this hyped concern about the U.S. consumer having too much debt), despite rising interest rates and skyrocketing energy prices over the past four quarters, individuals' net worth got better not worse. And it got better by a lot, even though it faced the headwinds of a housing bubble, rising interest rates, and rising energy costs. At the end of the third quarter of 2004, individuals' net worth stood at $46.1 trillion. Now, one year later, it is a cool $5 trillion higher.

Let me close with one final comment on this so-called housing or real estate bubble, which, in my opinion, will be the second most-hyped disaster that never happened, following the Y2K bug that was supposed to end the world and crash economies and stock markets around the planet. OK, back to real estate. Of the individuals' net worth on the balance sheet, real estate accounts for only 21 percent, or $10.7 trillion.

Now think about this so-called real estate bubble that is supposed to crush the U.S. individual investor and consumer alike. Well, no one is predicting that the value of real estate will go to zero; instead, the value of real estate in some locations will most likely go down and correct somewhat. Even if we had an unheard-of national correction of 10 percent, that would only wipe out $1.1 trillion of net worth from the real estate portion of individuals' balance sheets. And while that may sound like a lot, when you put into perspective that individuals have almost five times that amount sitting in cash today, you will see why I call this one of the most-hyped disasters that will never happen.

Oh, and by the way, watch out when individuals start spending all that cash buying stocks and lots of other stuff.

In closing, the one thing that I have learned in my almost 30-year career is to always follow the money. If you do that today, you will find that U.S. corporations are fine, as are U.S. individuals. And together, they combine to create just one more foundation and reason why the world is not about to end and global investors everywhere can relax. 2006 is shaping up to be a great year to go global from an international investing perspective. All you have to do to see why is follow the money to U.S. corporations and U.S. individuals, and it can lead you to become a global investor in 2006 as well!

Investment Footnote . . . What actually happened ↑

I was right. While the U.S. market returned 16.3 percent, as measured by the Dow, the rest of the investment world boomed as the MSCI–EM (Morgan Stanley Capital International–Emerging Markets) was up 23.5 percent and the MSCI–EAFE (Morgan Stanley Capital International–Europe, Australia, and the Far East) was up a whopping 29.2 percent.

Great Team, Great Super Bowl

FEBRUARY 6, 2006

While everyone knows that I am a die-hard Pittsburgh Steelers fan, the great team I want to talk about first is my new team—DWS Scudder. You see, this is my very first commentary as a DWS Scudder employee. Today, Scudder was rebranded DWS Scudder as our firm became fully integrated into Deutsche Bank's global mutual fund platform (which is branded globally as DWS). The three-letter acronym comes from the original name of DWS, which was Deutsche Gesellschaft fur Wertpapiersparen. This translates directly as "German Company for Security Savings."

This is the single greatest day in the history of Scudder Investments—to finally become an integral part of Deutsche Bank's global powerhouse DWS brand.

RINGING THE BELL

I had a special thrill today. I was invited to be one of the senior executives from DWS Scudder to ring the opening bell at the NYSE, officially launching DWS Scudder. This marked the fifth time in my investment career that I participated in either an opening or closing bell ceremony for either the NYSE or Nasdaq stock markets. But let me tell you, this one was clearly the best and the most exciting.

Talk about a great new team: DWS Scudder now has access to a team of over 700 investment professionals around the globe. Truly, DWS Scudder has become "One Global Force with One Focus: You."

BACK TO THE SUPER BOWL

Now that you know about my new super team at DWS Scudder, let's get back to the Super Bowl. I have watched all 40 Super Bowls—every single one of them. I watched this one by myself in a hotel room in New York. You see, in order to get to New York from Chicago on time to ring the bell early Monday morning, I had to travel on Super Bowl Sunday. (My apologies to the poor people in the hotel room next to me who were wondering why I kept screaming, "One for the Thumb.") The good news about traveling on Super Bowl Sunday (if there is any) is that it gave me the time to do some Super Bowl/stock market research.

SUPER BOWL EFFECT

All right, let's refocus this Super Bowl discussion on that research and to something Wall Street refers to as the "Super Bowl effect." The Super Bowl effect suggests that if the winner is either the National Football Conference (NFC) or the American Football Conference (AFC), it will tell us where the stock market will end up at the end of the year (as measured by the S&P 500 Index). For the first 39 Super Bowls (remember, yesterday was Super Bowl XL, or 40), the National Football Conference or NFC won 21 times. Of those 21 years, the stock market ended the year with a positive return 19 times, or an unbelievable 90.4 percent of the time! Meanwhile, the American Football Conference or AFC won the Super Bowl 18 times. Of those 18 years, the stock market ended the year with a positive return only 10 times, or a dismal 55.5 percent of the time. So if you want the stock market to go up, you better hope the NFC team wins. Or should you? Yesterday, the NFC team the Seattle Seahawks lost to my beloved Pittsburgh Steelers by a score of 21–10. But I am not so sure that is a bad thing for the markets . . . here is what I mean!

DR. BOB'S SUPER BOWL EFFECT

Today, I am officially releasing a brand-new, first-of-its-kind indicator called the "Dr. Bob's Super Bowl effect" indicator. I don't focus on or care about the NFC or AFC; all I focus on and care about is which team actually wins the dang Super Bowl!

Through the first 39 Super Bowls, only 16 teams have shared the Super Bowl trophy among themselves all 39 times. Now, the first thing I did to develop Dr. Bob's Super Bowl effect was eliminate the five teams that have only won one Super Bowl. I do not believe that one year can be treated as a trend or an indicator, so

I threw them all out! By the way, of the five that I threw out, only two of them, Chicago and Tampa Bay, won their Super Bowl trophy in a year when the stock market finished with positive returns. The other three of five "one-time" Super Bowl winners, the New York Jets, Kansas City Chiefs, and St. Louis Rams won their only Super Bowl in a year when the market was negative.

So that leaves me with 11 teams that have won multiple Super Bowls. Next, I eliminated six teams that left the stock market either positive or negative after winning their Super Bowls. Their victories predicted nothing, one way or another, for our markets.

That leaves me with the five teams that you should have been rooting for if you are an investor. You see, only five teams have a perfect track record of winning a Super Bowl in a year when the stock market ended in positive territory every single time.

Two of these five teams, the New York Giants and the Denver Broncos, did it twice, so they are both a perfect two for two. Two others of the five teams were a perfect three for three. The two teams that did it three times were the Green Bay Packers and the Washington Redskins. Finally, there is only one team that had a perfect four for four. One hundred percent of the time, all four times they won a Super Bowl, the market ended the year in positive territory. And I am sure that you have guessed it by now; that team is my beloved *Pittsburgh Steelers*!

Now for the good news: the Pittsburgh Steelers just won their fifth Super Bowl, finally getting that "one for the thumb"—a fifth championship ring to grace the hand's fifth digit, the thumb.

If the terrible towel can help the Steelers, I am willing to bet it can help our stock market as well. (The Terrible Towel is an idea created by Myron Cope, a broadcaster for the Pittsburgh Steelers. Needing a way to excite the fans during a 1975 playoff football game against the Baltimore Colts, Cope urged Steelers fans to take yellow dish towels to the game and wave them throughout. Pittsburgh won that game 28–10. To this day, these rally towels are more popular than ever.)

How do you spell five for five? Now there are two Super Teams: DWS Scudder and the Pittsburgh Steelers!

Investment Footnote . . . What actually happened

I was spot on as the Dow surged 16.3 percent in 2006.

Nothing Secret about This Bond

March 6, 2006

Without a doubt, the most famous Bond in the world is James Bond (also known as Secret Agent 007). While James Bond may be the most famous Bond, he is not the most important Bond. That title goes to the U.S. Treasury Bond market, the largest bond market in the world—and considered the safest bond market, as well. This is because it is backed by the full faith and credit of the U.S. government, which in turn is supported by the largest economy and largest stock market in the entire world. Why, then, is everyone so concerned about the bond market? In a word, it's the "curve"—as in *yield curve*.

FLAT OR INVERTED YIELD CURVE

While most investors have no idea what a flat or inverted yield curve is, they still worry about it. Let me try to explain. A yield curve should have a positive slope. In other words, the further out you go in years, the higher the yield you should receive. Think of it like this: If you lent someone money for one year, maybe you would charge them interest of 1 percent because you are getting all of your money back in one year. If, however, you lend someone money for 10 years, you should get paid 5 percent interest a year for all of the additional risk you are taking for those additional nine years. That is what a positive yield curve is: The further out you go in years from one to 10, the more you get paid in interest rates (a one-year loan at 1 percent and a 10-year loan at 5 percent). That positive yield curve makes all the sense and logic in the world today. So how come the yield curve in our bond market is flat or even inverted? Why would someone buy a 10-year Treasury bond and accept less interest or the same interest as someone who buys a two-year Treasury note?

ENTER CHINA

Let me try to explain this situation as I see it. The U.S. economy is the largest economy in the entire world with a population of just under 300 million. Our economy also has the largest and richest consumer base in the entire world.

Meanwhile China's developing economy has 1.3 billion people with nearly 1.1 billion of those people living in virtual poverty in rural parts of China. The challenge for China is to create millions upon millions of manufacturing jobs in urbanized areas of China over the next decade to move people out of poverty in those rural areas and into manufacturing jobs in urbanized areas. The only way you can create millions upon millions of manufacturing jobs is to ensure someone will buy all that you are manufacturing.

Enter the U.S. consumer and U.S. economy, still the largest in the world. China may actually need the United States more than the United States needs China—especially if they are going to create all of these jobs to move people from poverty.

How do you ensure that the U.S. consumer keeps shopping and buys everything made in China? You keep U.S. interest rates low. How can China keep U.S. interest rates low? By buying all the 10-year and 30-year Treasury bonds it can, regardless of the yield. That will keep the yield curve flat, or even invert it. China knows that the Federal Reserve Board will be forced to stop raising short-term interest rates, which would cause the yield curve to become even more inverted.

The result? U.S. interest rates stay low; the U.S. consumer stays happy and buys everything made in China. That allows China to create millions upon millions of new jobs—all because they continued to buy 10- and 30-year Treasury bonds. What a deal, what a bond!

REMEMBER THE DEFICIT

There is one final item that I think will end up supporting our bond market even more. I believe that the federal budget deficit will actually go down and not up this fiscal year, and here is why.

The consensus on Wall Street is that once you combine the cost of the war in Iraq with that of the ongoing war on terror and add to that last year's unprecedented weatherman axis of evil—Katrina, Rita, and Wilma—the federal budget deficit has nowhere to go but up. Let me explain to you why I think the consensus on Wall Street is wrong about the impact of Katrina, Rita, and Wilma. First of all, the majority of the federal government's responsibility in the aftermath of those horrific storms is for bridges, highways, roads, dams, and levies. In other words, the federal government is mostly responsible for major infrastructure projects. Let me remind you that major infrastructure does not happen over a three- to four-month period. It happens over a three- to four-year period. In other words, the federal government's cost will actually be spread out over three or four different fiscal years, which will lessen the impact in any one year on the deficit.

Also, don't forget that there is a revenue side to these horrific storms, as well. These three storms, in essence, wiped out the entire gulf coast region—homes and businesses alike. So now we are in the midst of one of the biggest building booms the United States has seen in the past 25 years as we rebuild our entire Gulf Coast region. As we rebuild an entire region of this great country of ours, a lot of firms stand to make more money than they ever dreamed of. But don't forget how the United States works. The more you make, the more you pay in taxes to the federal government. Maybe the single biggest legacy of Katrina, Rita, and Wilma will be that they formed the perfect tax storm to cause corporate tax receipts to skyrocket to the highest level in the past decade.

When you combine the facts that the federal government will be spending less and taking in more, I think the federal government budget deficit has nowhere to go but down. Once that happens, everyone will have wished they were in Bonds—not James Bond (Agent 007) but rather good, old-fashioned American bonds. And with the U.S. economy poised to grow at 5 percent, while inflation stays below 3 percent, I think now would be the time to look at "high-yield" versus "high-quality" bonds. They may turn out to be the biggest and best investment surprise in all of 2006!

Investment Footnote . . . What actually happened

I was right on both fronts as the consumer price index came in at 3.42 percent for March 2006. Meanwhile, first quarter gross domestic product (GDP) was 4.8 percent, which, rounded up, would be 5 percent. So my 3 percent inflation and 5 percent economy growth call was indeed correct.

Turkey to Tax Time II

OCTOBER 26, 2006

Examples of movie sequels that are widely considered to be as good as, or better than, the original include *The Godfather, Part II*; *Terminator 2: Judgment Day*; *Toy Story 2*; and *Spider-Man 2*. Well, I am about to share with you a new great blockbuster sequel. This one, however, will not be playing out on the silver screens of Main Street, U.S.A. This blockbuster comes to us from Wall Street.

TURKEY TO TAX TIME—THE ORIGINAL

Let's start at the beginning by focusing on the original Turkey to Tax Time. On October 25, 2005, I wrote a commentary titled "The Four Ts of Investing during Turkey to Tax Time." In that commentary, I pointed out that the six-month period between November 1 (called "Turkey" because Thanksgiving occurs in November) and April 30 (called "Tax Time" because income taxes must be filed in April) has historically been a period of significant outperformance for the U.S. equity markets.

In my commentary I pointed out, "If you go back to 1950 and look at the historical returns of the S&P 500 between Turkey to Tax Time (November 1 to April. 30) and compare them to the remaining six-month period between May 1 and October 31, the results are simply staggering." Since 1950, the average return of the S&P 500 during the six-month Turkey to Tax Time has been 9 percent. Meanwhile, the average return of the S&P 500 during the remaining six-month period of May 1 to October 31 was only 2.71 percent. That means that over the past 55 years, 75 percent of the return in the S&P 500 occurred during Turkey to Tax Time.

In that commentary I went on to forecast that last year's Turkey to Tax Time, November 1, 2005, to April 30, 2006, "will exceed the historical cumulative average return of 9 percent." And it did. I don't want to say I told you so, but I told you so! Last year's Turkey to Tax Time boasted a 9.64 percent return, which not only beat the historical average but was also the best Turkey to Tax Time investing period since the turn of the millennium.

THE SEQUEL

What about the sequel? As we are about to embark on the next Turkey to Tax Time investing period, I predict this one will be even better than last year's 9.64 percent return. In other words, the sequel will be better than the original, just like at the movies. I expect this Turkey to Tax Time will see double-digit returns (and 15 percent is not out of the realm of possibilities).

Why do I think the sequel could be so much better for investors? There are actually five reasons.

First, I'm confident that interest rates are no longer going up. In fact, the great debate on Wall Street now is when the Fed will begin cutting interest rates. This is extremely bullish for our markets. Second, I believe that profits will continue to grow on a year-over-year basis during this period at double-digit levels, fueled more by the ongoing productivity boom than by top-line revenue growth. Third, the price of oil has collapsed. Not only is this a great $100 billion de facto energy tax cut but it is also a boost to both consumer and investor confidence. You see, unlike a traditional tax cut that occurs basically one time and then goes away, this is a tax cut that keeps on giving each and every time we drive up to the pump. And this too is very bullish for our markets. Fourth, I think this so-called housing recession scare is history. From my perspective, we are not having and will not have an economic recession in this country because of a slowdown in housing. Most of the correction in housing has already occurred in many parts of the country, particularly California and Florida. And I believe that once the Fed starts to lower interest rates, the term "housing recession" will become as distant a memory as the term "Y2K." And removing the fear of a housing recession should also have a bullish influence on our markets. Fifth, and finally, we are in the midst of a global capital spending boom. This boom is not just happening in China as it prepares for the upcoming Olympics in 2008. It is occurring in Japan, and South America, and Australia and even right here in the good old United States of America. I feel certain that the synchronized global capital spending boom will stay in force for this entire period, which can only be bullish for our market.

In closing, let me remind you that if you missed the last Turkey to Tax Time, don't worry about it. The sequel is about to begin on November 1, 2006, and I believe it stands to be even better than the original.

Have a great day, keep a positive attitude, and I'll see ya at 13,000, which, by the way, could actually occur sometime during *Turkey to Tax Time II.*

Investment Footnote . . . What actually happened

I was correct, as the Dow broke 13,000 in 2007 and ended the year at 13,264.

"Super Bowl" Indicator

FEBRUARY 5, 2007

Let's begin with the "Super Bowl" indicator. Super Bowl XLI is now history and Da Bears lost. Even though they lost, it was still a super year for Da Bears. And it could be a super year for our stock market as well, according to the Super Bowl indicator. The Super Bowl indicator goes like this. The stock market will rise over the coming year if the winning team can trace its roots back to the original National Football League. Conversely, the stock market will fall if the winning team's roots can instead be traced back to the old American Football League. Well, I am sure you have guessed it by now. The roots of the winning team in the Super Bowl—the Indianapolis Colts—go back to the original National Football League when they were actually the Baltimore Colts.

How accurate has this Super Bowl indicator been? Well, through last year's Super Bowl, it had an impressive 80 percent success rate, which is why it is such a widely followed indicator. Just so you know, we investors couldn't lose with this past Super Bowl. That's because even if Da Bears would have won, their roots, too, can be traced back to the original National Football League. So, no matter who would have won Super Bowl XLI, the Super Bowl indicator would be predicting a positive stock market in 2007.

"JANUARY EFFECT" INDICATOR

Enough about Da Bears and the Super Bowl. Let's move on to Da Bulls. I do not mean the Chicago Bulls basketball team, but rather the stock market "bulls," of which I am a self-proclaimed founding member. Why are Da bulls so happy? Because of January, that's why. If you think the Super Bowl indicator is good, the "January effect" or "January indicator" is even better. On Wall Street, the smart money says: "As January goes, so goes the year." That's because, since 1926, if the stock market had a positive January, it would have a positive remainder of the year (February through December). This has held true again and again an astounding 80 percent of the time. And don't forget, this year the stock market, as measured by the Standard & Poor's 500 Index, was up 1.4 percent for the month of January. "As January goes, so goes the year."

Thus, the January effect tells us it should be a good year for the markets as well. And consider this: If we have 11 more months exactly like January's positive 1.4 percent monthly return, the market will end up 17.8 percent for the year. What's so special about that 17.8 percent number? Nothing much other than the fact that it happens to be the exact average return the stock market is up during every year an original National Football League team won the Super Bowl.

INDICATORNOMICS

Speaking of Da bull, remember this: While it is truly fun to look at these off-the-wall indicators, they are really not what drives our markets. And even if they did drive our markets, you would still have to decide how many indicators is enough. Do you stop at just the January effect and Super Bowl indicator? What about the "Presidential election cycle effect," which shows that over the past 60 years the third year of a presidential election cycle has never had a down year? And, yes, 2007 is the third year of President Bush's second-term presidential election cycle. That, again, is a good sign for our markets in 2007. Or, if you don't like politics, we can focus on the "hemline indicator," which is supposed to tell us the direction of the market based on whether skirt hemlines moved higher or lower that fashion year.

For as long as I can remember, individual investors have longed for an indicator that can accurately predict where the market is going. The truth is, there isn't one. Even though some of these anecdotal stories about Super Bowls and hemlines can paint a somewhat compelling investment picture, you should never make any investment decision based solely on such a simplistic analysis.

Instead, you should do what I do. First, call your financial advisor. (Yes, even I have a financial advisor; so if I need a financial advisor, how is it that you still think you can do it alone? That's a big mistake.) Then, focus on the things that really can drive markets. First, take a look at the economy, where the broadest measure of our economy, gross domestic product (GDP), just grew 3.5 percent for the fourth quarter. That suggests that our economy can grow 3 percent for all of 2007, and above the long-term economic growth trendline of 2.7 percent GDP. When the economy grows above trend, it is bullish for our markets. Second, focus on earnings. While today we find ourselves right in the middle of fourth quarter earnings season, I believe that when earnings season is over, we will have once again witnessed double-digit, year-over-year earnings growth. My actual forecast calls for an 11 percent year-over-year earnings growth increase. And again, if that happens, it, too, bodes well for a strong market in 2007 because, as we all know, it's earnings, not hemlines or Super Bowls, that drive the markets. And finally, and most important, look at the money. As I told you before, always follow the money.

Inflows into equity mutual funds were staggering in December according to the Investment Company Institute (ICI). Here are the eye-popping numbers. In December, equity mutual funds attracted a record $55.5 billion in net inflows. Actually, net inflows totaled only $10.7 billion, about the same as November's $10.8 billion. However, reinvested dividends, which always jump in December according to the ICI data, totaled a whopping $44.9 billion—the highest on record and double December 2005's $22.5 billion. For all of last year, equity mutual funds attracted a total of $229 billion, including the reinvested dividends. Money, not Super Bowl winners, will take the Dow to 14,000 this year.

Also, in December, funds that invested overseas (global and international, emerging, and regional) attracted $27.6 billion. This number included $14.5 billion in reinvested dividends. The total for 2006 was $166.6 billion. So they accounted for 73 percent of the equity mutual fund inflows last year. Now do you understand why my number one investment theme is "Go Global, Go Global, and go even More Global"?

There is one final thing to remember regarding these anecdotal statistics that appear to predict the direction of the market. These events actually may not even be correlated to one another. In fact, Professor David Leinweber, a visiting faculty member in the economics department at the California Institute of Technology, searched through billions upon billions of data points compiled by the United Nations to find the one indicator with the most significantly statistical correlation to the Standard & Poor's 500 Index moving higher in a given year. His discovery: "butter production in Bangladesh." Like I said, call your financial advisor.

CHINESE NEW YEAR (DA PIG INDICATOR)

In closing, now that I've told you that Da Bears, as in the Super Bowl indicator, and Da Bulls, as in the January effect, really don't matter, nor does Da Presidential Election Cycle, Da hemline indicator or even Da butter production in Bangladesh. So what about Da Pigs?

Finally, here is something that really matters—"the Pigs." On February 18, the Chinese New Year begins and you guessed it, it is the "Year of the Pig." As investors, you need to get exposure to this remarkable growth story that is going on in China today. While we are very pleased here in the United States that our economy can grow at 3 percent, the fact is the Chinese economy is growing three times faster than ours.

Every other week, a new city the size of Indianapolis, home of Da Colts who beat Da Bears in the Super Bowl, is being built. How is that possible, you might ask? Let me tell you from having traveled there and witnessed it firsthand with my own eyes. They have a supersized, motivated, billion-strong workforce working 17-hour shifts for only $30 a week. That is how it gets done and that also explains where all the steel, cement, iron, glass, etc., are heading as well.

As I finally bring this commentary to a close, I want you to remember two things. First, forget about Da Bears, Da Bulls, Da hemlines, and Da presidential election cycle, and instead focus only on Da Pigs; 2007 is the "Year of the Pig" in China. And when you do that, you will "Go Global, Go Global, and go even More Global." Second, please call your financial advisor today. Or, if you like, you can continue to go it alone; after all it's as simple as following butter production in Bangladesh!

Have a great day, keep a positive attitude, and I'll see ya at 14,000.

Investment Footnote . . . What actually happened

I was wrong. We didn't quite make it to 14,000, as the Dow ended the year at 13,264.

CHAPTER 5

Policy and Politics

Politics is the act of looking for trouble, finding it everywhere, diagnosing it incorrectly, and applying the wrong remedies.

GROUCHO MARX
American comedian and film star

INTRODUCTION

A policy is a deliberate plan of action to guide decisions and achieve rational outcomes. The term may apply to government, private sector organizations and groups, and individuals. Presidential executive orders and parliamentary rules of order are both examples of policy. Policy differs from rules or laws. While law can compel or prohibit behaviors, policy merely guides actions toward those who are most likely to achieve a desired outcome.

Policy or policy study may also refer to the process of making important organizational decisions, including the identification of different alternatives, such as programs or spending priorities, and choosing among them on the basis of the impact they will have. Policies can be understood as political, management, financial, and administrative mechanisms arranged to reach explicit goals.

Definitions of policy and research done in the area of policy are frequently performed from the perspective of policies created by national governments or public policy. Several definitions and key characteristics of policy have been identified within the framework of government policy. There is a lack of a consensus on just what is public policy. Here are a few of the definitions that Wall Street banters about.

The term *public policy* always refers to the actions of government and the intentions that determine those actions. Or, public policy is the outcome of the struggle in government over who gets what. Or, how about, public policy is whatever governments choose to do or not to do. Another subtle variation is: public policy consists of political decisions for implementing programs to achieve societal goals. And finally, how about this one: stated most simply, public policy is the sum of government activities, whether acting directly or through agents, as it has an influence on the lives of citizens.

Part of the reason for the lack of consensus on exactly what public policy means has to do with the newness of this concept. While the study of "politics" has a long history, the systematic study of public policy, on the other hand, is a twentieth-century creation. Its actual "roots" date back to 1922 when political scientist Charles Merriam sought to connect the theory and practices of politics to understanding the actual activities of government—in other words, public policy.

No matter how you define it, no matter how long it has been studied, public policy begins and ends with the government. With that in mind, it is important to remember that the fundamental purpose of government is the maintenance of basic security and public order, without which individuals would need to establish safety and public order for themselves.

When we think of public policy and government and their impact on our markets, we tend to think of them in terms of four different fronts. The first is *military defense*. The fundamental purpose of government is to protect citizens from their neighbors; however, a sovereign of one country is not necessarily sovereign over the people of another country. The need for people to defend themselves against potentially hundreds of non-neighbors necessitates a national defense mechanism, or a military.

Militaries are created to deal with the highly complex task of confronting a large number of enemies. A farmer can defend himself from a single enemy person, or even several enemies, but he can't defend himself from a thousand, even with the help of his strongest and bravest family members. A far larger group is needed, and despite the fact that most of the members of the group would not be related by family ties, they would have to learn to fight for one another as if they were all in the same family. An organization that trains people to do this is an army.

The second front is *economic security*. Increasing complexities in society resulted in the formations of governments, but the increase in complexities didn't stop there. As the complexity and interdependencies of human communities moved forward, economies began to dominate the human experience to the extent that an individual's survival potential was affected substantially by a region's economy. Remember, governments were originally created for the purpose of increasing people's survival potential; to achieve this goal, governments became very involved in manipulating and managing regional economies.

At a bare minimum, government, by prohibiting counterfeiting, ensures that the value of money will not be undermined; however, in almost all societies, governments attempt to regulate many more aspects of their economies. Very often, government involvement in a national economy has more than just the purpose of stabilizing it for the benefit of the people. Often, the members of government shape the government's economic policies for their own personal gains, or to push forward their personal political agenda.

The third front is *social security*. Social security is actually related to *economic security*. Throughout most of human history, parents prepared for their old age by producing enough children to ensure that some of them would survive long enough to take care of the parents in their old age. In modern, relatively high-income societies, a mixed approach is taken, where the government shares a substantial responsibility of taking care of the elderly. This is not the case everywhere, since there are still many countries where social security through having many children is the norm. Social security is still a relatively recent phenomenon, prevalent for the most part in developed countries.

The fourth and final front is *environmental security*. Governments play a crucial role in managing environmental public goods, such as the atmosphere, forests, and water bodies. Governments are critical institutions for resolving problems involving these public goods at both the local and global scale, whether these problems involve climate change, deforestation, or overfishing. In recent decades, economic markets have been championed as suitable mechanisms for managing environmental security. However, these economic markets have developed serious failures as they pertain to environmental security; thus, governmental intervention and regulation and the rule of law are required for the proper, just, and sustainable management of the environment. And, as if this weren't enough to get Wall Street's attention, now we have to throw politics in on top of all of these government and regulatory issues.

Politics, after all, is the process by which groups of people make decisions. The term is generally applied to behavior within civil governments, but politics has been observed in all human group interactions, including academic, religious, and corporate institutions.

From Wall Street's perspective, all of politics is looked at as either coming from the "left" or the "right." That is because most politicians divide politics into left- and right-wing politics, and use the idea of center politics as a middle path of policy between the right and the left. This classification dates back to the French Revolution era, when those members of the National Assembly who opposed the king sat on the left, while those who supported the monarchy sat on the right.

The meaning of *left-wing* and *right-wing* varies considerably among different countries and at different times but, broadly speaking, it can be said that the right wing is often linked to moral and social conservatism, law and order, and religion, while the left wing is often linked with the redistribution of wealth and resources toward the poorer and less successful sections of society.

On the pages that follow, you will get my perspectives and insights on exactly how and why public policy and politics will impact your investments.

Goodbye, Glass-Steagall . . . Hello, One-Stop Shopping!

DECEMBER 14, 1999

It finally happened—the financial services industry "walls," commonly referred to as Glass-Steagall, came tumbling down late last year.

The Glass-Steagall Act has been around since 1933. It was enacted as one of the responses to the great stock market crash of 1929, in which banks were also thought to be speculators on Wall Street. The original Glass-Steagall Act created a "wall" between the banking industry and the security industry so we would never again face the prospect of one-third of our banks failing at the same time the stock market collapses. Congress later adopted measures to create a similar separation or wall between the banking and insurance industries as well.

Why the sudden change? Well, over the years, study after study and exhaustive analysis upon analysis have failed to come up with any proof that banks were speculating in the stock market on Wall Street with depositors' money from Main Street, which in turn fueled our Great Depression.

Two forces have been combining to put pressure to repeal Glass-Steagall. First, this act has put our financial services industry at a competitive disadvantage globally. The reason is that, in most industrialized nations, banks are able to offer one-stop shopping, i.e., banking, securities, and insurance. It is impossible for us to compete if we can offer only one-third of the services other global financial services firms can offer global consumers.

The second force is the influence of the time-starved baby-boom generation. As the boomers head into their 50s, they want things made simple and convenient for them. In other words, they want and will demand one-stop shopping. They don't want to go one place for a savings account, another place to buy individual securities, another place for life insurance, another place for mutual funds, another place for homeowners' insurance, and so on. The boomers want the opportunity of going to one place for all their financial services needs. And with the repeal of Glass-Steagall, now they will get it.

This change will dramatically alter the financial services industry landscape as insurers team up with banks, which team up with securities firms, who team up with local banks, who team up with mutual fund companies. Better keep a scorecard handy—the names are going to change quickly as merger mania is about to reach new heights.

When it is all said and done, the firms that evolve as a result of the repeal of Glass-Steagall will be better positioned to compete in the global arena and will be able to offer the boomers what they demand—one-stop shopping!

Investment Footnote . . . What actually happened

I was wrong, as financials fell −10.5 percent in 1999.

A Modern-Day Mexican Revolution

November 1, 2000

When you hear the phrase "Mexican Revolution," you probably think back to the years between 1910 and 1920, when Pancho Villa rode his horse through the streets of Mexico during this turbulent time in the country's history. But a decade from now when someone talks about the Mexican Revolution, you may think more about Vicente Fox.

You see, with his election to president of Mexico, Fox just pulled off a modern-day Mexican Revolution, the impact of which could be felt for decades to come. His stunning presidential victory abruptly ended the Institutional Revolutionary Party's 71 years of control, and gives Fox an opportunity to create his own Mexican Revolution.

The Fox revolution will have little to do with political and military power, however. Instead, it will focus on the power of Mexico's economy and markets. I'm looking for three economic foundations to emerge from this modern-day Mexican Revolution.

DEREGULATION AND PRIVATIZATION

Fox supports the deregulation of the electricity, energy, and telecommunications industries, which is likely to lead to increased competition, lower costs, increased production, and higher profits. He wants to privatize Mexico's petrochemical plants. He wants to allow foreign investors to own shares of oil companies, which traditionally have been government-owned. Eventually, he would like to end all price controls. This major move to privatization and deregulation will set the stage for highly productive and profitable industries— and create abundant opportunities for international companies looking to invest in Mexico.

TAX REFORM

Fox's support came from Mexico's middle class and its energized younger voters. Both of these constituencies favor tax reform, which is much needed in Mexico. Oil taxes currently account for a third of Mexico's tax revenues, and this nondiversified tax revenue stream leads to a volatile economy. Fox plans to eliminate tax exemptions, thereby broadening the tax base without increasing taxes. This will increase total tax revenues and thereby lower Mexico's dependence on oil for tax revenue. Once this transition is complete, I expect to see a variety of other tax reform and reduction programs. And, as we have learned all too well in the United States, when you lower tax rates, the economy actually expands.

MY GOOD UNCLE SAM

Fox has repeatedly stated that Mexico needs a better relationship with its most important partner—the United States. With Fox in office, I expect Mexico to shift its foreign policies to better align itself with the

United States. This will likely lead to landmark agreements on trade and immigration issues that have haunted the two nations for decades. Under Fox's leadership, we could see the greatest Mexican cooperation ever on the war on drugs. When the cooperation starts, it will be hard to stop, and eventually we will realize that what's good for Mexico is also good for the United States, and vice versa. With the United States and Mexico on the same page, the whole world will take notice when the two countries flex their collective economic muscle.

Investment Footnote . . . What actually happened

Boy, was I right. In 2000, the Mexican stock market fell −20.73 percent. Then, just as I predicted, in 2001 it rose double digits, up 12.74 percent.

"A Taxing Time"

January 2, 2001

As we embark on another new year, this one may prove to be especially taxing for investors. The Big Three (and I'm not talking about the automobile companies, although they didn't have a good year either)—the Dow Jones Industrial Average, the Standard and Poor's 500 Index, and the Nasdaq—all had negative returns for the year.

In addition, it seems like everywhere you look the "bears" are having their way, pointing to one problem after another. It's almost like, pick your poison. Manufacturing is way down, and the other big three (auto companies) are now cutting back on production, citing weak consumer demand. Holiday season sales were especially disappointing, fueled by a sharp fall in consumer confidence. Technology activity is still slow, and layoff announcements are expanding along all industry lines, not just the dot-com companies. And, to make matters even worse, we have an evolving domestic crisis that hasn't officially been named yet; I'll take a stab at it by calling it the C.U.C. (California utility crisis). Like most crises, a majority of investors have no idea what the crisis is all about. All they remember is that California accounts for over 12 percent of the United States gross domestic product; thus, anything that's bad for California will eventually be bad for the entire United States.

I couldn't be happier. You see, these short-term problems are going to set the foundation for long-term opportunities for all investors, and here is why. Think of it this way: If everything were rosy today—manufacturing and technology demand rising, no lay-offs, the consumer driving the economy with record holiday sales, and no C.U.C.—what do you think the chances of a major tax cut would be? I don't care who is in the White House; the chances would be a big fat *zero*! The silver lining to these short-term problems is that they set the stage, giving a perfect foundation for President Bush's sweeping tax cut proposals. These short-term problems will make it easier than ever to adopt some major tax reforms early this year. Thus the odds just went up from zero to 100 percent.

Tax reform is going to happen. We are going to start encouraging people to save and invest instead of discouraging them. I look for expanded individual retirement accounts and liberalized 401(k) retirement guidelines that enable employees to increase contributions. A modest capital gains tax cut is also not out of the question, and you can expect some across-the-board business tax cuts and incentives.

The short-term problems that we have to face today are providing us with the opportunity to make some long-term fundamental changes that will have a positive impact on our markets for a decade or more.

It may be "a taxing time" today; however, tomorrow holds the promise of a less *taxing time*! Good luck, and thank you in advance, President Bush.

Investment Footnote . . . What actually happened

I was correct, as President Bush cut both the dividend tax rate and the long-term capital gains tax rate.

California Unplugged!

JANUARY 25, 2001

Well, it's official; the California electric utility crisis has now taken center stage as the event that will finally undo the U.S. economy and our stock market. I am sorry to inform all of you doomsayers that this California electric utility crisis will come and go just like the prior events that were supposed to lead to the collapse of our economy and markets. From the Southeast Asian currency crisis to the long-term capital management bailout, to the Russian default, to the dreaded Y2K, each of these much-hyped crises failed to deliver on their gloom-and-doom forecast. So will this newly hyped California electric utility crisis.

DEREGULATION WORKS

First and foremost, investors need to remember that deregulation works. This debacle in California will not stop the deregulation of electric utilities across the United States. This problem is not about deregulation but rather the misguided public policy approach to implementing deregulation in California. The fact that the California electric utility industry is in chaos is not the result of deregulation. Everyone would agree that seat belts are good things. What if, however, someone decides to put the seat belt on in such a way that it will support his or her sore neck? And when the car gets into an accident, the passenger's neck is broken and he or she dies from the injury inflicted by the seat belt. Does that mean we should outlaw seat belts? Absolutely not! Likewise, the fact that the misguided California deregulation is in chaos does not mean that deregulation, when properly implemented, is bad as well.

FAILURE FROM THE START

California electric utility deregulation was doomed for failure from the very start in 1996. Three separate components of this deregulation combined to guarantee failure, California style. First, this deregulation experiment freed wholesale prices for electricity while at the same time putting a price freeze on the retail price of electricity that could be charged to the ultimate California electricity consumer. Consider this strike one.

Second, the utilities are forbidden from entering into long-term supply contracts. What that means is that they have to buy electricity on the skyrocketing "spot" market while paying the current rate. The cost for buying a megawatt-hour of electricity during peak demand in California was about $10 when this deregulation experiment began. At the end of last year, it reached almost $350. And to make matters worse, remember that utilities can't pass any of that cost on to the ultimate consumer. Do I hear strike two?

Third, in a mind-boggling approach that you can find only in California, listen to what they did to all of the big power-generating plants before 1996. The state agreed to richly compensate the utilities for what they defined as "stranded assets." But wait, this is just the start. California valued those assets at a much greater value than fair market value. But it doesn't end there; California decided that any new entrant (competitor) to the California utility market must pick up part of the cost of these stranded assets. Wonder why there is no new competition in California? It's because once these new competitors are strapped with these old stranded asset costs, they simply can't compete on a price basis. Strike three.

DEREGULATION WORKS ELSEWHERE

Fewer than 1 percent of California residents have switched retail electric utility suppliers since deregulation. The reason is that there are no choices since deregulation because of the price disadvantage new entrants face.

Despite what's happening in California, deregulation of electric utilities works. In Texas and Pennsylvania, both very large states, deregulation has been successful. And the father of utility deregulation, Great Britain, is a great example of how it can work. After deregulation was implemented in Great Britain, almost one-third of Britain's customers switched to a new retail electric utility supplier.

ONE STEP BACK, TWO STEPS FORWARD

Despite what you hear from the media, this crisis is not that difficult to solve. All it takes is some strong political will in California. First, you have to take a step back and figure out what to do with the over $12 billion in debts that utilities owe to banks, creditors, and the power producers. That's easy; the state needs to step in and guarantee payment; then it needs to restructure and delay the payment schedule to allow these utilities to get back on their feet so that the state will never have to make good on their guarantee.

Now, after taking a step backward, you have to take one forward to today. Utilities must be freed to enter into long-term contracts to buy energy. They cannot be forced to buy in the spot market and subjected to every price move.

Last, another step forward must be taken for the future. California needs more power generation and it must reform its laws to encourage it. California's Silicon Valley is the home of the technology revolution—the same revolution that watched personal computer sales soar from 20 million five years ago to 60 million today. Oh, and by the way, we have to plug all of these computers in for electrical power. You don't have to be an analyst to figure out we've got a supply problem. Think about this technology revolution and how it eats up electricity. Then ask yourself, how is it that the largest state in the union, California, could think they could get by without building one single new power-generation plant in the past decade anywhere in the entire state?

The deregulation problems in California are unique to California; they will not spread to other states, and they certainly will not stop our economy or our markets.

Have a great day, and I'll see ya at 12,500!

PS: Please mail this commentary to a friend in California in case they are still unplugged!

> **Investment Footnote . . . What actually happened**
>
> Dead wrong. The Dow lost another −7.1 percent and barely stayed above 10,000, closing the year at 10,021.

It's the Stock Market, Stupid

JANUARY 9, 2003

Maybe one of the most famous one-liners in U.S. presidential politics was, "It's the economy, stupid." That line was made famous by James Carville, who was former President Bill Clinton's close political advisor and strategist. I am going to capture President Bush's $674 billion tax-cut package in a similar one-liner. When the president revealed his comprehensive tax-cut program, it was pretty obvious that he was telling the world, "It's the stock market, stupid."

EIGHT-PART PLAN

While the president's economic stimulus plan had eight components to it, more than half of the cost over the 10-year period would be for just one provision: ending the taxation of dividends for individuals. This one component will cost $364 billion over the next 10 years. When over half the plan's cost is centered on the stock market, it's easy to see why this proposal could be dubbed, "It's the stock market, stupid." In addition to the elimination of taxation of dividends, which was the cornerstone of his plan, there were seven additional components. The second largest component was to immediately phase in the expansion of child care tax credit, which would cost $91 billion. The third component of the plan was to move forward the marginal personal income tax rate cuts, scheduled for 2004 and 2006, to this year, 2003, at a cost over 10 years of $64 billion. Fourth was to move forward the marriage tax penalty relief from 2009 to this year, as well, at a cost of $58 billion. The fifth component of the plan expands the lowest 10 percent tax bracket for single and married couples—moving it from 6,000 to 7,000 for singles and from 12,000 to 14,000 for married couples. This proposed change would cost $48 billion. The sixth component involved changes in the alternative minimum tax (AMT), which would cost $29 billion. The seventh component was small-business "write-offs," or deductions, which would cost $16 billion. And eighth, and finally, was the establishment of re-employment accounts that provide the unemployed with up to $3,000 for training, childcare, transportation, and other expenses incurred when looking for a job. This component would cost $4 billion. So, all told, we have eight components that will cost $674 billion. As with any major changes in policy, it's important to figure out from an investment perspective who will benefit the most. I think there are three big winners.

THE OVERALL STOCK MARKET

The first winner is our stock market. President Bush's plan immediately lets every investor know that he is focused on the stock market. This proposal, however, does a whole lot more than simply eliminate the taxation of dividends for investors. It also hits at the heart of our problem—lack of investor confidence. By renewing the focus on dividends that have to be paid in cash quarterly, President Bush's plan is really changing all of corporate America. No longer can companies simply keep all of their cash until they can find a good (or bad) use for it. Investors now will want some of that cash paid out to them each quarter in a dividend that would be tax-free. Investors will know each quarter what a company is worth. And investors will be forced to focus on what's really important: cash flows in the companies that they invest in.

So now dividends will be treated better in our tax code than capital gains taxes. Do we risk businesses now not wanting to take risk to create capital gains? Not at all; we simply level the playing field by eliminating the tax on capital gains as well. First dividends, then capital gains, maybe even estate taxes . . . . Who knows, by the time we are done, we might even have only one simple flat tax.

THE RETAIL SECTOR

The second winner will be the retail sector. Any time you put more money in consumers' pockets, it's good for retail. Two things jump out from the president's plan that put cash into consumers' pockets now. First is the immediate phase-in of the child care tax credit. This proposal would immediately raise the child tax credit from $600 to $1,000, rather than phasing it in through 2010. The $400 difference would be sent to consumers as a rebate check. Second is the lowering of the overall personal income tax rates. Personal income tax rates were scheduled to be reduced in 2004 and 2006. President Bush's plan calls for those proposed cuts to be retroactive to January 1 of this year. The Internal Revenue Service would immediately lower the withholding taxes from everyone's paychecks and put more money in their pockets now. The combination of rebate checks and more take-home cash on your paycheck should provide a nice one-two boost to the retail sector.

DON'T FORGET TECHNOLOGY

The third winner is technology. Under President Bush's plan, small businesses would be able to triple the amount of tax write-offs for the purchase of new equipment. Currently they can write off $25,000. Under the president's plan, that would triple to $75,000. And the new equipment most likely to be purchased is technology. This incentive to small business should provide a nice boost to the technology sector.

FORGET THE DEFICIT!

One final note . . . I know many people are worried about the cost and what it will do to our already rising federal budget deficit. Let me put this in perspective for you. While keeping track of our deficit, it is important not to look at it in isolation. The deficit should be looked at as a percentage of gross domestic product (GDP). This is the most important way of looking at the deficit because it reflects our economy's ability to absorb the federal deficits. That is why one of the key economic measurements for a country to become eligible for membership in the European Monetary Union (EMU) is that their deficit as a percentage of GDP has to be less than 3 percent. Our deficit as a percent of GDP currently stands around 1.5 percent. With this new tax-cut program, it is projected to grow to just above 2 percent of GDP. To give you some historical perspective, the highest our deficit ever was as a percentage of GDP was back in 1943 when it was an unbelievable 31.1 percent. The highest our deficit has reached in the last 50 years as a percentage of GDP was in 1983 when it was 6.3 percent. A 2 percent budget deficit to GDP is not a problem. Also, don't forget that this economic stimulus package will help the economy grow, which will also lower the number. And whatever you do, remember— "It's the stock market, stupid."

Investment Footnote . . . What actually happened

I was right, as the Dow soared 25.3 percent.

A Not So Taxing Time
MAY 30, 2003

President George W. Bush signed into law this week a $350 billion tax cut plan. Well it's actually $330 billion in actual tax cuts and $20 billion in federal aid to state governments having trouble balancing their budgets. There are three very clear winners with the president's new tax policy: the economy, the stock market, and technology.

THE ECONOMY

The first winner is our economy. This new tax act accelerates tax cuts that Congress enacted in 2001 and makes them retroactive to January 1 of this year. The top marginal income tax rate will drop from 38.6 to 35 percent. Other rates will drop from 35 to 32 percent, from 30 to 28 percent, and from 27 to 25 percent. The Internal Revenue Service is already preparing new withholding guidelines for employees so that they immediately begin to start withholding less money. Here is why this is extremely critical at this point in time. The consensus on Wall Street is that our economy will be just fine in 2004. In other words, the monetary and fiscal stimulus that has been put in place should take hold by then and place our economy on the road to full recovery. The concern has always been how do we make it to 2004? Well, the president's tax cut plan just answered that question. This tax cut plan provides our economy with the necessary bridge to get from today to 2004. Think about it this way. The president's plan is placing more money in the pocket of every consumer right now. You don't need to worry about a wage increase to have more take-home pay . . . Uncle Sam is making sure that you will have more take-home pay. And remember, the consumer accounts for two-thirds of our economy. It's always a good sign when you give more money to two-thirds of what drives your economy. This plan provides our economy with the necessary bridge, supported by consumers, to get us to 2004 when our full economic recovery will be clearly under way.

THE STOCK MARKET

The second, and maybe the biggest, winner is our stock market. Whenever there is any proposed tax law change, the stock market always hopes for one of two things: it hopes either to receive a capital gains tax cut or a dividend tax cut. The stock market really doesn't care which one, simply cut one of them. The president's plan now cuts both at the same time. The top tax rate for dividends will now drop from 38.6 to 15 percent. The top tax rate for capital gains will drop from 20 to 15 percent as well. You simply couldn't ask for anything more. While the bears on Wall Street continue to growl that this compromise tax cut is not as good as the president's original plan to completely eliminate the dividend tax, I think the bears are wrong again. This plan is definitely better. You see, even though the president's original plan called for the complete elimination of taxation of dividends to individuals, his plan for establishing "excludable distribution accounts," or EDAs, as a back-door way of trying to cut capital gains taxes had a zero chance of passing: first, because it was a back-door attempt and second, it was way, way too complex. It would have created the full employment act for accountants, tax advisors, and lawyers. Thank goodness it didn't happen. In its place we have a straightforward tax cut for both dividends and capital gains. Here is why it is so important. It supports both aspects of our stock market value and growth. Think about it; the value style of investing has typically focused on undervalued companies who typically paid dividends. Now, those dividends are even more valuable because you pay fewer taxes on them. Meanwhile, the growth style of investing typically focused on companies who would, over time, return a capital gain as they grow in value. The capital gains that growth stocks return now are worth more, as well, because capital gains are also taxed less. Thus, the entire stock market benefits. Whether you are a value investor or a growth investor, you win. You now will be able to keep more of what you earn. I am not sure of what more we could ask for—unless of course the tax rates were dropped to 5 percent instead of 15 percent. Oh well, that will give us something to work on next year.

TECHNOLOGY . . . ONE MORE TIME

The third and final winner is technology. One of the real hidden gems in this tax cut is what it will do for technology demand. The reason it is a hidden gem is that it doesn't mention technology specifically. Under the new tax law, small businesses can expense for tax purchases up to $100,000 in equipment purchases. That's up fourfold from the current tax law that lets businesses expense only $25,000. In fact, it is even better than the president's original plan, which called for an increase to $75,000. How does this help technology? Well, the largest equipment purchase for small business is technology. And now they can write off four times more. I know that technology has already posted double-digit returns year-to-date; however, as a result of this new tax law, I believe technology will have an even better second half of the year.

In closing, the last three years have been a trying and taxing time on investors. Now, with these new changes, it's no longer such a taxing time.

Investment Footnote . . . What actually happened ↑

Wow, I was really right on this one. The economy grew at 7.5 percent for the third quarter of 2003 and, in the fourth quarter, it grew another 2.7 percent. Meanwhile, Nasdaq soared 50 percent in 2003.

Tax and Cash

JUNE 30, 2003

As I continue to travel across this great country of ours, I'm discovering that without a doubt the number one issue on most investors' minds has to do with the president's Tax Relief Act. Thus, I thought that I would take this opportunity to share some of those questions with you.

SHOW ME THE MONEY

The first question could be paraphrased as "Show me the money" or, specifically, when will the withholding schedules be adjusted and will any checks be sent out? The answer is that all withholding schedules will be adjusted on July 1 to reflect the lower marginal tax rates. In addition, checks totaling more than $14 billion will be mailed out in the third quarter to reflect the higher child tax credit, as well.

WHAT ABOUT REITs?

The second question could be paraphrased as "What about REITs?" or will real estate investment trusts (REITs) dividends be taxed at the lower 15 percent dividend rate? I am sorry to say that the answer is no. Dividends from REITs would be taxed at the higher ordinary rates because, unlike corporate dividends, REITs dividends are not currently taxed at the corporate level. Thus, there is no double taxation to get rid of.

WHAT ABOUT FOREIGN DIVIDENDS?

The third question could be paraphrased as "What about foreign dividends?" or will foreign dividends be taxed at the lower rate of 15 percent? The answer is yes for any company from a country with a tax treaty with the United States. As long as there is a tax treaty in place, that company's foreign dividends will be taxed at the lower 15 percent rate.

WHAT ABOUT SHORT-TERM GAINS?

The fourth question could be paraphrased as "What about short-term gains?" or, specifically, does this new tax relief act change the short-term capital gains tax rate? The short answer is . . . no. Stocks and mutual funds that are held for less than one year would continue to be taxed at ordinary income tax rates.

Let me shift gears now and move from tax to cash as I close out this commentary.

CASH IS KING

Everyone knows that cash is king, especially from the consumers' perspective. If we expect consumers, who account for two-thirds of our economy, to keep driving our economy, then those consumers need cash. Well, guess what? They have it—not just from their jobs, but from mortgage refinancings as well. Everyone knows about the record number of mortgage refinancings where consumers are rushing in to refinance their mortgage at a lower rate. What most investors fail to recognize, however, is that this is only half the issue. Not only are consumers locking in lower rates and lower payments, but they are taking out some cash as well.

Let me give you some perspective about the last three years. In 2000, consumers refinanced and took out $21 billion in cash. In 2001, they refinanced even more and took out $84 billion in cash. Last year, they really refinanced and took out a whopping $195 billion in cash. So far this year, they have already taken out $100 billion in cash. By the end of 2003, consumers will have taken out more than $200 billion in cash. Pretty impressive when you realize that the president's entire economic stimulus package that was just signed into law was $350 billion.

Here is some anecdotal proof that they are spending that money. The League of American Theatres and Producers reported that Broadway has set an all-time box office record for the 2002–2003 Broadway season. Broadway grossed $720,917,872 in the 52 weeks that encompassed this season. It's hard to believe that less than two years ago, after the tragedy of 9/11, most Broadway theaters were vacant. Everywhere you look, there are signs that things are picking up.

Investment Footnote . . . What actually happened   ↑

Dead right, as third-quarter GDP (gross domestic product) came in at 7.5 percent.

I Saw the Sign

SEPTEMBER 8, 2003

A couple of days ago, when I was conducting some research on stock dividends, the Ace of Base song "The Sign" came into my head. I couldn't get it out of my head—I hate when that happens. Then I realized that maybe it's a sign.

Here I am working on an analysis of the impact of dividend taxes being cut, which may be the single greatest sign that our markets have received in years that better times are in front of us, and no one is paying any attention to this extremely important sign. So I decided to write a commentary about it.

THE NEW WORLD ORDER

The investing world has completely changed. The new world order begins and ends with dividends. The lowering of the dividend tax rate to 15 percent was the final straw to put dividends on top of the investing world. This shifting focus toward dividends, however, was already under way. It was under way for two reasons: investors started demanding income and management discipline from the companies they own, and the way they got it was through dividends.

From an income standpoint, dividends are the perfect answer to provide an income stream regardless of where the overall market is headed. From a management discipline standpoint, dividends are an even better answer. You see, dividends force management discipline. The reason is that companies that pay a dividend have to come up with cold, hard cash every quarter to pay that dividend. You can't use accounting tricks and gimmicks or off-balance sheet games to pay dividends. They can only be paid in cash.

THE BEST IS YET TO COME

This new world order means that more and more companies will be both establishing a dividend if they don't already have one or increasing the dividend if they already have one in place. Let me give you an overall market perspective of why the best is yet to come in dividend yields. Namely, we have plenty of room to grow.

Here is some historical perspective to give you some idea of where things can be heading. Currently the Standard & Poor's 500 Index has a dividend yield of approximately 2 percent. That's a big increase from the 1.2 percent level in the year 2000. However, it's still extremely low from a historic perspective. In 1990, the S&P 500 dividend yield stood at 3.7 percent, almost double where it stands today. In 1980, the S&P 500 dividend yield stood at 4.5 percent. In 1970, it stood at 3.4 percent. In 1960, it was 3.3 percent. The S&P 500 dividend yield was a whopping 7.2 percent in 1950 and an equally eye-popping 6.3 percent in 1940. Anyway, I think you get the picture. Like I said, the best is yet to come.

IT'S A SIGN

Don't lose sight of the fact that dividends are an important sign for investors. Investing, after all, is not that difficult if you take the time to think about it logically. If a company raises the dividend, think about the sign they are trying to send us. They are telling us that they are confident about their future earnings. You would never raise the dividend unless you were extremely confident that the money will be there to meet that financial commitment. This sign is especially valuable in uncertain economic, market, and geopolitical times, like today.

SHOW ME THE MONEY

In the end, however, it's all about the money. Is there any proof you make more money in dividend-paying stocks? The answer is a resounding *yes*. The investment book *Triumph of the Optimists* studied that issue. Here is what the author did. A 101-year study examined the years 1900 to 2000. It examined the performance of the 30 percent of companies with the highest dividend yields at the beginning of each year and compared it to the companies that were in the lowest 30 percent of dividend yields. Here were the results. Companies with the highest dividend yields showed a total return of 12.2 percent a year while companies with the lowest dividend yields returned 10.4 percent a year.

Think of what that meant over the life of the study. If you had invested $1,000 in the lowest-yielding dividend stocks, you would be a millionaire today. Your investment would be worth $1,502,000. If, however, you did the right thing and invested $1,000 in the highest dividend-paying stocks, you would be a millionaire almost five times over. Your investment today would be worth $4,948,000.

If you are still looking for a reason to invest in dividend-paying stocks, I'll give you not just one reason—I'll give you 3,346,000 of them. That's the difference in the return of the highest-paying versus the lowest-paying dividend stocks in this study. Investors need to open up their eyes to this great investing opportunity.

In closing, let me remind you how the Ace of Base song ends. It goes like this: "I saw the sign, and it opened up my eyes. I saw the sign."

Investment Footnote . . . What actually happened

I was correct, as value, as measured by the S&P 500/ CitiGroup Value Index, was up 29 percent, while growth, as measured by the S&P 500/CitiGroup Growth Index, was only up 23.9 percent.

A 2004 Presidential Election Preview: And the Winner Is . . .

NOVEMBER 5, 2003

The 2004 U.S. presidential election will be upon us before we know it. In fact, in less than one year, it will be over. Until that time, however, the election will become a focus of investors not only in the United States but around the world as well. After all, when you are the largest economy and the largest market, every investor around the globe has a stake in who's running this place. Let me attempt to put this presidential election issue in some perspective for you.

WHY IS IT IMPORTANT?

To begin with, we need to remind ourselves why this election is important in the first place. I believe that this particular presidential election takes on added importance for two reasons: First, I believe it will most likely be a close election—and the closer the election, the greater the uncertainty. Remember, markets do not like uncertainty, and this could lead to increased market volatility next fall. The second reason is that the Democratic and Republican platforms differ on a very, very important issue to the financial markets—namely, tax cuts and tax policy. Well, before you can figure out who is going to win, you first have to figure out what the key issues are likely to be.

WHICH ONE IS IT, STUPID—THE ECONOMY OR THE WAR?

We know what the two most important issues will probably be in this upcoming election: the economy and the war. The problem is we do not know which will be more important to voters next November. Recall, if you will, that famous one-liner from Democratic strategist James Carville, aimed at President George H.W. Bush, the last time we were in Iraq; Carville quipped, "It's the economy, stupid," meaning George Bush, Sr. better stop worrying about Iraq and start worrying about our economy. Well, this time around maybe the one-liner aimed at President George W. Bush will be, "It's the war, stupid." From an economic perspective it will be all about jobs. With a 7.2 percent record economic growth in the third quarter of this year, no one can argue the fact that the fiscal and monetary stimulus has worked. However, as long as we hear the term "jobless recovery," it really doesn't matter how fast the economy grows; it only matters how fast employment grows. As the employment markets go, so go President Bush's reelection prospects.

From the war perspective, concern will revolve around continued military casualties. Most investors and voters have already long forgotten our easy military victory in Iraq. What they are focused on now is that "keeping the peace" is proving to be more difficult and more costly as well. Costly both in financial terms—reference the additional $87 billion to fund ongoing military and rebuilding expenses in Iraq—and costly in terms of loss of life. When every other day, one or two more soldiers die, voters and investors will question if we have an exit strategy. The president's reelection hopes may rise and fall with the ongoing U.S. casualty count in the war.

Now that we know the issues, let's look at the potential outcomes.

BUSH REELECTION

If the employment market recovers and some stability returns to Iraq, I believe George Bush stands a strong chance of winning reelection. If he does, he would most likely seek to make his first-term temporary tax cuts permanent. He might also push to reduce the dividend tax rate from 15 percent down to zero. Remember, that was the President's original proposal; he simply didn't have the votes in Congress to get it approved. His reelection would gain him a new honeymoon with Congress and a chance to push this through. I think he would also most likely phase in a total reduction of the long-term capital gains tax to zero. Phased in over three to four years, it would most likely drop from its current 15 percent level to 10 percent, then to 5 percent and then, finally, to zero. In addition, I think President Bush would make a major push at privatizing Social Security by creating private savings accounts as a key component of Social Security reform.

DEMOCRATIC VICTORY

Now, let's look at the other side of the coin. If the job market does not improve and we cannot develop an exit strategy in Iraq, President Bush is vulnerable and we may see a Democrat in the White House. But I think it would probably stop there. Because of the mix of Senate seats up for reelection as well as the House redistricting, I believe Republicans will most likely retain their control of both houses regardless of who wins the presidential election. From a Senate perspective, one-third of the seats are up for election every two years. In 2004 there are 34 seats at stake, 19 Democrat and 15 Republican. More important, both Democrat and Republican strategists alike feel that one-half of the Democrats' 19 seats are vulnerable. From a House perspective, all 435 seats are up for election every two years. The current makeup is 229 Republicans, 205 Democrats, and one independent. Historically, less than 40 to 50 of those 435 seats are truly challenged, as most are really uncontested. The reason is that congressional incumbents can build financial war chests fast. Thus, in the House, incumbents rule! Also, the impact of redistricting hurts the Democrats, especially in President Bush's home state of Texas. While no one knows what the final outcome in Texas will be, the consensus at this time is that the Republicans will either add two or three Republican House seats in Texas, or seven or eight. Either way, it makes the chances that much harder for the Democratic party to take the House back.

With a Democrat in the White House, regardless of which one of the current 9 or 10 candidates make it, their tax policy platform is the same; look for the following:

First, they say they would attempt to roll back most of President Bush's tax cuts. Second, they say they would veto any attempt by Congress to make any of the temporary tax cuts, like the one on dividends, permanent. Finally, I think it's safe to say that there would be no chance of privatizing Social Security with a Democrat in the White House. Also, I expect the Democratic focus to be on prescription drug benefits for Medicare, which could cause great uncertainty for the drug sector as the election approaches.

DRUG SECTOR SPOTLIGHT

Here is something to keep in mind regarding the drug sector as investors focus on the political risk that this sector now faces. While political risks are always important to look at for any sector, these risks are usually never as important as the underlying fundamentals of that sector. Thomas Bucher, the global healthcare sector team leader in our Frankfurt office of Deutsche Asset Management, continues to point out that the real issue in the drug sector is pricing power or lack thereof. More and more large drug-buying groups, such as private health plans, continue to negotiate higher discounts. This movement reflects the ongoing shift in power from drug manufacturers to buyers. I couldn't agree with Thomas more. While the election may drive the sector in the short run, in the long run I believe this shift in pricing power will be far more important.

AND THE WINNER IS . . .
DIVIDEND-PAYING STOCKS

In closing, let me answer the question you have been patiently waiting for: and the election winner is . . . *dividend-paying stocks*. That's right. Regardless of who is in the White House, dividend-paying stocks stand to win. If George Bush is reelected and pushes the dividend tax rate down to zero, it's easy to see why these stocks would be a clear winner. They will also win if a Democrat is in the White House. While the prospects for the dividend tax to fall to zero disappear, I think it is extremely unlikely that this tax law change could be rolled back with a Republican-controlled House and Senate. Even if it were somehow rolled back, dividend-paying stocks would still win. And the reason is that companies will continue to pay dividends regardless of the tax code. Remember, I don't care what the tax code is, institutional investors have figured out that the only way they can influence management discipline is to force companies to pay a cash dividend every 90 days. This trend will not reverse, regardless of tax policy. Second, the compensation shift from stock options to restricted stock (restricted stock receives dividends, stock options do not) means that more and more companies will initiate and increase their dividends regardless of tax policy. From the perspective of trying to figure out who will win the election, focus on two numbers: the jobs number and the number of military casualties.

From the perspective of trying to figure out why dividend-paying stocks win no matter who wins the election, you really need to focus on only one number: the S&P 500 dividend payout ratio. This ratio is measured as dividends per share divided by earnings per share. It peaked at over 70 percent in the early 1960s. And since World War II, the average has been 51 percent. Today it stands at only 31 percent. This number, more than anything else, tells you that companies have plenty of room to both establish and boost dividends—regardless of who is sitting in the Oval Office.

Investment Footnote . . . What actually happened

Correct again in 2004, as value, as measured by the S&P 500/CitiGroup Value Index, was up 13.3 percent; meanwhile, growth, as measured by the S&P 500/CitiGroup Growth Index, was only up 4.7 percent.

The Election Is Over, and Japanese Investors Win!

November 20, 2003

As Americans, we tend to be so self-centered that at times we think there is no election with importance other than the upcoming U.S. presidential election. When American investors say *election*, they assume that global investors know they are talking about the U.S. presidential election and its importance for the markets. Well, I hate to tell you, but the election is already over. Not the U.S. election, but rather the Japanese general election for the "lower house" of the Diet, their legislative branch. That would be similar to our House of Representatives in Congress. From my perspective, this election was every bit as important for the global markets as next year's U.S. presidential election.

NUMBER TWO AND TRYING HARDER

Try to keep things in the proper global perspective here. Japan is still the world's number two economy. That is absolutely amazing to me, considering the outright economic and market collapse that country experienced over the past decade. Yet once the dust settles, Japan is still the number two economy in the world, still holding a major key to the success of global economies and markets. In other words, forget what happened over the past 10 years; Japan is still a global force to be reckoned with, especially from an investment perspective.

WHY IT'S IMPORTANT

Let me share with you why I believe this particular Japanese election is so important. Prime Minister Koizumi's party, the LDP, had a bare majority of lower house seats in the last Diet (244 seats with 241 needed for a majority). But, in the past election, the LDP partnered with New Komeito (31) and NCP (10) to give it a clear majority of 285. Thus, from an outsider's perspective, this election is a nonevent because the ruling coalition is expected to retain its majority. The real question is Will Koizumi gain additional leverage with this election to move his platform forward?

AND THE SCORE IS . . .

The results show that Koizumi and his LDP won only 237 seats, just short of the 239 it won in the last election. However, that analysis missed the importance of this election. First, the coalition retains its majority; Koizumi stays in power and continues to pursue his agenda. The downside is he will probably have to make more concessions to his reform agenda, which in the long run is actually a positive. Even though building consensus takes more time in the short run, in the long run it puts you on more solid footing. Just look at President Bush in Iraq.

THE IMPACT

Enough of this postelection rhetoric. Let's move on to the impact. For me, the political and market impact is quite clear. Three things are likely to happen:

1. The LDP's reelection coalition means that there will probably be an early solution to the "nonperforming loan problem" in Japan's banks.
2. The International Monetary Fund (IMF) delivered its Financial Systems Stability Assessment of Japan, concluding, "The strengthening of the capital base of the banking system is clear . . . the government should develop a plan to recapitalize the banking sector." In my opinion, it will.

3. Reason works! It demonstrates what a Japanese bank can do if it has sufficient capital and its management is given the appropriate incentives to use it. Look for more to follow.

WHERE ARE WE NOW?

As an investor, your question should be, "Have these election results been reflected into the market?" My answer is "Not yet." But it won't be long. Witness the fact that Japan is poised to see the highest real-term pay increases among all the industrialized nations of the world, at 2.8 percent. To give you a frame of reference, the lowest industrialized country will be the United Kingdom, at 1.1 percent.

In addition to pay increases, consider this: Japan's latest industrial production number was revised to 3.8 percent from 3 percent—the single biggest revision in five years. This was fueled by higher demand in the electronics sector for products including cell phones and phone chips. Let me conclude by giving you a word of caution: Do not think that the Japanese upswing in cell phones and phone chips means a turnaround in the entire telecommunications sector. Michael Schmidt, Deutsche Asset Management's global sector team leader for telecommunications in our Frankfurt, Germany, office, astutely points out that developed countries (like Japan) will, on average, only be able to achieve cell phone growth rates in line with GDP. Thus, I am still bullish on Japan and bearish on telecommunications.

In closing, what I said on January 1, 2003, in my Top Ten Investment Themes still holds true today. Overweight the Japanese equity market!

Investment Footnote . . . What actually happened ↑

One hundred percent correct, as the Japanese stock market soared 37.8 percent in 2003.

Presidential Sectornomics

JANUARY 26, 2004

As the creator of Sectornomics™, a new investment principle in which the "sectors" in the market take on added importance, it is only fitting that I view the upcoming presidential election from that same perspective. In other words, as investors begin to worry about who will win and lose in the upcoming election—and what that will mean for the overall market—I believe I have a more important focus: namely, what sectors have the most to gain or lose from the upcoming election?

In my opinion three sectors have a lot at stake in this upcoming election: energy, defense, and health care. Let's take a closer look at all three, beginning with energy.

ENERGY

The energy sector is all about the much-ballyhooed energy bill. Regardless of which party controls the White House, I believe you are going to see passage of a comprehensive energy bill. What is at stake here is that the features of this legislation will vary greatly depending upon who is sitting in the White House.

In my opinion, a Democratic victory would, without a doubt, mean few (if any) tax breaks and incentives for oil and gas production. Instead, incentives and tax breaks would be geared toward alternative energy sources, especially fuel, cell companies, wind, and solar energy. I would expect the bulk of this tax break focus to be in the area of research. Last, but not least, I would expect a renewed focus on energy conservation, especially fuel efficiency programs.

If, however, George W. Bush is reelected, I would expect two major program initiatives in any comprehensive energy bill. First, look for large-scale tax incentives and breaks to boost domestic energy production and limit our dependence on foreign oil. In addition (depending on the final makeup of the House and Senate), I would expect the Republicans to make available federal lands for exploration and drilling, including the hotly debated Arctic National Wildlife Refuge.

DEFENSE

Next, let's look at defense, which always seems to have a lot to gain or lose as the political winds begin to shift. This presidential election is no different. I believe a Republican victory would be extremely bullish for the defense industry. Fundamentally, the Republican party is much more "hawkish" on defense. As a result, they tend to be much more willing to dramatically increase defense spending. You don't have to be an analyst to figure out that the defense sector outperforms the overall market in periods when defense spending is growing.

Fundamentally, a Democratic victory would be perceived as a major negative for the defense sector. That's because the Democratic Party has historically placed a higher funding priority on social issues such as health care. The political reality is, there is only so much money to go around and, thus, one of the most likely losers would be defense under a Democratic administration.

HEALTH CARE

Speaking of health care, let's move there next. Let me begin, however, by properly setting the stage. Remember that the recently adopted Medicare drug bill was viewed at opposite ends of the political spectrum by both of the major political parties.

Democrats called it unfair and in dramatic need of massive overhaul, while Republicans called it a great victory for seniors. With that as a backdrop, here is what I think we can expect. A Democratic victory would most likely mean making changes to the recent Medicare drug bill, probably by simplifying the benefits and perhaps increasing coverage. In addition, don't be surprised if there is a discussion of nationalizing the entire health care system.

If, on the other hand, President Bush is reelected, I would expect a push for private health care savings accounts as his long-term solution to our health care crisis.

In closing, while it will be fun to focus on who wins or loses the upcoming election, I believe savvy investors should instead focus on which sectors are positioned to be the big winners or the big losers.

Investment Footnote . . . What actually happened ↑

Right on all three industry and sector calls: health care up 0.2 percent, defense up 14 percent, and energy up a whopping 28.8 percent. Now that's what I call a trifecta.

Dr. Bob's ICU Index

FEBRUARY 22, 2004

As we move deeper into the presidential election season, investors are turning their focus from the markets to the campaign trail. Instead of wondering where the Dow Jones Industrial Average (DJIA) will be at the end of the year (12,500, if you ask me), they are instead wondering who will be in the White House.

In the spirit of that political focus I have created Dr. Bob's ICU Index for incumbent presidents. My ICU does not stand for "intensive care unit," but any incumbent president who doesn't pay attention to it will soon find that the intensive care unit cannot save their reelection campaign; they are going down in defeat.

Let me give you a little background on the original research that I am unveiling for the first time ever on Scudder.com.

RESEARCH THESIS

My research thesis for incumbent presidents began with the following premise: Most voters debate presidential politics with their heart and their soul and their mind. But when it comes to voting for president when an incumbent president is running for reelection, we vote with our pocketbooks. Thus, to get a peek at what could happen, all we need to do is find out what the most important issues are to voters' pocketbooks.

MISERY INDEX

I started my analysis with the old tried-and-true "misery index." This index, coined in the late 1970s, combined two things that make individuals miserable: inflation and unemployment. By combining the consumer price index with the unemployment rate, you were supposed to get a feel for how miserable voters felt. Well, I decided to take the misery index to the next level and used it as the foundation for Dr. Bob's ICU Index.

ICU COMPONENTS

My ICU Index is comprised of three components that are very important to investors, consumers, and voters alike—which means they could have a great impact on the prospects of any incumbent president. Here are my three components. The *I* in my ICU Index stands for *interest rates*, as measured by the 10-year Treasury bond. I believe interest rates are important because they impact housing and automobile purchases as well as credit card debt repayment. The *C* in my ICU Index stands for the *consumer price index*. Just as in the old misery index, I believe voters and investors hate it when they have to pay more for the exact same product or service because of inflation. Finally, the *U* in my ICU Index stands for *unemployment*, which, just as in the misery index, is a key component because high unemployment cannot be a good thing for consumers, investors, or, ultimately, for voters.

So, there you have it. My ICU Index is a pretty simple concept. All you have to do is add the three components together to see where we stand. Thus, the current ICU Index would be just under 12 percent. You get there by taking the *I* (interest rate of the 10-year Treasury), which is at about 4 percent. Add to that the *C* (consumer price index), which is below 2 percent. Now, let's round the combined total to 6 percent and then add in the *U* (unemployment), which currently stands at 5.8 percent, which would put our current ICU Index at a little under 12 percent, or 11.8 percent. Now what does that mean for our incumbent, President George W. Bush?

BACK-TEST TIME

As with any new research product, you need to back-test it to see if it reveals any trends. That is exactly what I did. I went back 50 years to 1953 (which, by the way, was the year I was born, although that had nothing to do with the study) and tried to identify trends for incumbent presidents using Dr. Bob's ICU Index. During that entire 50-year period, only three incumbent presidents failed to win reelection: Gerald Ford in 1976, Jimmy Carter in 1980, and George Bush, Sr., in 1992. What was their ICU Index? Gerald Ford's ICU Index was 21.08 percent. (The interest on the 10-year Treasury was 7.6 percent, the consumer price index stood at 5.8 percent, and unemployment weighed in at 7.7 percent). Jimmy Carter's ICU Index was a whopping 32.13 percent. (Interest on the 10-year Treasury was an eye-popping 11.5 percent, the consumer price index was even a more staggering 13.5 percent, and unemployment was 7.2 percent). Finally, when George Bush, Sr., was defeated, his ICU Index was 17.54 percent. (Interest on the 10-year Treasury bond was an even 7 percent. The consumer price index was an even 3 percent, while unemployment was 7.5 percent.)

WHAT DOES IT MEAN?

I believe this back-test proves my theory that investors and consumers vote with their pocketbooks regarding incumbent presidents; they are being held accountable for interest rates, consumer price, and unemployment. If those three indicators are high, the chances for an incumbent president's reelection are slim. Said another way, in the past 50 years no incumbent president has ever lost an election with a Dr. Bob ICU Index below 17 percent. George W. Bush's current ICU is below 12 percent. You do the math.

RAMIFICATIONS FOR THE MARKET

The potential ramifications for our equity markets are quite clear. A Bush reelection, which Dr. Bob's ICU Index is clearly predicting, may be the single greatest thing to ever happen to dividend-paying stocks. Here is why. George W. Bush has already told Wall Street what he thinks the tax rate should be on dividend-paying stocks: zero percent. The president simply didn't have the votes in Congress this past May and had to settle for a 15 percent tax rate. A Bush reelection would most likely tilt the makeup of both the House and the Senate and a zero percent tax rate on dividends would get much closer to becoming a reality. I liked dividend-paying stocks when the highest tax rate was 38.6 percent. I absolutely love dividend-paying stocks with the tax rate at the current 15 percent level. If my ICU Index is correct and Bush is reelected, the "word" has yet to be created to capture what a screaming buy dividend-paying stocks would become.

In closing, I believe history books will show Dr. Bob's ICU Index to be not only a great indicator for incumbent presidential elections, but the turning point for the "quality trade" in which dividend-paying stocks replace nondividend-paying stocks as the investment vehicle of choice. Choose wisely when picking presidents and stocks!

PS: I want to provide a quick follow-up to my February 6, 2004, commentary, "Indicator Overload," where I discussed the January effect, Super Bowl effect, Santa Claus effect, and Election effect. I have one final indicator: The Daytona 500 effect. Here is how it works: Leo Grohowski, my good friend and colleague (and boss), who happens to be the chief investment officer for Deutsche Asset Management Americas, analyzed the return of the DJIA between 1959 and 2003 based upon what make of car won the Daytona 500. For example the average return for the DJIA when a Dodge won the Daytona 500 was −17 percent and the average return for the DJIA when a Pontiac won the Daytona 500 was +6.3 percent. In fact, there are only two makes of cars that can boast positive double-digit returns for the DJIA when they win the Daytona 500. Those two makes are Chevrolet and Buick. Well, this year's Daytona 500 is history and the winner was Dale Earnhardt, Jr. More important from my perspective, guess what make of car he drove? You guessed it—a Chevrolet. That's one more in a long line of indicators pointing to double-digit returns again this year.

PPS: Sticking with the Daytona 500, did you see President Bush's presidential motorcade take a lap around the track? I do not ever recall a presidential motorcade taking a lap around a racetrack. Who knows, maybe the president got an advance look at my ICU Index for incumbent presidents and was taking his victory lap while plotting his strategy to lower dividend taxes to 0 percent.

Ladies and gentlemen, start your dividend-paying investment engines!

Investment Footnote . . . What actually happened ↑

I was right, as value outperformed in 2004. Value was up 13.3 percent, as measured by S&P 500/CitiGroup Value Index; meanwhile, growth, as measured by the S&P 500/CitiGroup Growth Index, was only up 4.7 percent.

I Told You So!

November 4, 2004

Back on February 20, 2004, I unveiled my ICU Index, which declared George W. Bush would be reelected president. A lot has happened since my February 20 market commentary. I have been confronted by Democrats and Republicans alike all across the country who disagreed with the concept of my ICU Index. Well, when it was all said and done, Dr. Bob's ICU Index correctly predicted the outcome of this presidential election just like it has for the past 50 years! I don't want to say I told you so but . . . I told you so!

ICU COMPONENTS

My ICU Index is comprised of three components that are very important to investors, consumers, and voters alike—which means these components would have a great impact on the prospects of any incumbent president. Here are my three components: The "I" in my ICU Index stands for interest rates as measured by the 10-year Treasury bond. I believe interest rates are important because they impact housing and automobile purchases as well as credit card debt repayment. The "C" in my ICU Index stands for the consumer price index. I believe voters and investors hate when they have to pay more for the exact same product or service because of inflation. Finally, the "U" in my ICU Index stands for unemployment, which is a key component because high unemployment cannot be a good thing for consumers, investors or, ultimately, for voters.

BACK-TEST TIME

As with any new research product, you need to back-test it to see if it reveals any trends. That is exactly what I did. I went back 50 years to 1953 and tried to identify trends for incumbent presidents using Dr. Bob's ICU Index. During that entire 50-year period only three incumbent presidents failed to win reelection: Gerald Ford in 1976, Jimmy Carter in 1980, and George H. W. Bush in 1992. What was their ICU Index? Gerald Ford's was 21.10 percent (the interest on the 10-year Treasury was 7.6 percent,, the consumer price index stood at 5.8 percent, and unemployment weighed in at 7.7 percent). Jimmy Carter's ICU Index was a whopping 32.20 percent (interest on the 10-year Treasury was an eye-popping 11.5 percent, the consumer price index was an even more staggering 13.5 percent, and unemployment was 7.2 percent). Finally, when George H. W. Bush was defeated, his ICU Index was 17.50 percent (interest on the 10-year Treasury bond was an even 7.0 percent, the consumer price index was an even 3.0 percent, and unemployment was 7.5 percent).

WHAT DOES IT MEAN?

This back-test proved my theory that investors and consumers vote with their pocketbooks; incumbent presidents are held accountable for interest rates, consumer prices, and unemployment. If those three indicators are high, the chances for an incumbent president's reelection are slim. Said another way, in the past

50 years no incumbent president has ever lost an election with a Dr. Bob ICU Index below 17 percent.

ELECTION DAY ICU READING

On Election Day President Bush's ICU Index was 12 percent. My ICU Index is a pretty simple concept. All you have to do is add the three components together. On Election Day the "I" (interest rate on a 10-year Treasury bond) was at 4.1 percent. Add to that the "C" (consumer price index), which was 2.5 percent. Then add the "U," the unemployment rate, which in this case was 5.4 percent. When you add them all together, the President's ICU Index was 12 percent! Add the fact that no incumbent president ever lost with an ICU under 17 percent, and George Bush was indeed reelected on these pocketbook issues. The ICU Index has never been wrong!

RAMIFICATIONS FOR THE MARKET

The ramifications for our equity markets are quite clear. A Bush reelection, which Dr Bob's ICU Index clearly predicted, will be the single greatest thing to ever happen to dividend-paying stocks. Here is why: George W. Bush has already told Wall Street what he thinks—the tax rate on dividend-paying stocks should be 0 percent. But the president simply didn't have the votes in Congress this past May to do that, and so had to settle for a 15 percent tax rate. But now, riding the coattails of the president's reelection, Republicans have increased their majority in both the House and the Senate; thus it appears that a 0 percent tax rate on dividends is almost certain to become a reality.

I liked dividend-paying stocks when the highest tax rate was 39.6 percent. I absolutely loved dividend-paying stocks at our current 15 percent tax-rate level. The words haven't been created to describe what I think of dividend-paying stocks if and when the tax rate goes to zero. Or, then again, maybe they have . . . I TOLD YOU SO!

Maybe the real winner of this election is everyone invested in dividend-paying stocks!

> ### Investment Footnote . . . What actually happened ↑
>
> I was right, as value outperformed in 2005. Value was up 3.5 percent, as measured by S&P 500 CitiGroup Value Index; meanwhile, growth as measured by the S&P 500 CitiGroup Growth Index was only up 2.5 percent.

Stocks, Bonds, and Bush!

November 9, 2004

There are now two questions on every investor's mind as a result of George W. Bush's reelection. First, what will it mean for the economy, and second, what will it mean for the stock market?

Before I give you my perspective on both of those issues, I want to remind you as an investor not to underestimate the importance of last week's election even though President Bush won by a small margin with 51 percent of the popular vote. That 51 percent, after all, was still the largest vote percentage victory since 1988. And remember, the Republicans picked up seats in both the House of Representatives and the Senate. But more important, for the first time in 50 years, Republicans start off with control of the Oval Office, control of the House, control of the Senate, and the majority of state governorships. In my mind, that makes this an even bigger mandate than what Ronald Reagan had in the 1980s. As the president uses his newfound political clout to pursue his agenda, it stands to have great impact on both the economy and the markets.

ECONOMIC IMPACT

First, from an economic perspective, let me begin by setting the stage. There were already some unique forces in position to help our economy as we head into 2005. First, the price of oil has stopped climbing, which boosts both business and consumer confidence.

In fact, this just might be the biggest tax cut of all when you consider oil has fallen from a high of \$55.20 a barrel to only \$49 and change. Second is the Florida rebuilding boom, resulting from the unprecedented four hurricanes this season. The Florida boom that is now under way will not be slowed down by winter weather; remember it's a Florida building boom, which has a year-round season.

Add the election to these two forces and there is no doubt in my mind that our economy is poised to surprise on the high side for 2005. The election should have two specific impacts on the economy. First, both consumers and CEOs alike feel better now that the election is over and all of the negative rhetoric is behind us. This bodes well for consumer and business confidence, which in turn bodes well for consumer and business spending—especially when you consider that there was not one single terrorist event in the United States leading up to this presidential election. And maybe even more important, there were no legal battles or extended controversy regarding the outcome. Mix this all together and we have very strong business and consumer confidence.

The second impact I see the election having on the market is that the prospects of permanent tax cuts have never looked brighter. The significance for the economy is that if these tax cuts are made permanent, they will serve as the foundation to improve the outlook for economic growth.

MARKET IMPACT

Now let's move on from the economic impact to the market impact. I believe this election was not so much about the overall market impact, but rather how certain programs on the president's agenda will impact certain sectors of our stock market.

Here is a "six-pack," if you will, of themes. (I use *six-pack* because my blue-collar Pittsburgh Iron City Beer heritage will never leave me.)

1. I believe Social Security will be privatized. Currently, individual taxpayers pay a 6.2 percent Social Security tax

matched by their employers' contribution of an additional
6.2 percent. I believe Social Security will be partially privatized by letting individuals self-direct 4 percent of their
6.2 percent to their own retirement accounts, which
would be a boon for financial services companies.

2. The tax cuts that President Bush pushed through in his
first term will most likely be made permanent in his
second term. In addition, the dividend tax rate could
go to zero. The big winners will be all the high-quality
dividend-paying stocks in our marketplace.

3. There will be major tax reform—whether it's the move
to a flat tax or the dramatic move away from income
taxes completely, to a value-added national sales tax.
One way or another, the tax code will more than likely be
overhauled to encourage people to save and invest
instead of penalizing them. Again, the big winner would
be financial services firms.

4. We could have major tort reform. It's long overdue to get
our legal system in order. And with President Bush's
known contempt of lawyers, it just might happen. There
are already signs across the country that tort reform is
starting state by state. In California, voters approved by
59 to 41 percent an initiative that permits an individual to
bring a lawsuit only if the person actually suffered injury
and only if they actually lost money or property. That
will slow down class action lawsuits in that state. And in
Colorado, voters overwhelmingly rejected by 77 to
23 percent a measure that would have repealed a requirement that property owners give builders a chance to
correct defects before filing a lawsuit. If this would have
passed in Colorado, consumers would have been allowed
to sue builders first and ask to correct defects later.
As tort reform catches on, the big winners will be the
tobacco industry as well as any company with potential
asbestos liability.

5. Both the health care and pharmaceutical industries will be celebrating George Bush's reelection because it means that there will be no government-negotiated prices for Medicare drugs. Let the marketplace set the price for drugs, not the federal government. This is a big win for the health care community and should greatly help this sector over the next four years—especially when you consider that when the government gets involved in buying a hammer from a defense contractor, the federal government shrewdly negotiates to buy a hammer that costs $12 at Home Depot for a mere $1,575. Thank goodness they will not be involved in setting drug prices. I get a headache just thinking about what a bottle of Tylenol would cost with the government involved.

6. Finally, I have no doubt that defense spending will continue to rise. Regardless of who was elected president, defense spending was set to rise as we continue to retool our entire defense industry to fight the war on terrorism. I believe spending on defense will go much higher and much faster under a Bush administration with a Republican House and Senate. Obviously, the big winners in this instance are the defense contractors.

In closing, I want you to think about this piece of presidential-election and market-cycle history. Did you ever wonder how the market performed during the first year of a president's second term, which is really the fifth year in office? Well, I have been thinking about it, and the answer is "quite well," thank you.

You see, in the past 25 years, there have only been two incumbent presidents reelected for a second term. The average return of the S&P 500 in the first year of a second term was a whopping 29.3 percent. In Reagan's first year of his second term (1985), the market was up 27.7 percent. And in Clinton's first year of his second term (1997), the market was up 31 percent.

Next year will mark the first year of President Bush's second term. From an investment perspective, 2005 can be summed up in just three words: stocks, bonds, and Bush!

Investment Footnote . . . What actually happened

I got two out of three right. The Dow was down just barely at −0.6 percent, while both of the broader indices were up: the S&P 500 was up 3 percent and the Nasdaq was also up at 1.4 percent.

Japanese Election Special—
The New Mailman Delivers
SEPTEMBER 12, 2005

In the sports world, Utah Jazz basketball star Karl Malone was given the nickname "The Mailman" because, like the real mailman, who always delivers in rain or shine, so too did Karl Malone. He always seemed to deliver a good game no matter whom he was playing or how he felt.

Now we have a new mailman, and this one comes from political circles. Japan Prime Minister Koizumi just "delivered" the biggest landslide victory in Japanese politics in almost 20 years. The cornerstone of Prime Minister Koizumi's campaign was to privatize the country's postal system.

LANDSLIDE

If ever the term *landslide* could be applied to an election, it would be this one. Prime Minister Koizumi's ruling Liberal Democratic Party, or LDP, won 296 of the 480 contested seats in the lower house. That 296 total is the second highest in the 50-year history of the Liberal

Democratic Party. But what makes this victory even more staggering is that the LDP's coalition partner—the New Komeito—won an additional 30 seats; so the coalition has 326 seats in the lower house, which is more than two-thirds of the 480 lower house seats. The significance of this is that with more than two-thirds control, the coalition will be able to pass bills that in the past have been voted down by the upper house.

POSTAL REFORM

Make no mistake about it. Prime Minister Koizumi will use this election landslide as his mandate to privatize the postal system, which, by the way, is about a whole lot more than simply delivering the mail in Japan. Japanese post offices also have investment products called *postal savings accounts*. These are, in essence, time deposits that pay guaranteed rates of return. They were established over a decade ago when the Japanese stock market was crashing and interest rates were soaring. Most Japanese investors didn't go to the post office simply to mail a letter; they went to invest in savings accounts with guaranteed returns. When you combine the insurance (guarantee) aspect of the post office (remember they guarantee the investments) with the actual savings accounts, it is actually one of the world's largest financial institutions.

From my perspective, this could prove to be not only a big boon to the financial services companies in Japan, but a boon to the entire financial services industry around the world as well.

IT'S THE ECONOMY, STUPID

In U.S. politics, perhaps the most repeated one-liner in history is former President Clinton's top advisor James Carville's quip, "It's the economy, stupid." Well, maybe that quote could be used to explain the Japanese election, because their economy has clearly turned the corner.

Over the last three years, the Japanese economy has come back from the dead. However, the economy has been driven mainly by exports to China (which are up 150 percent since 2001) and by government spending. Now, in addition to exports and government spending, consumer spending is finally picking up. And that's not all. Business spending on big-ticket capital expenditures is finally picking up too.

When you combine booming exports to China with continued government spending and then add in consumer spending and business spending, we may well see one of the strongest economic and broad-based rebounds in Japan in the past 20 years. And that, in turn, sets a strong and solid foundation for the Japanese stock market.

In closing, remember that it's still not too late. Remember, the mailman delivers every day, and I believe this investment story has a long way to go as well.

Investment Footnote . . . What actually happened

I was right. The Japanese stock market climbed +21.7 percent in 2005. And it didn't stop in 2006, as it posted another +5.9 percent return.

German Election Special—No One Delivers

September 19, 2005

My most recent election special commentary, dated September 12, focused on the Japanese elections. I titled it, "The New Mailman Delivers," since Prime Minister Koizumi registered a landslide victory. Prime Minister Koizumi's platform was one of massive government reform and privatization, especially in the postal system, which also operates a massive investment and insurance operation. Well, if the Japanese election special commentary was titled "The New Mailman Delivers," then yesterday's elections in Germany have to be titled "No One Delivers."

THE RESULTS

Current Chancellor Gerhard Schröder and his Social Democratic Party took 34 percent of the vote. Chancellor Schröder's current coalition partners, the Greens, won 8 percent of the vote and the new Left Party won almost 9 percent of the vote.

The challenger, Angela Merkel, and her Christian Democratic Union, along with their "sister" party, the Christian Social Union, won 35 percent of the vote. Just weeks ago, projections were that Angela Merkel could win an outright majority of over 50 percent of the votes. That would have made all talk of a coalition to govern Germany a moot point. Not anymore. Angela Merkel's preferred coalition partner, the Free Democrats, garnered almost 10 percent of the vote. (And remember, when trying to put together a coalition government to reach a majority—51 percent—even after the election is over, it isn't really over until a majority coalition is actually put in place.)

The only thing that is clear from this election is that no one has a clear mandate to govern Germany.

WHY THIS MATTERS

From my perspective, the election in Germany is not just important to Germany. It has ramifications for the European Union and the global markets as well. First of all, whenever there is an election taking place in one of the world's top five economies, the results stand to have an economic impact around the world. Germany is, after all, the fifth largest economy in the entire world, trailing only the United States, China, Japan, and India. But its impact is much, much greater than simply being the fifth largest world economy. Germany is also the largest economy in the 25-member European Union. When you look at the European Union as a whole, it is approaching the size of the number one economy in the world, the United States. That's why I believe what does or does not happen in Germany has ramifications throughout the rest of the European Union and the world.

WHAT DIDN'T HAPPEN

I think the best way to look at this election from an investment perspective is to consider what didn't happen. Angela Merkel—whom some were calling the next Margaret Thatcher (the former British prime minister in the 1980s, whose bold and sweeping reforms are credited with reviving the British economy)—didn't win an outright majority. The foundation of Angela Merkel's campaign was major reform in the three most critical issues in Germany, as far as investors are concerned: tax structure, rigid labor laws, and social programs.

Merkel promised to cut social and welfare benefits as well as to lessen some of the job and employment guarantees currently in place. Any reform in the cost structure of the labor market would be looked upon as a boon for the overall economy and market.

On the tax front, Merkel proposed a 25 percent flat tax on all income. Now, instead of these sweeping and dramatic market-friendly reforms, Germany is in gridlock. More important, at least from my perspective, if Germany had pulled off these major reforms in labor programs, social programs, and tax structure, there was a good chance that the other 25 members of the European Union would soon follow Germany's lead.

WHAT NEXT?

What happens next depends on the coalition that is finally put in place to govern Germany. It does not necessarily mean that these much-needed reforms, from an investment perspective, will not happen. It simply means that if they do happen, they will be implemented over a longer period of time and will most likely not be as dramatic in nature.

In the short run, I think these developments will probably put downward pressure on the euro, the common currency of the European Union, and the overall market in Germany. There is one thing that is the same the entire world over. Investors hate uncertainty. And uncertainty may be the only thing that this German election delivered to the markets.

Investment Footnote . . . What actually happened ↓

I was wrong. The German stock market didn't seem to care, rising 10.3 percent in 2005. And then, in 2006, it really boomed, jumping an amazing 36.4 percent.

The Election Is Finally Over!

OCTOBER 30, 2006

I know that you might be thinking this commentary is a little early, declaring that the election is finally over—but it actually depends upon what election you are talking about. Believe it or not, we live in a global economy and global marketplace that is interconnected. As investors in the United States, we have to be as aware of events (or elections) outside the United States as those inside the United States, especially if we invest globally. From a global perspective, the election that I am talking about occurred this weekend south of our border in Brazil.

ELECTION BACKGROUND

Let me begin by giving a brief background on the presidential elections in Brazil. On October 1, 2006, the first election was held for president of Brazil. No candidate received the absolute majority that was necessary to be elected. Incumbent President, Luiz Inacio Lula da Silva received 48.6 percent of the vote, while Geraldo Alckmin, the former governor of Sao Paulo, Brazil, received 41.6 percent of the vote. Unlike the United States, where whoever receives the most votes for president is declared president, in Brazil you have to have at least 50.1 percent of the votes. If not, there is a runoff vote, with the top two vote-getters going head to head. This is exactly what happened this past Sunday in Brazil. Maybe we could learn something from them on this issue.

That's not a typo. The election was held on a Sunday. Their elections are actually held on Sundays instead of Tuesdays, as we do here in the United States. The reason elections are held on Sundays is that most Brazilians do not work on Sundays, so it is much easier for them to vote on that day. Meanwhile, in America, we continue to have poor voter turnout as two-income families struggle with who will take the kids to day care and who will pick them up, and whether the voting polls will be open early or late enough to vote on a Tuesday. And there is one more interesting thing about voting in Brazil: it is mandatory. You are required to vote. If you don't vote, the next time you need something from the government like a passport, permit, or license, you will not get it. Needless to say, everyone votes in Brazil. Like I said, maybe we could learn something from them. That's another topic for another time.

THE CANDIDATES

Let me briefly touch upon the backgrounds of the two candidates. Geraldo Alckmin was elected deputy governor of Sao Paulo in 1994. In 2001, he took over as governor. He is generally credited with turning the fiscal fortunes of Sao Paulo completely around by privatizing and selling off $35 billion worth of state-owned companies. His platform was largely about economic change, tax cuts, reduction in government spending, and anticorruption.

Incumbent President Luiz Inacio Lula da Silva is Brazil's first "blue-collar" president, with charisma and an understanding of the poor and middle classes. He campaigned to continue the strong social safety net that he put into place for the needy as well as to increase government spending on key infrastructure projects. To say that these two approached the election from opposite corners would be an understatement.

THE RESULTS

The results of this election were overwhelming. Incumbent President Luiz Inacio Lula da Silva was a landslide winner for a second four-year term, gathering over 60 percent of the vote (which in political circles is the definition of a landslide)—actually 60.8 percent, to his challenger Geraldo Alckmin's 39.2 percent.

Even though the election was a landslide victory, looking beyond the headline numbers reveals a somewhat different story. President da Silva won almost 80 percent of the vote in the northeast where he was born and the residents are both poorer and less educated than in the south of Brazil. Also, it was this region that benefited the most from the president's program of increased welfare to poorer families. Meanwhile, Mr. Alckmin actually won in the more developed south by a 53 to 47 percent margin. He also carried his home state of Sao Paulo, which is home to both the industrial and financial centers of Brazil. The campaign was a bitter one where class warfare was clearly an issue, as these results prove.

THE IMPACT

What does all of this mean for investors? In other words, what is the impact of this presidential election? I believe there are three important elements to focus on with the results of this election.

First is continuity. What investors hate most is uncertainty. They would rather deal with a known rather than an unknown, regardless of policy differences. Investors know exactly what they are getting and what to expect from President da Silva. This is actually a good thing.

Second is moderation. While da Silva is a true blue-collar working-class president, he is not an extremist. While he has to be categorized as a "leftist leader," it is unfair and incorrect to paint him with the same "leftist" political brush as leftist leaders such as Bolivia's Evo Morales and Venezuela's Hugo Chavez. President da Silva is a moderate compared to those truly leftist leaders. After all, he ran unsuccessfully for president three times before he finally won in 2002. And back in 2002, his campaign rhetoric was leftist. In his first term, he ruled more as a centrist who actually embraced a conservative economic policy. And I expect more of the same in his second term. Again, this is actually a good thing!

Third, and finally, this election had nothing to do with the global commodity boom going on around the world. As the quality of life and quality of living improves around the world, so does the demand for commodities. One of the biggest beneficiaries of that commodity boom is Brazil which is witnessing unprecedented demand for its soybeans and iron ore. This commodity boom was going to continue regardless of who won the presidential election. Once again, this is a good thing!

In closing, President da Silva is now officially a "lame duck" president. You see, in Brazil, just as in the United States, presidents are constitutionally barred from a third successive term. I believe this means he just might be more supportive of labor and tax law changes as well as cutting government spending to make Brazil a more business-friendly environment. After all, he doesn't have to worry about getting reelected in the short run and can focus on longer-term issues. This election could be extremely bullish, not only for Brazil, but for all of Latin and South America as well.

And for you global investors in the United States, this is one more reason to go global, go global, and go even more global!

Investment Footnote . . . What actually happened ↑

I was right. While the U.S. market returned 16.3 percent, as measured by the Dow, the rest of the investment world boomed as the MSCI–EM (Morgan Stanley Capital International-Emerging Markets) was up 23.5 percent and the MSCI–EAFE (Morgan Stanley Capital International–Europe, Australia, and the Far East) was up a whopping 29.2 percent.

Tax Cuts Only for the Rich Are Enough to Drive a Man to Drink or Drive Him to Dubai

MARCH 16, 2007

As I find myself toward the tail end of my seven-country international tour, with only Oman and a stop in Dubai remaining, it is simply amazing to me how many questions and discussions I have had regarding U.S. tax policy and tax rates. But even more, I find it quite fascinating that so many people outside the United States actually care about and focus on our tax system and tax cuts. And most fascinating of all, is their misguided assumption that the United States only cuts taxes for the rich.

When I gave some more thought to it, I realized that most people inside the United States also have this same misguided concept. I guess when you think about it, it really shouldn't be a surprise. Every time there is mention of a tax cut, journalists and media talking heads alike quickly proclaim it as "another tax cut just for the rich" and, what makes matters worse, this proclamation is simply accepted as fact. No questions are asked. Not only that, we start inculcating this tax-cuts-for-the-rich premise early and often, as most college professors teach this concept to be the truth as well.

Anyhow, I struggled with how to explain that this is not true. I didn't want my explanation to take on major political overtones, so instead I came up with a great idea.

I remembered a story that my good friend Bob Peck told me about tax cuts for the rich. Bob and I worked together twice, first in my days at Van Kampen Funds, when he was the chief investment officer for bonds and I was the firm's chief investment strategist; subsequently, when I went to Kemper Funds (now DWS Funds), I recruited Bob to join me, once again as head of our bond group.

As the head of all bond investments, Bob had to constantly answer questions with a Washington, D.C., focus about such things as the budget deficit, trade deficit, and our tax code, including tax cuts.

While Bob Peck has since retired, and I miss him dearly, I will never forget his story about how tax cuts are not always just for the rich. Thus, I decided to write this special market commentary on that topic.

LET'S HAVE A DRINK

Let's put tax cuts in terms everyone can understand by going out and having a drink. Suppose that every day, 10 men go out for a beer and the bill for all 10 comes to $100. If they paid their bill the way we pay taxes in the United States, here is how it would work out.

The first four men (the poorest) would pay nothing at all. The fifth man would pay $1. The sixth man would pay $3. The seventh would pay $7. The eighth would pay $12. The ninth would pay $18. The tenth man (the richest) would pay $59. Think of each of these men as representing the tax brackets in the United States, where the bottom four brackets are not taxed and pay nothing at all. The fifth man, or tax bracket, pays taxes in the United States, but everyone in that tax bracket combined only accounts for 1 percent of our total tax revenue. That is why the fifth man pays $1. A dollar is 1 percent of $100. Meanwhile, the tenth man represents the top tax bracket in this country. When you add up all of the taxes the people in the top tax bracket pay, they account for 59 percent of all of our tax revenues. And thus, the tenth man paid $59, because that amount is 59 percent of their daily $100 beer-drinking bill.

This is exactly what the men decided to do as they drank in the bar every day, and they seemed quite happy with the arrangement. That is, until one day, the owner threw them a curve.

"Since you are all such good customers," he said, "I'm going to reduce the cost of your daily beer by $20. Drinks for the 10 of you now cost just $80."

The group of men still wanted to pay their bill the way we pay our taxes, so the first four men were unaffected. They would still drink for free. But what about the other six men, the paying customers? How could they divide the $20 windfall (or tax cut) so that everyone would get his "fair share"?

They realized that $20 divided by six is $3.33. But if they subtracted that from everyone's share, then the fifth and sixth men would each end up being paid to drink his beer.

So, the bar owner suggested that it would be most fair to reduce each man's bill by roughly the same amount on a percentage basis, and he proceeded to work out the amount each man should now pay.

The fifth man, like the first four, now paid nothing at all (a 100 percent savings). The sixth man now paid $2, instead of $3 (a 33 percent savings). The seventh man paid $5, instead of $7 (a 28 percent savings). The eighth man paid $9, instead of $12 (a 25 percent savings). The ninth man paid $14, instead of $18 (a 22 percent savings). And the tenth man now paid $49, instead of $59 (a 16 percent savings).

Each of the 10 men was better off than before, and the first four men continued to drink for free. But once outside the bar, the men began to compare their savings (or tax cuts).

"I only got a dollar out of the $20," declared the sixth man. He pointed to the tenth man and said, "But he got $10."" "Yeah, that's right," exclaimed the fifth man. "I only saved a dollar, too. It's unfair that he got 10 times more than I." "That's true," shouted the seventh man. "Why should he get back $10, when I only got $2? The wealthy get all of the breaks!"

"Wait a minute," yelled the first four men in unison. "We didn't get anything at all. The system always exploits the poor!" The nine men surrounded the tenth man and beat him up.

The next night, the tenth man didn't show up for drinks, so the nine men sat down and had their beers without him. But when it came time to pay the bill, they pulled their money out of their pockets (the amount they bring with them every night to pay for their share of the beer) and they discovered something very important. They didn't have enough money among all of them for even half the bill!

And that, boys and girls, journalists, and college professors, is how our tax system actually works today. The people who pay the highest taxes get the most benefit from a tax reduction. Tax them too much, attack them for being wealthy, and they just may not show up anymore. In fact, they just might start drinking overseas, where the atmosphere is somewhat friendlier—maybe in Dubai, the location of the final stop of my seven-nation tour.

ENTER DUBAI

I simply love that Bob Peck story. It really got me to thinking, however, that maybe not just wealthy individuals will leave this country if we don't treat them right. Couldn't major corporations do the exact same thing? Or maybe, they already have.

Consider the recent decision by Halliburton, the big energy services company from Houston, Texas. They decided to open a new corporate headquarters in Dubai and move their chairman and chief executive officer, David Lesar, there. While the company will also maintain a corporate office in Houston, maybe we are seeing the tip of the iceberg. As our government and political leaders continue to attack Halliburton, mainly for political reasons, because Halliburton was led by Vice President Dick Cheney from 1995 to 2000, the United Arab Emirates is welcoming them with open arms and support as it seeks to expand its global business presence. The reason for these politically motivated attacks is that any attack on Halliburton is an indirect attack on Vice President Dick Cheney, and any attack on Vice President Dick Cheney is an indirect attack on President Bush, and any attack on President Bush is an indirect attack on the entire Republican Party.

And it's not just Halliburton. What about all the publicly traded companies who no longer want to list their companies on our stock exchanges, like the Nasdaq or NYSE, and instead decide to list their company's stock on the London Stock Exchange? Who knows, our corporate tax structure may be partly to blame for driving these companies away from the United States.

DEATH, TAXES, AND GLOBAL INVESTING

In closing, it was once said that the only things for sure are death and taxes. Well, because of taxes, I would like to amend that a little by saying the only "sure" things are death, taxes, and global investing."

If all the wealthy people in this country get fed up and begin to move elsewhere, and all of our great companies like Halliburton begin to do the same, I believe you may have wished you had followed my investment suggestion to "Go Global, Go Global, and Go Even More Global."

Investment Footnote . . . What actually happened ↑

Boy, was I correct on this. The Dow returned 6.4 percent for all of 2007 and the rest of the investment world boomed even higher. The MSCI–EM (Morgan Stanley Capital International–Emerging Markets) was up 8.6 percent and the MSCI–EAFE (Morgan Stanley Capital International–Europe, Australia, and the Far East) was up a whopping 36.5 percent.

CHAPTER 6

Global Investing

Globalizing a bad thing makes it worse. But globalizing a good thing is usually good.

RICHARD STALLMAN
Software developer and activist

INTRODUCTION

Globalization can be defined as the transformation of a domestic product or phenomenon into a global one. It can also be described as a process by which the people of the world are unified into a single society, functioning together. This process is a combination of economic, technological, sociocultural, and political forces that combine into an investment issue. Thus, the term *globalization* is often used to refer to *economic* globalization: that is, an integration of national economies into the international economy, through trade, foreign direct investment, capital flows, migration, and spread of technology.

Sometimes the terms *internationalization* and *globalization* are used interchangeably, but they are not synonymous. *International* means between or among nations, hence internationalization refers to the increased importance of relations between nations, including the implementation of international trade relations, treaties, and the like. The basic unit and the optimum term here is *nation*. By contrast, the term *globalization* refers to economic integration on a global scale, into a global economy that blurs national boundaries. Carried to an extreme, globalization would erase all national boundaries for economic purposes; international trade would become interregional trade.

Modern-day globalization has its roots in the post–World War II era, and is the result of planning by economists, business interests, and politicians, who recognized the costs associated with protectionism and declining international economic integration. Their work led to the Bretton Woods conference and the founding of several international institutions intended to oversee the renewed processes of globalization, promoting growth, and managing adverse consequences.

These institutions included the International Bank for Reconstruction and Development, or the "World Bank," and the International Monetary Fund (IMF). They were facilitated by the General Agreement on Tariffs and Trade (GATT), which led to a series of agreements to lower barriers to international trade after World War II. A particular initiative carried out as a result of GATT is the World Trade Organization (WTO). More recently, these institutions have been facilitated by advances in technology, which have reduced the costs of trade and trade negotiation rounds.

Here is an interesting way to put the global story in some perspective. There are currently 322 international land boundaries that separate 194 independent states and 70 dependencies, areas of special sovereignty, and other miscellaneous entities. Ethnicity, culture, race, religion, and language have divided states into separate political entities as much as history, physical terrain, political fiat, or conquest.

In addition, most maritime states have claimed limits that include territorial seas and exclusive economic zones. Overlapping limits due to adjacent or opposite coasts create the potential for 430 bilateral maritime boundaries of which 209 have agreements.

Now you can understand why I say go global, go global, and go even more global. On the pages that follow, you will get my perspectives and insights on global investing.

Another "Big Bang" in Japan!

July 1, 1998

The official "Big Bang" in the financial markets in Japan occurred on April 1 of this year. This so-called Big Bang reform of Japan's financial markets enabled individual Japanese investors to invest in "non-yen"-denominated investments that could provide higher returns. The name was derived from the explosion of Japanese assets that would start flowing into other countries, especially the United States, in search of higher-yielding investments.

Now we are faced with an even bigger bang in Japan—the resignation of Prime Minister Ryutaro Hashimoto. Hashimoto resigned after his Liberal Democratic Party won just 44 of the 126 seats being contested in the upper chamber of parliament.

THE TAX MAN DID IT

This election was ultimately a case of the Japanese electorate believing Japan's economy needed major surgery, not a Band-Aid approach. At issue was how to move the economy forward with Hashimoto's perceived "flip-flopping" on permanent tax cuts.

In reality, the prime minister never flip-flopped. From the very beginning he pledged permanent tax system reform. However, until the comprehensive detailed plan was implemented, no one would know if it produced a net permanent tax reduction or cut. The voters in Japan obviously cast their vote for a permanent tax cut.

KEEP IT IN PERSPECTIVE

While the events in Japan will have a great impact on the rest of Southeast Asia, it is important to remember that the events in Japan will not determine the ultimate success or failure of the regional economies and markets. The key to the future of most Asian stock markets lies in the hands of their own domestic policy makers and corporations.

But all the focus is on Japan because two issues—growth and capital—are very susceptible to yen weakness, and these two issues could ignite the next level of the Asian crisis.

From the growth perspective, yen weakness is symptomatic of slow domestic growth in Japan, which makes a poor backdrop for exports from Asia, notably from Indonesia, Malaysia, and the Philippines. It also exerts downward pricing pressure on those exports that compete most directly with Japan in third-world markets.

From the cost and availability of capital perspective, yen weakness risks sparking a second round of major currency devaluations. Even if a doomsday scenario can be avoided, the mere threat of such a situation will probably keep interest rates and equity risk premiums higher and more volatile than they might otherwise be.

HISTORIC TURNING POINT

While the financial markets are always afraid of the unknown (meaning they hate change), there is no doubt that Hashimoto's resignation will go down in history as the turning point for the financial markets in Japan.

I firmly believe that this will be a long-term bullish event for Japan. I now expect a permanent tax cut to be put in place for a more economic future; major public works programs to be unveiled to turbo-charge the economy; the ill-conceived consumption tax to be rolled back; and the shambles of the banking system to be dealt with—weak banks will be left to fail and, finally, the banking system can turn the corner.

IS 4.3 PERCENT GOOD OR BAD?

The next time someone tells you how terrible it is in Japan, I want you to keep things in perspective by remembering this one number: 4.3.

In June, the unemployment rate in Japan soared to the highest level it's been since the end of World War II. That level that is causing so much concern is 4.3 percent. Meanwhile, in the United States in May the unemployment rate fell to a 29-year low. That record low level that has everyone so excited is (you guessed it) 4.3 percent!

It's all a matter of your frame of reference. When you compare 4.3 percent unemployment to the 1.0 percent unemployment level Japan is accustomed to, it is high. When you compare 4.3 percent to the double-digit 10 percent Americans have been used to, it does seem very low.

After all the hype of Japan's first "Big Bang" (reform of the financial markets), history will judge the second "Big Bang" (the 1998 elections and Hashimoto's resignation) as the "shot" that changed and ultimately saved Japan from going "bust."

Investment Footnote . . . What actually happened   ↑

I was correct, as the Japanese stock market soared in 1999 up 50.7 percent.

A Seabiscuit of an Investment

SEPTEMBER 15, 2003

One of the feel-good movies of the year is *Seabiscuit*. It's the heart-warming story of the longest of all long-shot horse's sudden rise to fame and glory. That long-shot horse's name was Seabiscuit. In the global marketplace we have our own Seabiscuit story unfolding this year. Japan is this year's Seabiscuit of an investment—the longest of all long shots, from an investing perspective, when the year began.

TOP 10 REVISITED

At the beginning of this year, I published my "Top 10 Investment Themes" for the year. One of my Top 10 themes when the year began was Japan. It was investment theme 9. Here is what I said back on January 2, 2003: "Overweight the Japanese equity market."

The Japanese economy has appeared to turn the corner, while the market has not yet caught up with the improving economy—which it will. But the real fuel to the market will be when Japan finally creates a process similar to the Resolution Trust Company and cleans up all of the bad bank loans once and for all.

As I traveled across the country earlier this year talking about my top 10 themes, each time I mentioned investment theme 9 (overweight the Japanese equity market), investors would snicker and some would even laugh. Well, they are not laughing anymore as Japan is one of the true feel-good investment stories of the year.

BANK REFORM

The real reflection point in Japan was in the form of much-needed bank reform. It officially began with the fifth largest bank in Japan, Resona Holdings. As its fiscal year was coming to a close, Resona was facing its third consecutive year of losing money. Resona was, however, forecasting very rosy and unrealistic rising profit forecasts for the next five years. These unrealistic and rosy forecasts were commonplace in Japanese banking. No matter how bad things looked, the banking system was still in denial.

Then something happened. Resona's outside auditors refused to approve these unrealistic profit forecasts, forcing Resona Holdings to seek a $17 billion government bailout, which officially put the bank under government control. This unprecedented event marked the first time auditors have ever pulled the plug on a major bank, and banking reform was under way. The days of denying problems in the banking system are a thing of the past, as are unrealistic and rosy profit projections that are designed to hide problems. This one simple act did more for investor confidence in Japan, as well as for the confidence of investors around the world looking to invest in Japan, than any other event in the past decade.

GOOD NEWS ALL AROUND

With banking reform as the foundation, Japan is now finally starting to flourish after 13 years of economic and market collapse. Virtually everywhere you look, things are better. Employment has turned the corner and is now trending upward. Wages are also trending higher. Business confidence is at its highest level in the past four years. Capital spending, as measured by Japanese machinery orders, is skyrocketing. In addition, real disposable personal income is up in Japan, which in turn has fueled a turnaround in the upward trend in consumer spending. And, believe it or not, housing starts are actually improving as well. And talk about pent-up demand. The Japanese economy has been waiting for 13 years to rejoin the global growth story. Thirteen years is a lot of pent-up demand that is about to be released.

CHINA HELPS

Staying focused on that global growth story unveils another key to Japan's sudden success—namely China. Industrial production in China is exploding, and this acceleration in industrial production is helping to boost Japanese exports, which in turn boosts Japanese industrial production.

Look how important China has become, not just from an export perspective, but from an import perspective as well. In the mid–1980s, 35 percent of Japanese exports were to the United States and only 3 percent were to China. Today, Japan exports 25 percent to the United States and 12 percent to China. The gap has greatly narrowed.

And China is equally important from an importing perspective. In the mid–1960s, 30 percent of Japanese imports were from the United States and only 3 percent were from China. Today, Japan only imports 15 percent from the United States and a whopping 20 percent from China. Clearly, the economic miracle in China is also taking hold in Japan.

FINAL LEG . . . TAX REFORM

The final leg of Japan's long-shot turnaround investment story is tax reform. Everywhere you look, tax reform is taking hold around the globe—everywhere that is except Japan. The United States has already cut dividend taxes and capital gains taxes this year.

Germany has also jumped on the tax reform band wagon. The top tax rate in Germany will be reduced from 48.5 percent to 42 percent, and the lowest rate will drop from 19.9 to 15 percent. France is talking about a 3 percent tax cut in the 2004 budget, which comes on top of a 5 percent cut in 2002 and a 1 percent cut this year. Belgium is cutting payroll taxes and the Czech government is cutting corporate taxes.

Like I said, everywhere you look around the globe there are signs of tax reform, except in Japan. Here is what has to happen next. First, Japan has to shore up the small business loopholes, which is a real injustice in Japan. You see, small businesses in Japan collect consumption tax revenues from Japanese consumers. However, that money doesn't always get remitted to the Japanese government. That loophole needs to be fixed now. The second thing that needs to happen is a modernization of the tax system—in other words, an electronic tax system where Japanese taxpayers can file their tax returns electronically over the Internet. This has not happened to date because any electronic system would need to be based upon a system where all taxpayers have a taxpayer ID number. This has been a sticking point with Japanese consumer advocate groups that claim this establishment of a tax ID number would result in an invasion of privacy.

Japan has got to find a way to join the global tax reform club.

In closing, if you are looking for a feel-good movie, try *Seabiscuit*. If, on the other hand, you are looking for a feel-good investment, it's still not too late to try Japan.

Investment Footnote . . . What actually happened

I was really right on this Japan call as the Japanese market boomed 37 percent in 2003, 12.5 percent in 2004, and another 21.7 percent in 2005.

Go for the Gold!

May 27, 2004

I recently returned from a trip to Asia where I spent time in both Japan and China. When I arrived home, the U.S. media were in the midst of declaring a major economic slowdown in China. I do not know where they were looking, but I can tell you from firsthand experience that they were not looking at the same China that I had just visited.

JUST THE FACTS

To me, there are three simple facts that put the Chinese economy in the proper perspective. First, China consumes 50 percent of the world's cement. Second, China consumes 40 percent of the world's steel. Third, China consumes 30 percent of the world's coal. And that consumption shows no sign of slowing down in the next five years. China is in the early stages of a major economic boom that I believe will take it through 2008 (which just happens to coincide with the 2008 Olympics in Beijing). I have never seen a nation, anywhere at any time, more focused on a single event than the 1.3 billion Chinese who are all focused on their one chance to showcase China to the world, namely, the Beijing Olympics in 2008.

SEEING IS BELIEVING

As an old "muni-bond guy," I remember stories about how, in the good old days, all you had to do was count the number of railroad tracks going into a community to know what kind of a debt rating the credit rating agencies would give that community. It was thought that railroad tracks were a great indicator of economic activity. Well, that was the good old days. Today we count the "national birds." From an economic perspective, national birds are cranes, as in building cranes. Now, it is thought that if you count the number of cranes in a city, you can get a good feel for its economic prosperity. I decided to do just that when I was in Shanghai, China, which many predict will someday be the greatest city in the world. So standing in Shanghai, I started counting the cranes and quickly realized I could not do it. It is currently impossible to actually count the number of cranes in Shanghai. As you look out, the cranes are 30 to 40 deep as far as the eye can see in every direction—north, south, east, and west. It is the most mind-boggling sight you have ever seen anywhere. In the best of economic times in the United States, you can count the number of cranes in any major city on both hands; in Shanghai they are impossible to count. What I saw first-hand tells me that there is simply no way China is headed for an economic slowdown.

THE RIVER TELLS THE STORY

Being the stubborn strategist that I am, if I couldn't count cranes (and it was too "old school" to count railroad tracks), I decided to count riverboat traffic. You see, on a map, Shanghai looks like it is on the South China Sea. Actually it is not; you have to go 60 miles up the Yangtze River to reach Shanghai. Those 60 miles are covered with factory after factory and shipyard after shipyard. So I decided to count the number of ships that passed in front of me in a 10-minute period. It was Thursday at 12 noon, so for the next 10 minutes I counted how many barges, oil tankers, cruise ships, houseboats, and shanties carrying lumber and food passed my eye. In 10 minutes more than 100 vessels passed by me on the Yangtze River—over 100! For a frame of reference, the Yangtze River is about half as wide as the Mississippi River. I think you could stare at the Mississippi River all day long and 100 vessels would not pass by, but at the Yangtze River it happened in 10 minutes! I couldn't believe it so I counted again, and again, and again. Three more times I counted the number of vessels that passed by me on the Yangtze River. I did it from 6 p.m. to 6:10 p.m., at 12 midnight to 12:10 a.m., and finally, from 6 a.m. to 6:10 a.m. You will not believe the lowest number of vessels that passed in front of me in any of those 10-minute periods—103! Words cannot begin to express what is actually going on in China.

BACK TO THE OLYMPICS

This unprecedented economic boom really got me thinking; then I connected the dots to Japan. Suddenly, everything became as clear as day to me. Here is what I mean: I was in Kobe, Japan, before going to China and needed to get to Kyoto. However, I was running late and it was clear that I would never make it by car. Everyone in Japan told me that even though they have an awesome national highway system (developed in the late 1950s in preparation for the 1964 Olympics in Tokyo), I would never get to Kyoto fast enough; I would have to take the bullet train.

Well, I take the train to work in Chicago. The last thing I wanted to do was hop on a train in Japan, but boy am I glad I did. The bullet train in Japan was created for the 1964 Olympics in Tokyo as well. It was built just in case all of the highway construction projects were not completed on time. You see, in the late 1950s most of the roads in Japan were dirt. Sounds like somewhere you might go today, like maybe China. Then it hit me: History does repeat itself. If you want a peek at the future, look into the past.

The story of the great economic and market boom in Japan in the 1960s through the 1980s was not about some unique Japanese business management model, or about this new found JITI (just in time inventory) concept. It was all about one simple thing—the economic boom leading up to the 1964 Olympics in Tokyo, Japan! And for the next 20 years the Japanese economy and market benefited from that economic boom.

History is about to repeat itself in China. This major economic boom is all about the Beijing Olympics in 2008. The benefits to the Chinese economy and market, however, will play out for the next 20 years. There is only one place to go for the gold . . . China!

> ## Investment Footnote . . . What actually happened ↑
>
> I was correct again, as the Dow was only up 3.1 percent. The rest of the world returned high double digits. The MSCI–EM (Morgan Stanley Capital International–Emerging Market) Index was up 17.6 percent and the MSCI–EAFE (Morgan Stanley Capital International–Europe, Australia, and Far East) Index was up 22.4 percent.

The Sun Is Still Rising . . . on Japan
July 28, 2004

Japan has long been referred to around the world as "the land of the rising sun." If you think about it, a "rising sun" denotes a new day full of great new opportunities. And from an investment perspective, there is no better motto for Japan today than "land of the rising sun," because the rising sun signals a new day for investors, with great new opportunities.

Having recently returned from a trip to Japan, three things strike me as laying a solid foundation for the Japanese equity markets. Those three things are the China connection, confidence, and reform. Let me briefly touch upon all three, beginning with the China connection.

CHINA CONNECTION

It was an eye-opening experience to see how the Japanese economy has become more closely tied to the Chinese economy than it is the U.S. economy. The numbers are absolutely staggering. Over the past 20 years, Japanese exports to the United States have been flat. Meanwhile, in the past four years alone, Japanese exports to China have increased by more than 160 percent. China is becoming a key to the Japanese recovery. And while there is some concern in the marketplace about a China slowdown, I do not share those concerns. Currently China is consuming 50 percent of the world's cement, 40 percent of the world's steel, and 30 percent of the world's coal.

To get an idea of how China is using all of those raw materials, one has to look no further than all of the infrastructure projects being built in preparation for the Beijing Olympics in 2008. Currently, China has over 15,000 different highway projects under way that will add 162,000 kilometers of road in China. For you older Americans who still protest the global use of the metric system, 162,000 kilometers would equal a little more than 100,000 miles. That would be enough to circle the globe at the equator four times. With all of these pending projects, I believe the talk of a slowdown is overdone.

CONFIDENCE

Let's now move on to my second investment foundation: confidence. I was taken aback by how confident Japanese businesspeople are. And that confidence extends to both large and small businesses. One of the primary reasons is that the business community gives high marks to the new head of the Bank of Japan's Central Bank, Governor Fukui (our Alan Greenspan), who has been in that role a little over a year now. While I was on the ground in Japan talking to business leaders, I couldn't figure out a way to quantify all of their confidence. However, now that I have returned to Chicago, the Japanese government has done it for me. Every quarter the Japanese government issues the Tankan report, which attempts to measure business confidence. The second quarter 2004 report has just been released, and three of the four business segments measured show record levels of confidence. Large manufacturing firms, large nonmanufacturing firms, and small manufacturing firms report the highest optimism readings seen in the past 13 years—since 1991. The only segment of the business community not displaying record optimism was the small nonmanufacturing firms that still lag in this recovery. Three out of four, however, isn't bad. I could see it in their eyes and I could witness the renewed hop in their steps, and now the Tankan report quantifies it for me.

REFORM

Let's now move on to the third and final foundation: reform, namely, bank reform. Last year the fifth largest bank in Japan, Resona Holding Company, went bankrupt. That was a critical turning point for Japan, a country that has a cultural aversion to failure and, as such, has kept money flowing to many insolvent banks. That all stopped with the collapse of Resona Holding Company. Letting a bank fail was only the first of two steps needed to begin to clean up the estimated $500 billion of bad loans on the books of Japanese banks. The second step is a consolidation of the banking industry. This step would combine troubled banks with weaker balance sheets with stronger institutions to avert a banking crisis. Well, step two is now in place. Mitsubishi Tokyo Financial Group, which is the second largest bank in Japan, is merging with UFJ Holdings, which is the fourth largest. UFJ's claim to fame is that it is the only bank in Japan with more bad loan problems than Resona Holding Company. That would be the exact same Resona Holding Company that went bankrupt last year.

This merger will create a bank with $1.5 trillion in assets. It will become the largest bank in the world, taking the top spot away from Citigroup. Japan is certainly the land of the rising sun in more ways than one!

Investment Footnote . . . What actually happened ↑

I was correct, as the Japanese stock market was up 12.5 percent in 2004.

An Olympic Investment!
August 17, 2004

While sports fans around the globe are currently focused on the 2004 Olympics in Athens, savvy investors are focusing on a different Olympic venue—the 2008 Olympics in Beijing, China. Now sports fans and investors alike can benefit from the 2008 Olympics in Beijing, China, and here is how.

HISTORY REPEATS ITSELF

First, I want to give you a quick history lesson on why I believe you would want to invest in the Beijing Olympics in 2008. On a trip to Asia earlier this year, I was in Kobe, Japan, and needed to get to Kyoto, Japan. I was running late and it was clear that I would never make it by car. Everyone in Japan told me that even though they have an awesome national highway system—developed in the late 1950s in preparation for the 1964 Olympics in Tokyo— I would never get to Kyoto fast enough. I would have to take the bullet train.

Well, I take the train to work in Chicago, and the last thing I wanted to do was hop on a train in Japan. But, boy, am I glad I did. The bullet train in Japan was also created for the 1964 Olympics just in case all of the highway construction projects were not completed on time. You see, in the late 1950s most of the roads in Japan were dirt. Does it sound like anywhere you know today, like maybe China? Then it hit me: I believe history does repeat itself. If you want a peek at the future, look into the past.

The story of the great economic and market boom in Japan from the 1960s through the 1980s was not about some unique Japanese business management model or quality circles, or about this newfound JITI (just in time inventory) concept. It was all about one simple thing: the economic boom leading up to the 1964 Olympics in Tokyo, Japan, which at the time was one of the biggest infrastructure buildups ever. And for the next 20 years, the Japanese economy and market benefited from that economic boom.

I'm convinced that history is about to repeat itself in China. This current major economic boom is all about the Beijing Olympics in 2008. The benefits to the global economy and global demand, however, have the potential to play out for the next 20 years.

SHORT-TERM OLYMPIC BOOM

China's current consumption levels are unprecedented. Currently, China is consuming 50 percent of the world's cement, 40 percent of the world's steel, and 30 percent of the world's coal.

To get an idea of how China is using all of those raw materials, one has to look no further than the infrastructure projects being built in preparation for the Beijing Olympics in 2008. Currently, China has over 15,000 different highway projects under way that will add 162,000 kilometers of road in China. For you older Americans who still protest the global use of the metric system, 162,000 kilometers equals a little more than 100,000 miles. That would be enough to circle the globe at the equator four times. With all of these pending projects, I believe the talk of a slowdown is overdone.

LONG-TERM ROLLER BLADERS

Longer term beyond just China, looking at all of Asia, don't forget about the Asia roller blade generation. The single most powerful economic force ever to move through any society in the history of time has yet to begin to make its true impact on economies and markets around the world. This most influential long-term demographic trend that is looming on the global horizon is what I call Asia's "roller blade" generation.

You see, you can classify roller bladers into two groups. The first group is all the roller bladers ages 10 to 24. The second group of roller bladers is comprised of everyone else who still acts like they are ages 10 to 24. The Asian roller blader generation is about the first group.

There is a population bubble about to burst in Asia. There are currently one billion Asians age 10 to 24—the Asian roller blade generation. The desires, tastes, and spending habits of this generation will radically reshape the business climate, social fabric, and political institutions of Asia.

In order to understand the potential impact of this population bulge in Asia, you must focus on the crucial point that Asia's roller blade generation was born into a world radically different from the one their parents entered.

You see, their parents, for the most part, were left largely scarred and desolated by World War II. For most of the postwar era, rebuilding societies and countries was the primary Asian goal. This, in turn, required hard work, dedication, individual sacrifice, high savings, production, and conformity. It was these exact attributes that have underpinned the industrial rise of Asia over the past half-century and have dramatically reshaped the world that the region's teeming population of youths currently lives in.

By contrast, Asia's roller blade generation is growing up in an era of prosperity, not poverty, and this roller blade generation has within its grasp opportunities and wealth that its parents did not have. Shopping is more characteristic of this group than savings. Their parents drank tea, wore sandals, ate rice, and bought things with cash; and their life centered on Buddhism.

That's not true for the roller blade generation. Think about what they prefer. While their parents drank tea, they drink Coca-Cola. Their parents wore sandals, they wear Nike running shoes. Their parents ate rice; they eat Chicken McNuggets at McDonald's. Their parents purchased everything with cash; they purchase everything with a credit card.

Let me put things in some perspective for you. Even if an unbelievable 25 percent of this population bracket never buys a single thing their entire lives, it's still the greatest consumption bubble of all time. So for argument's sake, I'm going to concede that 25 percent will never buy a single thing. That would mean that all I have left is the remaining 75 percent, or 750 million Asian roller bladers. Remember how the baby boomers here in the United States have changed the world because, after all, they are 76 million strong? Well, 750 million Asian consumers, after I concede the 25 percent, are still 10 times greater than the U.S. baby boom demographic explosion. When they get through with us, the world economic and global consumption demand will never be the same.

OLYMPIC STRATEGY

The question to investors is clear: how does one develop a strategy to benefit from the Olympic trends? The answer is quite simple. Think back to one of the most famous one-liners in film history, in *The Graduate*, when Mr. McGuire says the future is in plastics. Well, today the future is in commodities.

When you combine the short–term commodity boom of the Beijing Olympics in 2008 with the longer-term boom in commodities driven by the roller blade generation, investment strategists around the globe are going to have to update their old investment strategy asset allocation models of stocks, bonds, and cash to include commodities as well.

Let me end where I began. To me, there are three simple facts that put this commodity boom in the proper perspective. First, China consumes 50 percent of the world's cement. Second, China consumes 40 percent of the world's steel. Third, China consumes 30 percent of the world's coal. And that consumption shows no sign of slowing down in the next five years. China is in the early stages of a major economic boom that I believe will take it through 2008 (which just so happens to coincide with the 2008 Olympics in Beijing). I have never seen a nation, anywhere at any time, more focused on a single event than the 1.3 billion Chinese that are all focused on their one chance to showcase China to the world, namely the Beijing Olympics in 2008. And keep in mind, when the Chinese focus on something, they can do amazing things—remember that wall they built over there. Come to think of it, that used quite a bit of commodities as well! Go for the gold . . . go for commodities.

Investment Footnote . . . What actually happened

Commodities did indeed continue to boom up 11.21 percent in 2004, 22.5 percent in 2005, 13.51 percent in 2006, and another 20.56 percent in 2007.

It's for Real

OCTOBER 6, 2004

The Brazilian currency is called the *real*. Having just returned from a trip to Brazil, I found that not only is their currency real, so is their economy, their enthusiasm, and their passion to put the problems of the past several years behind them for good.

BELLWETHER EMERGING MARKET

I was most impressed with the never-ending flurry of economic activity on every street, everywhere I looked. Sometimes we forget that rising oil prices tend to move economic activity from industrialized oil-consuming nations to emerging-market, oil-producing nations. Clearly, with both Mexico and Venezuela in the top 10 of world oil-producing nations, the regional ripple effect has reached Brazil. Three observations about Brazil stick out the most.

Energy Conservation

First is energy conservation. While the United States continues to struggle with a comprehensive energy policy, Brazil has adopted some very simple, no-nonsense tips that work. A large percentage of cars in Brazil run on diesel fuel. The reason is quite simple: Brazilians realize diesel is cheaper than gasoline. Because of high inflation, Brazilians are very attuned to cost. They know that it is cheaper to transport goods using diesel fuel; thus, it stands to reason that it is also cheaper to transport themselves using that very same diesel fuel. Cars that weren't using diesel were hybrid vehicles using gasoline and alcohol. Brazil is proof that if you want to conserve gasoline, it is possible. One other fascinating thing: In Sao Paulo, based on the last digit of your license plate, you are restricted from driving in the city limits during peak/rush hour traffic in the morning and evening one day a week. I'm convinced that if Brazil can do it so can we.

Election Mandate

My second observation is about Brazil's just completed election (local elections, not national). Elections are held on Sunday instead of a Tuesday as we do here in the United States. The reason they are held on Sunday is that most Brazilians do not work on Sunday, so it is much easier for them to vote on that day. Meanwhile, in America, we continue to have poor voter turnout because two-income families struggle with who will take the kids to day care and who will pick them up, and will the voting polls be open early enough or late enough to vote on a Tuesday.

There is one other important aspect about voting in Brazil. It is mandatory. You are required to vote. If you don't vote, the next time you need something from the government, such as a passport, permit, or license, you will not get it. Needless to say, everyone votes in Brazil.

Investment Rich

My third observation is about how Brazilian investors' attitude toward risk tolerance differs from that of their American counterparts. In America, investors are investing in the market to create wealth. And since these investors are looking to the market to make them wealthy, they are generally willing to take on a great deal of risk.

In Brazil, it's just the opposite. Most Brazilian investors have already acquired their wealth elsewhere. Wealth in Brazil is about taking risks in business ventures; when these are successful, real wealth is created. When these wealthy Brazilians invest, the most important thing to them is protection of the wealth they already have, not creation of wealth. Most American investors constantly demand that their financial advisor give them a better return *on* their investment. In Brazil, all that investors really want is simply a return *of* their investment.

EMERGING MARKET ALLOCATION

In closing, I see that, as one of the real bellwether countries for emerging markets, Brazil is ringing the bell, if you will, regarding emerging market opportunity—in Brazil specifically, and in all emerging markets generally. Emerging markets just might give investors the trifecta they are looking for. First, they have lower valuations. Second, they generally have higher growth prospects. And third, and finally, rising oil prices have strengthened their markets' balance sheets.

In my opinion, this one's for real!

Investment Footnote . . . What actually happened   ↑

I really got this one right. The Brazilian stock market was up 28 percent in 2004, 45.2 percent in 2005, another 45.4 percent in 2006, and a whopping 72.3 percent in 2007.

A Tsunami with a Silver Lining
FEBRUARY 24, 2005

As I continue my travels throughout Asia, I'm realizing how quickly most Americans (myself included) have almost completely forgotten about the deadly tsunami that struck this region on December 26, 2004, killing over 170,000. Here, that disaster is still front and center on everyone's mind. Even in places far from the center of most destruction, they simply cannot forget this issue. I have just visited Malaysia, which had very little damage and small loss of life, yet you would have thought the tsunami struck them directly by the way this entire country has been engulfed by this disaster. To attempt to give you some frame of reference for this catastrophe, simply recall back to that horrific day in our country's history on 9/11 and multiply that 20 times and you will begin to feel the magnitude of this catastrophe. The loss of life was mind-boggling with over 170,000 dead. As investment strategists we are asked to move beyond the human and emotional impact of any disaster and figure out how it will impact the economies and markets. This is an especially difficult task standing here in Malaysia when you realize the magnitude of this tsunami. However, let me attempt to frame this issue for you.

SMALL GLOBAL IMPACT

First of all, you need to realize that any negative impact will be regional rather than global. That is because the countries that were impacted are still only a very, very small part of the global economy. In fact, India, Indonesia, Thailand, Malaysia, and Sri Lanka combined account for less than 10 percent of the global economy.

TOURISM, NOT MANUFACTURING OR INDUSTRIAL IMPACT

Within these regions, the greatest economic impact will be on tourism, not the manufacturing or industrial sectors. The reason is quite simple and logical. The catastrophic damage of the tsunami was felt the most along the coastal regions of these countries. The coastal regions, or beachfront property as we call it in the States, is typically the most expensive real estate there is. These beautiful, high-priced areas tend to be where all of the tourist action is located. Conversely, you seldom find any manufacturing or industrial factories in these high-rent districts. As a result, the tsunami will take a bite out of tourism, but this, too, you must keep in its proper perspective. In only one of the affected countries does tourism account for more than 5 percent of the economy, and that is Thailand, at only 6 percent. For all the others—Malaysia, Indonesia, India, and Sri Lanka—tourism accounts for less than 5 percent of the national economy. Thus, even though the tsunami will have a negative impact on tourism, it will not really impact the overall economies of these countries because tourism is such a small part of the whole. Meanwhile, the economically vital manufacturing and industrial facilities were all located inland from the coastal regions and were not damaged at all by the tsunami. The real economic engines were untouched.

COMMODITY BOOM AGAIN

In many respects, this disaster may actually fuel overall economic growth in the region. Building, rebuilding, and reconstruction will be massive undertakings. And money is flowing into the region from all parts of the world. There are highways to be built, hotels to be reconstructed, roads to be repaved, and infrastructure to be replaced. If anything, this tsunami could actually slightly lift overall economic growth.

Furthermore, as if we needed one more factor to fuel the current bull market in commodities, we just got it with this tsunami. These regions will be fighting China for steel, cement, lumber, copper, tin, and the like. When demand peaks even further, and supply remains constrained as it is, commodity prices have nowhere to go but up.

While the loss of life has been horrific and we can never underestimate that loss, from an economic and market perspective this tsunami actually has a silver lining as far as commodities are concerned. As this massive rebuilding fuels even greater demand for commodities, maybe I should call this the tsunami with the silver, gold, copper, steel, and tin lining!

Investment Footnote . . . What actually happened ↑

I was right, as commodities continued to boom, gaining 13.51 percent in 2006 and 20.56 percent in 2007.

The Hottest Global Theme: Europe's TMT Is Out, China's Top Is In!

March 7, 2005

I am just finishing the final leg of my Asian tour with stops in Hong Kong and then mainland China to check on Beijing's progress in preparing to host the 2008 Olympics.

COMMODITY BOOM IN FULL SWING

To say that the commodity boom is still in full swing would be a complete understatement. I think it is actually a bigger boom now than it was 10 short months ago, the last time I was here. I am looking at an entire city block that has suddenly appeared. Ten months ago there were no structures at all, just dust and dirt blowing in my eyes. Today, the entire city block is finished, including a 50-story building. The hustle and bustle is even greater today than it was 10 months ago. There are more highway projects, more buildings being developed, fewer Chinese riding bicycles, and more on mopeds and in automobiles. This transformation is moving ahead at breakneck speed. For me, one of the more memorable sights was hundreds upon hundreds of Chinese men pushing wheelbarrows of cement to a construction site. They looked like little worker ants off on the horizon. It wasn't a parade of cement mixer trucks; it was a parade of hundreds of Chinese laborers moving cement from one location to another. Remember, the cheapest resource in China is labor, and China uses that cheap resource in every way imaginable, even replacing cement mixer trucks.

FROM TMT TO TOP

Over the past half decade, there has been a gradual shift among global investors about what the hottest global investment theme is. Recall, if you will, a little over five years ago. After the Asia tiger's collapse, which was fueled by Thailand devaluing its local currency, the baht, everyone wanted to invest in Europe, especially in light of the newly formed European Monetary Union (EMU). But only certain sectors were attracting investors' attention: technology, telecommunications, and the media. These three sectors largely defined the investment landscape in Europe. In fact, they were such a rage that an investing acronym was born: TMT (for technology, media, and telecommunications). No one knows whom to credit with the creation of this global term, but it quickly swept across the globe! It seemed that investors everywhere only wanted to talk about and invest in the hottest global theme, which at that time was

Europe's TMT! Back then, if you didn't know what TMT stood for, you had no business investing globally. Today, the global investing rage is all about China and the dramatic growth that is being fueled in preparation for the Beijing Olympics in 2008. I would like to offer up a new investing acronym that captures this China investment boom. I call it China TOP. The *T* stands for technology and telecommunications. The *O* stands for oil, and the *P* stands for power. Let me explain the investment thesis behind all three of these, beginning with technology and telecommunications.

T = Technology and Telecommunications

China is not simply a consumer of technology; it is a major producer of technology as well. Currently, China exports $160 billion annually in technology products. Maybe even more impressive is the fact that they import the exact same level annually, $160 billion. Of that amount, almost half the imports are semiconductors. As a result, semiconductor fabrication plants are popping up faster than high-rises and highways.

The telecommunications story is even more compelling. China now has the largest group of mobile phone users anywhere in the world at 3.25 million and counting. When you compare this to the fixed-line phone users in China, which total right now around 300 million, that means that China has already hit the crossroads of more mobile phone users than fixed-line users.

One of the primary reasons for the fixed-line phone is for Internet access. Almost 100 million Chinese people now access the Internet through their fixed-line telephone company. As we leave the *T* in China TOP, remember this: China is now the number one market in the world for cell phones and the number two market in the world for computers.

O = Oil

Let's now move on to the *O* in China TOP—oil. To understand the amount of oil that will be consumed by China, one has to look no further than automobiles. Currently there are approximately 25 million automobiles in China. Over the next 10 years, China projects that number to be over 100 million. As more and more Chinese move into urban areas, we will see higher incomes. That means more people will be able to buy a car—and that means more oil demand. Currently about 40 percent of China's population is living in cities. Over the next 10 years, that number will approach 60 percent. It is a very simple cycle: the more people in urban areas, the more automobiles and the more oil that will be consumed.

$P = $ **Power**

Let's finally move on to the P in China TOP—power. It seems that the only thing that can slow the China boom is insufficient power. And the Chinese government knows that. Electrical power is without a doubt the key to China's economic future. Remember that all those computers need to be plugged into something.

Maybe this will put both the problem and opportunity into proper perspective for you: Of the 31 electrical power grids that cover mainland China, 24 of them suffered major shortages last year. To remedy that problem, the Chinese government plans to double the Chinese electric power capacity within the next five years. It may well be the biggest power buildup in the history of time.

In closing, if you are looking to become a cutting-edge global investor, look no further than Dr. Bob's newly founded China TOP! Pass the word: China TOP.

Investment Footnote . . . What actually happened

I was correct. China was one of the top markets in the world, posting a 130 percent gain in 2006 and a 96 percent gain in 2007.

China's Investment Puzzle: Bonds, Olympics, and the World's Fair

MARCH 9, 2005

As my trip to Asia generally, and China specifically, becomes a distant memory, let me leave you with these final three thoughts to ponder about China. By putting these three pieces together, you too will be able to solve China's investment puzzle.

U.S. TREASURY BONDS

My first thought is regarding U.S. Treasury bonds and the great concern in the United States that our bond market may be on the brink of collapse—that all it will take is for the Chinese government to quit buying U.S. Treasury bonds for our entire bond market to collapse. Let me try to explain why I do not believe that is going to happen. The Chinese government realizes that it must create hundreds of millions of manufacturing jobs over the next decade as Chinese workers move off the farm and into the city to improve their quality of living. Thus, manufacturing is really set to explode in China. In order to support all this new stuff made in China, the Chinese government needs someone with lots of money to buy all the things stamped "Made in China." Enter the U.S. consumer. Remember, we are still the largest economy in the world. Now, the best way to make sure that the U.S. consumer has plenty of money to spend on Chinese products is to keep U.S. interest rates low. And if you are the Chinese government, there is only one way you can influence that—by buying U.S. Treasury bonds. Here is how it works; I think it is a better conspiracy theory than the DaVinci Code. Think about it: The Chinese government buys U.S. Treasury bonds, which in turn keeps U.S. interest rates low, which keeps the U.S. consumer buying stuff made in China, which allows China to create more manufacturing jobs, which allows Chinese workers to improve their quality of life. And it all begins with the bond market.

I do not believe that the Chinese government can afford to break this cycle by stopping their purchase of Treasury bonds.

OLYMPICS

My second point to ponder concerns the Beijing Olympics in 2008. While I have written and spoken extensively on this topic, I do have some additional perspectives that I would like to share regarding Beijing, China, the host of the Olympics. Beijing currently has three separate subway systems. They are adding seven new subway systems. By the time the Olympics arrive, Beijing will have 10 separate subway systems. It will be one of the world's most comprehensive mass transit systems. And it's not just the subways. Let me describe what is going on with the highway infrastructure. Most of you in major U.S. cities can relate to this. In the United States we developed a beltway system around most major cities, where instead of driving through the city, you can take the beltway around the city. In Beijing there is currently not one beltway, or two, or even three, but five separate beltways surrounding the city, with each new beltway making a bigger circle. No U.S. city has two beltways circling the same city, but Beijing has five. And that's not all; they are building four more beltways before the Olympics. There will be nine separate beltways where you can circle the entire city of Beijing, and each one will take you closer to the city. There is no system like it anywhere in the world.

One final thought on the Olympics: It is not just about Beijing. Olympic events will be hosted in cities as far away as Shanghai and Hong Kong. From this point on, we should call the 2008 games the *Chinese* Olympics, not just the *Beijing* Olympics.

THE WORLD'S FAIR

My third, and final, point to ponder is the concern of many U.S. investors that China may collapse after the Olympics in 2008. I don't think China will have time to slow down, let alone collapse, after 2008 because two short years after that, Shanghai will host the

Worlds Fair! That's right. The next World's Fair is scheduled from May 1 to October 31, 2010, in Shanghai, China. The theme for this World's Fair is "Better City, Better Life." As an investor, don't underestimate what a World's Fair can do for a city or a country. Way back in 1893, Chicago hosted the World's Fair, with the theme, "Fourth Centennial of the Discovery of America."

Many historians believed that World's Fair began the transformation of Chicago from the hog-slaughtering cowtown it was to the cosmopolitan city it is today. That World's Fair unveiled two things that are still with us today: one is the Ferris wheel and the other is Juicy Fruit gum. One can only imagine what will be unveiled at the World's Fair in Shanghai. Oh, one more thing about that Chicago World's Fair in 1893, which is when Chicago got the nickname of "the Windy City." You see, it has nothing to do with the actual wind that blows off Lake Michigan. It was actually Charles Anderson Dana, the New York editor, who back in 1890 before Chicago was selected for the World's Fair, called Chicago the Windy City. He called it that because all the leading political and business leaders in Chicago were boasting that Chicago would prevail in getting the World's Fair!

In closing, every investor wants to know the next big thing. First, we had the creation of the European Union, and then we had the Internet and the dot-com craze. Now we have this China boom. What's next? I think I may know the next big thing after China. It will be China. And I believe I also know what the next big thing after that will be. You guessed it: China once again.

Maybe this investment puzzle isn't that difficult after all, since all the answers are the same: CHINA!

Investment Footnote . . . What actually happened

I was correct. China was one of the top markets in the world, posting a 130 percent gain in 2006 and a 96 percent gain in 2007.

Let's Party Like It's 1992

October 28, 2005

I remember that Prince hit, "Let's Party Like It's 1999," like it was only yesterday. I have taken a little liberty with it and changed the year to 1992. I have just begun my European travels in Spain—specifically, Barcelona. And everywhere I look, I am reminded of the 1992 Olympic Games held in Barcelona. More about that later. First I want to put Spain into some perspective for you, then I want to share my personal observations about Barcelona, and finally I will go back and discuss the impact of the 1992 Olympics.

A PERSPECTIVE ON SPAIN

In many respects, Spain is an economic paradox. On the one hand, it has pushed hard for privatization and deregulation for a large part of its economy. On the other hand, it continues to focus on ways for the government to control and regulate the labor markets. Maybe this paradox explains why Spain's economy seems never to quite catch up to the other major economies of Europe.

Spain is part of the Iberian Peninsula, along with Portugal, one of its land borders. To the north, it borders France, as well as the tiny principality of Andorra. The rest of Spain is surrounded by the Balearic Islands and the Mediterranean Sea to the east, the Bay of Biscay to the northwest, and the Atlantic Ocean to the west. Spain has the fifth largest population in the European Union at 40 million. Its population growth rate is 0.15 percent, which places it behind the average for the European Union, which stands at 0.20 percent.

In Spain, 15 percent of the population is below the age of 15 (less than the European Union average of 16 percent). And 18 percent of its population is 65 years of age and older—well above the European Union average of 15 percent. Thus, the aging dynamics become quite clear: You have both a below average youth population and an above average senior citizen population. And to further complicate this demographic dilemma, life expectancy in

Spain is 79.52 years, which places it well above the European Union level of only 78.10 years.

BARCELONA NOW

I am struck by two major phenomena in Barcelona today. The first concerns the youth of the city—virtually all of them smoke. This is not all that surprising when you consider over 50 percent of the youth population in all of Spain smokes. With a cigarette in one hand, they all carry the latest cell phone in the other. In fact, I saw numerous youth with more than one cell phone. And finally, I could not believe the vast, vast number of young people with multiple body piercings and prominent tattoos. As a youth in Barcelona, you are clearly in a small minority if you do not display body piercings in the nose and eyelid and tongue and lower lip and navel and so on and so forth.

From an investment perspective, it appears that the future for both the cell phone industry and the tobacco industry could not look brighter. I'm not sure how to tie in the tattoos and body piercings. Maybe the first cigarette company or cell phone company that gives away free piercings with a purchase will become the dominant market leader with the youth of Barcelona!

WORKFORCE

My second observation concerns the labor force. I have two specific observations on this front. First, it is hard for me to believe, as an American, that businesses still honor the traditional "siesta." This means the workday has two parts or shifts. The day begins with stores and shops opening from 10 a.m. to 2 p.m. Then they close for a three-hour siesta. The stores then reopen from 5 p.m. until 9 p.m. The number of tourists that want to shop between 2 p.m. and 5 p.m. is staggering. I have to think it will be extremely difficult to become fully integrated into the global economy when you are constantly taking a siesta.

My second labor force observation concerns the fishermen. They decided to have an unexpected wildcat strike and close the ports. All maritime commerce came to a complete stop. Here is the issue that the fishermen are striking over—they are demanding that 80 percent of their wages be *tax free*! The government only wants to allow 40 percent of their wages to be *tax free*! Talk about a workforce (and a government, for that matter) that is out of touch with the global labor markets. I did my own formal protest by starting a one-man fish boycott. Let 'em eat steak!

THE OLYMPIC IMPACT

Let me close by revisiting the Olympic impact. Everywhere I looked, the infrastructure buildup for the Barcelona Olympics in 1992 was evident. I am not talking about just the athletic stadiums and the new highways to get you there. It was also the Olympic Village to house the athletes, which was built in an area of Barcelona that used to be run down and had abandoned factories and warehouses. Now, it is a vibrant part of the Barcelona city center, serving as a model for urban living. In addition, much of the subway system was designed for the Olympics, and I can tell you from multiple firsthand riding experiences, that it is a very clean and efficient way to get around Barcelona quickly.

The one element that I underestimated the Olympics would have on Barcelona (and all of Spain) was a sense of pride. So many people from all walks of life commented on how gray and dirty Barcelona was as a city before the Olympics. No one ever cleaned anything up because there was no pride in the city. That changed with the 1992 Olympics. Without a doubt, the biggest impact these Olympics had on both Barcelona and Spain was the renewed sense of pride it created. And that pride is still present today more than 13 years later. That is why the streets are clean and the buildings are sparkling. I completely missed this new sense of pride as an impact of the Olympics.

From an investment perspective, this got me thinking about the 2008 Olympics in Beijing, China. I have written extensively about the infrastructure and commodity boom that these Olympics are already having on China, but never once did I mention the renewed sense of pride these Olympics are likely to produce, not only in Beijing but all of China as well.

Maybe the best investment idea to come out of Barcelona, Spain, is that this commodity-led China investment impact will probably last long after the closing Olympic ceremony in 2008.

After all, it's all a matter of . . . pride. Something it seems the youth of Barcelona and the fishermen have both lost sight of.

Investment Footnote . . . What actually happened

I was correct. China was one of the top markets in the world, posting a 130 percent gain in 2006 and a 96 percent gain in 2007.

Casablanca: More than Just a Movie

November 1, 2005

When most people in the United States hear the word *Casablanca*, they simply think of the movie of the same name. Having just left Casablanca, I can tell you from firsthand experience it is much more than just a movie. And it is much more complicated as well, especially from an investment perspective.

HISTORY

First, a little bit of history about Casablanca, the unofficial capital of Morocco on Africa's rugged northern shoreline. Casablanca was established over 8,000 years ago by Phoenicians wanting to set up a commercial center. That's not a typo—8,000 years ago. Remember, if you will, what a big deal Americans made of our country's two-hundredth birthday on July 4, 1976. Realizing that Christopher Columbus discovered our country in 1492, the discovery of

America was just a little over 500 years ago. This really puts into perspective the magnitude of the long, rich history of the world outside the United States, which most of us in the United States lose sight of. Remember, from a historical perspective we are one of the youngest nations; so our historical perspective is extremely narrow as compared to a place like Casablanca.

The latest chapter in Morocco's long history began in 1956 when it was granted full independence by both Spain and France. Morocco has retained its independence.

DRAMATIC GROWTH

Casablanca has witnessed a remarkable population explosion. At the beginning of the twentieth century, there were fewer than 20,000 people living in the city. Today, the city has a population of over 4 million people. As you can imagine, this dramatic growth has also brought along some pretty dramatic and what appear to be, at times, unsolvable problems.

The biggest and most obvious problem is disposing of trash. Casablanca is not a clean city, and its very narrow and walled streets tend to create a sense that there is no place for the trash to go. In reality, there almost isn't. Currently, both Germany and France accept 20 percent of the trash of Casablanca and dispose of it for them. Casablanca continually struggles to find a way to dispose of the other 80 percent, so it is truly hard to imagine the magnitude of this problem unless you see it firsthand. It is not just the trash. The buildings are dirty and somewhat run down, and the center city is an array of odors, none of which are pleasant. But this problem can be addressed over time.

POVERTY ABOUNDS

As you would expect with an emerging market like that of Morocco, there is a tremendous amount of poverty everywhere. The basic mode of transportation is mopeds that are so old and so full of rust that they appear as if they would crumble to the ground if you sat on them. But even beyond the poverty, those with jobs struggle to achieve an acceptable quality of living. The average wage in Casablanca is only $2,400 a year! Then, for every child, a parent must pay a 10 percent annual fee. So a person making the average wage of $2,400 has to pay a fee of $240 per child. Then, there is a flat tax of 35 percent imposed on all income.

I think it will take decades for the wealth level and quality of living in Casablanca and Morocco to improve to the point of being an investment opportunity for global investors. But I believe there is one lesson to be learned from Morocco; if a flat tax can be implemented in Morocco, why is everyone so convinced it is too complicated to ever happen in the United States?

This to me shows that the political leadership of Morocco understands the issues that need to be addressed. Their leaders are embarking on innovative solutions and, from my perspective, they are on the right path to both address and improve the quality of living for their citizens. There is no doubt in my mind that they will get there. Both investors and citizens, however, need to give the political leadership the time to address these issues because, after all, there are no quick fixes.

MUSLIM INFLUENCE

I found it especially fascinating to be in Morocco during Ramadan. Most people don't realize that Morocco is over 90 percent Muslim. In fact, the third largest Muslim Mosque in the entire world is in Casablanca. It holds 20,000 worshipers inside and another 80,000 in the surrounding open courtyard! And you can clearly feel how deep their beliefs are during this holy season. Ramadan is a "month of blessing," marked by prayer, fasting, and charity. This year it began October 5 and lasts through November 4. Muslims believe that during the month of Ramadan, Allah revealed the first verses of the Qur'an, the holy book of Islam. Muslims practice "sawm," or fasting, for the entire month of Ramadan. This means that they may not eat or drink anything, including water, while the sun shines. Thus, most restaurants are closed during daylight hours.

NOT JUST A MOVIE

Back to *Casablanca,* the movie. The underlying reason that this movie took on legendary status was that it was only one of a confluence of issues focusing on Casablanca in 1942. In addition to the release of the film, General Dwight D. Eisenhower was directing "Operation Torch," where 25,000 troops came ashore at Casablanca and other parts of Morocco's shoreline. The news of "Operation Torch" landing in Casablanca was broadcast around the world. And, finally, President Roosevelt and Prime Minister Churchill were in deep discussions regarding World War II. Even though these talks were actually held in Anfa, Morocco, these strategy sessions were referred to by the media and recorded for history's sake as "The Casablanca Conference." The entire world was watching and reading about "The Casablanca Conference." So it was the confluence of these three events that helped launch the movie to instant legendary status.

In closing, we are always looking for "the next big thing" on Wall Street. In my opinion, the next big thing from an investment perspective is still China, which should play out over the next decade. I think the next big thing after that will probably be India, which should play out over the next 20 years. And the next big thing after that could be northern Africa, and specifically Morocco, led by Casablanca. From what I've just seen, that investment opportunity is still 25 to 30 years away.

While Casablanca is clearly more than just a movie, sometimes Hollywood can create an image of a place that is more glamorous and exciting than it actually is. That is the case with Casablanca, especially from an investment perspective. And one more thing— the entire movie was shot in the studios of Hollywood. No one ever actually came to Morocco to shoot any part of the movie.

Finally, the issues facing Morocco are issues faced by other countries in Africa as well as other parts of the world. Do not underestimate the will of the people of Morocco. This may someday be one of the real gems of Africa and the world. Also do not underestimate the importance of strong and innovative political leadership, which is exactly what Morocco has. In the long run, that leadership can make Morocco a great place to invest in the future. Maybe then Hollywood can come here and make a movie about the miracle of Morocco!

Investment Footnote . . . What actually happened ↑

I was right. The next big thing still is China. China was one of the top markets in the world, posting a 130 percent gain in 2006 and a 96 percent gain in 2007.

Canaries, Dogs, and Cranes

November 4, 2005

I have just left two of the Canary Islands. I visited the city of Santa Cruz on the island of Tenerife and the city of Las Palmas on the island of Gran Canaria. The Canary Islands are part of Spain. There are actually 13 separate islands (7 large and 6 small) that stretch across 400 miles in the Atlantic Ocean between Spain and Africa. Over 1 million people live on the islands.

WHAT'S IN A NAME?

If you are thinking that the Canary Islands have something to do with little yellow canaries, you are dead wrong. In fact, I didn't see one single canary on either island. The islands were actually given their name by King Juba, who led an expedition there and discovered not little yellow birds, but rather large dogs everywhere. *Canis* is Latin for "dog" and is the genus type for all species of dogs, both domestic and wild. The islands then became not "Canis Islands" but "Canary Islands," named after the dogs. By the way, I didn't see any of those either.

SMALL TOURISM ISLANDS

What I expected to see were some remote-looking islands similar to the smaller islands in Hawaii that have nothing but lush vegetation. That is not what the Canary Islands are about today. Instead, both of the cities I visited reminded me more of Monte Carlo than Maui. For any of you who have not been to Monte Carlo, the entire mountainside facing the ocean is completely filled with hotels, stores, and condos—building after building and house after house, one on top of another, covering virtually every square inch of land. You could n't fit one more building in Monte Carlo if you tried. The same can be said for both Santa Cruz and Las Palmas. In fact, at first glance, both actually look like Monte Carlo. But the comparison ends there.

NEW STATE BIRD

From my observation, both the island of Tenerife and the island of Gran Canaria have adopted a new state bird: the "crane"—as in building cranes, which are everywhere you look—especially in Santa Cruz. There is every size of crane you can imagine, working on all types of projects—cranes, cranes, and more cranes. It is the biggest building crane explosion I have seen outside of China's current, unprecedented building and infrastructure boom. In the Canary Islands, there is indeed an infrastructure building boom, as they are embarking on massive highway construction projects that will take years if not decades to complete.

COMMODITY BOOM EVERYWHERE

From a pure investment theme perspective, what struck me the most was that I am halfway around the world on some supposedly remote islands and the "commodity boom" story is alive and well. Mind you, these are not major emerging markets like China, Brazil, and Russia, where you would expect to see cranes everywhere fueling the commodity boom. Instead, these are tiny little islands in the middle of nowhere. And they, too, are part of this unbelievable commodity boom investment theme. Just maybe it's places like the Canary Islands locations, which are off everyone else's investment radar, that are the reason why these commodity cycles can last for 15 to 20 years.

If you are looking for an investment theme from the Canary Islands, I think the answer is to consider buying commodities today, tomorrow, and next year.

Investment Footnote . . . What actually happened ↑

I was correct. The commodity boom continued posting a 22.54 percent gain in 2005, a 13.51 percent gain in 2006, and another 20.56 percent gain in 2007.

Put a Cork in It

NOVEMBER 8, 2005

I have just finished the final leg of my international trip with a stop in Portugal. Did you know that Portugal is actually the world's largest exporter of cork? In fact over 50 percent of the entire world's supply of cork comes from Portugal—more about that later.

THE PORTUGAL PERSPECTIVE

Let me begin by giving you a current perspective on Portugal. It is located in southwestern Europe and shares the Iberian Peninsula with Spain, which borders Portugal to the north and east. The Atlantic Ocean serves as its border to the south as well as the west. It has the ninth largest population in the European Union with a little over 10 million. It enjoys a population growth rate of 0.39 percent which is just about double the European Union rate of 0.20 percent.

The population of Portugal really begins and ends with Lisbon, which has a population of 3 million people, or 30 percent of the entire country's population. Let me give you some perspective of the magnitude of that relationship using the United States as an example. New York City has the largest population in the United States today at over 8 million people, while the U.S. population is 295 million. Think of how important New York City is today to the United States with only 2.7 percent of the nation's total population. For New York City's population to have the same relationship as Lisbon's to Portugal, it would have to increase tenfold to 88 million people. So if you want to understand how important Lisbon is to Portugal, simply imagine New York City 10 times larger than it is today and then try to imagine how important it would be to the United States. That is how important Lisbon is to Portugal.

In many respects, Portugal is a lot like California. It has basically the same geographic shape as California. In addition, it has the same climate and terrain. In fact, when you are going up and down the hills of Lisbon in a trolley car, you would swear you were in San Francisco. The relationship doesn't end there; they also have earthquakes just like California, only worse.

In fact, almost 250 years ago to the day in 1755, Lisbon was completely destroyed by an earthquake of almost 9 on the Richter scale. And because the epicenter of the quake was actually in the ocean, a tsunami immediately followed the quake and Lisbon was virtually wiped off the map.

That makes Lisbon a new city and an old city all at the same time—pretty much like the country of Portugal, which is an old country and a new country all at the same time. In fact, it was Portuguese explorers who discovered Brazil some 500 years ago in the name of the King, John Frederick I, Elector of Saxony. The King and the monarchy were overthrown in Portugal in 1910; Portugal was then governed by a republic that evolved into a pure dictatorship. Finally, in the 1970s, the dictatorship was overthrown and the country became a democracy. So, like Lisbon, it is old and new at the very same time.

ECONOMIC DRIVERS

Portugal's economy has witnessed the privatization and deregulation of many state-owned and state-controlled industries, including telecommunications and financial services.

A large portion of Portugal is still focused on agriculture. Abundant olive trees, vineyards, and wheat have given it a corner in the wine, olive oil, and cereal market. Natural resources cover over one-third of the country, mainly in the form of cork trees, pine trees, and eucalyptus trees. Portugal remains the third largest exporter of olives, dating back to 200 B.C. when the Romans first brought olive trees to Portugal. And, as I mentioned, it is the world's number one exporter of cork. Do not underestimate the extent to which cork is used. It is not just for wine bottles (even though that remains a very important element). Cork is also used to make shoes. And it is one of the main ingredients used to make cigarette filters. Now, it is being used for insulation as well.

Portugal also has significant mining resources in uranium, tungsten, and tin. Finally, tourism remains a very important element of Portugal's overall economy.

INVESTMENT THEMES

Two investment themes struck me about Portugal. The first theme or opportunity is global. More and more, the economies and markets of the world are becoming interconnected. How else can you explain a tiny country like Portugal being responsible for 50 percent of the world's supply of cork? From my perspective, this *global* theme is not just something that is going to play out in the next year or two, but rather for the next decade or two. I believe the beginning and end of every investment portfolio should be global and more global. It clearly is the new world order.

The second theme is the cigarette industry. When I traveled through Hong Kong and China last year, I vividly remember everyone with a cell phone in hand. In Portugal it seems to be a cigarette (or two) in hand. From what I saw, this goes on morning, noon, and night—both inside and outside. Young and old, from all walks of life, are smoking; in fact, many look to be under 16. Make no mistake about it: Cigarette demand is booming throughout Europe and especially Portugal. And while this may not be healthy for you, it can certainly be healthy for your investment portfolio.

AN IRONIC TWIST

Let me close with what I consider an ironic twist. The single most important resource in Portugal is cork. The two most prominent uses of that cork are "corking" wine bottles and making cigarette filters.

On Wall Street we call the alcohol and tobacco industries the "sin industries." In fact some investors refuse to invest in these so-called sin industries. And every time a state government needs more money, everyone says raise the sin taxes, meaning the taxes on alcohol and cigarettes.

Here is why this is so ironic to me. Over 98 percent of the population in Portugal is Catholic. And this 98 percent Catholic population has to rely on the so-called sin industries of wine and cigarettes to buy their cork. There has got to be some sort of investment theme there as well, but I just can't find it. In the meantime I'll "put a cork in it."

Investment Footnote . . . What actually happened

I was right. While the U.S. market returned 16.3 percent, as measured by the Dow, the rest of the investment world boomed as the MSCI–EM (Morgan Stanley Capital International–Emerging Markets) was up 23.5 percent and the MSCI–EAFE (Morgan Stanley Capital International–Europe, Australia, and Far East) was up a whopping 29.2 percent.

The Investing Secret of Oman

April 18, 2006

Who in the world would have ever believed that I actually found the key to successful international investing off the beaten path in a tiny country call Oman? More about that later. Let me first begin with a closer look at Oman.

WHERE IN THE WORLD IS OMAN?

I am sure that many investors have no idea where Oman is even located. Oman is a country in the southwestern part of Asia on the southeast coast of the Arabian peninsula. It borders the United Arab Emirates (UAE) in the northwest, Saudi Arabia in the west, and Yemen in the southwest. The coast is formed by the Arabian Sea in the south and east and the Gulf of Oman in the northeast. For your frame of reference, it's about the size of the state of Kansas.

Oman has a very long and storied past; it actually was part of the original Persian Empire. It was incorporated into that empire around 563 B.C. In its more recent history (over the past 500 years), Oman has been a major center for traders. In 1508, Oman was captured and controlled by the Portuguese. In 1659, the Ottomans took control of Oman from the Portuguese and then, in 1741, the Ottomans, too, were driven out when the present line of sultans was established. In 1891, Oman became a British protectorate; this lasted until 1971. The year before, in 1970, the sultan had been ousted and overthrown by his son, Qaboos bin Said, who continues to rule the country today under an absolute monarchy. As a note of interest to U.S. investors, Oman's military bases actually were used by U.S. forces involved in ground raids against Afghanistan in 2001. In general, Oman is a vast desert plain that is very hot and very dry.

ECONOMIC PERSPECTIVE

The economy of Oman begins and ends with oil, which accounts for over 90 percent of the country's exports. It produces close to one million barrels of oil a day. But it wasn't always that way. In the 1950s, a series of dry holes were drilled in the search for oil; most companies left Oman in 1960. Only Royal Dutch/Shell and Partex remained. Finally, in 1962, they struck oil. In 1967, Compagnie Française des Petroles returned to Oman to form a partnership with Royal Dutch/Shell and Partex and, in 1974, the government of Oman joined the partnership taking a 25 percent stake. One year later, the government acquired another 35 percent stake, which is where things still stand today. Petroleum Development Oman LLC is a limited liability company; 60 percent is owned by the government of Oman, 34 percent by Royal Dutch/Shell, 4 percent by Française des Petroles (now called "Total"), and the final 2 percent stake by Partex.

Oman's economy has made great strides over the past five years, fueled by the spike in the price of oil. Oman has used this newfound wealth to improve the infrastructure of roads, schools, and utilities. While they are making great strides, there remains much to be done in this still developing country. One remarkable achievement to me is that they have accomplished all of this despite the fact that they are the only oil-producing nation in the Middle East that is not a member of OPEC (Organization of the Petroleum Exporting Countries).

THE SECRET

Now, it's time to unveil the secret of international investing that I found in Oman. But I want you to first think of how global everything is even to a tiny country like Oman.

First, Portugal controlled Oman. Then Britain protected it. Royal Dutch/Shell, a British company, struck oil there. Then Compagnie Française des Petroles, a French company, joined in the oil partnership. Then the United States used Oman's bases to attack Afghanistan. We truly live in a global village. Now for the secret, which I actually found in the city of Salalah, Oman. Salalah is home to the tomb of Job. Regardless of one's religious beliefs, no visitor to Oman should miss the tomb of Job, which is located in a small white building with a golden dome. The secret to international investing is the principle that the Prophet Job lived by: patience. This is, after all, where the saying, "the patience of Job," originated.

You see, international investing is not that complicated, but you need to have patience. That's the secret. It's that simple. The way to become a long-term investor in a short-term world is to have the patience of Job. And I firmly believe that your patience as an investor is likely to be rewarded if you invest internationally.

PS: My commentaries on international investing continue with the following report, focusing on Egypt.

> ### Investment Footnote . . . What actually happened ↑
>
> I was right. While the U.S. market returned 16.3 percent, as measured by the Dow, the rest of the investment world boomed as the MSCI–EM (Morgan Stanley Capital International–Emerging Markets) was up 23.5 percent and the MSCI–EAFE (Morgan Stanley Capital International–Europe, Australia, and Far East) was up a whopping 29.2 percent.

Nile (Now) and Then

APRIL 24, 2006

There are very few places in the world today that have a greater economic and quality-of-life spectrum than Egypt. The disparity between the richness of the Nile River valley and the almost isolated state of the deserts provides one stark contrast. Then, when you include the major cities that border the Red Sea and benefit from the Suez Canal, it is truly like looking at Egypt as it is now (the urban, metropolitan Nile area) and Egypt as it was in ancient times (the farms and the deserts). As an investor, I think the exciting thing about this contrast is that it gives us a peek at where the rest of Egypt may be headed over the next decade. More about that later.

Let me begin by giving you a brief political and economical perspective on Egypt.

POLITICAL PERSPECTIVE

Egypt is located in northern Africa and shares land borders with Libya to the west, Sudan to the south, and Israel and the Gaza Strip to the northeast. The remaining border to the east is the Red Sea, while the Mediterranean Sea forms its northern border.

Egypt has one of the richest political histories in the world. It remains famous for its ancient civilizations and stunning ancient monuments, from pyramids to sphinxes to temples. While Egypt has been around for 5,000 years it wasn't until 3,100 B.C. that it had its first unified kingdom. In its more recent history, Egypt fell to the Persians, Greeks, Romans, Byzantines, and then, the Persians again.

The completion of the Suez Canal in 1869 made Egypt an important transportation hub. However, it also caused the country to fall heavily into debt. Because of Egypt's budget problems, the United Kingdom took control of Egypt in 1882 to protect its financial investment in the Suez Canal. Egypt finally acquired full sovereignty following World War II. The final chapter was written in 1953 when the current Egyptian Republic was established with General Muhammad Naguib serving as the first president.

Because Egypt controls the Sinai Peninsula (the only land bridge between Africa and Asia) and the Suez Canal (the sea link between the Indian Ocean and the Mediterranean Sea), it has been able to establish itself as a major force on all geopolitical issues in the Middle East.

ECONOMIC PERSPECTIVE

From an economic perspective, Egypt is the fifteenth largest country in the world, with a population of 77 million. Nearly 90 percent of the population lives near the banks of the Nile River or the coastal border of the Red Sea. Egypt's economy depends mainly on three components: first, the exports of oil, manganese, iron ore, and natural gas (yet another commodity boom example from around the world); second, tourism; and third, agriculture.

Due to a lack of any major structural economic reform since the early 1990s, foreign investment in Egypt has slowed. As a result, the Egyptian economy had been hard-pressed to grow at a 2 percent annual level throughout the 1990s. 2004 provided an economic turning point for Egypt with the implementation of several key economic measures in an attempt to attract more foreign investment. And it worked. Foreign investment in Egypt soared after implementation of customs reform and income and corporate tax reform; energy subsidies were reduced as several enterprises were privatized.

No discussion of Egypt's economy would be complete without at least one sentence on the Suez Canal. Here is the best perspective that I can provide you: Every single day of the year more than 100 ships pass through the Suez Canal. These ships carry almost 15 percent of the world's trade. There is no more important trade corridor anywhere in the world than the Suez Canal.

One final and very interesting economic note: There are over five million Egyptians working abroad, most of them in the Saudi Arabian oil fields. When they return home from working in the oil fields, it is a sight even more striking than any pyramid or sphinx; it is capitalism at its best. I was able to witness firsthand the return of about 2,500 Egyptian workers coming back from the Saudi oil fields on a cargo ship. Their belongings were unloaded first, in wire crates piled 10 feet high and 50 feet long. There were probably 75 of these metal cages, row after row after row. Next, a series of flatbed trucks delivered people in orange uniforms. They were porters helping the Egyptians with their luggage. I use the term *luggage* loosely. All of a sudden a whistle blew and what followed was the most unbelievable example of organized chaos I've ever witnessed. Remember that I used the term luggage loosely. Here is what I meant. These Egyptians returned home with hundreds and hundreds of carpets, big screen TVs, regular TVs, stereos, computers, air conditioners, and washing machines (yes, washing machines)! These Egyptians witnessed a better quality of life in Saudi Arabia, and they brought it back with them on their own backs.

THE NILE (NOW)

With that political and economic perspective, let's now move on to the Nile, focusing on what is happening in the major urban economic centers of Egypt.

Alexandria and Cairo are bursting at the seams with people and economic activity. The streets are packed with vendors, restaurants, and store after store selling everything you can imagine.

These major urban areas of Egypt have benefited from the increased flow of new foreign investment. The signs of building and infrastructure improvements are everywhere (one more commodity boom aspect). These cities have harnessed the same frantic pace of economic development as Hong Kong, Shanghai, Beijing, or even New York City. Their economic future could not be brighter.

"THEN" THERE IS THE FARM

As bright as the future of those living in the cities may be, when you focus on those living outside the major urban areas, it is truly like going back in time a thousand years. The agriculture component of the Egyptian economy could not be more primitive. The primary mode of transportation on these farms is a donkey, with an occasional camel here and there. Almost everything is done by hand; there are very few tractors or plows or any other farm equipment anywhere in sight.

The living conditions are also very primitive. In a stream where the women stand knee-high in river water to wash clothes, there is a dead horse floating a mere 20 yards away. That dead horse was one of three dead animals I saw floating in the river. As I said, it is what I imagined Egypt to have been like a thousand years ago.

THE AMERICAN FARMER

Now, before you give up on these backward Egyptian farmers, let me remind you of what happened in the United States. In 1900, almost 40 percent of the entire U.S. population worked on the farm in order to feed the United States. Today, less than 2 percent of the population works on the farm, feeding not only the entire United States, but many other parts of the world as well. How did this happen? With high-tech farm equipment that does the work of 10 farmers. And with our new information-based economy, farmers are now better equipped with information about how to protect crops from disease and pests. Wait until you see what happens in Egypt when they begin to go the way of the American farmer. The investment theme here is pretty easy to grasp. I think Egypt is going to continue to evolve into one of the great places in the world to invest. Also, they are not doing so bad in the here and now (Nile) either. At the end of the first quarter of this year, the Egyptian stock market (as measured by the Egypt CASE 30 index) on a year-over-year basis is up 74.3 percent. Meanwhile, the U.S. stock market (as measured by the Dow Jones Industrial Average) is only up 5.8 percent for the same time period. Maybe Egypt is about more than just Nile (now) and then. From my perspective, it is also about what will become a great place for international investors as well.

Investment Footnote . . . What actually happened ↑

I was right. While the U.S. market returned 16.3 percent, as measured by the Dow, the rest of the investment world boomed as the MSCI–EM (Morgan Stanley Capital International-Emerging Markets) was up 23.5 percent and the MSCI–EAFE (Morgan Stanley Capital International–Europe, Australia, and the Far East) was up a whopping 29.2 percent.

Star Wars

April 25, 2006

It seems that no matter where you are or where you look in the world today, you are reminded of the powerful forces of globalization. There may be no better example of that globalization than Tunisia, Africa. While Tunisia is very important historically, maybe the most famous event in its modern history was when it was chosen by Hollywood producer and director George Lucas as the location to film one of the greatest movies of all time, *Star Wars*. And now it appears that Tunisia (or *Star Wars* as I like to call it) is about to provide the newest link between Africa and Europe. More about that later; first, let's focus on Tunisia itself.

A HISTORICAL PERSPECTIVE

Tunisia is a tiny country (about the size of the state of Georgia) in northern Africa. Its border to the north is the Mediterranean Sea. Algeria provides its western border, while Libya surrounds the remainder of the country on both the southern and eastern borders. About 40 percent of the entire country is covered by the Sahara Desert.

At the beginning of recorded history, Tunisia was inhabited by Berber tribes. Its coast was settled by Phoenicians, starting as early as the tenth century B.C. In the sixth century B.C., Carthage rose to power and eventually became the dominant power in the Mediterranean after a series of wars with Greece. Tunisia was the center of the Carthaginian civilization and it challenged the dominance of both the Greek and Roman empires in the Mediterranean between the sixth and first centuries B.C.

In more modern history, Tunisia was declared a protectorate of France in 1883. Pressure for Tunisia's independence began in 1934 with the formation of the New Constitution Party. Finally, in 1957, the Republic of Tunisia was formed. It has had only two presidents since establishing its independence in 1957.

THE ECONOMY

Tunisia is attempting to diversify its economy beyond agriculture and chemicals. It remains one of the largest exporters of palm dates in the world, growing more than 100 different varieties. Its focus as a major producer of chemicals has not come without its costs and burdens. Both toxic and hazardous waste disposal are very ineffective in Tunisia and pose a great health risk. Tourism is one of the areas into which Tunisia hopes to expand in a much greater way over the next decade.

Unemployment remains one of the country's biggest hurdles. Currently running between 13 and 15 percent on a monthly basis, this unemployment rate completely understates the real problem. If, for example, you work contractually for only one day in the entire month, which happens more times than not, you are considered employed for the entire month by the government of Tunisia. If it weren't for this distortion, I believe that unemployment would easily be over 20 percent.

THE STAR WARS LINK

Let me now end where I began, by explaining my Stars Wars link between Africa and Europe. As you recall, *Star Wars* was filmed in Tunisia, which I believe is about to become a vital link between Africa and Europe in a seemingly never-ending global story. It all started on March 1, 1998, when Tunisia became the first Mediterranean country to enter into an "association" agreement with the European Union. Under this agreement, Tunisia must continue to remove trade barriers one at a time with the European Union over the next decade. Then, in 2008, Tunisia will become a fully associated member of the European Union. Other fully associated members include the countries of Norway and Iceland. So now, as an investor, when you are looking for reasons to invest in Europe, one of them may actually be in Africa in the tiny country of Tunisia.

In closing, Tunisia is providing investors in the United States with one more reason why their investments need to go global. I continue to say, go more global and then go even more global! Globalization is for real and it is everywhere, including the country that is the home of *Star Wars*—Tunisia.

Investment Footnote . . . What actually happened ↑

I was right. While the U.S. market returned 16.3 percent, as measured by the Dow, the investment world in Europe boomed just as I predicted, as the MSCI–EAFE (Morgan Stanley Capital International–Europe, Australia, and the Far East) was up a whopping 29.2 percent.

All Roads Lead to Change—in Italy

April 26, 2006

In order to explain fully what is going on in Italy today, I need to tweak one of the most famous proverbs about Italy's largest and most important city: "All roads lead to Rome." I am going to tweak that proverb and create a new one: "All roads lead to change in Italy," and here is why.

As my international travels come to a close in Italy, I see signs of change everywhere. These are major and dramatic changes that I think will reshape Italy and quite possibly the world. These changes are coming from three fronts: the recent prime minister elections; the Vatican (or more specifically, the Pope); and the Italian stock market, called the *Borsa Italiana*. More about these three major changes later. First, I want to provide you with some background on Italy from both a historical and economic perspective.

HISTORICAL PERSPECTIVE

Italy is a country in southern Europe. Virtually everyone, young and old, recognizes its boot-shaped appearance on a map. In addition to that boot-shaped peninsula, Italy also comprises two large islands in the Mediterranean Sea—Sicily and Sardinia. As a peninsula, Italy is surrounded on three sides, east, west, and south, by the Mediterranean Sea. It is bordered to the north by France, Switzerland, Austria, and Slovenia. The independent country of the Vatican City is an enclave within Italy. It is the smallest independent sovereign state in the world, with a population in the hundreds. The Pope has full legislative, executive, and judiciary powers in the Vatican.

Important cultures and civilizations have existed in Italy, rich in ancient history, since prehistoric times. Both the Roman Republic and the Roman Empire civilizations dominated this part of the world for many centuries. As a result, Italy was central to both European art and science during the Middle Ages and the Renaissance.

In more recent times, Italy became a nation-state by uniting under King Victor Emmanuel II. Italy's parliamentary government came to an end in the early 1920s when Benito Mussolini established a fascist dictatorship. Mussolini's alliance with Nazi Germany led to Italy's defeat in World War II. A democratic republic replaced the monarchy in 1946 and remains in place today.

ECONOMIC PERSPECTIVE

Italy's economy remains one of the 10 largest economies in the world, yet it never seems to command the respect it deserves as a key driver in Europe. That is because, even though it is in the top 10 in the world, it is only the fourth largest in Europe, trailing Germany, the United Kingdom, and France.

Italy has a rather diversified industrial economy driven by a population that is now approaching 60 million. In many respects, Italy's capitalistic economy is not "the tale of two cities" but rather what appears to be the tale of two distinct economies within one country.

First, we have the highly developed and industrial north, which is dominated by private companies and a thriving economic base, driven by the textile, clothing, footwear, and automotive industries. Meanwhile, in the south, you find a less-developed economy, driven almost solely by what has evolved into an almost "welfare" type of dependent agricultural industry, with unemployment levels greater than 20 percent. One critical economic issue to both north and south is that most raw materials needed for production are imported, as well as 75 percent of the country's energy requirements, which makes the overall economy highly susceptible to energy shocks.

Italy has done a wonderful job in recent years of pursuing a tighter policy on government spending, which in turn has helped reduce inflation and lower interest rates. But even with that progress, Italy's long-term economic challenges are very similar to the ones faced by other Western European countries; namely, major structural reform must be accomplished by lowering the current high tax rates and completely overhauling and transforming Italy's rigid labor market. And, in addition, Italy must address its overly generous public pension system before its rapidly aging population enters retirement.

PRIME MINISTER ELECTIONS

Let's move on to the first of the three major changes I mentioned. In the recent election for prime minister, incumbent Prime Minister Silvio Berlusconi was defeated for reelection by Romano Prodi. Berlusconi has served as the Italian Prime Minister since 2001. And while on the surface that may not seem like a long time, in Italian politics it's a lifetime. In fact, Berlusconi is the longest-serving prime minister since World War II. A little-known fact outside of Italian politics is that this is not the first time this election has happened. Ten years ago Prodi defeated Berlusconi in another race for prime minister of Italy.

This particular election was considered a referendum on the policies as well as the character of Berlusconi, who, as Italy's wealthiest individual, amassed his fortune in real estate and the media. The election was almost too close to call. Italy's highest court stepped in and upheld the narrow victory for Prodi. This close election shows how divided Italy is politically as well as economically.

With such a close vote, it would not be out of the question to try to put together a "German-style" grand coalition government. Regardless of the outcome, investors can be assured of change on the political front. Investors around the globe will be watching closely to see which policy direction the new prime minister decides to take. The stakes could not be higher.

VATICAN POLICY CHANGES

Let's now move on to the second major change. This one is taking place at the Vatican and is being driven by the Pope. All of Italy is "abuzz" on this issue. Pope Benedict XVI has been seen wearing several high-profile brands recently, and all of Italy is debating whether the Pope should ever endorse or even publicly use high-profile consumer products.

Unlike sports stars and movie stars, who command huge sums of money for an endorsement of a product, many believe the Pope should handle issues in a manner similar to the queen of England, who allows companies to discreetly mention patronage by the Royal Family.

Why is this suddenly a big issue? Well, because product placement is the new age of marketing. *Product placement* occurs when a company pays to have its product placed or filmed in a movie or television show, for example. If the actors want a soft drink on the set, Coke is willing to pay to have their brand be the drink of choice. When the previous Pope, John Paul II, was elected in 1978 there was no such thing as product placement, so it wasn't an issue with him at that time. The concept exploded over the past 10 years during the same time frame that Pope John Paul II's health deteriorated and he spent less time in the public eye, so such product placement was again a nonissue.

Now along comes Pope Benedict XVI, wearing Geox shoes, sporting Serengeti sunglasses, and listening to his customized Apple iPod. While I doubt that we will see corporate logos on the Papal garb like we do on race car drivers' colorful garb, make no mistake about it: a sea change is in the air. Global markets and capitalism are everywhere, even in the tiniest independent sovereign state in the world, the Vatican. This has got to be a good sign for global markets!

STOCK EXCHANGE MERGER MANIA

Let me now move on to the third and final major change in Italy. This one is being driven by the Borsa Italiana, Italy's stock exchange. Borsa Italiana is planning to sell 30 to 40 percent of the exchange to the public in an upcoming initial public offering (IPO) sometime in late summer or early fall. Once that occurs, Borsa Italiana will find itself right in the middle of the global stock market exchange merger mania. Borsa Italiana is the eighth-largest stock exchange in the entire world, based on trading volume.

Here is where we stand so far. The world's largest stock exchange, the New York Stock Exchange, has been in talks to merge with the number three exchange, the London Stock Exchange, as well as the number five exchange, Euronext, which is comprised of the stock exchanges in Amsterdam, Paris, Brussels, and Lisbon. Meanwhile, Euronext is also talking about a merger with Deutsche Borse (the number six exchange), which runs the Frankfort stock exchange.

Nasdaq (the number two exchange) has purchased a 15 percent stake in the London Stock Exchange. And, in the past, Borsa Italiana has said it would prefer a deal with the London Stock Exchange, given London's position as the financial capital of Europe.

Not to be left in the dust, the Dubai International Financial Center, which owns the Dubai Stock Exchange, just purchased a 2 percent stake in Euronext, as well. Let the games begin. All we know for sure, at this point, is that Italy will be one of the major players in this stock exchange merger mania. And that's great news for the Italian stock market.

In closing, let me end where I began. The roads of change do indeed seem to lead to Italy. Whether that change is good, bad, or indifferent is yet to be seen. But we do know one thing for certain: change creates opportunities and right now opportunities abound in Italy—even if the Pope eventually has a Nike "swish" on his sleeve.

Investment Footnote . . . What actually happened

I was dead right on this call. The Italian stock market soared 29.7 percent in 2006.

Das Ist Stadtische

JUNE 9, 2006

I recently returned from a trip to Germany where I was one of the keynote speakers for Deutsche Bank's Global Transaction Banking Conference, and all I could think about was "Das ist stadtische."

That is German for "that's so urban." So many Americans still view Germany as beautiful countryside filled with lush green fields and mountains along with the greatest festival in the world, Oktoberfest (which is held in September).

In reality, Germany is so much more than mountains and Oktoberfest. In fact, it has evolved into one of the most urbanized countries anywhere in the world today. While the mountains and Oktoberfest are still important, it is these urban centers that hold the future for all of Germany.

BACKGROUND

Let's begin with some basic background about Germany. Germany is one of the world's leading industrialized countries. It is located in central Europe and is bordered to the north by the North Sea, Denmark, and the Baltic Sea. Its eastern border is Poland and the Czech Republic; the southern border is comprised of Austria and Switzerland and, finally, its western border is comprised of France, Luxembourg, Belgium, and the Netherlands. A little known fact is that, due to its central location, Germany actually shares borders with more European countries than any other country in Europe.

ECONOMY

From an economic perspective, Germany is the largest European economy and the third-largest economy in the world behind the United States and Japan. Germany is actually the world's top exporter, ahead of both China and the United States, and the largest trading partner with every other European country. The biggest issue facing the German economy today remains the high unemployment rate and weak domestic demand, which combine to slow down economic growth.

As with most large economic nations, Germany's industrial sector has been in a steady state of decline while its service sector has boomed. Even with this shift away from its old industrialized economy, Germany is among the world's largest and most technologically advanced producers of iron, steel, cement, chemicals, machinery, and motor vehicles. In fact, major car manufacturers like BMW, Mercedes (DaimlerChrysler), Opel, Porsche, Volkswagen, and Audi are all German.

Germany is divided into 16 states, which are further subdivided into 439 districts and cities. The five largest cities in Germany are Berlin, Hamburg, Munich, Cologne, and Frankfurt. Due to the country's federal and decentralized structure, these major urban areas have evolved both together and somewhat equal. The federal structure has kept the population oriented toward a number of large cities, and has precluded the growth of any single city that would rival the likes of London or Paris for size. While outsiders may consider this a weakness, it is actually the key strength of Germany today.

INVESTMENTS

From an investment perspective, stock valuations in Germany remain reasonable and are still below their historical average. And while earnings are currently slowing, there is a great likelihood that earnings will improve during the second half of the year. In addition, a pickup in merger and acquisition activity in all of Europe, especially Germany, stands to propel the equity market during the second half of the year. Combine that with the fact that the European Central Bank is near the end of its interest-rate tightening cycle, and I think that is all the fuel you need for a strong equity rally in Germany for the second half of the year. Especially when you realize the secret to their economy and market just might be, "Das ist stadtische."

Investment Footnote . . . What actually happened ↑

This call was spot on as well, with the German stock market gaining 36.4 percent in 2006 and another 35.6 percent in 2007.

Investing in the Big J-C (Japan and China)

JULY 24, 2006

It seems like only yesterday when the hit Broadway musical *Jesus Christ (JC) Superstar* took the world by storm. In reality, it was 40 years ago. I remember that musical for two reasons: first, because it was controversial, and second, because it forced people to think differently. As a teenager in the 1970s, both of those radical concepts seemed very cool to me. Now, some 40 years later, I have my own extremely radical JC concept; only my JC is not Jesus Christ but rather Japan and China. In many ways, my JC will be much more controversial than the original JC Superstar musical ever was.

The reason my concept is so controversial is that, on Wall Street, we want you to pick one (Japan) or the other (China or the rest of Asia), but you don't get both. My JC will force you, all of Wall Street, and the entire investing world, for that matter, to change everything you have ever been taught about investing in Asia.

ASIA EX-JAPAN

Consider how most mutual fund companies offer products to invest in in Asia. You can invest in a product that invests in "Japan" or you can buy a product that invests in "Asia ex-Japan." If you want to track performance of the Asian markets using the benchmark Morgan Stanley indices, you can look at the Morgan Stanley Japan Index or the Morgan Stanley Asia Ex-Japan Index. Most Wall Street firms are organized exactly the same way; they have a "head" of Japan and a "head" of Asia ex-Japan. Why? This is the only region in the entire world that is treated that way by Wall Street.

In Europe, there is no such thing as investing in France or investing in Europe ex-France. No companies are organized that way nor are there any indices that track performance that way. It's the same in South America. There is no such thing as investing in Brazil or South America ex-Brazil, and again no one is organized that way and there are no indices set up that way. And it's the same with Africa. You don't get the choice of Egypt or Africa ex-Egypt. The only place in the entire world of investing where we do that is with Japan. That is so old school. You must break that habit if you are ever going to embrace how to invest in the big JC.

WORLD WAR II

The reason we are organized that way is World War II. After World War II Japan was disliked by most of the world—especially its neighbors in Asia. It was thought that the wounds of World War II were so deep that they would last forever and never heal. It was common belief that no one in Asia would ever want to do business with Japan as a result of Japan's aggression during World War II. This was especially true for China, because Japan actually invaded and controlled parts of mainland China during World War II.

So the entire investing world was set up to reflect these negative views on Japan. These outdated views are over 60 years old, and I say it is time to put them to rest forever. There is a new world order of investing called the big JC.

EXPORTS BOOMING TO CHINA

Let me prove it to you. Currently Japanese exports to China are exploding and Wall Street's response is that trend can't continue because you must choose Japan or Asia ex-Japan, but not both. This export boom is not going to stop anytime soon. In fact, it just might be one of the greatest investment opportunities in your lifetime. Think about this for potential: if the population of China walked past you, in single file, the line would never end because of the current rate of reproduction. Why wouldn't you want to do business with China? Let me put this export boom in some perspective for you. Ten years ago, according to the World Bank, Japanese exports to China totaled only $21.8 billion. Last year, Japanese exports had increased almost fourfold over that nine-year period to $80.1 billion. In addition, last year, for the first time in history, Japanese exports to China totaled $7 billion in an individual month, achieving that feat on four separate occasions. So far this year through the first five months, Japanese exports are on target to exceed $90 billion and just might approach $100 billion. Oh, and by the way, in four of those five months, trade exceeded $7 billion, matching the number of times that feat had ever been accomplished in history. So how does Wall Street respond to these facts? Exactly as you would have guessed—by saying this trend can't continue, because we all know that people in China are simply not going to buy things made in Japan because everyone in China hates everyone in Japan because of World War II.

THE CHINESE PERSPECTIVE

While it is common belief that most people in China hate most people in Japan, let me give you my perspective on this outmoded school of thought. While I am not a China expert, I have gained wonderful firsthand experience, having traveled there most recently on three separate occasions over the past year and a half.

Here is what I found during my recent travels to China. Allow me to generalize here a bit. If you draw a line at roughly age 40, I would tend to agree that most people in China 40 years of age and older do indeed dislike most Japanese, and many do hate Japan and will never ever buy anything made in Japan. However, there are a few other things about this group of Chinese, age 40 and older. Most of them work outside the urban areas on farms. Most of them live at or below poverty level. I don't mean to imply that they are irrelevant, but from a global economic perspective they are irrelevant. It is true that they do hate Japan and they will never buy anything made in Japan. But it is also true that they can afford to buy very, very little from any country.

How about the rest of the population in China, the group below age 40? This is the group that, for the most part, is college educated. This group also lives in the major urbanized areas of China. They have the best-paying jobs. They enjoy the highest standard of living. And their spending habits are driving the Chinese economy to grow at above 10 percent a quarter and 10 percent a year.

One more fact about this 40 and younger group. I think they missed the history class where they were told that they are supposed to hate Japan. Many of them don't even know that Japan invaded China in World War II. It's a generational thing! Think about it. We never, ever, ever get the big-picture generational things correct on Wall Street because we are always shortsighted, focusing on the here and now. Most investors are more interested in knowing what couple of stocks Jim Cramer will discuss on CNBC's *Mad Money* tonight than they are in any generational shifts.

Yet this generational shift is the exact reason to invest in the big JC. From a generational perspective, people 40 and older in China do indeed remember hearing about World War II and, as a result, may never buy anything made in Japan. Keep in mind, however, that they have no money. Meanwhile, people in China 40 and under simply want to buy the next cool thing, and they have the money to do so. If the next cool thing happens to be from Sony, they will buy it. Heck, they may even buy two of them. The fact that Sony is a Japanese company simply doesn't matter to them. They want anything cool and they want it now. Remember, it's a generational thing.

WE HAD ONE TOO

If anyone should get this generational issue, we should in the United States, because we had our very own around 40 years ago. And I participated in it firsthand. While I went to college in the mid-1970s I went back home each summer and worked in the steel mills in Pittsburgh. It was the single greatest motivation in my life. It simply scared me to death to think about not graduating from college and having to come back to Pittsburgh and work "a real job" in the steel mills for the rest of my life. You don't know what hard work is until you've been inside a steel mill.

Anyway, as I was about to graduate, almost everyone I worked with in the mill came up to me with the exact same message. First, they wished me luck. Second, they said that once I am successful I should never forget my roots in this steel mill—meaning I better never, ever, ever buy a foreign car made with foreign steel. The only car I could buy was an American-made car made with US Steel. I have to admit they scared the heck out of me.

That, too, was a generational thing in the 1970s. My parents never bought a foreign car. None of my neighbors ever owned one. In fact, no one in my family or anyone I knew owned one. Back then, Wall Street laughed at the idea of anyone in the United States ever buying a foreign car, because Wall Street knew that we would always buy American-made cars. It was a generational issue and Wall Street missed this one completely as well. Yes, my parents never bought a foreign car. But the generation that followed can't buy enough foreign, and Wall Street missed this trend completely— the same way they are missing in investing in the Big JC. Think about it. Where else can you get the upside of China's explosive growth with the downside protection of Japan—a mature industrialized economy that already embraces capitalism and already embraces the rule of law. Investing in the Big JC gives you the best of both worlds.

You are, however, going to have to think outside the box and forget the old-school Japan and Asia ex-Japan stuff. Remember, there is always more than one way of doing something. In fact, there are 293 ways to make change for a dollar. It's time for you to "change" the way you invest and invest in the big JC.

PS: Not all baby boomers like me fit this generational mode of only buying foreign cars. Who knows, maybe the steel mill had a greater impact on me than I realized. I drive a General Motors car. My wife drives a General Motors car. We bought our eldest daughter a Ford when she graduated from college and bought our youngest daughter a General Motors car when she graduated from college. Maybe that explains why I am such a die-hard Steelers fan!

Investment Footnote . . . What actually happened ↑

I was correct about the Big JC. Japan was up 5.9 percent in 2006 and China was up 130 percent in 2006.

"Sweden's Newest ABBA Group Is Performing Well"

August 21, 2006

Whether music fans or not, most people around the world recognize the music group ABBA. True music fans also know that ABBA is actually from Sweden, but it takes a real die-hard rock n' roll music fan to know that ABBA actually stands for the first letters in the first names of the members of the group: Agnetha Faltskog, Bjorn Ulvaeus, Benny Andersson, and Anni-Frid Lyngstad. These days, there is a new ABBA group that is performing quite well, and that is the real story of what's going on in Sweden. But before I introduce you to the newest members of ABBA, let me first put Sweden into some perspective for you.

GEOGRAPHIC PERSPECTIVE

Let's start with a brief geographic perspective. Located in northern Europe, Sweden is actually a little larger than the state of California. It is bordered by Norway to the west, Finland to the northeast, the Skagerrak Strait and the Kattegat Strait in the southwest, and the Baltic Sea and the Gulf of Bothnia in the east. The largest city in all of Sweden is Stockholm and it is also the capital. Stockholm is comprised of 14 separate islands that are all connected by an elaborate maze of 57 individual bridges. All of these canals and waterways have earned Stockholm the nickname, "Venice of the North," or "The Clean Venice," as I refer to it, since Venice remains a dirty and polluted city while Stockholm is one of the cleanest and safest cities in the entire world.

ECONOMIC PERSPECTIVE

Let's now move on to a brief economic perspective of Sweden. Sweden has developed a formula for the "axis of prosperity." First and foremost is its neutrality and peacefulness. Sweden was not involved in World War I or World War II, which is amazing considering its geographic location. The second element in the axis is its vibrant high-tech capitalist business environment. The third and final element is its extensive system of welfare benefits. The confluence of these three foundations has produced one of the highest standards of living anywhere in the world. However, the strength of their economy goes well beyond these issues.

Sweden has a very modern and efficient transportation and distribution system, excellent communication infrastructure, and a highly skilled and well-trained labor force. Timber and iron ore serve as the basic foundation of its natural resource base, which is one of the reasons Sweden's entire economy is heavily dependent upon foreign trade. From more of a political perspective, debate over the country's role in the political and economic integration of Europe delayed Sweden's entry into the European Union (EU) until 1995. In 1999, Sweden waived the introduction of the euro as its new currency and in 2003, Swedish voters officially turned down the euro because of concerns that the currency might ultimately have a negative effect on Sweden's democracy and sovereignty. As a result, Sweden's currency today remains the krona and not the euro, even though Sweden is part of the EU.

DEMOGRAPHIC PERSPECTIVE

Finally, let's move on to a demographic perspective. As I mentioned before, Sweden has one of the world's highest life expectancies. In 2004, the population of Sweden exceeded 9 million people for the first time ever, according to the World Bank. Almost 90 percent of its population is ethnic Swedish. The single largest nonethnically Swedish group is from Finland, which accounts for 2 percent of the population. The remainder of the population is comprised of ethnic groups from Denmark, Norway, the former Yugoslavia, and the Middle East, especially Iran, Iraq, and Palestine. Even though Sweden first became populated by hunters and farmers soon after the end of the Ice Age in 10,000 B.C., it remains a relatively young country from a purely demographic perspective, as a mere 17 percent of its entire population is 65 years of age and older.

THE NEW ABBA GROUP

Finally, it is time to introduce you to Sweden's new ABBA group. The first A in ABBA stands for "automobiles." The automotive industry is one of Sweden's top global exports. Both Volvo and SAAB are from Sweden and both are enjoying robust sales globally. The first B in ABBA stands for "boom in commodities." I don't know how many more examples we need to prove once and for all that the commodity boom is not dead; however, Sweden is another one. *Boom* doesn't quite capture the explosion in Sweden's commodity exports, which consist of iron ore, copper, lead, zinc, gold, silver, tungsten, uranium, and, of course, timber. The second B in ABBA stands for "benefits." It is hard to find a place with better health and social welfare benefits than Sweden. The government of Sweden provides for child care, a ceiling on health care costs, tax-funded education up to and including college, retirement pensions, dental care up to 20 years of age, and parental leave of 480 days between birth and a child's eighth birthday. Today, Sweden still has some of the most generous benefits around, and there has been massive reform in both education and health care benefits, which has set the foundation for an even stronger economy that is less dependent on government handouts. Finally, the second A in ABBA stands for "Absolut," as in Absolut vodka, whose home is also Sweden. Absolut vodka is one of the most dominant brands of vodka in the entire world today.

GO GLOBAL!

In closing, if you put them all together: automobiles, boom in commodities, benefits, and Absolut vodka, they not only spell ABBA but they spell out one more reason why investors need to go Global, go Global, and go even more Global. Sweden is simply one in a number of investment stories all about globalization.

One final thing about the "old" ABBA, the music group: It ushered in a new era of international prominence in pop music for Sweden. Following ABBA to the worldwide pop music stage from Sweden were Ace of Base and The Cardigans, to name a few.

Talk about a global force, after the United States and the United Kingdom (home of the Beatles), Sweden is the largest producer of music in the world! That should provide a sweet sound to savvy global investors!

Investment Footnote . . . What actually happened

I was right. While the U.S. market returned 16.3 percent, as measured by the Dow, the rest of the investment world boomed as the MSCI–EM (Morgan Stanley Capital International-Emerging Markets) was up 23.5 percent and the MSCI–EAFE (Morgan Stanley Capital International–Europe, Australia, and the Far East) was up a whopping 29.2 percent.

A Fairy Tale Comes True in Denmark

AUGUST 25, 2006

From a purely investment perspective, there are numerous fairy tales or myths about the economy. Today, three of the most common ones focus on economies that have to import food and energy and what will happen to them if there is no more food and energy to import. Remember, Wall Street loves to focus on these two elements. Wall Street even measures inflation exfood and energy. The second one focuses on economies that have to rely on foreign funding to pay for their debt. Again, it's pretty much the same question: What will happen when those other countries slow down or stop buying debt? And the third and final one focuses on the issue that labor unions and management will never be on the same page, so to speak, and unions will always be a problem. Who would have thought that the tiny country of Denmark would come up with an answer to all three of those economic fairy tales?

Before I explain how they did it, let me give you a little better perspective of Denmark itself.

GEOGRAPHIC PERSPECTIVE

Let's begin with a geographic perspective. Denmark borders two seas—the Baltic Sea and the North Sea—and is actually part of a peninsula named Jutland, which is attached to northern Germany, Denmark's only land neighbor. Denmark is also comprised of the islands of Funen, Zealand, Bornholm, and hundreds of smaller islands that together are referred to as the Danish Archipelago. Denmark is both the smallest and the southernmost of the Nordic countries.

ECONOMIC PERSPECTIVE

From an economic perspective, Denmark is about as modern and up-to-date as any country anywhere. Although it is mainly driven by a high-tech agriculture industry, economically, it goes well beyond the high-tech farm industry. Denmark also provides extensive government welfare measures that allow its citizens to enjoy a high living standard. Add to that a stable currency and you have all the ingredients for a sound economic base. But the part of the economic puzzle that I find most exciting is the fact that the government of Denmark is continuing in its efforts to streamline the bureaucracy and further privatize the state-owned assets and functions.

The government has become a model of success by meeting and exceeding all the economic benchmarks needed to advance to the third phase of the European Economic and Monetary Union (EMU), the adoption of the common European currency, the euro. However, even though Denmark met all the economic conditions in a September 2000 election referendum, the people of Denmark reconfirmed their decision not to join the 12 other EU members in using the euro. While Denmark still has its own currency, the Danish krone, they decided to peg their currency to the euro anyway.

When you combine above-average economic growth with comprehensive government benefits and a very stable political system, it is easy to see why Denmark enjoys one of the highest living standards, not just in Europe but in the entire world as well.

And it's not just the "high" standard of living, but rather the "high" tech standard of living as well. The people of Denmark are as tech savvy as any nation anywhere in the world. In fact, for the past two years, Denmark was ranked number one in the world by *The Economist* magazine on its intelligence unit's e-readiness list. A country's *e-readiness* is a measure of its e-business environment, which is a collection of factors that indicate how amenable a market is to Internet-based opportunities.

ECONOMIC FAIRY TALE

Let's get back to these three economic fairy tales that no one can seem to solve. The first one focuses on economies that have to import food and energy and what will happen to them if there is no more food and energy to import. In Denmark, this actually doesn't matter. Denmark is one of the few places in the entire world that is a net exporter of both food and energy. Denmark is a major exporter of oil, natural gas, meat, dairy, and fish products. Forget about this economic fairy tale impacting Denmark.

The second one focuses on economies that have to rely on foreign funding to pay for their debt. Again, it's pretty much the same question of what will happen when those other countries slow down or stop buying debt. Once again, this doesn't matter, because Denmark actually is one of the few places in the world that has *zero* net foreign debt! You can forget about this economic fairy tale as well.

Now the third and final one focuses on the labor union and management issue—that they will never be on the same page, so to speak, and unions will always be a problem. This is not the case in Denmark. In fact, relationships between unions and employers are very cooperative. Unions actually have a day-to-day role in managing the companies and union representatives sit on most companies' board of directors. Rules on work schedules and pay are negotiated without any government involvement. Need proof that this works? The current unemployment rate in Denmark is 4.5 percent and falling—one of the lowest in all of Europe. This economic fairy tale is dead as well.

DENMARK'S FAIRY TALE

In closing, even though Denmark has dispelled these economic fairy tales, other noneconomic fairy tales remain part of the rich culture and tradition of Denmark. In fact, Denmark is home to one of the most famous fairy tale writers of all time, Hans Christian Andersen. Two of his most famous fairy tales are "The Little Mermaid" and "The Ugly Duckling." It's okay to believe in fairy tales as long as they are not economic fairy tales. Denmark has proved beyond a shadow of a doubt that these economic fairy tales are fiction. It is only fitting that a country whose most famous national monument is "The Little Mermaid" would be the one to prove economic fairy tales are myths!

Investment Footnote . . . What actually happened

I was right. While the U.S. market returned 16.3 percent, as measured by the Dow, the investment world in Europe boomed just as I predicted, as the MSCI–EAFE (Morgan Stanley Capital International–Europe, Australia, and Far East) was up a whopping 29.2 percent.

From Vikings to Terrorists—Only the Names Change in Norway
August 28, 2006

As I travel through Norway, I am simply overwhelmed with the vast history of the latter-day Vikings and their savagery and pillaging. They were truly the "terrorists" of their time.

ALWAYS A REASON NOT TO INVEST

It suddenly hit me that there will always be a reason to be afraid and, in turn, always a reason not to invest. It is never going to go away. The only thing that will change is the name. While I know that many investors today are afraid of "terrorists," we can't even imagine the fear and terror that citizens of days gone by had of the Vikings. Centuries ago, when peasants huddled in their farmhouses as part of the masses of a terrorized Europe, they would actually whisper at the end of each prayer, "and deliver us from the Vikings, Amen." The Vikings left a legacy of exploration, savagery, and pillaging. As they swept through one village to another, they carried whatever they could to load aboard their ships. Items too cumbersome were simply set ablaze. The destruction was always catastrophic.

Now, if you are looking for a reason to be afraid of investing, you can always find one. If, however, you are looking for a reason to invest, I have found one off the beaten path right here in Norway. Before I tell you what I found, let me give you a little better perspective of Norway itself.

GEOGRAPHIC PERSPECTIVE

Norway is part of the Scandinavian peninsula along with Finland and Sweden. To the south, west, and north, Norway borders the North Sea and the North Atlantic Ocean and to the east, has three major land borders, mostly Sweden, but also Finland and (what few people realize) Russia. For a frame of reference regarding size, the entire country of Norway is about the same size as the state of New Mexico.

DEMOGRAPHIC PERSPECTIVE

The size of Norway's population is around 4.6 million. In recent years, immigration has accounted for more than half the population growth. The largest immigrant groups are Swedes, Danes, Pakistanis, Iraqis, and Vietnamese. Almost 90 percent of Norway's inhabitants are members of the state church, the Evangelic

Lutheran Church of Norway. Norway is a youthful country where over 20 percent of its population is 14 years of age and under while only 14 percent of the population is 65 years of age and over.

ECONOMIC PERSPECTIVE

From an economic standpoint, Norway has the best of both worlds—free capitalism along with government intervention. Many refer to Norway's economy as "welfare capitalism." The government controls the single most important industry, the petroleum sector. Actually, oil and natural gas account for more than one-third of all of Norway's exports. Only two countries—Saudi Arabia and Russia—export more oil than Norway.

The control mechanisms Norway uses over the petroleum industry are state ownership of major Norwegian field operators (Statoil is 70 percent government owned and Norsk Hydro is 43 percent government owned) combined with specific taxes (set at 78 percent) on operators' oil profits. In addition, the government controls the licensing of exploration and production of all oil fields.

The country is richly endowed with natural resources, including petroleum, hydropower, fish, forests, and minerals. Norway has obtained one of the highest standards of living in the entire world, mostly due to its petroleum production. It also boasts efficient economic policies, which create a great environment for doing business, as reflected in Norway's low unemployment rate.

Norway actually opted to stay out of the European Union during a referendum in 1972 and again in November 1994. However, Norway, along with Iceland and Liechtenstein, participates in the EU's single market via the European Economic Area (EEA) agreement. The EEA Treaty, between the EU nations and the EEA nations, is constituted as superior law in Norway, which makes Norway a full member of the EU's free trade market.

COMMODITY BOOM

As I draw this commentary to a close, I will state my reason for investing in Norway. It's quite simple—commodities. Remember, oil and gas account for over 50 percent of all of Norway's exports; only

Saudi Arabia and Russia export more oil than Norway, which, by the way, is not a member of OPEC even though it is the third-largest exporter of oil in the world.

Because of this dependence on oil and gas for its future, many in economic circles call oil and gas dependency the "Dutch disease." In response to this issue, Norway began searching for coal beneath its oil reserves. What was found is staggering. The government's rough estimate of the tons of coal (of unknown quality) beneath the oil reserves on the continental shelf of Norway is three times greater than all the known coal reserves in the entire world. Now that is what I call a commodity boom and just what we need to keep this global economic boom and market boom in full swing as well.

In closing, if you are looking for a reason to be afraid of investing, you can always find one somewhere between the Vikings and today's terrorists. But if you are looking for a reason to invest, look no further than the commodity boom in Norway.

PS: My next stop is Scotland!

Investment Footnote . . . What actually happened ↑

I was correct. The commodity boom continued to boom returning 13.51 percent in 2006 and another 20.56 percent in 2007.

Scotland Exports More than Whiskey— Just Ask Sean, Alex, or Harry

AUGUST 29, 2006

When someone says "Scotland," investors and travelers alike immediately think of Scotch whiskey. While it is true that Scotch whiskey remains an important part of the Scottish economy, this nation's booming export base involves much more than just whiskey.

GEOGRAPHIC PERSPECTIVE

First, let's put Scotland into its proper geographic perspective. Scotland occupies the northern third of the island of Great Britain. It shares its only land border to the south with England. It is bound by the North Sea to the east, the Atlantic Ocean to the north and west, and the North Channel and Irish Sea to the southwest. In addition to its mainland, Scotland consists of approximately 800 islands as well.

Scotland, while a nation, is not a sovereign state. It is part of the United Kingdom, along with England, Wales, and Northern Ireland. Scotland does, however, continue to have a separate legal and judicial system from England, Wales, and Northern Ireland. This Scots Law, along with the Church of Scotland and the Scottish education system, form the axis of the continuation of Scottish culture and the Scottish national identity even though the country is part of the United Kingdom. But, because it is not a sovereign state, Scotland does not enjoy direct membership in either the European Union or the United Nations. The United Kingdom represents Scotland with these organizations as well as England, Wales, and Northern Ireland.

ECONOMIC PERSPECTIVE

From a pure economic perspective, Scotland has been part of some major transformational shifts. The Scottish economy was concentrated mainly in heavy industry, including shipbuilding, coal mining, and steel. As heavy industry began to decline in the latter part of the twentieth century, Scotland began a transformational shift toward a technology- and service-based economy. It especially boomed in "Silicon Glen," the corridor between Glasgow and Edinburgh (the two largest cities in all of Scotland), where many large technology firms throughout Europe relocated. And there was one other significant transformation: the discovery of North Sea oil in the 1970s.

About one-third of the land in Scotland is under cultivation, principally in vegetables and cereals. The main cereal cultivation is barley, which, you guessed it, is the key ingredient for Scotch whiskey.

HOW ABOUT THOSE EXPORTS?

While the overall Scottish economy is closely linked with the rest of Europe, it is clearly an economy that lives and dies based solely on its exports. And today, its export business is truly booming. In addition to being one of the top exporters of whiskey in the entire world, there are numerous other products that serve as Scotland's export industry foundation as well.

As mentioned above, one of them is oil. Scotland is actually referred to as the Oil Capital of Europe because it is at the center of the North Sea oil industry. In fact, the Scottish waters of the North Sea and the North Atlantic contain the largest oil reserves in all of Europe.

The fishing industry is also one of the major exporters. With Scotland surrounded on three sides by water, it is easy to figure out why.

Financial services is also one of Scotland's key exports. Edinburgh, which serves as the financial services center of Scotland, is actually the sixth-largest financial services center in all of Europe. Key to this industry is the Royal Bank of Scotland, which is the second-largest bank in all of Europe.

Finally, they still do build ships in Scotland, making shipbuilding the final cornerstone of Scotland's export base. Even though shipbuilding has significantly diminished from its heights in the early twentieth century, it still forms the largest part of Scotland's manufacturing base.

So the next time someone says the word *Scotland*, I want you to think of oil, fishing, financial services, and shipbuilding in addition to your knee-jerk thought of Scotch whiskey; it is all five of these industries that form the strong economic export base for Scotland.

WHAT ABOUT SEAN, ALEX, AND HARRY?

I almost forgot about Sean, Alex, and Harry. You really don't need to ask them about exports because they actually are exports from Scotland. *Sean* is for Sean Connery, who grew up in Edinburgh and, as a boy, delivered milk to the Fettes School. You James Bond film buffs might recognize the name of that school. It is where the fictitious character of James Bond was educated. How ironic is that?

Alex is for Alexander Graham Bell, the inventor of the telephone, who was born in Edinburgh, Scotland. He went first to Canada, then to the United States, where he became one of the world's greatest inventors.

And finally, the *Harry* is for Harry Potter. J. K. Rowling, author of the famous Harry Potter books, wrote her first novel *Harry Potter and the Philosopher's Stone* in Edinburgh, splitting her time between writing in a cafe and writing in the public library. She has gone on to become one of the most famous and wealthy authors in history.

My next stop is the Netherlands!

Investment Footnote . . . What actually happened ↑

I was right. While the U.S. market returned 16.3 percent, as measured by the Dow, the investment world in Europe boomed just as I predicted as the MSCI–EAFE (Morgan Stanley Capital International–Europe, Australia, and the Far East) was up a whopping 29.2 percent.

The Netherlands Has Become the Land of the Good, the Bad, and the Ugly

AUGUST 31, 2006

I am not sure that there is another place in the entire world like the Netherlands. For in the Netherlands, especially in its capital city, Amsterdam, you have it all. There is so much "good," but there is plenty of "bad" and even some "ugly" all in one place. While every country has its good and bad points, nowhere are they as dramatic and "in your face" as they are in the Netherlands. More about the good, the bad, and the ugly later; first, let me bring you up to speed on the Netherlands itself.

GEOGRAPHIC PERSPECTIVE

The Netherlands is located in northwestern Europe. It is bordered by the North Sea to the north and the west, Belgium to the south, and Germany to the east. It is the European part of the Kingdom of the Netherlands, which also includes the Netherlands Antilles and Aruba.

The Netherlands is often mistakenly referred to as "Holland." That term is commonly used as a synonym for the Netherlands, but the word *Holland* actually derives from a region in the west of the country that currently accounts for only two of the 12 provinces, namely, North Holland and South Holland.

The Netherlands is completely flat. In fact, more than half its surface area is less than three feet above sea level and large parts of it are below sea level. That is one of the reasons for its extensive system of canals and dykes, which help prevent flooding. The highest point in all of the Netherlands, the Vaalserberg, in the southeasternmost point of the country, is only 1,000 feet above sea level.

ECONOMIC PERSPECTIVE

Moving on now to the economic perspective, the Netherlands has a prosperous economy in which the government has greatly reduced its role. The three economic drivers are agricultural and food processing, energy, and electrical machinery.

A highly technology-driven agricultural sector employs no more than 4 percent of the entire labor force, but provides large surpluses for the food processing industry and for exports. This food processing industry is dominated by two global powerhouses— Unilever and Heineken. A little-known fact is that the Netherlands actually ranks third in the entire world in the value of agricultural exports. Numbers one and two are the United States and France, respectively.

The second key industry is energy. Petroleum refining is dominated by another local global powerhouse—Royal Dutch Shell. Also, the Netherlands boasts one of the largest natural gas fields in the entire world in Slochteren. Only half these reserves have been used up, so these natural gas fields will continue to be a key economic driver for at least the next decade, if not longer.

Finally, the Netherlands is a key player in electrical machinery, and the global powerhouse doing it for this country is Philips. As you can see by all three of these leading industries, international trade is the key underlying driver of the Netherlands economy. As the global economy goes, so goes Netherlands' economy.

THE GOOD

With that as background, let's now move on to the Good, the Bad, and the Ugly, starting with the good. There is so much good, it is hard to know exactly where to start. When people think about the Netherlands they think of windmills and wooden shoes. Or they think of flowers, especially tulips. Each of these issues brings good and happy thoughts to mind. But there are more good things about the Netherlands than those for which it is traditionally known. It is also known for its elaborate canals and dykes. Bicycles seem to be everywhere. In fact, more people per capita use bicycles for transportation in the Netherlands than anywhere else in the world, even China! The day I was in Amsterdam it rained the entire day and people rode their bikes anyway in their raingear, holding an umbrella overhead while riding with one hand. And truly important, the Netherlands' art and culture may be second to none. In the early seventeenth century, the Netherlands had Rembrandt, and in the nineteenth and twentieth centuries, the Netherlands had Vincent van Gogh, not to mention the numerous other world-class artists and philosophers in between. If all that good doesn't put a smile on your face, nothing will.

THE BAD

But I am afraid that the smile will not stay on too long because, for as much good as there is, it is more than offset by the bad. Prostitution is legal in the Netherlands. One could make the case that there is prostitution everywhere so it does not matter whether it is legal or not. But it does matter, for in the Netherlands, it is smack in your face for all to see in a display window. At 10 a.m., middle-aged, overweight women selling their bodies from a store front window is a sight that words simply can't describe. And it's not just the sex and prostitution; it's the drugs. Marijuana is legal and can be bought in every coffee shop. You will learn quickly that if you want coffee, you go to a café, and if you want drugs, you go to a coffee shop to choose from a wild array of marijuana. Young and old alike smoke pot. One can argue the merits of legalizing these things or not, but you cannot argue the fact that, by legalizing them, the Netherlands has put sex and drugs right in your face, every minute of every day, unlike anywhere else in the world.

THE UGLY

As if the bad is not bad enough, you are probably trying to guess what could be uglier? Well, for starters, the Netherlands is the number one European producer of ecstasy, illicit amphetamines, and many other synthetic drugs. It is the gateway for the major sources for most cocaine, heroin, and hashish that enter into Europe. And it's not confined to just Europe. The Netherlands is the number one source of U.S.-bound ecstasy as well. Because of all the drug trafficking, the financial sector is thought to be extremely vulnerable to money laundering. Oh, and I almost forgot—more bicycles, over 250,000 annually, are stolen in the Netherlands than anywhere else in the world. Now, some of you may have more liberal opinions than I regarding sex and drugs, but everyone has to agree that stealing a bike . . . that is just plain wrong!

PS: The next stop is Belgium!

Greetings from Belgium, the Capital of Europe

SEPTEMBER 1, 2006

After reading the title of this commentary, most global investors may be thinking to themselves, "I didn't know there was such a thing as the capital of Europe." Well, there isn't officially, of course, but unofficially, I have just named Belgium the capital of Europe. I will tell you why a little later but for now let's focus on some key reference points regarding Belgium itself.

GEOGRAPHIC PERSPECTIVE

Let's start with a geographic perspective. Belgium is a country in northwest Europe bordered by the Netherlands, Germany, Luxembourg, and France. It also has a border with the North Sea.

Belgium has a population of over 10 million people in a country only 11,000 square miles in area, or a little smaller than the state of Maryland. The population density (the number of people per square mile) is one of the highest in all of Europe, after the Netherlands and the tiny country of Monaco. The areas with the highest population density are around Brussels and Antwerp—two cities that I visited while in Belgium. Almost all the population (97.3 percent) live in urban areas.

Four primary languages are spoken in Belgium. That's no typo: four primary languages! Dutch is spoken by about six

million people in Flanders to the north. French is spoken by some
3.5 million people living in the Walloons area to the south. There
are about 70,000 citizens who live in a German-speaking community in the east of the country that borders Germany. And, finally,
just about everyone speaks English. And I almost forgot that
the capital city of Brussels is officially bilingual (Dutch and
French). So if you want to get around in Belgium, you better know
how to speak Dutch, French, German, and English. Talk about
a truly global country; Belgium would have to be at the top of
the list.

ECONOMIC PERSPECTIVE

Let's now take a little closer look at the Belgium economy. Belgium
is located in the heart of one of the most highly industrialized
regions in the world, stuck between Germany and France. In fact,
Belgium was the very first continental European country to
undergo the Industrial Revolution in the early 1800s. It rapidly
developed mining and steelmaking, along with the chemical and
petroleum industries.

Belgium developed a wonderful transportation system of
highways, railways, ports, and canals. This enabled it to integrate
its industrial base with the rest of Europe. Antwerp is actually the
second largest port in all of Europe. Because of this great transportation infrastructure, the Belgian economy is strongly oriented
toward foreign trade. The main imports are food products, machinery, rough diamonds, chemicals, clothing, and textiles. The main
exports are automobiles, food and food products, iron and steel, finished diamonds, and plastics.

Belgium was one of the founding members of the European
Union (EU) and it strongly supports the extension of the powers of
EU institutions to more fully integrate the member economies. In
1999, Belgium adopted the euro, the single European currency,
which replaced the Belgian franc. Belgium is one of the few member states of the EU to have achieved a balanced budget. Finally, no
discussion of the Belgian economy would be complete without at

least pointing out that Belgium brews 600 different brands of beer—more than anywhere else in the world.

EUROPEAN CAPITAL

In closing, let me give you three reasons why I believe Belgium is the capital of Europe and that investing in Belgium would be a great part of a global strategy. First, after World War II, Belgium joined the North Atlantic Treaty Organization (NATO) and, together with the Netherlands and Luxembourg, formed the Benelux group of nations. Belgium is also one of the six founding members of the European Coal and Steel Community, founded in 1951. It was also a founding member of the European Economic Community and the European Atomic Energy Community. But, most important, Belgium is the headquarters for NATO.

Second, in addition to being the headquarters for NATO, Belgium is also the headquarters for the European Union. Belgium is home to a major part of the European Union's institutions, including the European Commission and the Council of the European Union. In addition, all committee meetings of the European Parliament are held in Belgium.

Third, and finally, as I mentioned earlier, four different languages are spoken in Belgium. Add these three things together and two things should become very clear. First, Belgium is indeed the capital of Europe. And second, Belgium is a great place for global investors to put some of their money in, as well.

Investment Footnote . . . What actually happened ↑

I was right. While the U.S. market returned 16.3 percent, as measured by the Dow, the investment world in Europe boomed just as I predicted, as the MSCI–EAFE (Morgan Stanley Capital International–Europe, Australia and the Far East) was up a whopping 29.2 percent. And in 2007 it was even better, returning 36.5 percent.

Greetings from Davos East in Krynica, Poland

SEPTEMBER 11, 2006

One of the fantastic things about working for a great global company like Deutsche Bank, with its 80,000 employees, are the limitless opportunities presented to us as investment professionals almost daily. Let me try to explain how I ended up speaking in Poland this past Thursday. In the spring of this year, I was one of the speakers at Deutsche Bank's first ever worldwide meeting for its Global Transaction Banking (GTB) Group held in Munich, Germany. In attendance at that meeting was Marcin Iwaszkiewicz, the head of Deutsche Bank's Global Transaction Banking in Poland. He was impressed with my investment message last spring in Munich and convinced Krzysztof Kalick, president of the board of Deutsche Bank Poland as well as our country manager for Poland, to invite me to speak at the sixteenth Annual Economic Forum in Poland as part of Deutsche Bank's panel. He did and I accepted, serving as a panelist along with Deutsche Bank's chief economist for Poland, Arkadivsz Krzesniak. Krzysztof Kalick was our panel moderator. They let me name the Deutsche Bank-sponsored panel session, so I called it "European Investment Megatrends." The title was a play on the title of my latest book, *Investment Megatrends*. I was hoping to pump up my European book sales and raise some money for the University of Dayton's R.I.S.E. (Redefining Investment Strategy Education) Forum through increased sales. (I have donated all the financial proceeds of my book sales to R.I.S.E.) And after all, I refer to R.I.S.E. as Davos West because Dayton is west of Davos and structured exactly like Davos, only for students.

One other interesting note: I actually spoke on another panel as well. That panel was sponsored by the Polish newspaper *Presspublica*. Their panel was moderated by Danuta Walewska, one of the paper's journalists. When she saw I was coming to the Economic Forum, she asked me to speak on her panel as well. About three months ago, I had received a call from a reporter from

Presspublica, who had seen me on TV as a guest co-host on CNBC Squawk Box Europe while I was in London. They had a few questions regarding geopolitical risks in the global capital markets. I gladly provided them with my answers and insights, which they needed and used in the story they wrote. You guessed it. That reporter was none other than the very same journalist, Danuta Walewska. The title of her panel was "Investment Conditions in the Countries of Central and Eastern Europe." A special thrill to me was that one of the other panel members was the former prime minister of Poland and current CEO of the Bank Pekao, SA, Jan Krzysztof Bieleck. Talk about a small world that is getting smaller every day. Thomas L. Friedman is right: *The World Is Flat*. (See, I plug other books as well as my own.)

DAVOS EAST

Let me start by giving you a little more background about this impressive Economic Forum that is informally called "Davos East." Davos, Switzerland, is home to the annual World Economic Forum. At that forum, political, business, labor, academia, religious, and media leaders conduct interview-style panel discussions rather than formal presentations in order to encourage spontaneous and dynamic exchange among the panelists and participants.

The Economic Forum, held annually in Krynica, Poland, is organized and structured the same way as the World Economic Forum in Davos; hence, the reference to "Davos East" (Krynica is east of Davos).

EUROPEAN CHALLENGES

The question of Europe's identity was the theme of this sixteenth Economic Forum that was held from September 6 through 9. Every year the Economic Forum brings together an international community of experts and leaders from political, social, economic, and cultural spheres. They meet to discuss the challenges faced by the contemporary world in general and Europe in particular. This year's Forum hosted almost 2,000 participants from 40 countries, who attended nearly 100 discussion panels and promotional meetings.

The Economic Forum organizers invite everyone who is interested in Europe's future to Krynica. Those who are drawn to the idea of a secure European community living in solidarity are welcome. Developing Europe's economy into the most competitive economic area in the world is another objective. The Economic Forum has already established a reputation as one of the most important gatherings of people from the worlds of politics, business, science, and the media from European countries, especially from Central and Eastern Europe.

I think the best way to judge a forum's influence is simply to look at who attended. Again, this forum was clearly a who's who from Central and Eastern Europe. Jaroslaw Kaczynski, the Prime Minister of Poland, was in attendance and speaking, as well as Viktor Yanukovich, Ukrainian Head of Government. In fact, the two of them met officially for the very first time at Krynica.

To give you some idea of the magnitude of this particular event, let me briefly mention some of the other speakers: the Minister of Economy for Lithuania, Navickas Vytar; the Minister of Economy for Slovakia, Lubomir Jahnatek; the Deputy Prime Minister of Georgia, Baracamidze Giorgi; the Deputy Prime Minister of the Czech Republic, Jaroslav Barta; the Under Secretary General of the United Nations, Marek Belka; the former Prime Minister of Poland, Minister for the European Integration, and current CEO of Bank Pekao, SA (and fellow panelist), Jan Krzyszt of Bieleck; the Secretary of State for Romania, Mugur Craciun; the Deputy Prime Minister of Cyprus, Serdar Denktar; the Minister of Economy and Trade for Moldova, Igor Dodon; the Minister of Economy and Transportation for Hungary, Gabor Eszes; the Minister of Trade and Industry for Finland, Mauri Pekkarinen; the Deputy Minister of Economy and Energy for Bulgaria, Nina Radeva; the Deputy Speaker of the Lithuanian Parliament, Ginataras Steponavieius; the Minister of the Economy for Poland, Piotr Wozniak; the Deputy Minister of Industry for Tajikistan, Makhmadszarif Khakdodov; the Minister of Finance for Poland, Stanislaw Kluza; the former President of Poland (from 1995 to 2005), Aleksander Kwasnieuski; the Minister of the Economy for Ukraine, Volodymyr Makukha; and last, but not least,the "unofficial" Minister of Wall Street, Dr. Bob of DWS-Scudder.

POLAND'S GEOGRAPHIC PERSPECTIVE

Let me now briefly put Poland into a clearer geographic perspective for you. Poland is located in Central Europe. It is bordered by Germany to the west, the Czech Republic and Slovakia to the south, Ukraine and Belarus to the east, and the Baltic Sea, Lithuania, and Russia to the north. In addition, Poland shares a maritime border with both Denmark and Sweden in the Baltic Sea. From a pure size perspective, it is slightly smaller than the state of New Mexico.

Poland formerly played host to many languages and religions. However, the outcome of World War II created a westward shift in Poland's territory that also created homogeneity. Today, 36,983,700 people (or 96.74 percent of the population) consider themselves Polish. The remaining minorities are mostly Germans, Ukrainians, and Lithuanians. Most Poles follow the Roman Catholic faith; 89.8 percent of the population are practicing Catholics, while the remaining population is mainly Eastern Orthodox.

With its transformation to a democratic, free-market–oriented country, Poland is making itself known on the global stage. In 1999, it joined the North Atlantic Treaty Organization (NATO) and in 2004 it joined the European Union.

ECONOMIC PERSPECTIVE

Moving on to Poland's economy, it is one of the most successful examples of transformation from a partially government/state-owned and -controlled capital market economy to a primarily privately owned market economy. Since its return to democracy, Poland has steadfastly pursued a policy of liberalizing its economy.

The privatization of small and medium government-owned and -operated companies and a liberal law on establishing new firms have allowed for explosive development in the private sector. Even restructuring and privatization of "the sensitive industries" (energy, communications, steel, railways, and the like) have begun. The biggest privatization so far was the sale of Telekomunikacja Polska, a national telecom company, to France Telecom in 2000.

Poland has a large agricultural sector of private farms that are evolving into a leading producer of food in the European Union. Now that Poland is a member, its economy is beginning to diversify away from its primary manufacturing base. In addition to the above-mentioned food, Poland's economy produces clothes, cars (including Leopard, a luxury car), buses, locomotives, planes, ships, and chemical products.

There are economic challenges, especially in terms of underinvestment. In addition, structural reforms in health care, education, and the public pension system have resulted in larger-than-expected fiscal pressures. Last, since Poland joined the European Union (EU), many young Polish people have left their country to work in other EU countries because of Poland's high unemployment rate, which is the highest of any EU member, at 15.7 percent. Both the former Prime Minister Jan Krzysztof Bielecki and I raised this issue in our panel discussions, and the two of us dubbed this problem "Poland's Brain Drain"— smart young people leaving Poland for other opportunities.

THE LONG ROAD TO DAVOS EAST

Let me shift gears now and give you my personal perspective of what I witnessed firsthand in Poland. Because Krynica is somewhat off the beaten path, I had to fly into Krakow and then take an almost four-hour drive to Krynica. (It usually doesn't take that long, but traffic was heavy because of the Annual Economic Forum.) At the outset, I wasn't too happy about a four-hour car ride after traveling over 16 hours just to get to Krakow. In hindsight, I am thankful that I had to take that drive because it opened my eyes up to a side of Poland that I would never have witnessed otherwise.

First of all, the part of Poland I was in is beautiful country, filled with hills, trees, and lakes. And not just a few lakes; Poland has 9,300 lakes to be exact. Second, the area was extremely clean. In fact, it reminded me of Chicago, which I consider one of the cleanest cities in the world. Not only was it clean, but there was a noticeable lack of graffiti. Third, the highways and transportation system were wonderfully modern and clean. The road to Krynica reminded me of the autobahn in Germany, the only difference being that the road to Davos East had only two lanes and neither of them was moving very fast.

One other thing that really impressed me about the highways was the noise barriers. First of all, I didn't expect noise barriers at all. Second, each one was different from the next. I quit counting when I got to over 20 different types of highway noise barriers. The third thing that impressed me while on my ride was what I saw when we went off the major highways and onto the country roads. There were walkers everywhere—young people and old people alike, walking to work and to school and to the stores. I haven't seen so many people walking in a long time. And they were walking in "style," as many of these country roads had beautifully colored paved brick sidewalks stretching for miles and miles on both sides of the road. You don't even see sidewalks like that in the most upscale neighborhoods of suburban Chicago. In fact, my neighborhood doesn't have any sidewalks.

The fourth thing that impressed me was all the workers in the fields, working the farms by hand, the women right alongside the men. In fact, I witnessed more women laboring on the farms than I did men. And most farms had a little stand at the end of the driveway where it looked like the grandmother had the job of selling food from the farm to any passersby.

The fifth and next-to-last thing that struck me was how well behaved and well dressed all the youth were in Poland: no blue jeans five sizes too big and no pants crotches hanging down to their knees with underwear showing. Also, I didn't see a single chain strapped to someone's wallet; and all these were clean-cut kids.

The sixth and final impression I had was at the hotel. I had breakfast, and the kids (under 20) who waited on me ran. And they did the same for other customers. They ran with my kielbasa wrapped in bacon, and they ran with my coffee (by the way, it was the best kielbasa ever, and I should know since I was raised on kielbasa and Iron City Beer in Pittsburgh). I have never witnessed anything like it, anywhere. In the states you are lucky if a waiter looks at you, let alone waits on you; in Poland they run to you. By the way, they didn't run to me with czernina, which is duck blood soup. I had to draw the line on Polish culture and cuisine somewhere, and I felt the duck blood soup was a good place.

In wrapping up my personal impressions, I would put the Polish work ethic up against any other country's work ethic in the world, and in my opinion Poland would win. They have some of the hardest-working and dedicated employees that I have seen in my travels around the world.

Need some final proof that Poland has arrived? The Polish Football Association (that's soccer for you Americans) and the Ukrainian Football Federation joined together to bid to host the European Football Championships (UEFA EURO) in 2012. They are one of three final candidates to host the 2012 European Championships.

Just as China hosting the Olympics in 2008 is a clear sign China has arrived, so, too, is this bid to host the European Football Championships in 2012 a sign that Poland has arrived.

And I vote that they host the games. Of course I don't have a vote on such matters, but I do have a vote and a say on where to invest globally, and in that perspective Poland is a two-thumbs-up yes!

Investment Footnote . . . What actually happened

Poland didn't let me or investors down as it soared 41.6 percent in 2006 and another 10.4 percent in 2007.

Beyond *The Firm*, Cayman Is Booming

DECEMBER 8, 2006

I recently returned from the Cayman Islands where I was a keynote speaker at the Cayman Captive Forum—2006, hosted by the Insurance Managers Association of Cayman (IMAC). Deutsche Bank's Off-Shore Group from the Cayman Islands sponsored the luncheon and asked me to be the keynote speaker. This marks the third time that I have spoken at this prestigious forum.

WHY A CAPTIVE FORUM IN THE CAYMANS?

You are probably wondering just what is a "captive" and why they have a forum about it in the Cayman Islands. First, the term *captive* is used to describe where to locate your captive insurance company. While the decision about where to locate varies from firm to firm, I can tell you from firsthand experience that those who establish their businesses in the Cayman Islands do so because of the vast network of service providers already there. Dan MacLean, managing director of Aon Insurance Managers (Cayman) and the new chairman of IMAC said it best: "It is easy to pass legislation to become a captive domicile, but it is harder to get the infrastructure and knowledge to support the industry."

Part of that infrastructure and knowledge—and one of the key reasons insurance companies locate in Cayman—is the Cayman Islands Monetary Authority (CIMA), which is run by my good friend and colleague, Mr. Timothy Ridley, O.B.E., with whom I was able to spend some time and gain some additional insights. Tim is, quite simply, one of the very best and brightest central bank leaders anywhere in the world today.

CIMA continues to receive plaudits for the oversight and flexibility it offers new captives. It has also delivered with the proposed amendments to the insurance law, via the Insurance Law Review Working Group, giving the industry the robust, modern framework required to serve clients in the years ahead without comprising standards. Let's back up for a minute and let me give you a little history of the background and economy of Cayman.

WHERE IS CAYMAN?

The Cayman Islands are located in the Caribbean Sea. The three islands are located about 500 miles south of Miami, 150 miles south of Cuba, and 180 miles northwest of Jamaica. Grand Cayman is by far the biggest island with an area of 76 square miles. The two sister islands of Cayman Brac and Little Cayman are located about 90 miles east of Grand Cayman and have areas of 14 square miles and 10 square miles, respectively.

THE CAYMAN ECONOMY

The economy of the Cayman Islands used to be built around turtling (which explains why there is a little turtle on Cayman Airlines planes). This industry began to disappear in the twentieth century, and tourism and financial services began to be the economic mainstays. From a trade perspective, the United States is the Cayman Islands' largest trading partner.

With an average income of $42,000, Caymanians enjoy the highest standard of living in the Caribbean. As I mentioned previously, tourism has become the driver of the Cayman economy. In fact, tourism accounts for over 75 percent of the annual gross domestic product (GDP) of the Cayman Islands. Of the millions of tourists that visit the islands annually, 99 percent stay on Grand Cayman. George Town in Grand Cayman also serves as a major cruise ship port, which brings in 4,000 to 22,000 tourists a day, depending on the number of ships in the port.

FINANCIAL SERVICES BOOM

The biggest story in the Cayman Islands today is not about tourism but rather the financial services industry. The Cayman Islands is now widely recognized as one of the leading offshore financial centers in the world. The Cayman Islands financial services industry encompasses banking, mutual funds, vessel registration companies, and partnerships, trusts, structured finance, the Cayman Islands Stock Exchange, and, of course, captive insurance. There are over 70,000 companies incorporated on the Cayman Islands, including 430 banking and trust companies, 720 captive insurance firms, and more than 7,000 funds.

The future of the Cayman Islands rests in the Financial Services industry. I have believed that from my very first visit over 10 years ago, and I believe it even more today. But don't just take my word for it. Here is a remark from a recent report on the Cayman Islands from the International Monetary Fund (IMF): "The Cayman Islands supervisory system benefits from a well-developed banking infrastructure with an internationally experienced and qualified workforce as well as experienced lawyers, accountants, and auditors."

COMMODITY BOOM

No discussion of the Cayman Islands would be complete without a brief discussion of the building boom going on. And remember, every building boom is really a commodity boom in disguise.

Basically, everywhere you look there are cranes—not the kind in the water but the kind that build buildings and hotels and condominiums. And it's not just the cranes; the Cayman Islands are also embarking on major infrastructure road projects as well. (They even built their first bridge. If you blink, you might miss it.) This is good for the Cayman Islands. And it is great for the ongoing global commodity boom as well!!

FRIENDLY AND RESILIENT PEOPLE

The people of Cayman are some of the warmest, kindest, and friendliest people I have met anywhere in the world. It is not something that they turn on just for tourists, but rather it's how they live every day of their lives—with the greatest respect for their fellow man. While their friendliness truly impresses me, it's their resilience that amazes me. The Cayman Islands were severely damaged by a Category Five (that's as high as it gets) hurricane, Ivan, on September 11 and 12, 2004, which destroyed many buildings and damaged almost 75 percent of the remaining buildings. Power, water, and communications were disrupted. Ivan was the worst hurricane to hit the islands in 86 years. Today, you wouldn't even know it happened, unless you are a veteran traveler to the Caymans like me and recognize the loss of the old, established trees that will take a century to replace. These are the most resilient people in the world. No wonder everyone wants to do business here.

WHAT ABOUT *THE FIRM?*

In closing, you are probably wondering about the title of this commentary right about now. Why did I call this commentary, "Beyond *The Firm*, Cayman Is Booming"? I haven't mentioned anything about *The Firm*. Well, here goes.

Large parts of John Grisham's best-selling novel *The Firm*, and the film of the same name, take place on the Cayman Islands. The main character works for a Memphis, Tennessee, law firm that uses Cayman Island banks for money laundering. The book and movie are fiction. It would be almost impossible for that to happen in the Cayman Islands today, not with my good friend Tim Ridley as the head of the Central Bank.

Investment Footnote . . . What actually happened

I was correct, as commodities returned 20.56 percent in 2007.

Greetings from Germany, the Motherland
MARCH 5, 2007

I have just arrived in Germany, my first stop on a seven-country international tour that includes stops in South Africa, Mozambique, Kenya, Seychelles, Oman, and the city of Dubai in the United Arab Emirates, in addition to the "Motherland" of Germany.

THE "MOTHERLAND"

I refer to Germany as the "Motherland" for three reasons. First, and foremost, it is after all the largest economy in all of Europe, driven by the largest population base in all of Europe as well. Second, DWS-Scudder, my employer, is part of Deutsche Bank, the largest bank in all of Germany and one of the largest banks in the entire world. Third, and finally, my family heritage is German; *Froehlich* translated from German means "happy."

So whether I look at Germany from the perspective of the largest and most important economy in Europe, or my job with Deutsche Bank, or my family's German heritage, Germany is indeed my "Motherland," no matter how you look at it.

ECONOMIC PERSPECTIVE

From a purely economic perspective, the German economy is not just the largest economy in all of Europe, but a global powerhouse as well. Globally, the German economy is the third largest in the world, trailing only the United States and Japan. In terms of exports, Germany has no equal in the entire world. Germany is the world's leading exporter, topping about $1 trillion in exports, according to the World Trade Organization. Most of the country's exports are in engineering (especially in automobiles and machinery). Of special note in terms of total capacity to generate electricity from wind power, Germany is first in the world in this area, and it is also the number one exporter of wind turbines.

But it would be a mistake to consider the German economy as only an export-driven economy. In fact, it is second in imports, trailing only the United States. Germany is one of the few industrialized nations of the world with a large trade surplus.

AS GERMANY GOES, SO GOES EUROPE

Because Germany is both the biggest and most important economy in all of Europe, one can make the case that as Germany goes, so goes all of Europe. Well, German consumers are indeed going and they are going to take all of Europe along with them. Currently, both Germany's consumer confidence and Germany's "willingness to spend" indicators are at their all-time highs.

This will bode well not just for Germany, but for all of Europe, especially when you consider that the savings ratio in Europe is actually double that of Japan, which most investors wrongly view as the nation with the highest savings ratio. Second, European employment expectations, which are key drivers to employment growth and employment confidence, are at six-year highs.

INVESTABLE THEME—
THE EUROPEAN CONSUMER

What does all of this mean from an investment perspective? It means two things, in my opinion. First, you need to "overweight" the European consumer for three reasons.

First, employment expectations and employment growth continue to rise. This is the single most important driver to consumption. Second, the European consumer is clearly underspending currently. That is why their savings ratio is double that of Japan. Thus, they have the money to spend but have lacked the confidence to spend it in the past. Third, consumer confidence is finally back, which in turn should lead to an uptick in consumer spending and consumer growth. That is why you need to "overweight" the European consumer.

The second investable theme just happens to be the number one theme of my Top Ten Investment Themes for 2007. After all, what's going on today in Germany and the rest of Europe is simply one more reason to Go Global, Go Global, and Go Even More Global.

Next stop on my international tour: South Africa.

Investment Footnote . . . What actually happened ↑

I was right. While the U.S. market returned 6.4 percent, as measured by the Dow, the investment world in Europe boomed just as I predicted as the MSCI–EAFE (Morgan Stanley Capital International–Europe, Australia, and the Far East) was up a whopping 36.5 percent in 2007.

Plenty of "Good Hope" from South Africa

MARCH 6, 2007

Greetings from the second stop of my seven-nation international tour, South Africa, where I found plenty of "Good Hope." More about that later, but first let me give you a better perspective of South Africa geographically, historically, and economically.

GEOGRAPHIC PERSPECTIVE

Let's begin with a brief geographic description. South Africa is a country located on the southernmost tip of the continent of Africa. It borders the countries of Namibia, Botswana, Zimbabwe, Mozambique, Swaziland, and Lesotho (which is actually an independent enclave entirely surrounded by South African territory).

South Africa is unique in Africa for two reasons. First, immigration from Europe reached higher levels in South Africa than all of the other nations on the African continent combined. As a result of this immigration, South Africa is a very ethnically diverse nation. It boasts the largest population of people from a mixed ethnic background in all of Africa. Black South Africans actually account for less than 70 percent of the total population of South Africa. The second reason is the strategic importance of the sea route around the Cape of Good Hope (I bet now the title is starting to make more sense to you). The closure of the Suez Canal during the Six-Day War exemplified just how important this sea route is to the entire world of trade and commerce.

HISTORICAL PERSPECTIVE

From a historical perspective, racial strife between the white minority and the black majority has played a major role in the country's history. This racial strife culminated in "apartheid," which was officially instituted in 1948 by the National Party even though segregation existed long before that date. The segregation laws that defined apartheid began to be repealed and abolished by the National Party in 1990 after a long and violent internal struggle and a series of severe economic sanctions from the external international community.

South Africa is now referred to as the Rainbow Nation, which was actually coined by South African Archbishop, Desmond Tutu, and later adopted and made internationally famous by then president Nelson Mandela. President Mandela used the term "Rainbow Nation" to paint a picture describing the country's newly developing multicultural and multiethnic diversity in the aftermath of the segregationist apartheid ideology. South Africa is now the most progressive of all the countries on the continent of Africa and one of the most socially progressive countries in the entire world, along with Belgium, Spain, and the Netherlands.

In addition to this most recent history, South Africa contains some of the oldest archaeological sites in the entire world. Extensive fossil remains found in caves suggest an existence of life in South Africa from about three million years ago. If you have traveled to Athens or Rome, you have come away with such a deep feeling of history that you know western civilization had its origins in those places. When you come away from Africa, you realize all of mankind may have started here. This is why, even today, most archaeologists refer to Africa as "the cradle of mankind."

One final historical perspective and the perspective that really put South Africa on the map, so to speak, relates to a new global trade route. Who knows, maybe my global investment story is not so new after all? Anyway, back to the trade routes.

The very first European navigator to sail around the southern tip of the cape of Africa was Portuguese explorer Bartolomeu Dias in 1488. When he returned to his "motherland" of Lisbon, Portugal, he brought exciting news of the discovery he called "Cabo das Tormentas" or the "Cape of Storms." But the sponsor of his explorations, Henry the Navigator, decided on a different name, "Cabo da Boa Esperance," or "Cape of Good Hope," for it brought with it the promise of a sea route to the riches of India, which was eagerly anticipated by all of Europe. Who knows, maybe the switch from Cape of Storms to the Cape of Good Hope was the first account of putting the correct public relations and political "spin" on an event.

From firsthand experience, I can tell you that we should have kept the name "Cape of Storms." These are some of the roughest seas in the entire world, routinely boasting over 30-foot waves (higher than a typical three-story building). That makes the Cape of Good Hope even more violent than the South China Sea during monsoon season, which I have witnessed firsthand as well.

ECONOMIC PERSPECTIVE

Let's move on to the final background perspective; this one focuses on the economy. Let me start with the conclusion, which may shock you, because many people perceive that the entire continent of Africa is immersed in poverty. Actually, South African's per capita gross domestic product (GDP) places it as one of the 50 wealthiest countries in the entire world today. It gets there because it has a very well-developed legal, financial, energy, communications, and transportation network. Its modern infrastructure supports an efficient distribution of goods and services to all major urban areas in the region.

This highly developed system in South Africa is very central-ized, however, occurring around just four areas: Cape Town, Port Elizabeth, Durban, and Johannesburg. Beyond these four economic centers, development is marginal and poverty reigns everywhere. This has resulted in large income gaps; actually, you can think of South Africa as having a dual economy, which is one of the reasons Wall Street still designates it as a "developing" economy. As a result of this disparity, South Africa has one of the highest rates of income inequality in the world.

Even with all that inequality, South Africa still accounts for over 30 percent of the economy for the entire continent of Africa. South Africa is also the continent's largest energy producer and energy consumer.

INVESTMENT THESIS

With the geographic, historical, and economic perspectives of South Africa out of the way, let's now focus on what is the best investment thesis in South Africa. There are actually two of them—"feed the world" and "fuel the world," which come together to create a third investment thesis that I will talk about at the end.

Let's start with the investment thesis, "feed the world." My good friend and colleague Oliver Kratz (one of the best investment managers in the business, in my opinion) coined this phrase to explain one of his top-down investment themes that he focuses on in his Global Thematic Fund. Nowhere could that global agribusiness theme be more apparent than in South Africa today.

South Africa has a large agricultural sector and is a net exporter of farm products. There are over 1,000 agricultural cooperatives and agribusinesses throughout the country. The largest group of exported items includes sugar, grapes, sunflower seeds, citrus, nectarines, and wine. In fact, South Africa is the eighth largest wine producer in the world.

The largest locally produced crop is maize (corn), and it is this product that clearly puts the "feed the world" dilemma in perspective. South Africa produces 9 million tons of corn every year. However, it consumes over $7\frac{1}{2}$ million tons of that total. Forget about feeding the world; farmers are simply trying to feed South Africa. And it isn't just corn; raising livestock is also very popular on South African farms. And once again, South Africa produces over 85 percent of all of the meat that is consumed by South Africans. So maybe, first it is "feed South Africa," then "feed all of Africa," then "feed the world." No matter how you cut it, it all bodes well for the global agribusiness for years and years to come.

Let's move on to my second investment thesis, "fuel the world." This term has become synonymous with the world's global commodity boom, and nowhere is this boom more apparent than in South Africa. In South Africa, it's not just a "fuel the world" commodity boom, but a "build the world" as well.

The airport in Cape Town is currently undergoing a major renovation and expansion. Workers are also building a major airport parking complex. There are cranes and workers every-where. In the central city, there is even more of a commodity boom and an even more frantic pace of building. In the downtown area, one hotel after another is being built. What is the reason for this unprecedented building boom? South Africa will play host to the single most exciting team event in all sports, the World Cup. South Africa will host the World Cup in 2010, and this commodity boom is necessary to get everything in order and ready. You may recall that the last World Cup (2006) was held in the "moth-erland" of Germany. Cape Town will be the location for several of the World Cup matches to be held all throughout South Africa in 2010.

While, on the surface, having South Africa host a major inter-national sporting event may seem like a bit of a stretch, it really isn't. In fact, in 1996, Cape Town itself was one of five candidate cities shortlisted by the International Olympic Committee to launch an official bid to host the 2004 Summer Olympics. Although the 2004 Summer Games ultimately went to Athens, Cape Town came in an impressive third place. It actually beat out such cosmopolitan cities as Buenos Aires and Stockholm. With a successful hosting of the 2010 World Cup, there is a lot of hope, "Good Hope" actually, that Cape Town may host the 2016 or 2020 summer games. After all, it's as easy as "feeding the world," "fueling the world," and "build-ing the world," and all it takes to do all of that is a continued com-modity boom.

Now, when you put these two investment theses together, you can create a third and even more dominant investment thesis. And that investment thesis is go global, go global, and go even more global, especially when you are trying to both "feed the world" and "fuel the world" at the same time. No wonder most of the people, jobs, and economic activity are occurring outside the United States. That is where the action is, and that is where the investment oppor-tunities will be.

There really is plenty of hope, both in and for the "Cape of Good Hope," and all of South Africa, as well, especially if you go global!

> ## Investment Footnote . . . What actually happened ↑
>
> I was correct. While the Dow returned 6.4 percent for all of 2007, the rest of the investment world boom percent and the MSCI–EAFE (Morgan Stanley Capital International–Europe, Australia, and the Far East) was up a whopping 36.5 percent.

Hakuna Matata, Not from Mozambique

March 8, 2007

Greetings from the third stop of my international tour, Mozambique, where I found an impoverished nation still recovering from a bitter civil war in the 1970s, and something major to worry about everywhere you looked.

That makes this part of Africa at odds with the animated movie about Africa, *Lion King*, where there were "no worries." Fans of that Disney movie will remember that the African translation for "no worries" is "Hakuna Matata," the song that everyone sang throughout that movie.

Well, in Mozambique, no one is singing "Hakuna Matata." Why is there so much to worry about everywhere you look in Mozambique? Let me try to explain by putting a few things into perspective for you.

WHERE IS MOZAMBIQUE?

Mozambique is a country in southeastern Africa bordered by the Indian Ocean to the east, Tanzania to the north, Malawi and Zambia to the northeast, Zimbabwe to the west, and Swaziland and South Africa to the southwest. It is a member of the Community of Portuguese Language Countries.

EARLY HISTORY

When Portuguese explorers reached Mozambique in 1498, Arab slave-trading settlements had already existed there. From the year 1500 on, Portuguese trading posts and forts became regular ports of call on the new route to the east. Later, traders and prospectors penetrated the interior regions, seeking gold and slaves. Although Portuguese influence gradually expanded, its power was limited and it was exercised through individual settlers and officials who were granted extensive autonomy. As a result, investment lagged while Portugal devoted itself to the more lucrative trade with India and the Far East and to the colonization of Brazil.

THE FIGHT FOR INDEPENDENCE

After World War II, while most European nations were granting independence to their colonies, Portugal maintained that Mozambique and other Portuguese possessions were overseas provinces of the "motherland." As a result, emigration to the colonies from Portugal soared, especially to Mozambique. Over time, calls for Mozambican independence developed and in 1962 several colonial groups formed the Front for the Liberation of Mozambique, which initiated an armed campaign against Portuguese rule. However, Portugal had occupied the country for more than four hundred years, and not all Mozambicans desired independence. Fewer, still, sought change through armed revolution. Despite massive "arms shipments" from China and the Soviet Union, the Front for the Liberation of Mozambique and other loosely linked armed guerilla forces proved no match at all for the Portuguese forces. After 10 years of sporadic warfare, the Front for the Liberation of Mozambique had not made appreciable progress toward capturing either significant territory or population centers. Then, suddenly, a socialist-inspired military coup overthrew the "motherland's" quasifascist Portuguese government. Soon after that, independence was granted to all of its colonies and on June 25, 1975, Mozambique became an independent nation.

VIOLENT CIVIL WAR

The new independent government, under President Samora Machel, gave shelter and support to South African and Zimbabwean liberation movements, while the governments of first, Rhodesia, and later South Africa (which was still operating under apartheid laws at the time) fostered and financed an armed rebel movement in central Mozambique called the Mozambican National Resistance. Hence, civil war, sabotage from neighboring nations, and total economic collapse characterized the first decade of Mozambican independence. Also, at the same time, there was a mass exodus of Portuguese nationals and Mozambicans of Portuguese heritage out of Mozambique. Deteriorated and weak infrastructure, government takeover and nationalization of privately owned industries, massive economic mismanagement, fraud, and corruption are what resulted. During most of the civil war, the government was unable to exercise effective control outside the urban areas, many of which were completely cut off from the capital. Over 1 million Mozambicans died during the civil war and another 1.7 million took refuge in neighboring states. This doesn't even begin to account for the millions upon millions that were displaced internally, as well. Now do you understand why there is no "Hakuna Matata" in Mozambique?

THE LONG-TERM FUTURE COULD BE BRIGHT

While there is plenty to worry about today, the longer-term future could be bright. Resettlement of the war refugees, along with some major economic reforms, led to an economic rebound in the mid–1990s, which saw the economy grow at close to 7 percent. By the late 1990s, the economy boomed to over 10 percent growth annually until devastating floods in 2000 crippled the economy again. It has since fully recovered and is again on pace for 6 to 7 percent economic growth.

This pace can only be maintained with continued foreign investment and ongoing economic reforms. Mozambique's economic future is tied to the agriculture and tourism industries. From my personal perspective, it will be decades upon decades until tourism takes off and becomes an important part of the Mozambique economy. Not so with agriculture; it is their future today, tomorrow, and decades from now.

THE FUTURE IS IN AGRICULTURE

The future of Mozambique's economy is all about agriculture. In fact, Mozambique is simply another excellent example of why my good friend and colleague, Oliver Kratz, who manages our Global Thematic Fund, has long been touting the global agribusiness as one of his top investment themes.

Currently in Mozambique, more than 75 percent of the population engages in small-scale agriculture, which still suffers from inadequate infrastructure and investment. But here is why, I believe, the future is so bright. Currently, over 88 percent of Mozambique's "farmable" land is still uncultivated. Who knows, maybe Mozambique will one day play a major role in how we "feed the world"?

And, if that occurs, who knows, maybe someday my children's children will be standing in Mozambique singing, "Hakuna Matata." Only time will tell.

Investment Footnote . . . What actually happened ↑

I was correct with my "feed the world" theme, as corn gained 16.24 percent in 2007 and overall commodities rose 20.56 percent.

Out of Africa

MARCH 12, 2007

Kenya is the fourth country of my seven-country international investing tour. After this I am "out of Africa," as Kenya is my final stop on the continent of Africa. Many people forget about the direct relationship between Kenya and *Out of Africa*, so I thought I would remind you.

It was Robert Redford (who played Denys Finch-Hatton, a Kenyan bush pilot who died in a fiery plane crash) and Meryl Streep (who played Baroness Karen Blixen), who starred in *Out of Africa*, a film about the Baroness, who comes to Kenya to live on a coffee plantation on the outskirts of Nairobi.

She grew to love those around her and fought against all odds to see that the coffee plantation survived. But survive, it did not. Her 1937 account of those years in Kenya, that she titled *Out of Africa*, is the premise of the movie and one of the most impassioned narratives of that era. Now, I too find myself leaving Africa, but not before I tell you what I found in Kenya.

GEOGRAPHIC PERSPECTIVE

Let me first begin by giving you a geographic perspective of Kenya. The Republic of Kenya is a country in Eastern Africa. It is bordered by Ethiopia to the north, Somalia to the east, Tanzania to the south, Uganda to the west, and Sudan to the northwest. The Indian Ocean runs along its southeast border.

From the coast on the Indian Ocean, the low plains rise to central highlands. These Kenyan Highlands comprise one of the most successful agricultural production regions in all of Africa. Kenya is comparable in size to the state of Texas in the United States.

HISTORICAL PERSPECTIVE

Let's move on to a brief historical perspective of Kenya and the most important territory within Kenya—the island of Mombasa.

Back in the twelfth century, a group known as the "Shirazi" established their rule over Kenya, especially the coast and the tiny island of Tonike, today called Mombasa, which was and still is Kenya's most important territory. These Shirazis were of Persian stock; they intermarried with the local people, and from these relationships, a new Bantu-Arabic language known as "Swahili" was created. It is still spoken today.

Explorers and ships from as far away as the Far East and the Middle East came and went for the next 400 years. Trade with the inland areas of Kenya boomed as coffee, tea, ivory, and slaves were all very marketable commodities. All of this went on rather peacefully until the Portuguese arrived in large numbers in 1528. They were tracing the path charted by one of the most famous and celebrated of all Portuguese explorers, Vasco da Gama, who explored here when he was searching for trade routes to India.

By 1592, Mombasa finally came under Portuguese rule. The goal of the Portuguese was simple. They wanted to protect this most viable and valuable port city and control all of the trade that passed through it. Portugal continued its authority until the Omani Arabs literally starved them out. And, because of this rather violent history, the city was renamed Mombasa, which replaced its original name, Tonike, by the Arabs. Mombasa translated means "Island of War" in their language.

ECONOMIC PERSPECTIVE

Let's fast forward to more recent times and take a look at Kenya's modern-day economic backdrop.

From 1991 to 1993, Kenya had its worst economic performance since its independence in 1963. Economic growth as measured by gross domestic product (GDP) stagnated, and agricultural production was collapsing at an unheard-of 4 percent annual rate. Inflation was 100 percent by mid-1993. Let's put this in perspective for a moment. Wall Street today worries when inflation tops 3 percent and, in Kenya, it was a shocking 100 percent! But that wasn't all; the government's budget deficit was over 10 percent of GDP.

From this low point in 1993, the government of Kenya embarked on major economic reform and liberalization. A new minister of finance and a new head of the Central Bank of Kenya undertook a series of economic measures with the assistance of the World Bank and the International Monetary Fund (IMF). As part of these changes, the government eliminated price controls, tariffs on imports, and foreign exchange controls, and even began to privatize a wide range of government-owned businesses. The economy responded and, for the next few years, it grew at almost 4 percent GDP.

Then, in 1997, the economy entered a period of stagnant growth, due in part to adverse weather conditions. It has improved slightly since then as rainfall has returned to more normal levels.

What it hasn't recovered from yet is something else that happened in 1997. The government of Kenya refused to meet agreed-upon commitments made earlier to the IMF on reforms. As a result of its refusal, the IMF quit lending money to Kenya, and the World Bank put $90 million of credit on hold. Kenya still has not recovered because it can't improve its economy fast enough to combat the massive poverty that afflicts 60 percent of its population.

The main challenges remain the same. The government must take action on corruption. They must enact antiterrorism and money laundering laws. And they must build and rehabilitate their almost nonexistent infrastructure. Witness the fact that the drive from Mombasa to the capital city of Nairobi, about 400 or so miles away, takes 14 hours by car.

INVESTMENT THESIS

I believe the long-term economic future of Kenya will be determined by its ability to be a major player in one of the greatest investment themes ever: "Feed the World."

Kenya is already a major producer and exporter of coffee, tea, sugarcane, corn, wheat, and rice. In addition, grain and sugar milling is one of its only successful industries.

The poverty, abject living conditions, and deplorable environmental conditions of this third-world country almost bring one to tears. Their only way to escape this cycle is to join the commodity boom and help "Feed the World."

In closing, in 1908 Sir Winston Churchill called Mombasa, Kenya, "The Gate of Africa." Right now, that gate is locked, closed in my opinion. The keys that will unlock that gate are taking action against corruption and enacting laws to combat terrorism and money laundering. And Kenyans must build and rehabilitate their almost nonexistent infrastructure. For if they do that, Kenya can not only be the "Gate to Africa," but the "Gate to the World," as well, as we all figure out how to "Feed the World."

Investment Footnote . . . What actually happened ↑

Again, I was correct with my "feed the world" theme, as corn gained 16.24 percent in 2007 and overall commodities rose 20.56 percent.

While No Man Is an Island, Seychelles Is Lots of Them

MARCH 15, 2007

Greetings from the fifth stop of my seven-nation international investing tour, the Republic of Seychelles. Seychelles is not just an island or even eight islands like those which comprise our state of Hawaii. Instead, the Republic of Seychelles is actually an archipelago nation of 158 separate islands in the Indian Ocean. It is located off the eastern coast of mainland Africa and northeast of the island of Madagascar. Other nearby island countries include Zanzibar to the west, Mauritius and Reunion to the south, Comoros and Mayotte to the southwest, and Maldives to the northeast.

HISTORICAL PERSPECTIVE

The history of Seychelles dates back only 500 years. While it is widely believed that Arab traders were the first to visit the uninhabited Seychelles, the first recorded sighting of them took place in 1505 by the Portuguese.

Seychelles was used as a transit point for trading between Africa and Asia. It was also occasionally used by pirates until the

French began to take control of the islands in 1756, naming them after Jean Moreau de Seychelles, the French finance minister at the time.

The British contested control over the islands with the French and eventually gained the upper hand as the French ceded the islands to Britain in 1814. Seychelles was granted its independence from the British on June 29, 1976.

ECONOMIC BACKDROP

Let's move on to the economy. Since its independence in 1976, per capita economic growth has expanded nearly sevenfold. This growth was led by the tourism sector, which, while employing 30 percent of the workforce, accounts for 70 percent of the overall economy, and by tuna fishing. While Seychelles also exports coconuts, coconut oil, vanilla, and tortoise shells, its economy begins and ends with tourism and tuna fishing.

The biggest challenge facing Seychelles is to expand its economic base beyond tourism by promoting the development of more fishing and farming. The country's tourism sector has been hit extremely hard over the past 15 years by a confluence of independent events and factors. First, as the 1990s began, tourism took a major dive, because of Seychelles' very rich and very overvalued currency, which is still overvalued today. In fact, the "black market" value of the Seychellois rupee is barely half the official exchange rate. And without a major devaluation, the tourism industry remains vulnerable to continued major downturns due to the exchange rate. Second, as a result of the first Gulf War, tourism here took another major hit. Third, and finally, tourism again took a big blow and is still recovering following the complete collapse after the terrorist attacks of 9/11.

Beyond its overdependence on tourism, Seychelles has two other major problems it must address. First, it must begin to privatize its public enterprises and put them where they rightly belong, in the hands of business. Currently, the government controls and has a major presence in all petroleum product distribution, insurance, banking, all imports, telecommunications, and basically anything else it can get its hands on. That, by the way, is actually the major cause of the second problem, their budget deficit.

To give you some frame of reference, we worry and complain about our budget deficit here in the United States. While our deficit is currently running at a little under 3 percent of our economy, or gross domestic product (GDP), in Seychelles, the deficit is currently running at 123 percent of GDP. According to the World Bank, that makes Seychelles the most highly indebted country per capita GDP in the entire world.

AND THE ANSWER IS . . . FOOD

With an extremely high debt level and an overvalued currency, in the short run, Seychelles provides no immediate investment opportunity. But in the longer run, over the next five years or so, I believe it could begin to provide some excellent investment opportunities. All it needs to do is privatize all of its public enterprises and then devalue its overvalued currency. And finally, it needs to encourage, develop, and support an expansion of its fishing and farming industries as the industries of the future. For, if it does that, I believe, because of its unique location between Africa and Asia, it can revert back to its gloried past when it was a trading hub. In my opinion, no country is better positioned to help "feed the world" than Seychelles because of its proximity to the two continents with the greatest opportunities and greatest need to be fed; namely, Asia and Africa. All it takes is food.

Investment Footnote . . . What actually happened

I was correct with my "feed the world" theme, as corn gained 16.24 percent in 2007 and overall commodities rose 20.56 percent.

Lions and Tigers and Bears, Oman!

March 19, 2007

Greetings from the sixth stop of my international tour, Oman. This commentary is dedicated to my lovely wife, Cheryl, who has accompanied me on this seven-country international trip. She actually came up with the catchy title, "Lions and Tigers and Bears, Oman." She has obviously logged a lot of hours with our two daughters, Marianne and Stephanie, when they were young and afraid to watch *The Wizard of Oz* without Mom sitting between them. Then, for the next two days, after watching the film, everyone in the Froehlich household would be singing the jingle from *The Wizard of Oz*, "Lions and Tigers and Bears, Oh My."

Cheryl has decided that the hard part of writing a market commentary is coming up with a catchy title, and she has already done that for me. The easy part is to simply tie it all together to make some sense of the "Lions and Tigers and Bears" part. You know what? She was right. Let me begin by focusing on the "Lions."

A HISTORY AS PROUD AS THE "LIONS"

As I sit here in Muscat, Oman, I quickly realize that very few places on earth have a history as rich and proud as Oman, especially its capital city, Muscat.

Muscat is one of the oldest cities in the Middle East. It has been established since the second century A.D. Its history and economy back then were all about the commodity frankincense. In fact, over 3,000 pounds of frankincense were transported each year by ship to Greece, Rome, and the rest of the Mediterranean. The center of this trade was in a place called "Khour Rouri," which the Greeks called "Muscat."

The first foreign presence in Muscat was the Portuguese explorer Vasco da Gama, who landed in Oman on his way to India. The Portuguese returned in 1507 to sack and capture Muscat.

In 1649, the Imam Sultan bin Saif defeated the Portuguese and drove them back to India.

As a result of this victory, they now found themselves armed with the captured warships of the Portuguese navy, which were far superior to anything in the Oman military. With this newfound military power, the Imam established an empire that spanned from Zanzibar to Pakistan. Slaves were brought in from Zanzibar to work in Oman and to be traded elsewhere. This was a period of great prosperity and relative stability in Muscat and Oman as a whole.

However, this period lasted only 30 years. The country was torn apart by strife and civil unrest upon the death of the Imam in 1679. In 1737, Muscat was invaded by the Persians, and when Ahmad bin Said finally defeated them, he was elected Imam.

As the nineteenth century rolled around, Saudi Arabia attacked Oman. The Saudis were later defeated by Sayyid Said bin Sultan. The Sultan then decided to set up a colony in Zanzibar and, in essence, ruled Oman from a foreign island. Later, in 1853, the Sultan transferred the title of "capital" of Oman to Zanzibar. Thus began the decline of the fortunes of Muscat and Oman, from which they are still trying to recover over 150 years later.

In the early twentieth century, Sultan Taimur bin Faisal became Sultan and the territory was officially renamed "Muscat and Oman," with the Sultan ruling Muscat and the Imam ruling Oman. Then, in 1947, after independence from India, the Sultan, with military help from Great Britain, defeated the Imam and immediately unified all of Oman. Less than 20 years later, the Dhofar War began in 1964. It was a Communist insurrection staged from the People's Democratic Republic of Yemen against the Sultan of Oman. This insurrection was defeated by Omani forces with military help again from Great Britain and Iran.

Then, six years later, Prince Qaboos bin Said, son of Sultan Said bin Taimur, staged a palace coup and claimed the throne. This coup was the beginning of a new, consolidated, modern sultanate. Now that's a coup only a proud "lion" would dare attempt.

CATCH A TRADING "TIGER" BY THE TAIL

Maybe the biggest event in Oman's recent history occurred on July 20, 2006, when they landed a major deal with the biggest economy and largest consumer base in the world, the United States of America.

On that day, the United States Congress approved the U.S.–Oman Free Trade Agreement. This Agreement immediately ended all taxes, duties, and tariffs on trade in both industrial and consumer goods and gave American farmers duty-free access to the market for Oman's products, namely, dates, frankincense, and fish.

The biggest export from Oman, however, is oil, and that accounts for over 90 percent of all exports. Oman remains the only oil-producing nation in the Middle East that is not a member of OPEC (Oil Producing and Exporting Countries).

Even though Oman is dominated by the commodity oil, its most famous commodity is frankincense. We all know the story: when Christ was born, he received from the Magi the gift of frankincense, which in those days was actually more valuable than gold. Oman's Dhofar regions were then, and still are today, one of the three major frankincense-growing areas in the world.

During the time of Christ, frankincense was carried overland in camel caravans and later processed in such faraway places as Alexandria, Egypt, before being shipped to European ports. As I said earlier, an amazing 3,000 tons were exported annually during the height of this commodity's popularity.

Oman's amber frankincense has lost its glow today. Other less costly incense is marketed from several countries, including India. And the younger generations of the Omani families, who have long harvested the trees for frankincense, have found more profitable jobs in the oil fields. Thus, in Oman today, the memory of the sweet fragrance of frankincense lives on mainly in the Scriptures, the history books of ancient times, and in the modern-day tourist traps called *souqs*.

Let's get back to this Free Trade pact and not forget that it will also liberalize the Omani market and open it up to buy U.S. goods as well.

SUBPRIME MARKET BEARS EVERYWHERE, EVEN OMAN

Well, I have covered the "Lions and Tigers" part and now it's time for the "Bears." Even though I am halfway around the world in Oman, the "bearish" focus here is on the U.S. subprime mortgage market. Let me once again put this problem in the United States in perspective for you even though I am standing here in the Middle East.

Actually, the latest news on delinquencies and foreclosures wasn't so bad, though it could worsen later this year.

We had record foreclosures in the fourth quarter, according to the Mortgage Banking Association. Last quarter, 0.54 percent of all outstanding loans entered the foreclosure process. That's 0.08 percentage points higher than the third quarter and the highest ever recorded in the Mortgage Bankers Association survey. The previous record was 0.50 percent in the second quarter of 2002. To me, this is a rounding error and a nonevent even though it is a record.

Now, I will admit there are problems in the subprime market where the fourth-quarter foreclosure rate was 4.53 percent, with more problem loans ahead as the delinquency rate in this category rose to 13.33 percent from 11.63 percent a year ago.

However, now I want you to pay close attention to this important fact: The Mortgage Bankers Association survey is based on 44 million loans, including 38 million that are in the prime category, or 86 percent of the total. Last quarter, only 2.57 percent of the prime loans were delinquent, with 2.27 percent for fixed-rate prime loans and 3.39 percent for prime adjustable rate mortgages. Foreclosures amounted to 0.50 percent of all fixed prime loans, up from 0.42 perent a year ago. As I said before, this is not a big problem; it is a rounding error.

Think of it this way. The subprime mortgage market is a small part of the overall mortgage market. The mortgage market is a small part of the overall fixed-income market. The fixed-income market is only one part of a financial services company's overall "trading" revenue. And trading revenue is just one part of overall earnings for major financial services companies. In my opinion, this subprime mortgage collapse is and will be a nonevent for major financial services firms and our stock market.

OH MY, IT'S BACK TO OMAN

Oh my, now that we have discussed the "Lions and Tigers and Bears," it's time to close with a final point about Oman. Let me give you a different perspective on this subprime mortgage problem so you can see exactly how ridiculous this so-called disaster is.

Suppose that, as a result of the U.S.-Oman Free Trade Agreement, consumers in the United States buy most of their fish as an import from Oman. Now, if the price of fish from Oman rises tenfold, will it cause the U.S. consumer and U.S. economy to collapse? The answer is "no" and here is why.

Consumer spending on fish is a small part of overall protein spending that includes meat as well. This is just like the subprime mortgage market as a small part of the overall mortgage market.

Spending on protein is only a small part of overall food expenditures, just like the mortgage market is a small part of the overall fixed-income market. And expenditures on food are a small part of overall shopping expenditures, just like the fixed-income market is only one part of a financial company's overall trading revenue. Finally, expenditures on shopping are only one part of a consumer's overall expenditures, just like trading revenue is just one part of overall earnings for a major financial services company.

Next time you hear someone talk about the subprime mortgage crisis, simply sing my favorite tune, "Lions and Tigers and Bears, Oh My, and Oman."

Regarding Oman, this time from an investment theme perspective, I found a story where you didn't have to be the Wizard of Oz to figure things out. It is a story about the "great commodity shift" in Oman centuries ago. Back then, Oman's present and its future were all about commodities and the commodity was frankincense. Currently, Oman's present and its future are still all about commodities; this time, however, the commodity is oil. Oman benefited from a commodity boom centuries ago in frankincense, and currently it is benefiting from the latest global commodity boom—oil. As an investor getting exposure to what's going on in Oman today, this is, I believe, as simple as overweighting commodities, which by the way is investment theme 5 of my top ten investment themes for 2007.

PS: My next commentary is a report on the seventh and final stop on my international investing tour, the United Arab Emirates and the city of Dubai.

Investment Footnote . . . What actually happened

I was right. The commodity boom continued in 2007, up a whopping 20.56 percent.

From Camels to Cadillacs in Dubai

March 23, 2007

The earliest recorded mention of Dubai is in 1095 A.D. in an Arabic book where Dubai is referred to as "a vast place." Well, it still is a vast place today. Only now, it is vast on a global scale, not just on a Middle Eastern scale as it was in 1095 A.D.

Also, in 1095 A.D., the mode of transportation in that part of the world was camels. Today, instead of camels, think Cadillacs, BMWs, Porsches, or whatever cars you equate with the highest end of quality, luxury, and spending in the world.

While this is only my second visit to Dubai in the past year, I have finally realized that I have found a place that puts me at a loss for words; even pictures cannot capture what I have found and am witnessing firsthand: the miracle of what is going on in Dubai today. There is an economic, cultural, social, and political evolution going on that I believe will position Dubai to become the greatest place on the face of the earth.

Dubai to me today feels like what it must have been like in the United States in the mid- to late 1700s, when everyone knew the United States was poised to become something great. While history has shown us that the United States did indeed evolve into something great, in my opinion, Dubai will some day be recorded in the history books as the greatest place on the earth to live, work, and play.

At the risk of sounding too much like the self-appointed ambassador of Dubai—or, more correctly, the ambassador of the United Arab Emirates (UAE), since Dubai is not a country and has no ambassador—let me back up and give you a frame of reference regarding the United Arab Emirates.

But not without first making a quick mention of Honorable Saqr Ghobash, the current Ambassador of United Arab Emirates to the United States, whom I had the pleasure and honor of meeting within his embassy in Washington D.C., earlier this year. He stands out as one more example of the political wisdom and global insight that the United Arab Emirates and its leaders have regarding the global marketplace and global economy. I am honored to call him a colleague and a friend. Now back to a quick history of the United Arab Emirates.

HISTORY OF THE UNITED ARAB EMIRATES

The United Arab Emirates is a Middle Eastern country situated in the southeast of the Arabian Peninsula in southwest Asia on the Persian Gulf. It is comprised of seven emirates: Abu Dhabi, Ajman, Dubai, Fujairah, Ras al-Khaimah, Shatjah, and Umm al-Quwain.

Before 1971, they were referred to as the "Trucial States of Oman," in reference to a nineteenth-century truce between Britain and several Arab sheikhs. The UAE borders Oman and Saudi Arabia.

HISTORY OF DUBAI

On December 2, 1971, Dubai, together with Abu Dhabi and four other emirates, formed the United Arab Emirates after former protector Britain left the Persian Gulf. Ras Al Khaimah joined the UAE in 1972 as the seventh emirate. In 1973, Dubai and the other emirates adopted a single, uniform currency: the UAE dirham.

Today, Dubai has the largest population and is the second largest emirate by land area, after Abu Dhabi. Dubai is distinct from other members of the UAE in that revenues from oil account for only 6 percent of its gross domestic product (GDP). With enormous construction and development in all industries, Dubai has attracted worldwide attention through innovative real estate projects, sporting events, conferences, and ongoing additions to the Guinness Book of World Records.

DUBAI ECONOMY

It is only fitting that I end my international trip here in Dubai, the mecca of the world of finance, shopping, leisure, real estate, and glamour. After leaving South Africa, I witnessed two of the most impoverished countries in the entire world, Mozambique and Kenya. Night and day does not evoke the distinction between what is happening on the western coast of Africa and what is happening several hundred miles away in Dubai. In some respects, if we could send just 10 percent of the investment dollars going into Dubai today to the countries along the western coast of Africa, we could probably solve 50 percent of their problems. That is another topic for another time.

BACK TO THE DUBAI EONOMY

The economy of Dubai is centered on the ports of the city and on tourism. In fact, the Port of Jebel Ali, which was constructed in the 1970s, has the largest manmade harbor in the world. In addition, Dubai is developing increasingly as a hub for the financial services industry and technology industries, as well.

One of Dubai's most forward-thinking and innovative concepts is the government's decision to create industry-specific zones throughout the city. Dubai Internet City, now combined with Dubai Media City, is one such zone, whose technology members include firms like Microsoft, EMC, Oracle, and IBM and such media organizations as CNN, Reuters, and the Associated Press. Dubai Knowledge Village is an education and training zone that will become home to 10 separate universities.

REAL ESTATE BOOM

While the government's decision to create these industry-specific zones may seem like their greatest idea, it wasn't. I believe their greatest idea is their forward-thinking decision to diversify from an oil-reliant economy to one that is tourism- and service-industry driven; this, in turn, has caused real estate to boom. In fact, the large-scale construction going on in Dubai today has made it the fastest growing city in the entire world.

This real estate and property boom is primarily driven by Dubai's megaprojects, both inland, such as Dubai Marina, the Burj Dubai Complex, Dubai Waterfront, Business Bay, and Dubailand, as well as its world-famous and innovative offshore projects, such as the Palm Islands and the World Archipelago.

Dubai is already home to some iconic skyscrapers, such as Emirates Towers, which comprise the twelfth and twenty-fourth tallest buildings in the world, and the Burj al-Arab, located on its very own island in the Persian Gulf. The Burj al-Arab is currently the tallest hotel in the world.

Currently, Dubai is constructing what will become the world's tallest structure, the Burj Dubai. The final height is still a closely guarded secret, but estimates so far point to a height of somewhere between 180 to 200 stories high. As 2007 began, it was already over 100 stories tall. By the way, right next to the Burj Dubai is another massive project, the world's largest shopping mall, to be called the Dubai Mall. Also under construction is what is planned to become Dubai's new central business district, Business Bay. Once completed, the project will be home to an unbelievable 500 skyscrapers built around an extension of the existing Dubai Creek.

In 2005, Dubai announced the construction of the Dubai Waterfront. This will be seven times the size of the island of Manhattan in New York City. Dubai Waterfront will be a mix of canals and islands full of hotels and residential areas, which will add 500 miles of man-made waterfront. It will also contain the Al Burj, which is planned to surpass the Burj Dubai once it is completed and will be the tallest building in the entire world.

Dubai has also just launched Dubaitech. This is a new park to be targeted at biotech companies working in the pharmaceutical, medical, genetic research, and biodefense fields.

Finally, one of Dubai's most recent plans is for a 30-story condo skyscraper that will actually rotate at its base, making a 360-degree revolution once a week. This will be the world's first rotating skyscraper, and it will be located in the center of the Dubailand Complex.

OFFSHORE LAND RECLAMATION PROJECTS

Maybe the two most amazing developments in Dubai are their off-shore land reclamation projects. First is the famous three Palm Islands of Jemeria, Jebel Ali, and Deira. When completed, these islands will be the largest man-made islands in the world, created in the shape of a palm tree. Their ingenious design will create a new coastline housing more than 100 luxury hotels, 12,000 residential villas, 10,000 shoreline apartments, luxury homes, restaurants, and even theme parks.

The second project is the World Archipelago, a collection of almost 300 man-made islands designed to resemble the countries and continents of the world. Each island will be custom designed to create a special environment, and the only means of transportation between the islands will be boat or helicopter.

Just the fill material needed to create these man-made islands is mind boggling. The fill material alone would be enough to create a wall $6\frac{1}{2}$ feet high and 2 feet deep that would circle the earth three times at the equator. Keep in mind, this is simply what is needed to make the islands, before construction on them begins.

Maybe this will help put these land reclamation projects in some perspective for you: due to their immense size, each of these projects, the three Palm Islands and the World Archipelago, will all be visible from outer space with the naked eye.

INVESTMENT THESIS

I believe the investment thesis found here is very simple; in fact, it supports three of my top ten investment themes. The first is global real estate, the second is commodities, and the third is global investing. In my opinion, there is no other place on the face of the earth that can make a more compelling case for investing globally, especially in real estate and commodities, than Dubai.

ONE FINAL FORECAST

Let me end this commentary where I began, when I said that what is happening in Dubai cannot be captured in pictures nor explained in words, and then proceeded to attempt to explain it. Think of Dubai this way. Have you ever gotten tired of reading about all the war and violence in the world today and ever wondered "why can't we all just get along"? Well, we can in Dubai. It is unlike any other place on the face of the earth, where people from all faiths and religious beliefs and all different national and political beliefs live together as one, and everyone respects every other person's point of view and opinion. I wish that I could send every political leader and every business leader in the world to Dubai to prove to them all that it can be done with political insight and vision.

As a strategist, I am required to make forecasts all the time, such as my current forecast that the Dow will cross 14,000 this year and that the best investment theme for 2007 will be Go Global with investments.

Now, I will reveal to you the forecast and prediction that I have the most confidence in: I believe Dubai will some day be recorded in the history books as having been the greatest place on the earth to live, work, and play.

In the meantime, Go Global, Go Global, and Go Even More Global.

Investment Footnote . . . What actually happened ↑

I was correct. While the Dow returned 6.4 percent for all of 2007, the rest of the investment world boomed even higher. The MSCI–EM (Morgan Stanley Capital International–Emerging Markets) was up 8.6 percent and the MSCI– EAFE (Morgan Stanley Capital International–Europe, Australia, and the Far East) was up a whopping 36.5 percent.

The Pretzel Thief and Global Investing

March 26, 2007

I find myself sitting here in Frankfurt, Germany, in the airport, at the end of another long international trip. I have struggled the past few days trying to come up with a more compelling way of explaining to investors in the United States why they need to be more global with their investments. This is especially true after this most recent seven-nation tour, where almost everywhere I turned the investment answer was Go Global, Go Global, and Go even More Global.

PRETZELS AND BEER

Even though it is still morning, I thought I would grab myself a soft pretzel and a draft beer and think about how I can help with this major disconnect in the United States, where most investors, in my opinion, do not have enough investment exposure outside of the United States.

Then, suddenly, it hit me. I know exactly how to explain the misconceptions of global investing and I will do it with pretzels and beer.

THE GREAT PRETZEL THIEF

I am reminded of a story that happened to a good friend of mine, over a decade ago, whom I worked with at Van Kampen Funds. He was waiting at an airport late one night with several long hours ahead of him before his delayed flight home. He hunted down the only open airport shop where he bought a *Wall Street Journal* and a bag of pretzel sticks. Then, just as I would have done, he bought a draft beer to wash down the pretzels.

He was very engrossed in his *Wall Street Journal,* attempting to catch up on the news of the day, when he happened to see a man sitting beside him. As bold as could be, the man grabbed a pretzel or two from the bag of pretzels that lay between them.

My friend tried to ignore what had just happened to avoid a scene. All the while, reading his *Wall Street Journal,* he just continued to munch on the pretzel sticks, drink his beer, and watch the clock, hoping that time would pass quickly.

As time passed, the gutsy pretzel thief diminished my friend's stock of pretzels. By now, my friend was getting more irritated as the minutes ticked by thinking, "If I weren't so nice, I would blacken his eye." But the elderly gentleman was in his 70s, so my friend simply let it pass.

With each pretzel my friend took, the old pretzel thief took one too. When only one pretzel stick was left, my friend wondered what the pretzel thief would do. With a smile on his face and a nervous laugh, he actually took the last pretzel stick and broke it in half. He offered my friend half as he ate the other. That was the last straw; my friend snatched it from him and thought, "Oh brother, this guy has some nerve and he's also rude. Why, he didn't even show any gratitude!"

My friend couldn't remember the last time he had been so annoyed. He finally sighed with relief when his flight was called. He gathered his belongings and headed to the gate. He refused to look back at the ungrateful pretzel thief. My friend boarded the plane and sank in his seat. As he went to retrieve his *Wall Street Journal*, he reached in his briefcase and gasped with shock and surprise at what he found.

There was a bag of pretzel sticks in front of his eyes. But if his are here, he moaned in despair, the others on the seat at the gate were actually the old man's, and all the old man really tried to do was share. Too late to apologize, he realized with grief, that he was the ungrateful rude one.

How many times in our lives have we been convinced of something in our own mind, only to discover later that what we believed to be true was not?

I will allow my friend to remain nameless as he knows who he is, and because we have all felt like my friend at one time or another, convinced of something only to find out later it was not true.

GO GLOBAL

Well, for most investors, that feeling usually occurs when they are thinking about global investing. Because of their misconceptions, most investors are convinced of certain things regarding global investing only to discover later that they may not be true.

For example, some may have the misguided concern that you can't trust any companies outside the United States and that if you invest in them, they may end up taking all your money. To that I would like to say three things: Enron, WorldCom, and Arthur Andersen. These are three U.S. companies that cost U.S. investors billions.

The lesson here is that people who want to be immoral and unethical know no boundaries. Risk is everywhere, not just outside the United States. You will never be able to eliminate risk completely, but a financial advisor may be able to help you identify it accurately and measure it wisely. And when you do that I believe that you will go global, go global, and go even more global.

And why wouldn't you? After all, look at what is outside the United States. Basically, all the earth's land, all the people, all the jobs, most of the economic activity, and a majority of the world's natural resources are outside the United States. This is pretty simple: if they have all the land, all the people, all the jobs, most of the economic activity, and a majority of the world's natural resources, in my opinion they should also have a majority of your investment dollars.

Here is my newest investment theme. Sit back, grab a beer and some pretzels, and go global, go global, and go even more global. But most of all, remember the pretzel thief. When you remember him, you may decide to go global, so that you won't find out "later" how wrong you were about global investing—just like my friend found out "later" how wrong he was about the pretzel thief!

Investment Footnote . . . What actually happened ↑

I was correct. While the Dow returned 6.4 percent for all of 2007, the rest of the investment world boomed even higher. The MSCI–EM (Morgan Stanley Capital International–Emerging Markets) was up 8.6 percent and the MSCI–EAFE (Morgan Stanley Capital International–Europe, Australia, and the Far East) was up a whopping 36.5 percent.

INDEX

About the Author

Dr. Bob Froehlich is the chairman of the Investor Strategy Committee for Deutsche Asset Management. This committee is the first of its kind on Wall Street providing a link between investment trends, investment strategies and, ultimately, investment products for the individual investor. He is highly regarded on Wall Street as a dynamic and entertaining lecturer, as evidenced by his more than 1,000 speaking requests per year. He has delivered a speech on investing on six continents: North America, South America, Europe, Australia, Africa, and Asia.

Dr. Bob has the unique distinction of being the only "Wall Street" strategist who has been invited to both open and close the markets for the Nasdaq OMX and the New York Stock Exchange. He appears regularly on a variety of financial television programs on CNBC, CNN, Bloomberg, and FOX News as well as other domestic and international networks.

Froehlich is one of the regular guest cohosts of CNBC's highest rated program, *Squawk Box,* and a regular guest cohost for CNBC Europe's *Squawk Box* based in London and CNBC Asia's *Squaw Box* based in Singapore. He was the first and remains the only person ever to be a *Squawk Box* guest host in all three locations. In addition, Froehlich was one of the first guests on one of CNBC's most innovative programming concepts, a show called *Worldwide Exchange.* It is the first financial news program ever to be simulcast around the world live. He was also selected as one of the original regular guest financial commentators when CNN launched its new network, CNNfn, in December 1995. At FOX News, Froehlich has become one of the regular special guests on their highest rated weekend show, *Bulls and Bears.* In October 2007, when Fox launched its new business network, Fox Business, it too called on Froehlich to help launch the new network by appearing as a guest on the very first day.

Dr. Bob is a prolific writer. His timely and insightful investment commentary interpreting current events driving the markets can be found on Deutsche Asset Management's retail Web site www.dws-investments.com. This weekly commentary has gained Froehlich acclaim within the brokerage community as one of the most important strategists of our day. In addition to this weekly commentary, Dr. Bob has written three books prior to this one.

Dr. Bob is married (Cheryl) with two daughters (Marianne and Stephanie) and currently resides in Chicago.